Modern Short Fiction of Southeast Asia

A Literary History

Asia Past & Present: New Research from AAS
A series edited by Martha Ann Selby

"Asia Past & Present: New Research from AAS," published by the Association for Asian Studies, Inc. (AAS), features scholarly work from all areas of Asian studies. In addition to scholarly monographs, translations, essay collections, and other forms of scholarly research are welcome for consideration. AAS particularly hopes to support work in emerging or under-represented fields.

Formed in 1941, the Association for Asian Studies (AAS)—the largest society of its kind, with more than 7,000 members worldwide—is a scholarly, non-political, non-profit professional association open to all persons interested in Asia.

For further information, please visit www.asian-studies.org.

© 2009 by the Association for Asian Studies, Inc.

All Rights Reserved. Written permission must be secured to use or reproduce any part of this book.

Published by:
Association for Asian Studies, Inc.
1021 East Huron Street
Ann Arbor, Michigan 48104 USA
www.asian-studies.org

Library of Congress Cataloging-in-Publication Data

> Modern short fiction of Southeast Asia : a literary history / edited by Teri Shaffer Yamada.
>
>   p. cm. — (Asia past & present; no 1)
> ISBN 978-0-924304-52-1 (pbk. : alk. paper) 1. Short stories, Southeast Asian—History and criticism. 2. Southeast Asian fiction—20th century—History and criticism. I. Yamada, Teri Shaffer.
>
> PL3508.4.M63 2009
> 808.83'10895--dc22
>
>   2008055025

Modern Short Fiction of Southeast Asia

A Literary History

edited by
Teri Shaffer Yamada

ASIA PAST & PRESENT

Published by the Association for Asian Studies, Inc.
Asia Past & Present: New Research from AAS, Number 1

About the Cover

Front cover: *Mermaid* (*Yethuma*) (2006)

Back Cover: *Anyeint* (2008)

Both paintings by Htein Lin. Reproduced with permission of the artist.

About the Artist

Htein Lin was born in Burma in 1966 and began painting and performing at a young age, including as a comedian in university "anyeint" troupes. He led protests in his home town during Burma's "democracy spring" in 1988, and following the brutal military crackdown fled to the Indian border where he joined the All Burma Students' Democratic Front (ABDSF).

Htein Lin's journey as a political activist, wanted by the authorities, took him from India, across the jungles of northern Burma to Kachin state, where he was lucky to survive an internal ABDSF power struggle, until he surrendered to the Burmese government and was allowed to return to university in Rangoon.

He then worked as an artist and comic film actor, and pioneered modern performance art in Burma. In 1998, he was arrested and sentenced to seven years' imprisonment, charged on the basis of plans for politics in an intercepted letter from an erstwhile "comrade": he was unaware of the letter until his arrest. In prison, he was forced to improvise to continue painting.

In November 2004, six and a half years into his sentence and over 200 paintings later, he was released. The authorities informed him that, following a review of his files, they concluded that there had been no case against him.

He currently lives in London where he continues to paint, write and perform.

For further information, please visit www.hteinlin.com.

Contents

Acknowledgements / vi

Contributors / vii

Introduction / 1

1. Thai Short Fiction of the Modern Era / 19
   Susan F. Kepner

2. Contemporary Trends in Thai Short Fiction / 43
   Suradech Chotiudompant

3. The Short Story and Contemporary Lao Literature / 79
   Peter Koret

4. Modern Short Fiction in Cambodia: A History of Persistence / 111
   Teri Shaffer Yamada

5. The Short Story in Myanmar/Burma / 153
   Anna Allott

6. Storytelling across Boundaries: Malaysian Short Stories / 193
   Shirley Geok-Lin Lim and Wong Soak Koon

7. Conflict and Change: The Singapore Short Story / 213
   Mary Loh and Teri Shaffer Yamada

8. Some Landmarks in the Development of the Indonesian Short Story / 243
   Harry Aveling

9. The Modern Vietnamese Short Story / 271
   Peter Zinoman

10. The Story of the Philippine Short Story in English / 293
    Cristina Pantoja Hidalgo

11. The Contemporary Short Story in Filipino / 321
    Rosario Torres-Yu

Literary Authors' Index / 351

Acknowledgments

The first essays for this collection were solicited over ten years ago as a companion volume to *Virtual Lotus: Modern Fiction of Southeast Asia* (Ann Arbor: University of Michigan Press, 2002). Most of those essays have been revised many times during the past decade. I would like to acknowledge my deepest appreciation to the remarkable scholars who contributed to this volume; their patience through this lengthy process has been extraordinary. I would particularly like to mention my gratitude to Prof. Harry Aveling, whose friendship and intellectual expertise have fostered our collaboration on a series of articles relating to Southeast Asian literature and translation since the beginning of this project. The contribution of Robert Vore and U Saw Tun, who developed the original concept for the essay on Myanmar, also needs to be recognized. My own essay, "Modern Short Fiction in Cambodia: A History of Persistence," benefited greatly from several close readings and comments by Judy Ledgerwood. Finally, I would like to thank the Association for Asian Studies, whose encouragement of Southeast Asian studies over the years has fostered new scholarship on this underrepresented area.

Contributors

Anna Allott is Senior Research Associate in Burmese Studies at the School of Oriental and African Studies, University of London, with over fifty years in the field of Burmese Studies. From 1980 to 1996 she served as Honorary Secretary of the Britain-Burma Society. She has written extensively on Burmese literature, including *Inked Over, Ripped Out: Burmese Storytellers and the Censors*, a Freedom-to-Write report (New York: American PEN Center, 1993).

Harry Aveling is a Professor of Indonesian/Malay in the Department of Asian Studies at La Trobe University, Australia, and Adjunct Professor of Southeast Asian Literature at the Center for International Studies, Ohio University. In 1991 he was awarded the Anugerah Pengembangan Sastera award by the Federation of Malay Writers Associations for his contribution to the international recognition of Malay literature. His publications include *Shahnon Ahmad: Islam, Gender, and Power* (Bangi: Penerbit Universiti Kebangsaan Malaysia, 2000); *Osho Rajneesh and His Disciples: Some Western Perceptions* (Delhi: Motilal Banarasidass, 1999); *Sahaj Prakash: The Brightness of Simplicity* (with Sudha Joshi) (Delhi: Motilal Banarasidass, 2001): and the bilingual anthology *Secrets Need Words: Indonesian Poetry, 1966–1998* (Athens, Ohio: Ohio University Center for International Studies, 2001), which was short-listed for the 2003 New South Wales Premier's Translation Prize.

Suradech Chotiudompant lectures at the Department of Comparative Literature, Faculty of Arts, Chulalongkorn University. He has written essays on international authors such as Jorge Luis Borges, Italo Calvino, and Gabriel García Márquez, as well as Kanokpong Songsomphan and Siriworn Kaewkan from Thailand. His interests include literary theory, Latin American literature, postmodernism, magical realism, and contemporary Thai literature.

Cristina Pantoja Hidalgo is a Professor of Creative Writing and Literature at the University of the Philippines. She has written twenty books, many of which have won national awards, including the Carlos Palanca Grand Prize for the novel *Recuerdo* and four Manila Critics Circle National Book Awards, and has edited several books. She has also been awarded the Gawad Balagtas for fiction by the Writers Union of the Philippines. Her stories and essays have been published in both the Philippines and the United States. Her latest book is *Over a Cup of Ginger Tea: Conversations on the Literary Narratives of Filipino Women* (University of the Philippines Press, 2006). She served as Director of the University of the Philippines Press and is currently the University of the Philippines Vice President for Public Affairs.

Susan F. Kepner teaches about mainland Southeast Asian cultures and literatures and Thai language at the University of California, Berkeley. She has published many translations of Thai literature and is the author of *The Lioness in Bloom: Modern Thai Fiction about Women* (Berkeley: University of California Press, 1996). In 2002, Silkworm Books of Chiang Mai, Thailand, republished her translation of Botan's *Letters from Thailand* and in 2005, *Married to the Demon King: Sri Daoruang and Her Demon Folk*.

Peter Koret is an independent researcher with an interest in Buddhism, culture, and politics in Southeast Asia. His primary focus is on literature (both modern and pre-modern) in Laos and Thailand. He has taught at the University of California, Berkeley, and Arizona State University. Examples of published works include "Past, Present, and Future in Buddhist Prophetic Literature of the Lao," in *Buddhism, Power, and Political Order*, edited by Ian Harris (London: Routledge, 2007) and *"Luep Phasun* (Extinguishing the Light of the Sun): Romance, Religion, and Politics in the Interpretation of a Traditional Lao Poem" in *Contesting Visions of the Lao Past: Laos Historiography at the Crossroads*, edited by Christopher E. Goscha and Søren Ivarsson (Copenhagen: Nordic Institute of Asian Studies Press, 2003). He is the author of two forthcoming books, *A Crab in the Shell of a Snail: The Story of the First Female Monks in the History of Thailand and the Legal Case Against Them* (Chiang Mai: Silkworm Books and *The Gestation Period for Miracles*, a biography of Narin Phasit, a religious and political reformer in early twentieth century Siam (Chiang Mai: Silkworm Books).

Shirley Geok-Lin Lim is Professor of English at the University of California, Santa Barbara. She received her doctorate from Brandeis University in 1973 and has also taught at the National University of Singapore, National Institute of Education of Nanyang Technological University, and served as Chair Professor at the University of Hong Kong. Her research interests include Asian American and postcolonial cultural productions and ethnic and feminist writing. Her creative works include the genres of memoir, novel, short-story, and poetry such as *Among the White Moon Faces: An Asian American Memoir of Homelands* (New York: Feminist Press at the City University of New York, 1996), *Sister*

Swing (Singapore: Marshall Cavendish Editions, 2006), *Two Dreams: New and Selected Stories* (New York: Feminist Press, 1997), and *Monsoon History: Selected Poems* (London: Skoob Books, 1994). Lim has authored, edited or co-edited a number of scholarly works on literary criticism, ethnic identity, gender and Diaspora including *Transnational Asia Pacific: Gender, Culture, and the Public Sphere* (Urbana: University of Illinois Press, 1999), and *Transnational Asian American Literature: Sites and Transits* (Philadelphia, PA: Temple University Press, 2006).

Mary Loh is a Singaporean playwright and critic. She obtained her master's degree in literature from the National University of Singapore with her thesis entitled "Style, Strategy and Structure in the Singapore Short Story in English" (Department of English Language and Literature, National University of Singapore, Singapore, 1994). In 1989, she collaborated with two local Singaporean writers to produce the anthology *Mistress and Other Creative Takeoffs!* (Singapore: Landmark Books, 1990).

Wong Soak Koon taught comparative literature in the School of Humanities, Universiti Sains Malaysia, until her retirement. She received her bachelor's degree (first class) and master's degree from the University of Malaya and her doctorate from the University of California, Berkeley, where she studied under a Harvard-Yenching Doctoral Fellowship. She was Fulbright Senior Scholar at the Women's Studies Program of the University of California, Santa Barbara, in 1998. In 2001 she was awarded an Asian Public Intellectual Fellowship by the Nippon Foundation to carry out research on the teaching of literature and critical literacy at the University of the Philippines, Diliman. She has published on Conrad, Kipling, feminist literary criticism, and Malaysian–Singaporean literature in English. She coedited "Feminism: Malaysian Critique and Experience," a special issue of the *Journal of Malaysian Studies*, in 1994; and in 2001 she coauthored *Risking Malaysia: Culture, Politics, and Identity* (Bangi: Penerbit Universiti Kebangsaan Malaysia).

Rosario Torres-Yu was Dean of the College of Arts and Letters (2000–2003), Vice Chancellor for Student Affairs (1993–96), and Chair of the Department of Filipino and Philippine Literature (1985–88), University of the Philippines, Diliman. A prize-winning creative writer and dedicated scholar, she has been a devout chronicler of the life and works of the labor leader and National Artist for Literature, Amado V. Hernandez. She co-authored *Amado V. Hernandez: Tudla at Tudling, Katipunan ng mga Nalathalang Tula, 1921–1970* (Quezon:

Palimbagan ng Pamantasan ng Pilipinas, 1986), and *Langaw sa Isang Basong Gatas at Iba Pang Kuwento* (Diliman, Quezon City: University of the Philippines Press, 1996). Her scholarly articles on trade unionism are used as references in graduate classes in Philippine studies and industrial relations. Her book, *Sarilaysay: Tinig ng 20 Babae sa Sariling Danas Bilang Manunulat* (Manila: Inilathala at Ipinamamahagi ng Anvil Pub., 2000) received the first Gawad sa Natatanging Publikasyon sa Filipino of the prestigious University of the Philippines President's Academic Distinction Awards. Torres-Yu obtained her doctorate in Philippine studies from the College of Social Science and Philosophy, University of the Philippines, Diliman.

Teri Shaffer Yamada received a master's degree in Southeast Asian languages and literatures in 1975 and a doctorate in Buddhist Studies from the University of California, Berkeley, in 1985. Currently she is Professor of Asian Studies in the Department of Asian and Asian American Studies at California State University, Long Beach. Her research interests include modernity and Southeast Asian literature. To this end she edited and compiled the short story collection *Virtual Lotus: Modern Fiction of Southeast Asia* (Ann Arbor: University of Michigan Press, 2002). She has written numerous articles on modern Southeast Asian literature, modern Cambodian literature, and the Cambodian diaspora. Currently she is involved in the development of modern literature in Cambodia with the Nou Hach Literary Project.

Peter Zinoman received his doctorate in Southeast Asian history from Cornell University in 1995. He is Associate Professor of History and Southeast Asian Studies at the University of California, Berkeley. Currently, he is serving as Director of the Center for Southeast Asian Studies and Editor-in-Chief of the *Journal of Vietnamese Studies*. His research interests include the cultural, social, and political history of Vietnam, as well as the history of twentieth-century Vietnamese literature. He is the author of *The Colonial Bastille: A History of Imprisonment in Vietnam, 1862–1940* (Berkeley: University of California Press, 2001); and co-translated *Dumb Luck: a Novel* (Ann Arbor: University of Michigan Press, 2002).

Introduction
Teri Shaffer Yamada

Is Southeast Asia's resistance to generalization an inevitable result of the region's inherent fragmentation, or is it simply that not enough is known to perceive underlying patterns? . . . The aim, after all, is not to be able to say "yes" or "no" to the existence of "Southeast Asia," but to frame a meaningful analysis. This depends on clarity, including the use of a consistent conceptual vocabulary (Sutherland 2005, 28–29).

A field of knowledge rests upon a particular political economy of scholarship—its social conditions of production, of demand and supply, distribution and consumption (Thongchai 2005, 115).

Geographically, Southeast Asia is located south of China and east of India, an area also incorporating thousands of islands that form the Indonesian and Philippine archipelagoes. Although these geographical borders appear to be somewhat fixed, the region itself as a concept is still contested—largely disputed in academic discourse through the disciplines of anthropology, history, political science, and economics (Kratoska 2005a, 1–19). And, even though certain aspects of literary theory have been utilized by anthropologists, historians, and others in their analyses of various Southeast Asian countries, we have yet to embark on a serious discussion of the role of modern literature in the cultural, historical, and political development of the entire region (Yong 2003).[1]

This collection of essays begins to redress the underrepresented and fragmented historical representation of modern literature in Southeast Asia's recent history.[2] It strives to establish a basic historical frame for the unique modern literary development of nine Southeast Asian nations: the Philippines, Malaysia, Indonesia, Singapore, Vietnam, Cambodia, Thailand, Laos, and Myanmar, excluding only East Timor and Negara Brunei Darussalam.[3]

To provide some coherence among the essays, each was organized around the "theme" of the modern short story as a developing genre in the region. This choice was based on the amount of significant research already completed on the short story in Southeast Asia. Its social importance became the subject of analysis in Jeremy Davidson and Helen Cordell's *The Short Story in South East Asia: Aspects of a Genre* (1982) and Tham Seong Chee's *Essays on Literature and Society in Southeast Asia: Political and Sociological Perspectives* (1981). Neither collection, published several decades ago, included the entire region. Although some of the best work on modern Southeast Asian literature has been published since then, most are case studies on a single country within the region.[4]

Each essay in this collection provides a diachronic analysis of the modern literary history of the specific country it addresses. As a set of diachronic case studies, the collection clarifies historical patterns across Southeast Asian nations since both the form and content of the developing short story genre archive a response to political, social and economic changes in the modern period.[5] This collection also establishes a basis for comparisons among Southeast Asian countries before globalization further transforms their literary history into a transnational discourse, with authors writing from the subject-position of multiple national identities, the topic of a subsequent volume. Finally, as a collection of literary case studies, *Modern Short Fiction of Southeast Asia* enables us to situate the region's short fiction within a broader academic discourse of Asian and world literature studies or modern intellectual history. This intent echoes the efforts of Wang Gungwu, M. Guerrero and David Marr, editors of *Society and the Writer: Essays on Literature in Modern Asia* (1981), who have begun the process of incorporating Southeast Asia into a larger pan-Asian discussion.[6]

Another intent of this essay collection is to reflect a more integrative, interdisciplinary emphasis within Southeast Asia area studies. Some innovative historians have incorporated literary theory and other disciplines into their research methodology since the 1980s (Yong 2003).[7] Although criticized for some of their findings, studies by Anthony Reid, David Marr and A. C. Milner exemplify outstanding interdisciplinary research that incorporates material culture, social anthropology, technological developments, economics, and political economy into the data set for analysis.[8]

Some of these integrative approaches also use literature, not just literary theory, as part of the data set although the use of literature for historical analysis has met more resistance than the use of material artifacts associated with archaeology and anthropology. Scholars who have incorporated an integrative studies approach into traditional historical practices have produced dramatic results, leading to a reexamination of (1) the theme of "Indianisation" and; (2) "the extent to which exaggeration of that theme led to serious errors of interpretation of earlier archaeological materials" (Wang, Guerrero, and Marr 1981, xiii). This type of interdisciplinary approach has facilitated a reexamination of ancient maritime trade as more than just a route linking India and China and challenged the facticity of descriptions about Khmer kingdoms found in the early Chinese chronicles (Reid 1993; Marr and Milner 1986). These revisions, based on an interdisciplinary approach in research about Southeast Asia, have fostered an increased appreciation of literature as a component of historical experience. For example, Benedict Anderson ultimately advocated the usefulness of literature as data later in his career when he came to appreciate how the contents of Javanese literary texts could facilitate understanding of Javanese intellectuals' struggle to accommodate changing political conditions (1990, 13).

History and literature mirror each other. Much has been written about the interrelationship between intellectual history and literature since the 1980s when Stephen Greenblatt, the originator of New Historicism, took up the utility of literature for historical analysis.[9] The theoretical work of cultural critics such as Hayden White, Daniel Aaron, Michel de Certeau and others explores the pragmatic value of this combination.[10] Neil Jamieson demonstrates how effective this combination can be in a variety of his studies on Vietnam.[11]

Other talented scholars have produced interdisciplinary studies on specific Southeast Asia nations that intentionally integrate history and literature. David K. Wyatt successfully incorporates history and literature as a product of Thai intellectual expression in *Thailand: A Short History* (1982). Nidhi Eoseewong's *Pen and Sail: Literature and History in Early Bangkok* (2005) is a brilliant example of the actual synergy of history and literature, and the importance of viewing them not as separate but as complementary disciplines. David Chandler has fused the two with some success in his studies on Cambodian history.[12] In the area of Vietnam there is Hoang Ngoc Thanh's *Vietnam's Social and Political Development as Seen through the Modern Novel* (1991). Benedict Anderson has incorporated this approach in several essays included in *Language and Power: Exploring Political Cultures in Indonesia* (1990). Finally, editors Keith Foulcher and Tony Day have produced *Clearing a Space: Postcolonial Readings of Modern Indonesian Literature* (2002), which contains several articles—one by Goenawan Mohamad, "Forgetting: Poetry and the Nation, a Motif in Indonesian Literary Modernism after 1945" (2002)—that reveal the complementary nature of history and literature. Joseph Fischer, in *Foreign Values and Southeast Asian Scholarship* (1973), illustrates how this interdisciplinary approach productively deconstructs and advances some earlier scholarship on Southeast Asia.[13]

Ultimately, we may have to reconsider the Western categories that have been applied to the development of Southeast Asian literature: modernization, westernization, traditional, modern, postmodern, postcolonial. Paul Tickell warns us that in the case of Indonesia such categories may have outlived their applicability as descriptive frames (1987).

I believe that we may avoid some of the pitfalls of Western categorizations by reframing how the creative stimulus of "colonial influence" has shaped modern literary development in Southeast Asia. Such influence can be seen in the rapid development of the modern novel and short story genres in many countries within the region. Both genres emerged from "traditional" roots through an expansion of cultural space. They became "new" forms of creative expression brought about by the questioning of tradition caused partly by a colonial encounter. This movement away from a status quo aesthetic embodied in traditional literary forms, usually written in verse, was facilitated by new ideas and technologies associated with the colonial encounter. These include the valorization of mercantilism; the importance of vernacular language, literacy, and public education; print technology; romanized scripts; foreign language study; and translations of Western literature. Herbert T. Phillips describes "cultural transformation" of this sort in terms of modern Thai literature.

> It is in its social dimensions, however, that contemporary literature differs most markedly from the earlier genres. Paralleling so many of the other changes that have occurred in Thai society as a whole, the Thai literary enterprise has been transformed into an extraordinarily open-ended intellectual process, with contemporary authors writing about as many things as people speak about. This open-endedness is not total: political censorship in Thailand is real, even if it is capricious; also, the uncertain economic state of many writers, particularly the less-established ones, and the fickleness of public preferences, always constrains what is actually written and published. But in contrast to both oral and classical literature, contemporary literature is self-consciously felt to be a mode or vehicle for intellectual exploration, discovery, and experimentation. (1987, 15–6)

This opening of cultural space for new forms of creativity produced unanticipated consequences in a number of Southeast Asian nations. One was the use of vernacular languages by intellectuals, for example, in Indonesia and Vietnam, as a means to resist the very colonial authorities who had advocated their implementation. In short, the modernization of traditional literary languages—that is, the use of daily speech practices to compose written literature—became a dominant factor in the complex matrix of social factors shaping new forms of the novel, short story, and poetry. This shift from classical language and verse to the use of an increasingly natural language of ordinary conversation and dialogue for the representation of everyday life using prose marks what we call "modern" about Southeast Asian literatures. The genre that most reflects the modern is the new short story form that emerged out of this cultural space of transformation.

Just as in the West, the modern short story would develop differently in each Asian nation. In the West the short story developed specific characteristics in France, Germany, England, and the United States. With the influence of Anton Chekhov (1860–1904) in the era that followed WWI, however, the aesthetic of the short story became more unified irrespective of national boundaries. It became more focused on the depiction of interior states as fragments of everyday reality in the form of "a tight symbolic structure and ironic and distanced point of view" (May 1994, 212).

Unlike the West, where a somewhat shared literary aesthetic emerged in the 1920s, the modern short story had no comparable development across the region of Southeast Asia. As a genre it developed at a different pace and degree within each country and with little influence among nations within the region.[14] Likewise, the colonial experience was different for each nation, with the Western literature introduced into a specific country somewhat in conformity with the "canon" of each colonial power: France, Great Britain, the Netherlands, Spain. The colonial enterprise facilitated the modernization of Southeast Asian languages across the region and introduced Western forms of "realism" and "romanticism" through the fiction of Alexandre Dumas, Charles Dickens, Guy de Maupassant, and other Western writers.[15] The introduction of detective and mystery novels was received enthusiastically as a truly new form of literature in those parts of the region colonized or influenced by Great Britain. By the 1920s and 1930s, most nations were translating works of modern Western literature that would influence indigenous writers. Translations of Chinese literature also influenced the development of modern literature in much of the region (Aveling and Yamada, 2008). And Tamil literature influenced the modern short story in Singapore.

As Sutherland advocates, future projects on Southeast Asia need to "frame a meaningful analysis" that uses a consistent conceptual vocabulary (2005). In the context of modern literature, I would suggest Pierre Bourdieu's concept of cultural production. It provides one possible solution as a comparative analytical frame for the entire region, especially in the context of State censorship and its influence on the form and content of literary production, a problematic issue found in all Southeast Asian nations (1993).

According to Bourdieu, the "field of literary production" (*le champ littéraire*) is situated both within and relationally subordinate to the "field of power," which includes such factors as state censorship. In the context of literary production, the state can be defined as the dominant player in the field of power in terms of the following factors: its synergistic deployment of censorship laws and the direct violence or intimidation necessary to enforce them; its ability to promote and enforce a favored ideology; its control or manipulation of literary prizes by being the source of funding for monetary awards and by determining the specific topic of an award cycle; its sponsorship and legitimization of writers' organizations by being the source of their funding and by stipulating who receives the leadership positions within the organization; and its ability to enforce economic and political constraints on publishers and publications, which includes control over the distribution of paper and the stipulation that all publications must be approved prior to distribution.

Bourdieu then suggests that the field of literary production, positioned subordinately to state power, will naturally be influenced by it. According to the degree and design of state domination, a writer's product will be positioned in the field of literary production somewhere along the continuum of art for art's sake to social art. When the state is concerned with public perceptions, it may attempt to intimidate writers, thus manipulating them through coercion or self-elected accommodation to produce a "politically correct" literature, such as socialist realism. The result of strict State control is typically a literature that praises or ignores the state or a literature in which criticism of the state has been so encoded that it remains nominally undetected. Burmese writers are masters of this technique. In this context, writers who refuse to be intimidated or who situate themselves as "free-speech" advocates on the margins of political correctness do so at their own risk. Most of the essays in this collection illustrate the consequences of such bravery, for example, Anna Allott's "The Short Story in Myanmar/Burma," (Chap. 5) and Harry Aveling's "Some Landmarks in the Development of the Indonesian Short Story," (Chap. 8).

Examples of state intervention in the form and content of literature are bountiful in Southeast Asia: Indonesia's New Order regime, North Vietnam's socialist government, Myanmar's State Law and Order Restoration Council (SLORC) and its more recent transmogrification as the State Peace and Development Council (SPDC), and Singapore's managed democracy. State management of literary expression and publication frequently takes the form of literary contests with a stipulated subject matter and censorship laws. This type of political management and its influence on the form and content of fiction are illustrated throughout this collection.

State management directly or indirectly shapes the content of literature. It also influences the development of narrative strategies that may not have occurred otherwise. These narrative strategies include situating a current political event in the distant past; the use of traditional epic heroes and villains to represent contemporary politicians; and flight into fantasy, which usefully obfuscates the writer's criticism of the government.[16] These narrative strategies have been used most productively in Myanmar, Indonesia, and Vietnam while allegory is a preferred strategy of coded criticism in Cambodia.

Two essays that focus more intently on the influences of censorship are Teri Shaffer Yamada's "Modern Short Fiction in Cambodia: A History of Persistence" (Chap. 4) and Anna Allott's "The Short Story in Myanmar/Burma" (Chap. 5). Yamada establishes a causal matrix for the lack of a significant advancement in the short story as a genre in Cambodia, an anomaly in the region, although since 2000 some significant development in the short story form has occurred, largely among writers in the capital city of Phnom Penh. In contrast to Cambodia, Burmese writers have created a sophisticated and mature form of the short story genre in spite of severe state censorship as shown in Anna Allott's essay. Censorship can be subverted through new narrative forms and codes, an interesting development seen not only in Myanmar but also in Vietnam and Indonesia. Aspects of censorship are also discussed in Peter Zinoman's "The Modern Vietnamese Short Story" (Chap. 9) and Harry Aveling's "Some Landmarks in the Development of the Indonesian Short Story" (Chap. 8). Peter Koret also explores this issue in "The Short Story and Contemporary Lao Literature" (Chap. 3).

It is this phenomenon of state censorship that links the experience of modern writers of the region to their colleagues elsewhere in Asia. The governments of Laos, Vietnam, and Cambodia, as well as China, required writers to shape their work according to the ideology of socialist realism during certain periods of the twentieth century; some writers elected to use flight into fantasy during periods of strict censorship in the Philippines, Cambodia, Myanmar, and Indonesia, as well as in China and Japan. State censorship is a productive area of comparative study for Southeast Asia and its neighbors. Another is the remarkable emergence of women writers in Asia after World War II and their increasing importance in the current literary arena.

Although censorship in its various forms is common among the nations of Southeast Asia, other experiences are dissimilar. Thailand was never formally colonized, unlike its neighbors. Its modernization process, however, was deeply influenced by European and subsequently American interests as seen in Susan F. Kepner's "Thai Short Fiction of the Modern Era" (Chap. 1). Kepner discusses the importance of life in Britain experienced by the Thai aristocrats who became the first modern writers in a "country" developing into a constitutional monarchy. Thai writers have mirrored social circumstances and influenced changes in Thai society over the decades. Many of them have done so with a keen sense of humor. Kepner's essay also focuses on the emergence of women writers after World War II and their interest in personal relationships and romance. She ends her essay by advocating the importance of contemporary

Thai films, which are often based on novels and screen plays by prominent writers, as a necessary complement to the study of modern fiction.

While Kepner focuses on a historical overview of Thai literature in the modern period, Suradech Chotiudompant's complementary "Contemporary Trends in Thai Short Fiction" (Chap.2) explores new forms of writing since the 1980s, including experimental fiction and a form of Thai magical realism influenced by the translations of Gabriel García Márquez. Thailand has become a productive site of new pan-Asian collaborations, currently seen in Pen-Ek Ratanaruang's Thai/Japanese/Chinese films, which are shot in multiple locations and languages. This trend of hybridity and complexity will only continue, along with the difficulty of describing a "national literature," as the twenty-first century continues to unfold (Saxenian 2006). Descriptive categories, once quite useful, such as national literature or ethnic literature, are rapidly breaking down with "nomadic" writers publishing in multiple languages from multiple locations.

Another site of rapid globalization is Singapore. It is also an exception to the more common "colonial" pattern of literary development seen in other Southeast Asian nations. This difference occurred when the fledging government of Singapore, after achieving independence from the Malay confederation in 1965, adopted English as the nation's national language. Thus Singapore's modern literary tradition became even more complex, linking it to other British Commonwealth writers. Mary Loh and Teri Shaffer Yamada's "Conflict and Change: The Singapore Short Story" (Chap. 7) traces the young Singapore government's quest to develop a "national literature" in English, one it could exploit to unify an ethnically pluralistic and linguistically diverse society. This politically motivated use of a colonial language as a neutral discourse has some parallels with the adoption of English as a unifying language in India.

The desire for peaceful social unity under the umbrella of a shared national identity expressed in one "unifying" language is also seen in the development of modern literature in Malaysia, as explored in Shirley Geok-Lin Lim and Wong Soak Koon's "Storytelling across Boundaries: Malaysian Short Stories" (Chap. 6). In contrast to Singapore, English was relegated to a minor language in Malaysia after its independence from Great Britain.

One more variation on the English language issue occurs in the Philippines, a country whose rapid change of colonial masters from Spain to the United States produced a complexity of literary trends in English, Spanish, and indigenous languages.[17] This complexity is traced in two essays, Cristina Pantoja Hidalgo's "The Story of the Philippine Short Story in English" (Chap.10) and Rosario Torres-Yu's "The Contemporary Short Story in Filipino" (Chap. 11). Unlike the situation in Singapore, English in the

Philippines has lost its value as a national language yet remains the elite language of literary expression (Fernando 1986).

As the essays in this collection show, the nations organized around the designation Southeast Asia share certain patterns of literary development. Once these patterns are recognized they may allow for an integration of these nations into a broader discourse about Asian literature and intellectual history, so heavily dominated by the triad: India, China, and Japan. One pattern—censorship and literary repression alternating with periods of relative creative freedom of expression—can be seen throughout the broader region of Asia as well: in post-Partition India, Japan after World War II, and China after the Cultural Revolution. In each case, after a period of state repression, writers, artists, and filmmakers freely produced texts in a relatively unrestricted literary field. It is possible that Bourdieu's theoretical frame may be used productively in the future to comparatively explore the literatures of modern Southeast Asia and beyond. It is my hope that these essays will facilitate this process.

Notes

[1] Since the mid-1990s, a cultural studies approach to specific Southeast Asian nations has become more popular. These include William van der Heide's *Malaysian Cinema, Asian Film: Border Crossings and National Cultures* (2002), Adrian Vickers' *Being Modern in Bali: Image and Change* (1996), and Leakthina Chau-Pech Ollier and Tim Winter's *Expressions of Cambodia: The Politics of Tradition, Identity, and Change* (2006).

[2] A literary history, as opposed to a history of literature, attempts to acknowledge the synergistic role that literature plays in the cultural and political changes occurring in a country or region. An example of a fragmented representation of the region in recent publications is Yao Souchou's *House of Glass: Culture, Modernity, and the State in Southeast Asia* (2001).

[3] One of the best works on Southeast Asian literature is Dingwall 1995, now, unfortunately, out of print.

[4] Some studies of a broader scope include D. M. Roskies's *Text/Politics in Island Southeast Asia: Essays in Interpretation* (1993) and Luisa Mallari-Hall and Lily Tope's *Texts and Contexts: Interactions between Literature and Culture in Southeast Asia* (1999).

[5] There are a number of regional surveys focusing on history and culture but not literature, including Clark D. Neher's *Southeast Asia: Crossroads of the World* (2001), Niels Mulder's *Inside Southeast Asia: Religion, Everyday Life, Cultural Change* (2000); Charles Keyes's *The Golden Peninsula: Culture and Adaptation in Mainland Southeast Asia* (1995). A more historically focused work is David Steinberg's *In Search of Southeast Asia: A Modern History* (1987).

[6] Keyes, Kendall, and Hardacre (1994) mention this gap in comparative studies as they establish the links between East and Southeast Asia in terms of religions, modernity, and the crisis of authority. See their "Introduction: Contested Visions of Community in East and Southeast Asia," in that volume (1–16).

[7] The academic domain of Southeast Asian history prior to New Historicism is well represented by Donald K. Emmerson in his "Issues in Southeast Asian History: Room for Interpretation—A Review Article" (1980). O. W. Wolters's works (1982, 1986) also represent an early interdisciplinary effort to include literature and culture along with history in order to inform our understanding of Southeast Asia.

[8] These include *Southeast Asia in the Ninth to Fourteenth Centuries* (1986), edited by David G. Marr and A. C. Milner, which contains essays incorporating art

and archaeology into the historical analysis; and Anthony Reid's two-volume *Southeast Asia in the Age of Commerce, 1450–1680* (1988). A serious critique of previous historical work on Southeast Asia is found in Paul Kratoska's "Locating Southeast Asia" (2005a) in Kratoska, Raben, and Nordholt, *Locating Southeast Asia: Geographies of Knowledge and Politics of Space* (2005b).

[9] For a description of New Historicism and how it incorporates literature into historical analysis, see Hunter Cadzow's "New Historicism," in *The Johns Hopkins Guide to Literary Theory and Criticism* (Cadzow 1994).

[10] See Hayden White's *Tropics of Discourse: Essays in Cultural Criticism* (1978), *The Content of the Form: Narrative Discourse and Historical Representation* (1987), and *Figural Realism: Studies in the Mimesis Effect* (1999); Daniel Aaron's "What Can You Learn from a Historical Novel?" (1992); and Michel de Certeau's *The Writing of History* (1988).

[11] See Jamieson's *Understanding Vietnam* (1993) and "Shattered Identities and Contested Images: Reflections of Poetry and History in Twentieth-Century Vietnam" (1992).

[12] Three essays in Chandler's *Facing the Cambodian Past* (1996) incorporate literature as part of the historical analysis: "The Legend of the Leper King (1978)," "Normative Poems (*Chbap*) and Pre-colonial Cambodian Society (1982)," and "Songs at the Edge of the Forest (1978)."

[13] Other revisionist texts include Craig J. Reynolds's *Seditious Histories: Contesting Thai and Southeast Asian Pasts* (2006).

[14] There is some influence between Malaysia and Indonesia due to the similarity of the languages (Bahasa Malaysia and Bahasa Indonesia) and the influence of Islam; yet, Indonesia has a very avant-garde artistic and literary scene, which has developed experimental forms of contemporary fiction, whereas Malaysia's writers appear to be more constrained by the influence of Islamic didactic values.

[15] Writer-scholars in Vietnam were introduced to realism through the Chinese philosopher-writer Han Yu in the ninth century. Romanticism also existed before the colonial period. A psychological depth of characterization exists in Nguyen Du's *The Tale of Kieu* (1973).

[16] Examples of these narrative strategies include the following short stories in English translation. Situating a current political event in the distant past is seen in Burmese writer Ne Win Myint's "Thadun" in Yamada's *Virtual Lotus* (2002, 4–10). The use of traditional epic heroes and villains to represent contemporary politicians and critique current social issues is seen in Indonesian

writer Yudhistira ANM Massardi's "Interview with Ravana" (70–74), Leila S. Chudori's "The Purification of Sita" (96–102), and Thai writer Sri Daoruang's "Sita Puts Out the Fire" (201–9). Flight into fantasy which usefully obfuscates the writer's political criticism, is seen in Indonesian writer Seno Gumira Ajidarma's "GRRRR!" (87–95). For further information on some narrative strategies used by Southeast Asian writers, see Grant Olson's *Modern Southeast Asian Literature in Translation: A Resource for Teaching* (1997).

[17] In all colonized countries, writers emerge who use the language of the colonizer or the colonized or sometimes both. On this issue in Southeast Asia, see Tham Seong Chee's "Introduction" in *Essays on Literature and Society in Southeast Asia* (1981, vii–ix).

References

Aaron, Daniel. 1992. "What Can You Learn from a Historical Novel?" *American Heritage* 43.6 (October): 55–62.

Abu Talib Ahmad and Tan Liok Ee, eds. 2003. *New Terrains in Southeast Asian History*. Athens: Ohio University Press.

Anderson, Benedict R. O'G. 1990. *Language and Power: Exploring Political Cultures in Indonesia*. Ithaca: Cornell University Press.

Aveling, Harry, and Teri Shaffer Yamada. 2008. "Southeast Asian Traditions," edited by Mona Baker and Gabriela Saldanha. In *Routledge Encyclopedia of Translation Studies*, 527-533. London: Routledge.

Bourdieu, Pierre. 1993. *The Field of Cultural Production: Essays on Art and Literature*. New York: Columbia University Press.

Cadzow, Hunter. 1994. "New Historicism." In *The Johns Hopkins Guide to Literary Theory and Criticism*, edited by Michael Groden and Martin Kreiswirth, 534–39. Baltimore: Johns Hopkins University Press.

Chandler, David. 1996. *Facing the Cambodian Past: Selected Essays 1971–1994*. Chiang Mai: Silkworm Books.

Davidson, Jeremy H. C. S., and Helen Cordell, eds. 1982. *The Short Story in South East Asia: Aspects of a Genre*. London: University of London.

de Certeau, Michel. 1988. *The Writing of History*. Translated by Tom Conley. New York: Columbia University Press.

Dingwall, Alastair, ed. 1995. *Traveller's Literary Companion: South-East Asia*. Lincolnwood IL: Passport Books.

Emmerson, Donald K. 1980. "Issues in Southeast Asian History: Room for Interpretation—A Review Article." *The Journal of Asian Studies* 40.1: 43–68.

Fernando, Lloyd. 1986. *Cultures in Conflict: Essays on Literature and the English Language in South East Asia*. Singapore: Graham Brash.

Fischer, Joseph, ed. 1973. *Foreign Values and Southeast Asian Scholarship*. Berkeley: Center for South and Southeast Asia Studies, University of California.

Foulcher, Keith and Tony Day, eds. 2002. *Clearing a Space: Postcolonial Readings of Modern Indonesian Literature*. Leiden: KITLV Press.

Goenawan Mohamad. 2002. "Forgetting: Poetry and the Nation, a Motif in Indonesian Literary Modernism after 1945." In *Clearing a Space: Postcolonial Readings of Modern Indonesian Literature*, edited by Keith Foulcher and Tony Day, 183–211. Leiden: KITLV Press.

Greenblatt, Stephen, ed. 1982. *The Power of Forms in the English Renaissance*. Norman, OK: Pilgrim Books.

Groden, Michael, and Martin Kreiswirth, eds. 1994. *The Johns Hopkins Guide to Literary Theory and Criticism*. Baltimore: Johns Hopkins University Press.

Hoang Ngoc Thanh. 1991. *Vietnam's Social and Political Development as Seen through the Modern Novel*. New York: Peter Lang.

Jamieson, Neil, L. 1992. "Shattered Identities and Contested Images: Reflections of Poetry and History in Twentieth-Century Vietnam." *Crossroads: An Interdisciplinary Journal of Southeast Asian Studies* 7.2: 71–134.

———.1993. *Understanding Vietnam*. Berkeley: University of California Press.

Keyes, Charles. F. 1995. *The Golden Peninsula: Culture and Adaptation in Mainland Southeast Asia*. Honolulu: University of Hawai'i Press.

Keyes, Charles, Laurel Kendall, and Helen Hardacre, eds. 1994. *Asian Visions of Authority: Religion and the Modern States of East and Southeast Asia*. Honolulu: University of Hawai'i Press.

Kratoska, Paul H., Remco Raben, and Henk Schulte Nordholt, 2005a. "Locating Southeast Asia." In *Locating Southeast Asia: Geographies of Knowledge and Politics of Space*, 1-19. Athens: Ohio University Press.

Kratoska, Paul H., Remco Raben, and Henk Schulte Nordholt, eds. 2005b. *Locating Southeast Asia: Geographies of Knowledge and Politics of Space*. Research in International Studies, Southeast Asia Series, no. 111. Athens: Ohio University Press.

Mallari-Hall, Luisa Joy and Lily Rose R. Tope, eds. 1999. *Texts and Contexts: Interactions between Literature and Culture in Southeast Asia*. Quezon City: University of the Philippines.

Marr, David G., and A. C. Milner, eds. 1986. *Southeast Asia in the Ninth to Fourteenth Centuries*. Singapore: Institute of Southeast Asian Studies; Canberra: Research School of Pacific Studies, Australian National University.

May, Charles E. 1994. "Chekhov and the Modern Short Story." In *The New Short Story Theories*, edited by Charles May, 199–217. Athens: Ohio University Press.

Mulder, Niels. 2000. *Inside Southeast Asia: Religion, Everyday Life, Cultural Change*. Chiang Mai: Silkworm Books.

Neher, Clark D. 2001. *Southeast Asia: Crossroads of the World*. DeKalb: Center for Southeast Asian Studies, Northern Illinois University.

Nidhi Eoseewong. 2005. *Pen and Sail: Literature and History in Early Bangkok*. Chiang Mai: Silkworm Books.

Nyugen Du. 1973. *The Tale of Kieu*. Translated by Huynh Sanh Thong. New York. Vintage.

Ollier, Leakthina Chau-Pech, and Tim Winter, eds. 2006. *Expressions of Cambodia: The Politics of Tradition, Identity and Change*. London and New York: Routledge.

Olson, Grant, ed. 1997. *Modern Southeast Asian Literature in Translation: A Resource for Teaching*. Tempe: Arizona State University Program for Southeast Asian Studies.

Pen-Ek Ratanaruang, dir. 2004. *Last Life in the Universe*. New York, Palm Pictures.

Phillips, Herbert P. 1987. *Modern Thai Literature: with an Ethnographic Interpretation*. Honolulu: University of Hawai'i Press.

Reid, Anthony. 1988. *Southeast Asia in the Age of Commerce, 1450–1680*. 2 vols. New Haven: Yale University Press.

———. 1993. *Southeast Asia in the Early Modern Era: Trade, Power, and Belief*. Ithaca: Cornell University Press.

Reynolds, Craig J. 2006. *Seditious Histories: Contesting Thai and Southeast Asian Pasts*. Seattle: University of Washington Press.

Roskies, D. M., ed. 1993. *Text/Politics in Island Southeast Asia: Essays in Interpretation*. Southeast Asia Series, no. 91. Athens: Center for International Studies, Ohio University.

Saxenian, AnnaLee. 2006. *The New Argonauts: Regional Advantage in a Global Economy*. Cambridge: Harvard University Press.

Steinberg, David Joel, ed. 1987. *In Search of Southeast Asia: A Modern History*. Honolulu: University of Hawai'i Press.

Sutherland, Heather. 2005. "Contingent Devices." In *Locating Southeast Asia: Geographies of Knowledge and Politics of Space*, edited by Paul H. Kratoska, Remco Raben, and Henk Schulte Nordholt, 20–59. Athens: Ohio University Press.

Sweeney, Amin, ed. 1987. *A Full Hearing: Orality and Literacy in the Malay World*. Berkeley: University of California Press.

Tham Seong Chee, ed. 1981. *Essays on Literature and Society in Southeast Asia: Political and Sociological Perspectives*. Singapore: Singapore University Press.

Thongchai Winichakul. 2005. "Trying to Locate Southeast Asia from Its Navel: Where Is Southeast Asian Studies in Thailand?" In *Locating Southeast Asia: Geographies of Knowledge and Politics of Space*, edited by Paul H. Kratoska, Remco Raben, and Henk Schulte Nordholt, 113–132. Athens: Ohio University Press.

Tickell, Paul. 1987. "The Writing of Indonesian Literary History." *Review of Indonesian and Malaysian Affairs* 21.1:29–43.

Van der Heide, William. 2002. *Malaysian Cinema, Asian Film: Border Crossings and National Cultures*. Amsterdam: Amsterdam University Press.

Vickers, Adrian, ed. 1996. *Being Modern in Bali: Image and Change*. Yale Monographs no. 43. New Haven: Council on Southeast Asian Studies, Yale University.

Wang Gungwu, M. Guerrero, and David Marr, eds. 1981. *Society and the Writer: Essays on Literature in Modern Asia*. Canberra: Research School of Pacific Studies, Australian National University.

White, Hayden. 1978. *Tropics of Discourse: Essays in Cultural Criticism*. Baltimore: Johns Hopkins University Press.

———.1987. *The Content of the Form: Narrative Discourse and Historical Representation*. Baltimore: Johns Hopkins University Press,

———. 1999. *Figural Realism: Studies in the Mimesis Effect*. Baltimore: Johns Hopkins University Press.

Wolters, O. W.1982. *History, Culture, and Region in Southeast Asian Perspectives*. Singapore: Institute of Southeast Asian Studies.

———.1986. "A Reading of Vietnamese Annals." In *Southeast Asia in the Ninth to Fourteenth Centuries*, edited by David G. Marr and A. C. Milner, 369–410. Singapore: Institute of Southeast Asian Studies; Canberra: Research School of Pacific Studies, Australian National University.

Wyatt, David K. 1982. *Thailand: A Short History*. New Haven and London: Yale University Press.

Yamada, Teri Shaffer, ed. 2002. *Virtual Lotus: Modern Fiction of Southeast Asia*. Ann Arbor: University of Michigan Press.

Yao Souchou. 2001. *House of Glass: Culture, Modernity, and the State in Southeast Asia,* Singapore: Institute of Southeast Asian Studies,

Yong Mun Cheong. 2003. "Southeast Asian History, Literary Theory, and Chaos." In *New Terrains in Southeast Asian History*, edited by Abu Talib Ahmad and Tan Liok Ee, 82–103. Athens: Ohio University Press.

1

Thai Short Fiction of the Modern Era

Susan F. Kepner

In the first decade of the twenty-first century, most works of short fiction by Thai writers continue to reflect the conventions, styles, and literary factions that predominated over the past century. However, major innovations are taking place, led by a few relatively new writers. Whether or not these innovations should be labeled "postmodern" is debatable. What is certain, however, is the emergence of groundbreaking positions and practices in fiction writing that are exerting a notable influence on what is written, and by whom, and on the works of short and long fiction that are being read, written, and talked about by Thai readers. The genre that is most noticeable to the world beyond Thailand is that of screenwriting. Over the past decade, many excellent films have been written, directed, and produced, intended not only for Thai audiences but with international film festivals and global distribution clearly in mind.

In this essay, I shall examine Thai short fiction of the early modern period, trace the factions and fashions of the short story during the twentieth century, and discuss some important contemporary writers and their best known works—whether they reside and write in Thailand or elsewhere. As far as possible, I have chosen to describe written works that are available in English translation and films that are available in digital video disc (DVD) format with English subtitles.

Early Modern Short Fiction

In Siam, as in most of Southeast Asia, the oral tradition contributed folktales and verse, while works of "high" literature (viz., dance dramas such as the *Ramakian*, the Thai version of the *Ramayana)* were composed in poetry. Prose writing was used for practical matters, including the writing of royal chronicles; correspondence, both official and personal; and the copying of *jataka* tales—tales of the Buddha's former lives, called *chadok* in Thai, used by monks to teach people both how to conduct themselves in an appropriate manner and the repercussions of failing to do so.

The debt that modern short fiction owes to Thai folktales is unmistakable and freely admitted by many writers. In all decades of the twentieth century, stories that have the earthy, amusing, and touching qualities of the most popular folktales were favorites with Thai readers. While short stories per se did not exist before the late nineteenth century, the mode of expression we see in the earliest modern fiction is similar to the writing style of casual correspondence of the mid-nineteenth century. A good example is the correspondence of King Mongkut (1851–68), writing to his ministers in Europe, many of whom were his brothers, cousins or lifelong friends. The letters are down-to-earth, colloquial, and opinionated, filled with anecdotes that are by turn touching, insightful, and hilarious. A collection of these letters, translated by M. R. Seni Pramoj and M. R. Kukrit Pramoj, is available in English translation.[1]

The first modern Thai short stories were written during the reign of King Chulalongkorn (1868–1910). They relied heavily on humor to express their authors' frustrations and impatience with the nation's social and political status quo. During the 1870s and 1880s, young aristocrats returning from European universities established modern journals that they hoped would eventually resemble the publications they had enjoyed and admired in Oxford, Tübingen, or Paris. The first journal published by these Western-educated princes was called *Darunowat* (Advice to Young Gentlemen, 1874–75).[2] It contained news of the day, humorous tales, and "short stories" that read like transcriptions of conversations between high-spirited young gentlemen sharing their exasperation over the intransigence and old-fashioned notions of their fathers and uncles.

The stories that appeared in *Darunowat* were awkward, tentative works, reminiscent of folktales in some ways yet studded with events and issues of the day. The princes who wrote them, far from looking down their educated noses at the bawdy aspects of Thai folktales, made it clear that not only were they familiar with these tales but they quite adored them. In "Four Fishermen" (1874), considered by the literary scholar Chua Satawethin to mark "the dawn of the Thai short story," the four main characters are named "Pointy Butt," "Lots of Snot," "Flap Ears," and "Eats with Three Hands" (Sumali 1987, 33). It is the kind of story that would be denigrated a few decades later as "merely" a derivative of the folktale—as distinguished from stories in which more or less realistic people have largely believable experiences in contemporary society—in other words, stories that bear more recognizable kinship with the modern, Western short story.

1910 to Mid-Century: The Progress of Fiction

King Vajiravudh (1910–25), the first Thai king to be educated in the West (at Oxford and Sandhurst), was a gifted and prolific poet and playwright. He translated many works from English and French into Thai and founded the Royal Academy of Literature. Under its auspices, Thai literary genres and forms were carefully defined and modern prose standardized. The king himself experimented with all genres, even writing detective stories featuring the intrepid Nai In, but he was most interested in Thai poetry and creating new forms of theater, combining Thai and Western traditions.

After 1932, when the absolute monarchy was overthrown by a small group of foreign-educated bureaucrats and military officers (during the reign of Vajiravudh's brother, King Prajadhipok, 1925–35), magazines and newspapers proliferated and great strides were made in extending literacy. However, while the nation's new leaders were enthusiastic about social and economic advances, including a nationwide literacy campaign, they were less enthusiastic about disillusioned writers who shared their disappointment over the political and social realities of life in the post-absolute-monarchy era. Censorship, rather than decreasing, became in some ways more rigorous than it had been under two centuries of absolute monarchy.

The Literature of Social Preservation and the Literature of Social Consciousness

After the overthrow of the absolute monarchy in 1932, the national ideology of "nation, religion, and king"—first expressed by King Vajiravudh, during the 1920s—was altered to reflect the primacy of non-royal leaders, and progressive social and economic policies. Yet it was during the 1930s that the first great works of the "literature of social preservation" were written by members of the old elite. In 1935, Dok Mai Sot (the pen name of M. L. Buppha Kunjara Nimmanhemin), a great-great-granddaughter of the second king of the Chakri dynasty, wrote *Phuu Dii*, perhaps her most popular and enduring work. It is a novel entirely concerned with the plight of impoverished gentry in an era that the author portrayed as one of drab banality further diminished by a waning respect for moral certainties.[3]

Although her novels were her most popular works, Dok Mai Sot also wrote short fiction, and a translation of her story "The Good Citizen" appears in an anthology published by the Thai National Identity Board.[4] This volume contains another short story by a prominent early modern writer, Riem-Eng (one pen name of Malai Choopinit).

Siburapha (the pen name of Kulap Saipradit) was a highly respected journalist and fiction writer whose career began in the 1930s. His entire life was devoted to progressive social causes, and he is one of the most prominent early writers of the literature of social consciousness. Short stories available in English translation include "Lend Us a Hand" (1950), which begins with a rich man rebuffing the wife of a poor, sick neighbor who in the past had "lent him a hand" and ends with the poor man and his friends helping to pull the rich man's car out of the mud so that he can take his sick wife to the hospital (Siburapha 1990, 163–75). Another is "The Awakening," a story that takes aim at two targets. The first is U.S. military might and military aid to Thailand.

> That afternoon, there was to be an official presentation of military weapons which America had sent to the Thai government. They had made announcements inviting the people to go and view the new weapons, and it had also been announced that there would be monks blessing the weapons of destruction so that they might be successful and victorious. When the children heard the news, they had begged their father to take them. (181)

The second target of the story is the Thai elite for its victimization of farmers and laborers. In a conversation with his friends, the main character remarks:

> Just take us, working here in Bangkok. Have you ever seen your rich and your well-to-do give us any help? . . . When we were still living with our parents and our grandparents, working in the rice-fields, the rich made money and rice available for us to borrow . . . When you fell upon hard times, when you had no rice to eat or grow, and they gave you rice, did they do it because they loved you? And when you had rice, how much of it did they take away? How many times their original loan was it? (182–3)

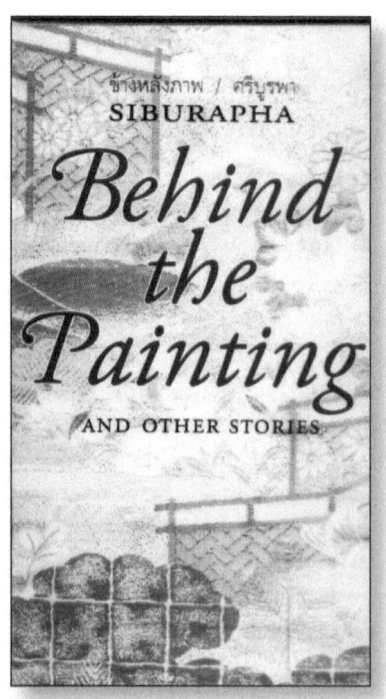

Courtesy of Silkworm Books

It is a matter of supreme irony that the work of fiction for which Siburapha is best known is his short 1938 novel *Behind the Painting*. It has never been out of print, and three film versions have been made, the latest in 2002, available with English subtitles. All of the characters in the story are wealthy, attractive, and educated, and the heroine, Khunying Kirati, is titled as a result of her high birth and marriage. If anyone is standing behind this "painting," to the point of invisibility, it is the socially and economically marginalized, uneducated Thais of the 1930s. But Thais of all political persuasions continue to love this story for its tragic, operatic themes; its splendid settings (Japan and Thailand at their most picturesque); and the unforgettable speeches of its heroine. Khunying Kirati had been married off at the age of thirty-five to a man her father's age only to fall in love with a younger Thai man studying in Japan while the couple is there on their honeymoon.

> It was awful to think that this body, which was still young and fresh with beauty, would have to be wedded to a man of fifty. Was it true that this beautiful figure could exist unloved and with no hope of love? (Siburapha 1990, 100)

The most famous lines in the novella appear on its last page, as Khunying Kirati dies of tuberculosis (a common fate of Thai women in 1930s fiction as in life). She is speaking to Nopporn, the young man who recovered from his infatuation with her and returned to Thailand to marry a suitable young woman.

> "You fell in love there [in Japan] and your love died there. But for someone else, love still flourishes in a wasted body." . . . She wanted to say a last word to me, but her voice had gone, and all her strength. Thus it was, that on a piece of paper she wrote, "I die with no one to love me, yet content that I have someone to love." (Siburapha 1990, 152).

1965-1980: The Courage to Write

Between the mid-1960s and the late 1970s, the impact of both domestic and international politics on everything in Thailand, including literature, can scarcely be overestimated. The "literature of social consciousness," or, as it came to be called during the 1960s and 1970s, "literature for life," grew and quickly surpassed earlier experiments with progressive literature and art during the 1930s and 1950s. In 1973, antimilitary and prodemocracy demonstrations in Bangkok culminated in the exile of the top military leadership and ushered in three years of open political activity. Key factors influencing Thai life and literature during this era include: (1) a conviction on the part of many Thais that their leaders were unapologetically corrupt and indifferent to issues of civil rights and popular participation in the processes of government; (2) Thai cooperation with the United States in the ongoing war in Vietnam, Cambodia, and Laos, which resulted in the presence of six U.S. air bases and hundreds of thousands of U.S. and other foreign troops on Thai soil, as well as the direct involvement of Thai military forces in the war; and (3) a burgeoning population of urban university students who lacked the patience of their fathers and grandfathers with the slow pace of political and social change and were willing to challenge the status quo at considerable risk to themselves.[5]

Short stories, novels and poems of the 1960s and 1970s that were written to portray social injustice and influence social change ranged from the powerful and touching to the didactic and unintentionally condescending. In Rachel Harrison's introduction to *A Drop of Glass and Other Stories* (1985), her anthology of the short stories of Sri Daoruang, she quotes one critic who insists, "The writer should create the spirit of the people. [He] must first blend his own spirit with that of the people and when the two spirits become one he will then be able to create a more beautiful spirit for the people, one which recognizes their needs and their desires" (Sidaoru'ang 1994, 23).[6] In fact, the majority of the reading public tended to choose exactly the kind "escapist" and "polluted" fiction (or television shows or films) that were most despised by left-wing intellectuals.

Useful works on the short fiction of this era include anthologies compiled and edited by Bowie (1991) and Anderson and Mendiones (1985), both of which include excellent introductions to the period, writers, and works. Anthologies produced by Thais that focus on this period include *The S.E.A. Write Anthology of Thai Short Stories and Poems* (Nitaya and Gross 1998), and a Thai P.E.N. anthology entitled *Short Stories and Poems of Social Consciousness* (1984). Many fine writers whose work is not mentioned specifically in this essay are included in these volumes, including Ussiri Dhammachoti, Vanich Charoongkij-anant, Anchan, Sila Khomchai, and the poets Naowarat Pongpaiboon, Chiranan Pitpreecha, Saksiri Meesomsueb, and Paiwarin Khao-Ngam.

Women Writers Getting Personal

By the end of the 1960s, several women writers were producing innovative short fiction. While the "early moderns" among women writers were all members of the upper class and products of European convent schools, compulsory education had gradually expanded throughout Thailand after 1932, and by 1960 literacy statistics in Thailand were impressive. Most villagers could read fairly well, and townspeople regularly read newspapers and magazines.

Suwanee Sukhontha (the pen name of Suwanee Sukhonthieng) holds a special place among women writers of this era. She grew up in a comfortably middle-class family in Phitsanulok. Her father was a respected physician. She graduated from the Fine Arts University in Bangkok, had an affair with one of her professors, married him following his divorce, and had three children. She taught at the university for a few years, left her husband, and eventually was dismissed from her position for having an affair with one of her students.

Notorious, fearless, and very well liked, Suwanee turned her creative efforts from the fine arts to fiction writing and the founding of the popular and influential magazine, *Lalana*, which launched the careers of many women writers. Suwanee's style displays elements of the folktale: earthy, suggestive, self-deprecating, and sarcastic. Her work also reflects an international phenomenon of the late 1960s and early 1970s: women writing the truths of their lives transformed into fiction with minimal alterations.

The charm and outrageousness of Suwanee's writing are epitomized in the story "Alone in Her Room with Her Snake, Brooding on Thoughts of the Past." A woman has come to detest her lover and housemate, who is cruel and unfaithful. She stalks the weekend markets, searching for the most horrible snake that can be bought, the snake that will inflict the most painful bite and produce the most hideous death.

> How does it feel to be a person who is able to kill another? I am such a person.
> My hatred and disgust gathered quietly at first, only a pinprick in my heart. Then tendrils of loathing sprouted and blossomed, permeating every pore, every molecule of my body.
> I hated your constant boasting, as though you were better than anyone else; the callous lies you told to make people think you were so great. I loathed your coarseness and vulgarity. I detested your derision and sarcasm. I abhorred the way you took advantage of people and thought only of yourself.
> Alas! You disgusted me so much that I scarcely knew how we could still live in this house together. And when I thought of all the times we had sex, I wanted to hold my breath until I died.[7]

The woman finds the perfect snake, installs it in an architecturally tasteful crate, becomes fascinated with it, and even has clothes made to match its shiny, colorful scales. She trains it to do its job—it kills her lover—and then, although she has gotten away with her careful crime, the snake gets lost in her house. "Now, every night I lie in bed, unable to sleep. When I close my eyes, all I see is her forked tongue, flickering like fire."[8]

Tragically, in 1954 Suwanee Sukhontha was murdered at the age of fifty-three, leaving her many writer friends and readers to wonder if she would have gone on writing about faithless men and angry women or if she would have focused her substantial gifts on other topics in other times.

Another important woman writer of short fiction who emerged during the 1970s is Sri Daoruang (the pen name of Wanna Sawatsri). She was born in 1941 in rural Phitsanulok (also the birthplace of Suwanee Sukhontha). In the early 1970s, while working in a Bangkok factory, she met and married the political activist and editor Suchat Sawatsri.[9] He and their friends encouraged her to write and be conscious of herself as a working-class writer. Over the past three decades, she has proven her independence as a purely creative writer. Her genius lies in writing imaginative, sometimes bizarre, short stories about life in contemporary Thai society, and she is particularly adept at writing about relations between men and women.

It is interesting that so much of this writer's work has been translated into Western languages, perhaps more than the work of any contemporary Thai writer. I believe it is the short fiction of Sri Daoruang, especially stories written during the 1980s and 1990s, that most nearly predicts the current postmodern trend in Thai writing. Perhaps the best example of her quirkiness and singular imagination is the series of short stories in which she takes characters from the *Ramakian* and installs them in a modest neighborhood in suburban Bangkok. Alas, Tosakan the Demon King has to make the payments on his television set like everyone else.[10]

Courtesy of Silkworm Books

Thai Short Fiction in the New Century

From the late nineteenth century to this day, regardless of a writer's political or social views or intentions, most Thai fiction has been:

1. Instructive and didactic
2. Reflective of a strong or at least identifiable point of view on the ideal nature of society
3. Focused on the experience of Thais within the context of Thai society or on the experiences of Thais in non-Thai settings[11]
4. Respectful of an author-reader contract concerning the nature, purpose, and construction of a proper story and concerning subject matter that is acceptable or unacceptable

During the closing decade of the twentieth century and the opening decade of the twenty-first, some Thai writers are creating fiction that differs markedly from the characteristics noted above and is:

1. Demonstrative, rather than didactic
2. Focused on the individual, rather than society, or the ideal nature of society
3. Primarily concerned with presenting the spectacle of contemporary life as a kaleidoscope of cultures, languages, attitudes, and behaviors
4. Willing, even eager, to alter or even obliterate the traditional author-reader contract

Two writers who have enjoyed rapid success in the first decade of the twenty-first century, and whose work demonstrates all of the points listed above, are Win Lyovarin and Prabda Yoon. Both were artists before they were writers, a fairly common situation in the Thai literary community. Win was born in 1956 in southern Thailand, earned a BA in architecture and an MBA in marketing, and has worked as an architect and interior and graphic designer in Thailand, Singapore, and the United States. An example of Win's short fiction currently available in English translation is "The Chaniang Pot by the Window" (Win Lyovarin 2001).

The short story entitled "Life's Lexicon: Everyman's Bangkok Edition," demonstrates the range and strangeness of his subjects and his style.

> If Bangkok were a book, it would be a thick one, filled with ten million characters, with stories of all sorts of confused flavors mixed up in it, like the Thai movies they stopped making 20 years ago. If Bangkok were a woman,

she'd probably be the honky-tonk kind, pleasuring herself with the cheap sides of Western culture. She'd paint her mouth and pretty up her face thick and sloppy with synthetic cosmetics, trying to hide the disrepair. If Bangkok were a drink, it ought to be mixed like this: 10% natural sweetener, 40% synthetic sweetener, 30% lead, 20% dirty sediment.[12]

Win earned the 1997 S.E.A. Write Award for best novel of the year with *Pracha Thippatai Bon Sen Khanan* (variously translated as "Democracy Shaken and Stirred" and, "Democracy on Parallel Paths"), an interesting, challenging mélange of history and fiction that follows important political characters and events of the Thai twentieth century. An English translation of the novel is by Prisna Boonsinsukh (Win Lyovarin 2003).

Prabda Yoon was born in Bangkok in 1973, the son of a well-known journalist Suthichai Yoon. At eighteen, he earned a full scholarship to the Cooper Union for the Advancement of Art and Science, in New York. In 1996, he received a BA in Fine Arts, and after working briefly in New York as a graphic designer he returned to Thailand and began writing fiction. He rocketed to fame soon after his return with brilliant short stories about people, most of them Thai, trying to figure out how to live (occasionally, even whether to live) in the contemporary world. But his stories about these people are never instructive or didactic, nor are they reflective of a strong point of view on the nature of an ideal society or focused particularly on the experience of Thais within the context of Thai society. They are set in many places: Lumpini Park, a Bangkok rooftop, the streets of New York, a snowy field in Alaska.

Prabda's first collection, *Muang Mumchaak* (Land of Right Angles), focused on his experiences living in New York. The second collection, *Khwamnachapen* (which may be translated either as "What Ought to Be" or "Probability" 2000b), was concerned with the lives of young urban Thais like himself. In 2002, this work was awarded the S.E.A. Write Award for Literature.

If Prabda Yoon's writing represents new directions in Thai fiction, at the same time it honors and even exemplifies the tradition of humor and satire that marks a lengthy roster of Thai literary works. He read widely as a boy, and his father sent him books while he was in New York—many of them old works by early modern writers whom Suthichai himself had loved when he was young.

> My hero was a humorist. His name was Op Chaiwasu. I also read Noi Inthanon, Manat Chanyong, and some others. As a teenager I was drawn to short fiction by people like Chamlong Fangcholachit, but I soon discovered translated books, and then I went to the U.S. and kind of lost touch with Thai books.[13]

But those old Thai books, those stories by wonderful humorists and great storytellers, did not lose touch with Prabda; they inform his work and they resound in his work. No matter that he spent years in New York; those years did not expunge his love of earthy Thai humor and the sense of play in the works of writers such as Op Chaiwasu.

How does this writer's work exemplify a shift to a postmodern sensibility? In the story "Probability," the narrator and hero (or, antihero) is a young man who, having stumbled through a few early career failures, particularly in art, is now a successful creative director in a Bangkok advertising agency. As a boy, orphaned when his parents died in a car accident, he had gone to live with his grandfather, an eccentric noodle shop owner who showed old black and white "Dracula" movies to the neighbors every Friday night. He tells us that, although his grandfather bore an alarming resemblance to the Lon Chaney Dracula of the movies, the evidence was against it.

> Despite his appearance, Grandfather was just a normal rice porridge seller during the day, and he was not much different at night. No changing into a bat, flapping his wings and flying around biting the necks of the neighbors and scaring the wits out of everybody. I never saw him raise his arms, shaking and terrified, shielding his face from the sight of garlic. He could eat all the garlic he wanted. Anyway, Grandfather was a Buddhist, and said his prayers faithfully every night before his head hit the pillow . . . Grandfather told me that Dracula wasn't anything like Thai ghosts, who wander around sticking out their ugly tongues and making their eyes bulge out, going around hating people, seeking revenge and haunting them, or hacking their chests open . . . vampires were worse off than Thai ghosts, Grandfather said, because they were unable to die. They were forced to live forever as evil beasts, and that was why he considered them to be the most unfortunate of beings.[14]

From Transylvania to Thonburi and back again . . . no problem. The depictions of family life in Prabda's work reflect traditional Thai sensibilities and notions of family values, but they are frequently mocked and subverted. The narrator remembers his relationship with his father when he was a little boy.

> There was one time in my life when I considered suicide. I was feeling ill-used and downhearted because my father would not buy me the plastic robot, even though it cost much, much less than the bottle of wine he had just bought. I went to his bureau and took out one of his neckties and tied it around my neck like a noose. I went to my father holding the necktie up above my head with one hand to show my intention, and with tears

streaming down my face I informed him that I was going to hang myself. This picture is indelibly printed in my mind, because it was a prize-winning performance. My father stared at me for a moment, and then walked away saying, "After you're dead, don't forget to call home." But at that time, I had no income, and also no cell phone.[15]

Another, very different story in this collection takes place in Bangkok and a field near Fairbanks, Alaska. A Thai woman has a son who, when he was four years old, came to her bedside early one morning and solemnly presented her with two handfuls of grass, saying, "Snow for you, Mother." He has been doing this every morning since, and he is now in his thirties. She patiently saves money until at last she is able to buy two tickets to Fairbanks, Alaska; perhaps the sight and feel of real snow will cure his strange behavior. Standing on the frozen field, bundled up in his new parka, the son looks confused at first, then smiles, picks up snow in both of his mittens, and trudges toward her. "Snow for you, Mother," he says, smiling happily.[16]

It is a devastating moment. Nothing will change; he will always be a four-year-old boy who brings her handfuls of snow every morning. Later, back home in Bangkok, reflecting on the great sacrifice she has made on behalf of her strange, beloved boy, she says to herself, "What a fortunate person is my son, to have such a mother."

She has made her peace with reality; she has reached the state of *plong-tok*, the acceptance of the way things really are, even when they are pretty bad. Yet, there is no traditional message in this story. Here is a mother, here is a son and this is how their life is in this world. The author is not wrapping it all up with a moral, unless it is that life is what it is and people may as well accept it.

These two writers, Win and Prabda, are very popular at this time. They are thought to represent the vanguard of Thai fiction at the outset of the new century. They, and a few others, have set standards and expectations that are difficult or impossible to attain for writers who have not studied abroad, do not easily read European languages (especially English), and cannot emulate their international outlook. The influence of foreign (Western but also Japanese and Chinese) fiction and film, either translated or subtitled, is very great and far more accessible than foreign education and travel. Nonetheless, there is a gap between more and less privileged Thai writers that is obvious, and growing.

Another problem that is continually raised and discussed within the Thai literary community is easy to understand and perhaps impossible to solve. Most Thais are reading less fiction than they did in previous decades. They watch television, buy or rent DVDs, and go to the movies. In the introduction to southern writer Kanokphong Songsomphan's 1996 short story collection, *Phaendin Uen* (The Other Land), which won the S.E.A. Write Award, the (unidentified) publisher writes:

> It is not that books are not being published, or magazines. Every day, thirty new paperbacks appear . . . Although the sheer number of books and magazines increases in every decade, what do people read? They read the news, articles that are "useful," that are relevant to their jobs. Or they read for entertainment, to decrease the stress that results from living in a competitive society. Very few people read in order to think . . . to open their mind to the world, to knowledge, much less to seek for meaning in their life . . .[17]

The publisher goes on to say that he is cheered by the presence of a new generation of writers in Thailand, represented by Kanokphong, who is presenting stories about contemporary life in the south, a part of Thailand that currently is in turmoil. Even if the reading audience for fiction (of this kind) is not large, he concludes, fiction that chronicles everyday life is of the utmost value for decades and centuries from now it will be fiction, not history books, that allows human beings to vividly experience their ancestors' lives and times.

There are some fundamental contradictions involved in the art of literature and the business of publishing at the outset of the twenty-first century in Thailand. Some new writers are doing groundbreaking work, and excellent films are being written and produced and appreciated around the world. At the same time, Thais are reading less and particularly reading less fiction. Of those people who do read fiction, very few read short stories or novels by outstanding writers such as Win Lyovarin and Prabda Yoon, and even fewer read what remains of the literature of social conscience. Romances written by Thais and adventure stories translated from foreign languages are quite popular—and thick, glossy magazines that feature fashion ads, beauty tips, and society news outsell all of them.

Thais Writing in English

The first Thai to find success writing in the United States was S. P. Somtow (the pen name of Somtow Sucharitkul), a writer and musician who began his writing career with horror and science fiction. Of his many books, *The Ultimate Mallworld*, a sci-fi fantasy, has had the most enthusiastic following. It was first published in 1984 (as *Mallworld*), and a new edition appeared in 2000. Most recently, he has written an opera, *Mae Naak* (2003), based on a well-known ghost story that also has been made into a very successful film.[18] Somtow always has written in English. His father was a Thai diplomat, and Somtow was educated at Eton and Cambridge. He divides his time between homes in Los Angeles and Bangkok. His very entertaining, more or less autobiographical novel, *Jasmine Nights* (1994), was translated into Thai by his mother, Thaitao Sucharitkul, a novelist who writes in Thai and lives in San Francisco and Bangkok.

Rattawut Lapcharoensap was born in Chicago and raised in Bangkok. His collection of short stories, *Sightseeing*, was published in 2005 by Grove Press and has been reviewed most favorably in many publications, from the *New York Times Book Review* to *People*. He graduated from Triamudomsuksa Pattanakarn School in Bangkok, then earned a BA from Cornell University and an MFA in creative writing from the University of Michigan. His short stories have appeared in *Granta*, *Zoetrope*, and other literary magazines, as well as in Harcourt's Best New American Voices series. In the story "Don't Let Me Die in This Place," the narrator is an old, sick American man living in Thailand with his son, Thai daughter-in-law, and grandchildren.

> I'm lying here now . . . in this bed, in this hot, godforsaken, mosquito-infested country, thousands of miles away from ever seeing another Orioles game, with two grandchildren I can barely talk to, a daughter-in-law who mocks my paralysis during mealtimes, and a son who seems indifferent to my plight, all of them sleeping soundly in this house, dreaming their nice little dreams, and I'm so pissed off I'm making a fist in the dark with my good left hand. (Lapcharoensap 2005, 135).

In the story "Farangs," the tourist scene on Phuket Island is described by a young Thai man whose long absent father was an American GI and whose best friend is a pot-bellied pig named Clint Eastwood. When they are translated into Thai, Lapcharoensap's stories no doubt will speak to readers who also like the stories of Prabda Yoon.[19]

Films

Very little of the newest Thai short fiction has been translated so far. If we include screenplays for films, however, we may get a reasonably good idea of the post-modern (or internationalized) trend in Thai literature. Just before Prabda Yoon's third book of collected short stories was published in 2001 (*Uthokphay nay duang taa* [A Flood in the Eyes]), he wrote the screenplay for Pen-Ek Ratanaruang's film *Last Life in the Universe*, which was released in Thailand and abroad in 2003 to great acclaim.[20]

Last Life in the Universe demonstrates all of the criteria I enumerated in describing the postmodern position. The film is supremely demonstrative and visual, never didactic. Its only "purpose" is to give the audience an hour and a half in which to observe the anomie, strangeness, and confusion of the characters' lives. Like living chips in a cosmic kaleidoscope, they drift, they rise, and they fall. The main male character is Japanese, not Thai. The main female character is Thai. People in the movie communicate in Thai, Japanese, and the universal language, English. They converse, they share, but they do not talk specifically about how they feel about anything.

My own favorite character in the film is a house. The house belongs to the Thai woman, a prostitute who works for the Japanese business community and looks forward, more or less, to moving to Japan. The house is an architectural, cultural artifact and remnant of the 1960s or early 1970s—an American-inspired, ugly stucco monument to economic development, Westernization, modernization, and so on. But it has been neglected for years. The house itself is filthy, the garden is a vast patch of weeds, and the swimming pool is grown over; with the tree that has taken root in the middle of it, it has the appearance of a jungle ruin, a modernistic, monstrous repository of lost dreams, lost souls, of civilizations imagined but never achieved. The woman lives in this ruin, with its plastic furniture, its eight-track tape player, its faint echoes of disco parties on the patio long ago. Each character in the film sees the house through his or her own lens, and while we may guess at its meanings for them, we cannot know if our guesses are correct. The Japanese man attempts to clean and fix the house, and establish order; the woman climbs over and around the mess to sleep, eat, bathe, and go out every evening, dressed in her schoolgirl uniform, to consort with her Japanese businessmen.

I look at this house, and it is impossible not to think *annicang*—"impermanence"—that central Buddhist concept. What does she see, or think, this girl? What does he think, this young Japanese man adrift in the universe? And what are we supposed to think about all of it? As is the case with so many of the stories Prabda has written, and other Thais are writing now, we are given no instructions.

We have to think for ourselves.

Conclusion

A few Thais began writing short fiction during the late nineteenth century in elite journals such as *Darunowat*, founded by princes returning from Western universities. Journals, novels, and short stories proliferated following the overthrow of the absolute monarchy in 1932 and the rise of an educated class comprised of Thais who were educated, opinionated, and eager to share their ideas.

Two major social/political factions among writers developed, producing a literature of social preservation, and a literature of social consciousness. Thai readers in general have tended to prefer historical fiction, novels about romance, marriage and families; adventures; and humorous stories and essays. Recently, nonfiction books, especially self-help and advice books concerning career advancement, fashion, beauty, and personal relationships have been popular, including many works translated from Western languages.

Literary prizes have usually gone to fiction and poetry representing the literature of social consciousness. As is true in other countries in the region, these books are read mainly by politically involved people, academics, students, writers, and artists. The prize giving is a somewhat circular process. In 1999, Supannee Varatorn, of the Department of Library Science of Chulalongkorn University, wrote that in a study of 169 national book award books for adults, "89 . . . novels were the works of 39 authors . . . The findings showed that a number of authors more or less had a monopoly of the national award novels" (3–4).

At the beginning of the twenty-first century, two new developments are of particular interest. The first is the rise of an "internationalized" genre of fiction exemplified by the (prize-winning) works of Win Lyovarin and Prabda Yoon. The second is the importance of films that are conceived by directors who reflect the same internationalized views and objectives and who work with new writers. The relationship between director Pen-Ek Ratanaruang and writer Prabda Yoon, on the movie *Last Life in the Universe*, is a case in point.

Writers who have not had the advantages of foreign travel and education are being marginalized by this trend, and feel understandably resentful. While their writing also bears witness to their era and validates the experiences of the majority of Thais, who are not world travelers with foreign educations, their work is well less known and less likely to be read by the very people they wish to reach.

The reading public has not dwindled as much as it has turned from fiction to television, DVDs, and movies—and to "leisure reading." The poet Saksiri Meesomsueb, a winner of the S.E.A. Write Award and the Silpathorn Award, made the following remarks at the Silpathorn Awards ceremony in August 2005.

> I think Thai people read more today, but the quality of reading is lower . . . Writers who show an intensive interest in the literary art have not been well accepted. Reading has become more about pleasure and relaxation, rather than finding out what lies inside those alphabet characters . . .[21]

In a sense, this statement may be accurate, but the fact remains that the awards continue to go to "writers who show an intensive interest in the literary art" such as himself.

The interesting questions, at this point in Thai literary history, are no different than they were twenty or fifty or seventy years ago. Who writes, what is written, and why? Who reads, what do they choose to read, and why? If the questions have not changed, the answers assuredly have.

Notes

[1] See Mongkut, *A King of Siam Speaks* (1987). The King's wit in some of the letters does seem to be enhanced by M. R. Kukrit Pramoj's own erudite and witty English writing style. A collection of letters King Chulalongkorn sent to his daughter during his travels in Europe in the first decade of the twentieth century was published in Thailand but is not available in translation. These letters also are much admired for their simplicity, warmth, and naturalness of expression. The edition of the letters entitled *Klaay Baan* / "Far From Home," was published in Thai by the Chulalongkorn University European Studies Programme (Chulalongkorn 1997).

[2] Information on *Darunowat* is taken from Sumali's, "Thai Prose Fiction of the New Path/way 1874–1910 (1987).

[3] Excerpts from *Phuu Dii* appear in Kepner 1996. The title is difficult to translate; literally, *phuu dii* means "good people," but to Thais it signifies "people of aristocratic lineage." Dok Mai Sot's first, very short novel (or novella) has been translated into English with the title *A Secret Past*, by Ted Strehlow (Dok Mai Sot 1992).

[4] Prasert Na Nagara, *Treasury of Thai Literature: The Modern Period (1988)*, 28–40.

[5] For information on political events during this era, see David L. Morell and Chai-anan Samudavanija, *Political Conflict in Thailand: Reform Reaction, Revolution* (1981); for information on the literature of the period, see Benedict R. O'G. Anderson and Ruchira Mendiones's *In the Mirror: Literature and Politics in Siam in the American Era* (1985); Katherine A. Bowie's *Voices from the Thai Countryside: The Short Stories of Samruam Singh* (1991); and Rachel Harrison's, *A Drop of Glass and Other Stories* (1994), an anthology of Sri Daoruang's short fiction.

[6] This author's name is spelled several ways, including Sidaoru'ang by Harrison; Sri Daoruang by me; and Sridaorueang by her husband Suchat Sawatsri, the editor of a recent collection of her stories (Sridaorueang 2004).

[7] Unpublished translation by Jodi York.

[8] Ibid.

[9] Suchat Sawatsri is still an editor, but in recent years he has shifted his attention to his career as an artist.

[10] These stories are included in Kepner 2004, *Married to the Demon King: Sri Daoruang and her Demon Folk*.

[11] This last element refers to works such as M. C. Akatdamkoeng's *Lakhon Haeng Chiwit* (1929) and Seni Sauvapong's *Wanlaya's Love* (1951), which are set partly in Europe, partly in Thailand, or, the most famous novella of Thais abroad, Siburapha's *Behind the Painting* (1938). In these works, virtually all of the characters are Thais relating to other Thais, and they are mainly concerned with Thai cultural and social issues.

[12] Unpublished translation by Peter Montalbano 2005.

[13] Email communication, Prabda Yoon, March 2005.

[14] Unpublished translation by Susan F. Kepner 2005.

[15] Ibid.

[16] Unpublished translation by Steve Charyasathit, 2005.

[17] Introduction to Kanokphong Songsomphan, *Phaedin Uen (The Other Land)*. Kanokphong passed away in 2006.

[18] Somtow Sucharitkul, *Mae Naak*. Bangkok Opera Foundation, 2003.

[19] Editor's note. At the House of World Cultures' conference in Berlin, September 2005, Prabda Yoon discussed the difficulty for him of writing in English because he felt that language did not express Thai humor as subtly as Thai, especially in terms of word play; whereas, Rattawut finds Thai to be not as effective for his expressive ability.

[20] Editor's note: for two excellent articles on contemporary trends in Thai film see Harrison (2005) and Anchalee and Knee (2006).

[21] Pungkanon Kupluthai, "Silpathorn Award Winners," in The Nation, August 27, 2005.

Bibliography

Anchalee Chaiworaporn and Adam Knee. 2006. Thailand: Revival in an Age of Globalization." In *Contemporary Asian Cinema: Popular Culture in a Global Frame*, edited by Tereska Ciecko, 58–70. New York: Berg.

Anderson, Benedict R. O'G. and Ruchira Mendiones. 1985. *In the Mirror: Literature and Politics in Siam in the American Era*. Bangkok: Duang Kamol.

Akatdamkoeng, M. C. (Akatsadamkng Raphiphat) 1999. *Lakhon Haeng Chiwit* (1929). Bangkok: Phraephitthaya Arkartdamkeung Rapheephat. *The Circus of Life: {A Thai Novel}*, translated from the Thai by Phongdeit Jiangphattanarkit; edited and introduced by Marcel Barang. Bangkok [Thailand]: Thai Modern Classics, 1994.

Bowie, Katherine A., ed and trans. 1991. *Voices from the Thai Countryside: The Short Stories of Samruam Singh*. Monograph, no. 6. Madison: Center for Southeast Asian Studies, University of Wisconsin.

Chat Kobjitti. 1983. *The Judgement*. Translated by Laurie Maund. Bangkok: Laurie Maund.

Chulalongkorn, King of Siam. 1997. *Klaay Baan* / [Far from Home] Bangkok: European Studies Programme, Chulalongkorn University.

Dok Mai Sot. 1992. *A Secret Past*. Translated by Ted Strehlow. Ithaca: Southeast Asia Program, Cornell University.

Harrison, Rachel. 2005. "Amazing Thai Film: The Rise and Rise of Contemporary Thai Cinema on the International Screen." In *Asian Affairs* 36.3: 321–38.

Harrison, Rachel, trans. 1994. *A Drop of Glass and Other Stories*, by Sidaoru'ang. Bangkok: Duang Kamol.

———. 2002. "'A Hundred Loves,' 'A Thousand Lovers': Portrayals of Sexuality in the Work of Thidaa Bunnaak." *Journal of Southeast Asian Studies*, 33.3: 451–70.

Kanokphong Songsomphan. 1996. *Phaedin Uen* [The Other Land]. Bangkok: Nakorn

Kepner, Susan F. 1996. *The Lioness in Bloom: Modern Thai Fiction about Women*. Berkeley: University of California Press.

———. 2004. *Married to the Demon King: Sri Daoruang and Her Demon Folk*. Chiang Mai: Silkworm Books.

Khamsing Srinawk. 1991. *The Politician and Other Stories*. Translated by Domnern Garden. Singapore: Oxford University Press.

Lapcharoensap, Rattawut. 2005. *Sightseeing: Stories*. New York: Grove.

Mongkut. 1987. *A King of Siam Speaks*. Translated by M. R. Seni Pramoj and M. R. Kukrit Pramoj. Bangkok: Siam Society.

Morell, David L., and Chai-anan Samudavanija. 1981. *Political Conflict in Thailand: Reform, Reaction, Revolution*. Cambridge, MA: Oelgeschlager, Gunn and Hain.

Nitaya Masavisut, and Matthew Grose, eds. 1998. *The S.E.A. Write Anthology of Thai Short Stories and Poems*. Chiang Mai: Silkworm Books.

Phillips, Herbert P. 1987. *Modern Thai Literature: With an Ethnographic Interpretation*. Honolulu: University of Hawai'i Press.

Pungkanon Kupluthai. 2005. "Silpathorn Award Winners," *The Nation*, August 27.

Prabda Yoon (Prapda Yun)

———. 2000a. *Muang Mumchaak* (Mu'ang Mumchak). Krung Thep: Samnakphim Kaimarut.

———. 2000b. *Khwamnachapen*. Krung Thep: Sutsapda Samnakphim.

———. 2001. *Uthokphay nay duang taa* (Uthokkaphai nai duangta). Krung Thep: Sutsapda Samnakphim.

Prasert Na Nagara, et al. 1988. *Treasury of Thai Literature: The Modern Period*. Bangkok: National Identity Board, Office of the Prime Minister.

Reynolds, Craig J. 1987. *Thai Radical Discourse: The Real Face of Thai Feudalism Today*. Ithaca: Southeast Asia Program, Cornell University.

Seni Sauvapong (Seinee Saowaphong). 1996. *Wanlaya's Love* (1951). Translation from the Thai and postscript by Marcel Barang. Bangkok: TMC.

Siburapha. 1990. *Behind the Painting and Other Stories*. (1938) Translated by David Smyth. Singapore: Oxford University Press.

Sidaoru'ang. 1994. *A Drop of Glass and Other Stories*. Translated by Rachel Harrison. Bangkok: Duang Kamol. (see also Sridaorueang and Sri Daoruang)

Somtow, S. P. (Sucharitkul) [1984] 2000. *The Ultimate Mallworld*. Atlanta, GA: Meisha Merlin.

———. 1995. *Jasmine Nights*. New York: A Wyatt Book for St. Martin's Press.

Sridaorueang. 2004. *The Citizen's Path: Three Decades of Sridaorueang*. Edited by Suchat Sawatsri. Bangkok: Neo Way.

———. 2003. *Mae Naak*. Compact disc produced by the Bangkok Opera Foundation. (Available at www.bangkokopera.com.).

Srisurang Poolthupya, ed. 2001. *ASEAN Short Stories and Poems by S.E.A. Write Awardees, 1999*. Bangkok: Thai P.E.N. Centre.

Sumali Wirawong, ed. 1987. *Roy kaew naew maay khong thaay*, 2417–2453 [Thai Prose Fiction of the New Path/way 1874-1910]. Bangkok: Thai P.E.N. Centre.

Supannee Varatorn. 1999. "National Award Books as Quality Information Resources in Thailand." *Proceedings of the Sixty-fifth Annual Conference of the International Federation of Library Associations and Institutions*. Bangkok, Thailand: August 20-28, 1999.

Suvanna Kriengkraipetch and Larry E. Smith. 1992. *Value Conflicts in Thai Society: Agonies of Change Seen in Short Stories*. Bangkok: Social Research Institute, Chulalongkorn University in cooperation with East-West Center, Honolulu, Hawai'i.

Suwanna Kriangkraipetch, ed. 2004. *Mong khaam baa nak-khian: Ruang-san thaay nay thatsana nak-wichan* [Looking over the Shoulders of Writers: Thai Short Stories as Viewed by Literary Critics]. Bangkok: Chommanat.

Thai P.E.N. Anthology: Short Stories and Poems of Social Consciousness. 1984. Bangkok: P.E.N. International, Thailand Center.

Wedel, Yuangrat, with Paul Wedel. 1987. *Radical Thought, Thai Mind: The Development of Revolutionary Ideas in Thailand*. Bangkok: Assumption Business Administration College.

Win Lyovarin. 2001. "The Chaniang Pot by the Window." 60–92. In *ASEAN Short Stories*, edited by Srisurang Poolthupya, Bangkok: Thai P.E.N. Centre.

———. 2003. *Democracy Shaken and Stirred*. A novel translated by Prisna Boonsinsukh. Bangkok: 113.

Recent Thai Films Available with English Subtitles

As of 2008, these films could be ordered from Amazon.com, eThaiCD.com, and various other Web sites. For information about some Thai films, see filmbangkok.com.

Apichatpong Weerasethakul, 2000. *Mysterious Object at Noon.*

———. 2004. *Tropical Malady.*

Cherd Songsri. 2002. *Behind the Painting.*

Ekachai Uekrongtham. 2004. *Beautiful Boxer.*

Nonzee Nimibutr. 1999. *Nang Nak.*

Pen-Ek Ratanaruang. 1999. *SixtyNine (6ixtyNin9).*

———. 2001. *Monrak Transistor.*

———. 2003. *Last Life in the Universe.*

Prachya Pinkaew. 2003. *Ong Bak.*

Surapong Pinijkhar. 2004. *The Siam Renaissance.*

Youngyooth Thongkonthun. 2002. *Iron Ladies.*

2

Contemporary Trends in Thai Short Fiction
Suradech Chotiudompant

Thailand in the late twentieth and early twenty-first centuries has come a long way. Urban development and the influx of Western influences have geared the traditional Thai lifestyle toward a new cosmopolitan, globalized consumer culture. This shift is by no means universal and comprehensive as it encounters resistance in various forms and at different levels. Thai literary works produced in this contemporary period make manifest this complex condition whereby the process of globalization is ongoing yet taking shape in a unique, specific, local context. Despite the economic downtrend of the late 1990s, one can sense the vibrant atmosphere of the literary industry as a whole, as Thai writers, of both older and newer generations and in both traditional and alternative forms, touch on a number of contemporary issues, ranging from urban capitalism to the unrest in the South. This essay aims to outline the variety of trends and movements in Thai short stories written during the contemporary period.

Chusak Patarakulwanich (2002, 21–28) categorizes modern Thai fiction in three groups: the romance, the best seller, and the experimental. Although this classification may be valid for the genre of the novel, that of the short story may need different groupings. As the nature of the style is its concision, it is more suitable for those Thai writers who wish to experiment within its limited space to give the most dramatic result rather than to spin a yarn of romance. Taking this idea in mind, one can then see that most Thai short stories seek to tackle social issues in a serious manner rather than providing romantic escapism.

Most Thai short stories are first published in current affairs magazines such as *Matichon Weekly* and the *Nation Weekly* or in the "Jutprakai" literary section of *Bangkok Bizweek*. Some also appear in lifestyle magazines such as *Praew*, *Hi-Class*, and *Sakulthai*. There are also occasional publications that anthologize short stories such as the *Sanamya* collection from the *Men Wanakam* and the *Rahu-omchan* collection from the Kanokphong Songsomphan Foundation. Also worth mentioning is the legendary *Chokaraket* collection published under the supervision of Suchart Sawatsri, a famous Thai literati who has been directly involved in the popularization of contemporary Thai literature for more than four decades. Its influence is lasting and powerful, as most writers discussed in this essay have published their works in it. The Chokaraket Prize, bestowed on the best stories published in its volumes, has been regarded as a guarantee of their high quality and distinctive style. The S.E.A. Write Award is another prize coveted by many writers as it guarantees fame and monetary success for those who win it. Given annually, the award each year focuses on only one type of work (the novel, the poem, or the short story); thus, every three years most aspiring Thai short fiction writers will submit their works and long to be prestigious winners.

This system of awards has become an essential factor in creating public recognition for literary works. Literary prizes, especially the S.E.A. Write Award, are powerful enough to make an anonymous writer a national celebrity overnight, which in turn generates interest in his/her works and a great number of critical pieces. The selective process of Thai short fiction in this essay is partly influenced by such competitions. This factor will be taken into consideration alongside the need to build a continuing history out of the wide variety of Thai short fiction published in the last thirty years.

Masters of Realism: Social Consciousness and Rural Depiction

In the 1980s, the Thai literary scene was adorned with masters of the short form of fiction who were mainly from outside Bangkok. Ussiri Dhammachoti from the west coast and Phaitoon Thanya from the South represented the trend of the short story in this period. Ussiri, originally from Hua Hin, received the 1981 S.E.A. Write Award for his collection of short stories *Kunthong, You Will Return at Dawn* [1987]. Some of his stories center on political issues such as the 1976 students uprising and social issues such as poverty-stricken rural society, urban dog-eat-dog culture, and the widening gap between rich and poor people. Based on a traditional lullaby about a brave man from the country called Kunthong who decides to fight the Burmese, "Kunthong, You Will Return at Dawn" refers to the political disillusionment of a student participating in the 1976 uprising. Also called Kunthong, the student demonstrates his courage by joining other students to protest against the autocratic government. However, they are defeated and hide in the forest to escape the authorities. In this story, the protagonist's mother is anxiously awaiting her son's return. To her dismay, it transpires that her son is "dead."

> "He is dead," a youth of Kunthong's age tells her.
> Mother sobs . . . her son is dead!
> Did you see his corpse?" Mother asks.

"No, not his corpse. I met him, and he asked me to tell you that he is dead."

"Who is he staying with?" she asks again.

"With his sword . . . the sword that is stained with blood and hate!" says the young man.

The sun glares from the mid-day sky as Mother's boat makes its way homeward with all the stuff that she had prepared for Kunthong. Who is it that has made her gentle boy so angry? Who is it that has made him decide to die away from his mother and his home? She could not find an answer. (Ussiri Dhammachoti, [1978] 1987, 189; translation by Chamnongsri L. Rutnin)

The "death" of her son is symbolic, denoting his disillusionment with the political situation, especially when one considers that most of the students who participated in the 1976 uprising eventually decided to leave their cherished ideals behind and return to Bangkok.

While "Kunthong, You Will Return at Dawn" focuses on the psychology of the student who loses his innocence in the political turmoil, other stories in this collection address the condition of rural people, who are both poverty-stricken and steeped in their traditional beliefs, resisting change. "On the Route of a Rabid Dog," for instance, shows the lives of two rural people juxtaposed with a mad dog. The first is a man who still wants to sleep with his younger wife despite his old age, and the second is a drunken father who forces his son to tell him where his wife has hidden their money. Ussiri depicts a rural culture that favors immediate sensual and physical gratification without thinking carefully about its possible ramifications. These shortsighted villagers are compared to a mad dog that finally faces its death.

The sun moves lower and is partially hidden by the mountain range. Its bright, copper rays suffuse the western sky. The laterite road that runs across the village looks dark against the glow of the sunset.

At this evening hour, the thin brown dog covered with dry red dust runs along the laterite road into the village . . .

And falls down, dead.

Red dust sticks to the saliva around its mouth, its body stiff, its eyes open and its swollen tongue jammed between its jaws. (Ussiri Dhammachoti [1978] 1987, 182; translation by Chamnongsri L. Rutnin)

The dog's death may symbolize the hopeless situation of the villagers, who will find no way out other than facing their own tragic ends should they remain in this base way of life.

Phaitoon Thanya is another well-regarded short story writer of this period. Like Ussiri, he has published short stories that focus on social problems to raise social consciousness. His collections include *Building Sand Piles* (1986) and *October* (1994), the former a recipient of the 1987 S.E.A Write Award. While Ussiri's narratives center around the plight of rural Thai villagers across the country, Phaitoon mainly chooses the southern landscape for his settings and deals with such themes as social injustice, greed, materialism, and the conflict between the new and traditional ways of life. In "The Red Turtledove," he encapsulates the conflict between the old and the new in the South. The protagonist is a kindhearted science teacher who decides to adopt a red turtledove despite the

Building Sand Piles by Phaitoon Thanya
Courtesy of Nakorn Publishing House

protests of his mother and uncle, who believe the bird brings bad luck. When his mother's pig dies and his girlfriend mysteriously falls ill, he has no choice but to get rid of the bird. However, before making his decision, he feels so dissatisfied with his family that he flees his home to sleep in a temple. His action brings him both guilt and remorse.

> I was truly sorry about the awful way I'd acted that evening; my mother was no doubt saddened by the stubbornness of her son. I became filled with regret. I was wrong to turn against my own mother, who had such good intentions. I shouldn't have run out on her like that. But if I had stayed, eventually she would have made me get rid of the bird. How could I do that? I had been raising it myself, and I had promised its mother that I would take care of it as well as I could. If I let it go now, wouldn't I be breaking my promise? Besides, it wasn't strong enough yet. It wasn't fully grown: if I let it go off on its own, who knows what might happen to the poor thing? And there was this: since I'm a science teacher who doesn't believe what can't be proven, and if I were to do what my mother and my uncle wanted me to do, wouldn't that mean that I was even more foolish than they were? No, I couldn't do it. (Phaitoon Thanya 2001, 91–92; translation by Tom Glass)

The protagonist's internal conflict reflects the confused mind-set of young Thai rural people whose modern lifestyle is in stark contrast to the old, traditional set of beliefs.

While "The Red Turtledove" portrays the defeat of the newer ways of thinking in the face of the indelible superstitions of southern Thai people, "Building Sand Piles" has more optimistic overtones. The central character is a young girl who is prevented from playing with her chauvinistic male friends. While they are busy playing boisterously in the canal, she is left alone building sand piles despite the waves that constantly crush them. Her dream of building a big pagoda out of sand is not crushed, however, as she gathers sand and turns it into a magnificent construction against all odds. One of her male friends is perplexed at what she is doing.

> "There it goes again," said the boy after another wave swept through. "It's all gone."
>
> "It's not all gone" the girl insisted.
>
> "What do you mean? If it's washed away already, how can it still be here?" The boy was confused.
>
> "The sand isn't all gone. The sand is still right here."
>
> "I told you it's gone. It's all washed away, can't you see?"
>
> "It's not true." The girl scooped up more sand. "The sand's still here, see?" She held up a handful. "They say it comes with the water. The water brings the sand every day. It will never run out. We have to keep building." She spoke with confidence.
>
> "And then it will get washed out again. Those guys are still playing. Any minute now another wave will be here."
>
> "So we'll build it again. If we make it as big as the pagoda in the temple, it can't be destroyed. Let the waves come. They'll never wash away everything." Her eyes shone brightly as she spoke. (Phaitoon Thanya 2001, 27–28; translation by Tom Glass)

This story is highly symbolic and can be read and understood on many levels. The little girl's persistence may represent a sense of optimism that some of the rural people in the South share, the hope that one day the dream of peace and equality in a conflict-free state will come true.

The short narratives of Ussiri and Phaitoon are similar on many counts: they both use realism in their literary presentation, and the rural underdog is a central character in their narratives. In this light, their narratives can be labeled "literature for life," produced in the faith that good literature should reflect the harsh realities of the underprivileged. This is in contrast to literary works by some writers of the previous generation, such as Dok Mai Sot, which tend to focus on the privileged group of aristocrats or the upper middle class in Bangkok (see also Anderson and Mendiones 1985, 44; and Mattani Mojdara Rutnin 1988, 57–62).

This strain of realism continues in Thai literature of the 1990s and 2000s, as exemplified by the works of Chamlong Fangcholachit, whose literary career spans more than two decades. His collections of short stories, such as *The Caravan* (1980), *The Prime Minister's Visit to the Bank* (1986), *The Gentleman with a Lighter* [1996] (2006), *Car Boot Sale* [2000] (2004), and *Ligor, They Have Changed* (2005), mainly feature realist settings and characters with the clear aim of portraying the subtleties and intrigues of contemporary Thai society. Chamlong's short narratives mainly deal with issues of human dignity and suffering, especially after the 1997 economic crisis, and the lives of rural people in the face of harsh capitalism and a corrupt bureaucracy.

In "Car Boot Sale," a short story in the eponymous collection, he vividly depicts the atmosphere of a car boot sale to show how flexibly Bangkokians have adjusted to the economic crisis. For most people gathering at the sale, this is their first retail experience. This engenders a feeling of shame since some of them occupied executive posts in esteemed companies when the economy was buoyant. Their uneasiness is maintained, as they are presented with uncomfortable questions about their previous jobs and their downfalls. Chamlong is a well-rounded author who takes an interest in more than urban life. Life in the southern part of Thailand is another subject close to his heart. In *Ligor, They Have Changed*, the collection that won the Seven Book Award, Chamlong addresses the social problems those southerners face. "They Have Changed" deals with the psychology of parents who are overly proud of their children. In it Boonta graduates from a university and marries a good-looking, wealthy man from the city, and Ratri is employed as a retailer in a trendy mobile phone shop. Their successes make their mother arrogant, and she distances herself from her neighbors. For this reason, "They Have Changed" details an interesting change in the rural space whereby young people move to the city and bring money back to their families.

> Boonta brought her good-looking boyfriend to visit her parents only once. The neighbors began to notice the gradual change in the couple's comportment until they became like different people. Soon after, there appeared things that the neighbors never expected to see. When their daughters went back to Bangkok, they didn't want to converse with the neighbors, with whom they had been acquainted all their lives. (Chamlong Fangcholachit 2005, 26; translation mine)

The change in attitude of the old couple reflects how some rural people value material progress and use it as a benchmark to judge others. The migration of their offspring becomes a source of comparison, a sort of "keeping up with the Joneses," where people are evaluated by the wealth and material success of their offspring. Morality is generally ignored, and fewer people take an interest in their spiritual improvement. Unlike those stories previously discussed, the rural is seen here not as a degenerative space breeding superstition and irrational beliefs but rather as an idyllic space tainted by the urban values of capitalism and materialism. In a nutshell, Chamlong's work can be considered as a continuation of the realist trend of the previous decade in portraying contemporary social phenomena when the impact of materialism and capitalism becomes visible in the psychology of rural people, significantly changing their worldviews and ways of life.

Beyond Realism: Rural and Urban Conflicts

While these three veteran writers prefer to work and revel in the traditional mode of realist representations in short fiction, other writers of the same and younger generations have tried their hands at other genres. One such writer is Vanich Charoongkij-anant. His short stories, which sometimes touch on the relationship between the modern and the older, superstitious ways of life, are distinguished in their use of ambiguity, thereby playing with the reader's reactions. In "The Song of the Leaves" from *Down the Same Lane* [1983] (1984), for instance, the author charts the life of Somchao, a young girl who, willy-nilly, is supposed to inherit from her grandmother the art of singing traditional music. The old woman tries very hard to train her granddaughter to be a good singer so that she can take her place in temple fair performances, despite the girl's clearly nonchalant attitude. The story portrays the difference in worldview between these two women from diverse generations.

> When Grandma was asleep, Somchao would wander off to some of the neighbors' houses to borrow those film star magazines with pictures and stories of the stars. Whenever Grandma went anywhere to sing, Somchao would always accompany her—at least she could be put to use in singing the refrains or marking the rhythm with the wooden clappers or the metal *ching* [Thai cymbals] or merely by clapping her hands. Somchao deigned to go just because Grandma went, if Grandma couldn't go Somchao wouldn't go either. (Nitaya Masavisut and Grose, 1996, 24; translation by Chamnongsri L. Rutnin)

At last, when they both go to a temple fair despite the old woman's ailing health and coming blindness, the old woman can sing only the beginning of the song and then agrees to be led to the side of the stage. Seeing her grandmother's poor state, Somchao immediately lays down the clappers and takes the place of her grandmother. Defying the public expectation of a mediocre performance, Somchao surprises everybody as her voice is so hauntingly and unmistakably that of her grandmother. The author's abrupt ending at this point leads to a powerful ambiguity: we do not know whether Somchao is possessed by her grandmother's spirit or whether this streak of genius is rooted in her blood. In ending the story thus, Vanich raises the issue of cultural disparity between people of different generations, yet retains the faith that Thai tradition will carry on regardless.

A similar ambiguity can be found in "The Barter," which is included in the same collection. Like "The Song of the Leaves," "The Barter" centers around the conflict between the old and the new ways of life, as represented in a situation in which an architect who falls in love with an old *sala* [Thai pavilion] in a temple subsequently moves it to Bangkok to become part of a riverside restaurant. However, the pavilion is believed to be haunted, as there are a growing number of creaks heard by the restaurant staff at night. The climax is reached when the creaks and screeches are heard on a Friday night when the restaurant is jam-packed. Apart from these worrying noises, the pavilion appears to be breaking apart; its roof tiles start falling off and crashing into the river. After the tremors and confusion, the restaurant is closed. The pavilion is now misshapen. Only a monk and a rural craftsman, who have lived with the pavilion since it was built, know the reason for the catastrophe.

> "We are going to pull it down, uncle," [the architect] said sadly to In Jaang [the rural craftsman] – mainly because he was at a loss to find anything else to say.
>
> "Yes, take it down . . ." In Jaang told the architect " . . . and put it up again with the pillars paired rightly."
>
> "Why, uncle? Are the pillars paired wrongly? But what difference does it make?" The architect felt a rising excitement.
>
> "They have stood together for a hundred years, how can you have the heart to go and separate them?"
>
> In Jaang replied with a tremor in his voice and tears running down his cheeks, as he turned to look at *sala hoi khao* [the *hoi khao* pavilion] with an inexpressible pity spreading through the depths of his heart. (Nitaya Masavisut and Grose, 1996, 50; translation by Chamnongsri L. Rutnin)

Like "The Song of the Leaves," the author's reticent ending is a powerful gesture signaling how superstition and faith have become deeply rooted in the rural mind-set. The tragedy may symbolize the conflict between the modern way of life, which enshrines physical wealth, and the traditional lifestyle, which entails beliefs in supernatural entities and inexplicable phenomena. The ambiguity of the ending reiterates this conflict, as the reader is not provided with the answer as to why the pavilion falls down.

A veteran writer of renown, Chart Kobchitti, delivers a sharp critique of contemporary society through his uniquely surreal narratives. As in his novels *The Judgement* (1981) and *Time* (1993), recipients of the S.E.A. Write Award, his collections of short narratives, such as *The Personal Knife* (1984), *The OK City* (1989), and *Facial Massage Service* (2005), tend to expose the reader to provincial moral deterioration, urban alienation, political corruption, and unattainable friendship in the wake of ruthless materialist development. Most of his very short stories have an intense emotional impact via the use of sarcasm and vivid symbolism.

In "The Ghostly City," from the *The OK City*, Chart tells of an old man whose experience of resurrection sheds light on the corruption of Thai politicians. Without knowing of his own death, the old man is transported to the netherworld, in which politicians are busy selling their policies. The surreal image of these politicians is telling: each face has twenty mouths, which proclaim the feasibility of their projects sugarcoated in sweet rhetoric. In addition, their arms have become shorter and some of them have no arms at all, only stout torsos (Chart Kobchitti 1989, 54). The old man tries to dissuade the public from believing in such projects, only to be imprisoned by the authorities. This surreal trip by the old man is analogical to the contemporary state of Thai politics, in which politicians' promises are seen as mere sweet talk intended to get them elected. For Chart, this fantastic presentation of the old man's dream state shows the reader another dimension of Thai society, one that is equally or more powerful than its realistic counterpart.

Continuing in the same vein, Chart grotesquely satirizes a corrupt politician who asks for help from a rural witch doctor in the short story "Facial Massage Service." In the course of his treatment:

> The deputy minister closes his eyes, hearing the scratching sound of foot skin as the feet rub his face, along with the chanting of the witch doctor. Sometimes when the feet press so hard on his nose he can't breathe, he needs to gasp for air, thus letting some dirt from the feet scratch against his teeth and fall into his mouth. Soon Deputy Minister Pithakthai alternately feels some heat and then warmth on his face. In that trance, he feels his worries start to dissipate and disappear as if they never happened. Deputy Minister Pithakthai Bamrungraj really believes that these worries never existed.

With the power of the witch doctor's feet, he feels as if he were a new deputy minister without blemish. The feet that are rubbing against his face start to emit the lovely smell of fragrant rice, boiled and still warm. The deputy minister now willingly breathes in the smell of the feet, as the chanting of the witch doctor becomes fainter and slower and finally stops. (Chart Kobchitti 2005, 122–23; translation mine)

The witch doctor rubs his feet on the politician's face to make it coarser and thicker so that the politician will be able to survive his own corruption scandal by means of shameless lies. This profane action is clearly a literalization of the Thai pun "the thick face" meaning "lacking in moral conscience," as well as a carnivalesque act of using the feet, deemed the lowest part of the body, to rub the face, considered the most revered part of the body according to traditional Thai belief. As in "The Ghost City," "Facial Massage Service" can be seen as portraying the harsh realities of Thai politics with recourse to a surreal, albeit at times violent and ridiculous, way of storytelling.

With the works of Gabriel García Márquez having been translated into Thai during the 1990s, some writers from the South find magical realism relevant, believing that this complex genre may provide an alternative to the overused genre of realism. As one of the most important literati of the "Nakorn" Group, which comprises other southern authors such as Phaitoon Thanya, Sathaporn Srisajchang, Pinyo Srichamlong, and Chamlong Fangcholachit, Kanokphong Songsomphan was among the first Thai authors to introduce the genre of magical realism to Thailand and has remained one of its most professional practitioners. His collection of short stories *The Broken Bridge* [1991] (2000) won the 1992 National Book Award, and his subsequent collection *The Other Land* [1996] (1997) received the S.E.A. Write Award. In the latter collection, the story "The Witch of the Valley" demonstrates his mastery of the magical realist genre. The central character, an old woman who is believed to be a witch and, according to public belief, can perform various miracles, lives in an old thatched house on an estate that has been bought for development. A battle between the woman and the estate becomes a conflict between the traditional, rural world of spiritual beliefs and the modern conception of development, which leaves no space for local lore. The ending demonstrates the insignificance of this battle in contrast to the power of nature: a three-day rain washes away all traces of the conflict and closes the entrance to the village, depriving it of any contact with the external world for another year (Kanokphong Songsomphan [1996] 1997, 277–279).

The current decade has seen the publication of four more collections of Kanokphong's short stories, *The World That Turns around Itself* (2004), *Around*

Our Own House (2005a), *National Tales* (2005b), and *The Poet's Death* (2005c), the last three of which were published after his premature death in 2006. With these recent publications, we see the writer's significant shift from magical realism to a more self-reflexive form of interior monologue. In "Her Problem" from *Around Our Own House*, Kanokphong describes an old woman from the vantage point of her internal thinking through the use of stream of consciousness. By following closely the inner thinking of the woman, the writer gradually reveals what the character herself does not know that she is a victim of consumerism and capitalism, which breed in her shame over her poverty and jealousy of other people's wealth.

> I shouldn't have stopped to talk with her. Suda. You arrogant toad! You thought you were the wife of a teacher, so you couldn't eat canned fish. Such a toad! She was walking, while furiously thinking. What type of a teacher's wife is she, still needing to get up early to scrape rubber trees? "The washing machine is still working, but the spinner is out of order," she drawled. "It doesn't spin. My clothes are not spun dry." She laughed and became furious. When I have a car, she thought, I will drive it in front of her house ten times a day. You toad! You teacher's wife! Can't eat canned fish. Your husband is still in debt with the house loans. You haven't finished paying off all those debts, not even in these ten or twenty years. You unthinking toad! She trod heavily, becoming more furious. (Kanokphong Songsomphan 2005a, 53; translation mine)

By ingeniously unraveling the tangled psychological subtleties, the author manages to effectively portray the personality of a rural woman whose life is under the domination of consumer culture, in which standards of life are judged by having such luxury products as a washing machine and a spin dryer.

Also from the South, Jiraphat Angsumali is another noteworthy writer who does not opt for realism, as his literary output shows his craftsmanship in the use of magical realism. Both his latest novel, *Shadow Play* (2005), and his collection of short stories, *Perversion* (2002), were short-listed for the S.E.A. Write Award. Various short stories in *Perversion* deal with supernatural events that happen in the South and the superstitious public. "Perversion 69" is a powerful story that tackles the theme of social transgression. The narrative centers on the obnoxiously profane action of a monk who breaks the religious code by sleeping with a woman. Knowing this, her husband decides to kill them both. The villagers are somewhat surprised but try to figure out what number this killing would represent in order to use it in lottery gambling. The narrative features perversion on many levels: sexual and religious perversion, as well as that in the minds of the villagers who mercilessly exploit the situation for their own selfish gain. This perversion of existing human codes corresponds with that of nature.

> The strong sea wind brought raindrops and saltwater vapor to his face. He [the husband] only felt an eye rash. The sea was still tumultuous and frightening. The cypress leaves made a sharp noise like someone's sinister laughter. [. . .] The wind was getting stronger. He tried to make a decision, after long consideration.
> Tut . . . tut . . . tut . . .
> Big *lang* fish fell from the sky amid the rain onto the sand and under the big cypress tree. Not just one or two fish, but a whole school spreading across the beach up to the road alongside it. Many straddled the branches of the cypress and big *jik* trees along the beach road. Most were still alive, struggling to live, thrashing their tails, gaping as if fighting for a slim chance of survival. (Jiraphat Angsumali 2002, 37–38; translation mine)

This use of a supernatural event parallels the human corruption in which social norms and codes are violated. Another story in this collection worth noting is "The Spirit Medium," which, as the title suggests, entails a man who has devoted his life to becoming a medium for a Chinese god during the vegetarian festival in Phuket. The reason for this spiritual commitment is that the god saved his life following a fatal accident. However, his decision is in conflict with his wish to look after his ailing mother, who is in need of care yet still adamantly wants him to stay at the Chinese temple. To please her, he leaves her behind and goes to stay at the temple during the festival. In the end, while the frail, ailing old woman stands motionless in the pouring rain, only to be rescued by a kind neighbor, her grandson is at work being possessed by the Chinese god. This juxtaposition is touching as the two people both lose consciousness and somehow connect with an indescribable spiritual world through the power of their beliefs. Jiraphat tellingly ends the narrative as follows.

> The small body [of the mother] was crooked, like a mass of something without feeling. A waft of cool breeze came through the window, along with remote sound of Chinese crackers. The smell of incense and candles faintly lingered in the air.
> The vegetarian festival was in its last night, when the gods were preparing to return to heaven through the gate of eternity. Nine lights adorning the gate would be extinguished, and smooth wooden poles, a bridge between the two worlds, would be brought back to earth as the din of the last Chinese cracker came to an end. (2002, 97; translation mine)

Vanich Charoonkij-anant, Chart Kobchitti, Kanokphong Songsomphan, and Jiraphat Angsumali have significantly broadened the scope of Thai short fiction, showing that realism is not the only way to represent contemporary Thai society. These writers have widened the choice for literary settings to mirror their mainly rural spaces and touched on topics that are related to these spaces.

The Metropolis and the Experiment

While the trend of realism evolved into magical realism and other alternative literary styles that similarly aim to portray the state of rural Thai society, one should not ignore a significant trend that has emerged in the capital. Several regional writers have migrated to Bangkok, and some of their short stories use the capital city as a setting and deal with such urban themes as alienation and loneliness in various manners. One of the writers who made their mark in this trend is Sila Khomchai. His short story "Mid-Road Family" does not present the urban condition in a totally negative light. In his subtly satirical tone, the author portrays how flexible urbanites can be in adjusting themselves to the demanding city lifestyle. The title "Mid-Road Family" suggests the great amount of time urbanites spend on the road, rather than in their houses, and the daily activities that take place in the car during heavy traffic jams. The beginning of the short story may reveal a startling picture for some yet a familiar one for Bangkokians.

> My wife is a thorough and wonderfully organized woman. When I remarked that I had to meet my boss for an important client meeting at three in the afternoon at a riverside hotel in Klong Saan, she said that in that case, we would have to leave the house at nine o'clock in the morning so that she could make her appointment just before noon near Saphan Khwai.
>
> But her thoroughness and organizational skill go much further. In the back seat of our automobile she has always ready a basket of *fast food*, a cooler full of iced drinks, an assortment of salty and sweet snacks, green tamarind, star gooseberries, a plastic trash bag, and a spittoon. Often there are changes of clothes hanging from the rear-view mirror. It looks as though we are going on a picnic. (Teri Shaffer Yamada, 2002, 210–11; translated by Susan F. Kepner).

The story is distinct in its exhibition of the mind-set of Bangkok city dwellers, who learn to accept the city's traffic jams as part of their lives rather than thinking of ways to solve the problem. They simply adjust their lives around these traffic jams and still manage to be happy. Throughout the course of the story, Sila tells how the couple manages to make love in the car and how the husband learns of his wife's pregnancy in the car too. The ending does not see any solution to the urban crisis but rather describes another adjustment by the couple.

> I take the driver's seat. When the traffic begins to crawl forward again, I think about the little one, the child who will make our family complete. And I think about a big car, big enough for a father, a mother, and a child. And all the things we'll need in our car, for family activities.
>
> A new, bigger car. . . A necessity, and the greatest source of happiness for the family that lives its life in the streets of Bangkok. (Teri Shaffer Yamada, 2002, 217; translated by Susan F. Kepner).

If every family in Bangkok thinks like this family, the problem of traffic jams will only worsen. Sila poignantly portrays the mind-set of middle-class Bangkokians who need to think of themselves and their families first in their day-to-day struggle to survive in the city; they have neither the time nor the energy to see the big picture or think of ways to strike at the root of urban problems.

While Sila subtly paints both the mental and physical landscape of urbanity through his realist lens, Win Lyovarin and Prabda Yoon represent a new generation of writers who tackle the city in a bolder manner of experimentation. Their works deal not only with day-to-day issues of social disparity and inequality but also with philosophical issues on a more metaphysical level as influenced by international literary and philosophical works. In this light, both Win and Prabda represent the trend of urban internationalism, which is distinctive in its formal experimentation and the use of international settings and characters.

A Creature Called Human, by Win Lyovarin
Courtesy of the author

Win's collection *A Creature Called Human* (1999) represents an apogee of Thai literary experimentation, especially because most of the stories exhibit a turn from realism to various forms of stylistic play. "An Affair," the first story, is a lucid example, displaying the psychology of two urban people who agree to have an affair. The narrative makes manifest urban alienation and longing for companionship, while at the same time it shows that intimate relationships are difficult, if not impossible, to attain. This longing and the impossibility of making proper human contact are rendered at the level of storytelling as the whole narrative is simply a series of words and linking elements are all omitted.

> A bathroom / taking off clothes / a mirror / a reflection / a man / age / 27 / I / yuppie / handsome appearance / single status / youth / freedom / fun / taking a shower / warm water / refreshment / quietness / a living room / a window / a horizon / lights / Bangkok / a clock / two o'clock in the morning / loneliness / a remote control / a hi-fi stereo / compact discs / music / softness / melodies / waltz / Johann Strauss / Chivas Regal.
> (Win Lyovarin 1999, 8; translation mine)

This careful chain of words attests to the loss of human contact, and what remains are merely words and phrases with no clear connection, signifying the urban condition whereby material objects are more important than relationships.

"The Chaniang Pot by the Window," another short story in the same collection, also exhibits Win's experimental streak, as he attempts to portray an "impossible" conversation between a patient and a nurse. Through this dialogue, the author touchingly describes the frail, suicidal mental state of the patient, whose car accident has rendered him paralyzed. As he was a breadwinner, the accident has proven to be a tragedy for his family, especially since his wife is pregnant. Now deprived of the means to earn money for her family, she has no choice but to resort to an abortion. Despite this bleak situation, the nurse, Ket, tries to cheer the man up and puts a plant pot near his bed so that he will learn to cope with his life once again. The retelling of their impossible conversation reveals the difference in attitude toward life between the two people.

> The next morning Ket came into the room laden with parcels. The young nurse pulled an object out of a plastic bag. It was a plain red-lime-colored terra cotta flower pot with a rough texture, about six inches tall. There was also a wavy-edged tray to put the pot on. She took a small paper envelope out of another bag. The paralyzed patient's eyes fixed steadily on the nurse.
> [*What is that?*]
> She was smiling with those eyes again. "Some *chaniang* seeds."
> [*What are you going to do?*] . . .
> "In a few days they will sprout."
> [*Why are you planting it?*] . . .
> "My grandfather believed that planting trees is building up life.

Watching the trees sprout leaves is a drill in patience. It is learning to love. And all these lead to an understanding of life."

[*Aha! Your grandfather was also a philosopher. But suppose your grandfather was lying here in this bed, would he still be saying the same thing? All right, if I didn't die first out of boredom I would be able to see it grow. But I think it would see me die first before I could see it grow.*]

"You must believe in the power of the will to live. You must go on fighting for your family, for your wife and for your child. Just think of your wife having to fight all alone. Think of. . ."

[*And has anyone ever thought of me? It is not any of my fault that that damn truck hit me and paralyzed me and I have to lie here waiting for death. Has anyone shown any interest in me? Everyone says the same thing, that I will live. But do they know that living is much more difficult than dying?*] (Srisurang Poolthupya, 2001, 79–82; translation by Malithat Promathatavedi)

By portraying the incredulous mental state of the patient, Win exposes us to the harsh contemporary world in which people need to struggle to make a living. Money has become a major issue that determines happiness, not only our own but that of our families. In addition, moral encouragement for the underdog, such as the nurse's didactic preaching, is considered shallow, as it simply makes people carry on living and shouldering all these responsibilities without solving real problems of the terrible dog-eat-dog state of modern society.

A Creature Called Human received the S.E.A. Write Award in 1999. This created a stir in literary circles, as most winners of the previous era were realistic in their literary style. One could sense in Win's stories an anxiety resulting from the economic boom, which has in turn created problems of rampant materialism and moral corruption in the city. Win has continued with this spirit of bold experimentation in subsequent works such as *Truth or Dare?* (2003), a collection of short narratives in which he teasingly asks the reader to judge whether they are real or simply his own concoctions, and *Galaxial Lights* (2005), a collection of science fiction short stories. He also experiments with illustrations in three of his works, *Life in a Day* (2001), *The First of the Remaining Days* (2004), and *The Side of the Earth That Turns against the Sun* (2006), which showcase the ingenious juxtaposition of short prose with meaningful pictures.

This celebratory atmosphere of literary play in Win's works contrasts with a more subdued, contemplative mood in the works of Prabda Yoon, whose *Probability* won the S.E.A. Write Award in 2002 thanks to "its unique literary style and its original and multifarious ways of storytelling," according to the awards committee (quoted in Prabda Yoon [2000] 2002, 203). However, this unique and creative literary style is presented in a general mood of pensive contemplation. Although he was educated in the West, Prabda is mesmerized by Eastern art and philosophy, and this interest has also shaped the overall atmosphere of his works since his first collection of short stories, *City of Right Angles*, which often feature international characters and settings.

"In Plain Eyes" is a short story in the collection *Probability* that typifies Prabda's work. The story centers around two men who meet in Lumpini Park in downtown Bangkok. Plong (which in Thai means "to let go") has a magical ability to judge whether people are good or bad. He likes to come to the park to "see into" joggers who are from all walks of life, including the narrator, whose name Praj means "the learned." Taken at face value, this story focuses on a rather eccentric man who likes to sit in the park and judge people, but on a deeper level it touches on the themes of virtue and vice, along with the Buddhist idea of *samsara* (the endless cycle of birth and rebirth to which ordinary people are subjected). Plong likes to study humans rather than animals or objects because in humans there is an unequal ratio of virtue and vice, making them a meaningful object of study (Prabda Yoon [2000] 2002, 41). In addition, Plong discourses on the necessity of the combination of virtue and vice that makes up the world as it is. He redefines *vice* as follows.

> Vice often comes with resourcefulness, with the art of survival, and with the special ability to simulate or pretend. The wicked can pass themselves off as the good, while the good can never understand the wicked. Everyone knows that human society cannot remain at work with goodness; everyone knows that vice is an important element in governing the world. If everyone is good, there will be no politicians. And if there are no politicians, human society will lack systems, regimes, orders, and bombs, the last of which is a key weapon in cleansing errors to start anew. This is not unlike the pressing of a button to undo all mistakes so that one can redo them once again. What vice offers is a chance; virtue is not that creative. Vice is art and entertainment, and virtue is boredom. (41; translation mine).

This philosophical rethinking of the common themes of evil and goodness may be the reason why Plong decides not to tell the narrator why he considers him a good person but prefers to close his eyes. The closing of eyes may symbolize Plong's understanding of *samsara*. Perhaps his insight is linked to Lord Buddha's enlightenment despite its distance of two centuries in time and thousands of kilometers in space. Plong's insight takes place in Lumpini Park, resonating with a park in India of the same name, which is the birthplace of Lord Buddha. This bridging of esoteric Eastern philosophy and contemporary characters and settings is typical of Prabda, who uses eccentric, at times quirky, everyday happenings as a platform on which to discuss such philosophical ideas as the meaning of life and the essence of being.

"Under Your Father's Grandeur" is another short story that shows Prabda's skill as an innovative writer. There are two main protagonists in this story, an anonymous aspiring writer and Prabda, the son of a media tycoon. The story plays on the true biography of the writer, whose father, Suthichai Yoon, is the founder of the *Nation*, one of the two national English-language newspapers in Thailand. Prabda's path to fame has therefore provoked accusations of nepotism. Whilst on a ferry from Hong Kong to Kaoloon, the anonymous writer makes a pact with Prabda that they will work together: he will write stories under the pseudonym of Prabda Yoon, as his manuscripts are unlikely to be considered for publication under his real name. Prabda, in turn, will reap the benefit of these creative literary pieces and use them as part of his identity formation as a leading celebrity who has both the looks and the brains. Nevertheless, after a while, both realize that the situation makes them uncomfortable: while the real Prabda recognizes that it is the anonymous writer who controls his life, the writer realizes that his real self must be sacrificed in order to perpetrate his favorite activity—writing stories. One day Prabda organizes another trip for both of them to Hong Kong, this time to contemplate what they have done.

> "When we come to think about it, it's a sad story." Suddenly Prabda Yoon's tone changed.
>
> "Yes, what we've done was fun. But I think you also realize that it's terribly awkward. It's as if we felt at last that neither of us had a real self. When people look at me, I don't know which of us they see. When I see the outside world, I don't know whose eyes I am using. Nowadays, whenever I need to sign my name, I only see some ink scribble. It's not my name. It's not my handwriting."
>
> "I feel the need for some separation," Prabda Yoon confessed at last.
>
> He wanted to have freedom enough to do what people think Prabda Yoon shouldn't do, can't do, or never does. He wanted to escape from literature, arts, and entertainment. But how? We have come too far, I thought.
>
> "I've been thinking," Prabda Yoon started to explain seriously what he'd been thinking. "I need to ask you to expose everyone to the truth, from how we met here, on this ferry, to every detail of our complicity. I'm willing to let myself be considered a liar in exchange for a lifestyle that I really want."

Nobody will believe you, I told him. Everyone will think that this is another trick of Prabda Yoon. It's another way of writing a complex and multilayered short story about a zealous young writer. It's just a fake but smart strategy that will get people talking in order to make one more popular. (Prabda Yoon 2005a, 124; translation mine)

In the Borgesian spirit of split identity, Prabda's story makes manifest how people no longer act according to their own wills but according to what society dictates. Free will is tainted with individualism and the desperate need to distinguish oneself under the impact of capitalism and consumer culture. The story is also distinctive in that it turns against itself as a story and the reader is no longer able to consider whether this story is true or just another fiction by Prabda. Both choices are presupposed by the writer.

Compared to Win, who likes to make a bold experiment in form, Prabda's experimentation lies in wordplay or quirky situations that befall his characters, leading to the contemplation of philosophical issues of life and existence. Prabda's works, however, are not confined to the genre of short stories; he has also tried his hand at writing novels, such as *Rain at All Times* (2005b) and *Sleep under the Cold Mist* (2006), and screenplays, such as *Last Life in the Universe* (2003, cowritten with Pen-Ek Ratanaruang) and *Invisible Waves* (2006), the films of which are distributed worldwide and have received critical acclaim.

It is not surprising that the works of both Win and Prabda have been relatively well received internationally and are taken to be representative of the contemporary Thai literary scene. To a certain degree, their narratives touch on such common themes as urban alienation and loneliness and the effects of capitalism such as consumerism and individual difference. Their choice of setting is primarily Bangkok or, in Prabda's case, other metropolises, including New York and Tokyo. This has made their narratives easier to translate in cultures that are experiencing similar processes of globalization.

Patriarchy and Resistance

Writers such as Sridaoruang, Anchan, and Duenwad Pimwana are prominent in portraying this issue. In the period leading up to the 1990s, Sridaoruang's short stories were a strong representation of the Thai female voice, as her works touch on wide-ranging issues from gender and social inequality to urban consumerism. Through her unique blending of myths and the contemporary world, Sridaoruang manages to paint a powerful picture of contemporary Thai society in which the ancient and the modern ways of life coexist and continue to challenge each other. One of the best examples is "Matsi," a story about an anonymous woman who is arrested for her attempt to desert her children at a bus stop. Interrogated by a policeman, the woman claims that her children have become too much of a burden for her as her husband has left her for another woman. The policeman reprimands the woman for her lack of maternal instinct. The way the policeman chastises her is like the way a monk preaches to the public in a religious sermon. However, when she asks the policeman to release her so that she can be ordained, the policeman accuses her of irresponsibility. The conversation between them becomes increasingly heated.

> "Many people choose to be ordained, and no one complains about that . . ." she stubbornly complained.
> "Well, they do not have any responsibility. They don't pass the buck like you. They aren't ordained so that they can leave their children. In other words, they don't dodge responsibilities by using religion as a pretext. If your children are willing to live by the roadside, does it mean that you will be able to curb your desires?" [The policeman] emphatically directed his words at her with strong emotion.
> "And why can men do it?" The woman did not relent.
> "Who . . . who would do such a thing?"
> "Well . . . Phra Wetsandorn." (Sridaoruang 1994, 131; translation mine)

It is no wonder that the policeman is stunned by her response, as Phra Wetsandorn was one of Lord Buddha's avatars before he attained the divine self. Phra Wetsandorn is a well-respected man, whose decision to leave his wife, Matsi, and his children behind, is considered a highly sacred act of self-sacrifice in Thai culture. When the woman relates her attempt to forsake her children to Phra Wetsandorn, she is regarded as blasphemous. The policeman subsequently considers her insane and decides to forward her case to a psychiatrist. "Matsi" can be regarded as a feminist critique of patriarchal values that are deeply ingrained in such traditional Thai institutions as the police and religion. If Phra Wetsandorn's act of leaving his family behind is deemed sacrosanct, that of the woman is considered irresponsible and inappropriate. The story raises the question of whether gender is involved in this discrepancy and, accordingly, whether religion is as bias free as people thought.

Such questioning of gender inequality continues in the works of Anchan, a writer of the later generation. Though based in the United States, Anchan still produces literary works that draw a lot of interest and criticism in Thai literary circles. Her short story "The Permanently Scorched Boiling Pan," in the collection *Jewels of Life* (1990), is a poignant picture of a female victim of violence in her own family. While she is from a middle-class background brought up by protective parents, her husband is from a poor family that needs to struggle to survive. Their marriage is based on her total reliance on him, both economically and sexually. He is the breadwinner of the family who always complains about her failures in doing business. He is also the one who initiates sexual advances, even though the story strongly conveys her repressed desires. Her role is limited to domestic chores, child raising, and basically making the house quiet and keeping the children away when he is back from work. However, with her middle-class upbringing she is not suited to this type of domestic work. Errors such as breaking glasses and charring boiling pans often become the pretext for his physical violence. With her inferior position, the house is no longer a place of love and commitment but has become a battlefield where the husband is on the lookout to find fault with his wife and the wife is left with no other recourse than shameful submission and self-deprecation. Toward the end, the wife finds two lizards on the window, the smaller, female one pursuing the male relentlessly even though the latter makes it clear that he no longer wants her companionship. She thinks:

> You shameless lizard! You shamelessly follow [the bigger, male lizard] and never think of going away. She inwardly expressed her criticism and felt disgusted and ashamed of the behavior of the female lizard until she found this unbearable. Her tears gushed out, and she looked around like a mad person. She looked for something to throw at the lizards to drive them from her sight. Go! Go away! Why do you keep following? I told you to go! (Anchan 1990, 82; translation mine)

Her frustration at the sight of the female lizard can be interpreted as her own self-hatred, as she feels herself powerless and worthless. This state of self-deprecation is related to the inferior position of the wife in a Thai family whereby she has no economic independence.

If "The Permanently Scorched Boiling Pan" illustrates female subjection to patriarchy, "Mother!" another story in the same collection, points towards the importance of women, especially of the mother in molding a child's personality. The story is told from the perspective of a little boy whose mother has recently died. Through his dreams, the story charts his progress in coming to terms with his mother's untimely death. His dreams feature a ghoul that keeps chasing him and his mother's appearance through the aid of his crayons. To his terror, it is always a race against time to draw his mother before the ghoul has fully materialized. However, the last dream in the story shows the boy's growth and independence as he learns a precious secret from his mother.

> You [the mother] cry and then smile before telling me your last secret. You say that whenever I want you, you would be there. I would find you in the words and rhythm of the songs that I sing, in the ABCs that I write, in the sketches that I draw, and in the plasticine that I love to mould. You said that you would be right here, in my small but immeasurably imaginative heart. (Nitaya Masavisut and Grose, 1996, 60; translation by Kuruvin Boon-Long)

Thanks to its vivid, lyrical description of his dreams, Anchan's "Mother!" was honored as the outstanding short story in 1985 by the P.E.N. Thai Center. Anchan subverts the myth of patriarchy in this short story by empowering the figures of women, the mother and grandmother, without whom the little boy would not have grown up to be a proper man.

Like Anchan, Duenwad Pimwana has published a number of short stories that deal with gender and inequality. In "Power," the author touches on the relationship between a wife and a mistress (the so-called minor wife in Thai) who compete for the love of a man. On discovering her husband's infidelity, the wife takes a pistol and embarks on a journey to his new love nest, hoping to kill the culprits when caught red-handed. However, while entering the house she overhears their conversation and the mistress's refusal to elope with him. The mistress says:

> I don't let the time drag on. Please don't say anything anymore. I'm satisfied with the knowledge that you love me more than your wife. My refusal to meddle with you has become the source of my pride. This pride has enabled me to live with sufferings. (Duenwad Pimwana [1995] 2004, 66; translation mine)

The mistress finds her power through the dignity of her decision not to destroy the marriage of her beloved man. Her words dissatisfy him, as he can no longer stay in a loveless marriage in which his wife wants to have power over him. In his opinion, "that woman [his wife] does everything for the sake of her own power. The woman who wants to have power over her husband and children will have love for nobody else and won't want love from anyone" (67). Overhearing this, the wife decides not to kill them but realizes that she has learnt a valuable lesson. From then on, she becomes a sweet, doting wife who carefully tends to her husband's needs. Power, according to her, also comes from subjection.

However, from another perspective, "Power" not only shows how a woman can win a man's heart and where her power can be situated; it also illustrates how women are locked in a patriarchal framework in which men are the boss. Power in this light still resides in the hands of men, whether they realize it or not, and the only reason women wield their power is to save their marriages or keep their men with them as long as they can. In this light, the invisibility of patriarchy, bestowing on women an illusion of power, renders the patriarchal system yet more powerful.

While "Power" elucidates how women are unconsciously imprisoned in the patriarchal order, "The Attainer" shows how they can learn to strike back in these complex power relations. The story focuses on the relationship between a young woman and an older man whom she believes to be wise and sophisticated. She feels she has learned a lot about life from him since they first met while she was at the university. She realizes that she no longer needs a family and learns to cope with life all by herself. On hearing this, the middle-aged man becomes worried that she will never experience the beauty of sex. Whether out of his goodwill or not, he offers himself to her, implying that, as he has taught her many a valuable lesson, this will be another one and he is willing to participate in this apparently selfless initiation rite. Despite her protests, he asks her to concede or leave his place. Seeing the man's naked body, she begins to vomit. However, she does stay at the man's house all night without any sexual activity, apparently falling asleep out of exhaustion. In the end, it is the middle-aged man who feels ill at ease with the situation, unable to sleep and becoming inexplicably agitated. He no longer wants to be her "god" but wants to have a man-and-wife relationship with her. In the morning, when she wakes up, he decides to clear the air by asking her not to think of him as a god any longer. She responds thus:

> "When you want reverence and respect, you want me to consider you a god. When you want a wife, you want me to consider you an ordinary person."
>
> For a moment, the middle-aged man felt giddy. "Was it because of last night?" he asked.
>
> "Yes—last night you taught me. I wanted to learn about sexual relationships from you, but you didn't teach me. You just wanted to exploit me. But—though you felt like you got something from me, I didn't feel I lost anything. I got what I wanted to learn."
>
> "Was it?" the middle-aged man sarcastically retorted. "If so, do you still consider me your god?"
>
> "Yes, you're a god. You don't need to be in haste to become an ordinary person. You just taught me last night that a god was just an ordinary person."
> (Duenwad Pimwana [1995] 2004, 122–123; translation mine)

This conversation suggests that power has changed hands from the man to the young woman. She has become "the attainer" who learns of her own independence and sophistication in a world where men look for sexual exploitation and try to sugarcoat such an act in various guises. The story ends with the woman leaving the man's place, probably never to return. Unlike "Power," "The Attainer" reveals the possibility of women's liberation when they reject male companionship and become independent.

These three women writers deal with the similar theme of gender relations in patriarchal Thailand. While they do not portray the optimistic vision of a society completely rid of patriarchal values, their stories offer themselves as a critique of total subjugation to such values and suggest some possibilities for negotiation and resistance.

Other Voices in the Contemporary Literary Scene

The towering presence of Kanokphong, Win, and Anchan in this decade should not blind us to the variety of other trends and movements in contemporary Thai fiction. A writer from the South, Siriworn Kaewkan, has recently created a stir on the Thai literary scene. His lyrical novella *The Shattered World* [2001] (2004), is evidently a Thai magical realist narrative in the style of García Márquez. In this novella, one of the main central characters, Abdul-Hamid, represents an older world that resists development. He is brought up amid local beliefs that entail such magical happenings as sea walking and animal transformation. The ending occurs with the defeat of the central character and his decision to transform himself into a turtle.

In his subsequent collection of short stories, *Tales from Bangkok* (2003), Siriworn shifted his interest in regionalism to the urban space of Bangkok. Some of the stories in this collection detail the lives of eccentric Bangkokians such as a navigator on top of the Baiyoke Building, the highest skyscraper in the Thai capital. He attempts to remap his whole conception of space with Bangkok as the new center. According to this spatial reconfiguration, the navigator has come to the conclusion that India becomes the West and the United States is the East. This insight has a significant impact on him.

> The East! The East!
> Then he went quiet for quite a while.
> Then he lit a new cigarette.
> Then he picked up the world map again, as if he still retained his normal sight.
> Then he tore the map, separating Europe and America along the Atlantic Ocean and attaching them through the Bering Strait.
> Imagination from the map was crucial, Old Srimin thought, but illusion from the map was evil! . . .

From this moment onward, now he shouted loudly, everything we have learned will be void! World history will be void! (Siriworn Kaewkan 2003, 63; translation mine)

In his next collection, *The Story of Lost Ariya and Other Stories* (2006), Siriworn blends his philosophical rethinking with lyrical prose in taking issue with a variety of topics from urban development to unrest in the Far South. "One Afternoon in April When the Rain Was Boiling Hot" is about an old witch doctor-cum-matriarch who has experienced a series of tragedies in her life yet maintains a positive attitude. Her granddaughter, facing similar tragedies in the modern day unrest in the Far South, cannot keep up a similarly positive perspective. The death of the matriarch symbolizes the permanent loss of the lightness and congeniality that have always held the southern community together. The narrative is nostalgic and tragic at the same time, as it shows the cul-de-sac of harsh realities that most southerners now face. The author's prose is both lyrical and telling, especially when he describes the scene in the present day Far South.

I decided to open the curtain, thinking that the sunlight was still shining brightly and puddles were still bubbling hot on the street in front of the house.
But alas. . . .
The sunlight had vanished from Pattani. In its place was dull grayness, as if the whole world had been drowned in an abyss of sadness.
I couldn't understand how the old matriarch could stand all this when there's nothing but sullen grayness in her life. (Siriworn Kaewkan 2006, 106–107; translation mine)

When the matriarch was young, the rain was magically bubbling hot: the sun was shining brightly even though it was raining. This magical realist scene is symbolically telling as it harkens back to yonder days when southern people were able to enjoy life despite religious and territorial conflicts, something that has become impossible of late.

Prachakom Lunachai is another writer who masterfully portrays the urban condition despite his provincial origins in the Northeast. His prolific literary output consists of novels such as *The Moonlit Shore* (1997), *A Flower in the City* (2002), *The Pentagonal World* (2003a), and *In Deep Sea* (2003b); collections of short stories such as *A Spare Glassball* [1996] (2003), *The Underground City* [2000] (2002a), *Desirous Pollen* (2002b), and *Moonlight Tales* (2005a); and the autobiographical *Writing Dreams* (2005b). Like Siriworn's, some of Prachakom's short narratives involve the shift from rural to urban space as well as the conflicts arising from such spatial change. Also adept at various literary forms, he uses a wide range of literary techniques to take issue with class inequality, uneven development, and urban alienation. In "The Two-Century Legend of Sutham," he discusses the issue of legend making, especially how a story is turned into a legend endorsed by the public and how consumer culture turns this legend into a moneymaking business. Prachakom tells how two protagonists, Pat and Peter, explore the legend of Sutham in a province where the public never questions the existence of the woman behind the legend. They believe that Sutham is a hero who long ago saved a woman named Sarocha, along with other villagers, from a landslide that destroyed the whole village. An event is organized in which they search for a woman who perfectly resembles Sutham, and a film is made, which is a realistic rendering of the legend. Both Pat and Peter go in search of the real Sutham only to find that there was no such man and the tale is simply a myth. To their dismay, Pat says:

> Most of the incident [of the destructive landslide] is true, not just the mountain, the village, and the company that received the concession to build a quarry. From the evidence I have gathered, the whole mountain suffered a major landslide as it appeared in the film. The film and the books differ only in minor details and the characters' features. But in reality there was neither Sutham nor Sarocha. All one hundred households were buried under the mud pile with no survivors.
> (Prachakom Lunachai 2002a, 32; translation mine)

"The Two-Century Legend of Sutham" is a critique of the manipulation of information in the age of mass communication, where the public, left unguided, is portrayed as lost in this maze of "real" illusions not dissimilar to Jean Baudrillard's hyperreality. Films and other manifestations, such as the museum and streets bearing the name of Sutham, all engender belief in the sacredness of the legend. Not only do they make the residents proud of their hometown; they also provide capitalists a way to milk money from gullible tourists.

Moonlight Tales by Prachakom Lunachai
Courtesy of Matichon Publishing House

"Takhu," a short story in the collection *Moonlight Tales*, which was shortlisted for the 2005 S.E.A. Write Award, is distinctive in its homage to Franz Kafka's "Metamorphosis." In this magical realist narrative, the transformation into an animal called Takhu does not happen to an alienated wage slave, as in Kafka's narrative, but to a middle-class man who received his doctoral education in the West and returned to live in Bangkok. The story is told from the vantage point of his sister, who has to feed him with bark from special trees that their father has planted. For her, this transformation comes as a shock.

> Nitaya was proud of her brother. From the praises sung by his friends, Komet was not only well versed in economics but in music and arts. Before he went to study abroad, he had already produced a great number of academic works, including reviews of films, music, paintings, and literary works.
>
> He was a genius. The world had made him a well-rounded scholar who was knowledgeable in all disciplines. Nitaya once believed that he would become a world-renowned person. He would be great.
>
> But one bright, fine day Komet simply turned into the first ever two-tailed creature with a six-forked tongue.
>
> From the great person in the world of the future to an animal that had never existed, not even in fairy tales. (Prachakom Lunachai 2005a, 264–265; translation mine)

The transformation in this case signals the sense of alienation a middle-class person can feel after a lengthy period of education in the West. It also provides a symbolic satire on the education that has turned a human into an inscrutable creature. Whereas Kafka's Gregor Samsa is a victim of the modernist system of empty bureaucracy, Komet's alienation comes from the irresolvable discrepancy between Western training and the Thai way of life.

Paritas Hutangkul is another writer who takes an interest in contemporary issues of urban capitalism and consumerism. His collections of short stories, such as *The Witch in the Building* (2002) and *Digital Sloka* (2005), present various dimensions of city life. In "The Witch in the Building," for example, he tells the story of a girl from the north of Thailand who decides to come to Bangkok to look for a job. As there are few choices left for her, she makes up her mind to become a prostitute with the help of her own sister, who is a hairdresser by day and a sexworker by night. But she needs to have courage in order to take up her new career. The way Paritas tells this story is distinctive in that it parallels L. Frank Baum's children's novel *The Wizard of Oz*. Like Dorothy, who embarks on a lengthy journey to ask the Wizard of Oz to help her find her way home, Muan Sai Kham, the young girl in the short story, needs to travel to ask a witch to give her courage. The trip is sponsored by Auntie Yai, a brothel owner. While Dorothy is portrayed as innocent and her story lacks an economic dimension, Muan Sai Kham's story is set in contemporary Thailand, filled with economic hardships and the need to become successful in materialistic terms as one is surrounded by sensual temptations. The dialogue between Muan Sai Kham and her sister, Muan Sai Pin, illustrates this.

> "Sai Pin, I don't think I can [go to see the witch]. I can't do it. I'm sorry."
> "Sai Kham, why are you suddenly scared? You've already got money to do this. I know you want to be a celebrity. But it's difficult, and you can't get rid of those shitty men. Believe in Auntie Yai. Have faith in Auntie Yai. With both of us working together, we can save enough money to open a grocer's store in our village." (Paritas Hutangkul 2002, 93; translation mine)

What the witch does in this story is help Muan Sai Kham shed her shame over her decision to become a prostitute. While Baum's text is full of childhood innocence, Paritas's parody signals that the return to such an idyllic world is unattainable in a contemporary society engulfed in a tantalizing consumer culture, inducing people to think only of material gain and ignore their spiritual side. Shame becomes nothing but an obstacle that hinders people from gaining more material wealth.

"The Infernal Shopping Mall" is another significant story in the same collection. The main characters are a group of mall strollers who are suddenly held hostage and ordered to lie on their stomachs and hand the criminals all their money. It later transpires that the whole hostage scene is a set-up, filmed for an advertising campaign. The protagonist is in this group along with an old man who is not happy with the whole setup. When they protest, they find the following answer from the production team.

> Yes. We know that you're angry because we may have overstepped. But this is the world of creativity. However, have some money to relieve your stress, two hundred thousand baht each. Besides, all your panic-stricken expressions will give you national fame. (Paritas Hutangkul 2002, 40; translation mine)

By portraying a situation in which the boundaries between reality and the unreal have become fuzzy, the story is distinctive in its use of the shopping mall as a space of exploitation whereby mall browsers are in turn commodified and "bought" to be part of a sales campaign. Despite the angry protests of the old man, the protagonist accepts the money after long deliberation. His decision saddens the old man as it means that he is willing to be exploited as a commodity. Like "The Witch in the Building," "The Infernal Shopping Mall" sarcastically portrays our plight in the face of a harsh consumer culture, which, in generating and intensifying our desire for material products, has dehumanized us and turned us into mindless consumers susceptible to manipulation and exploitation.

The Princess, a collection of short stories by Binla Sankalakhiri (2003), offers an interesting alternative to the (magical) realist or the experimental works by escaping to the land of the fairy tale. Under a seemingly innocent and cynicism-free facade lies a strong message of hope and optimism. In "The Eighth Color of the Rainbow," the author tells a modern fairy tale about a little spoiled princess. Unlike the classical versions, which portray happy families residing together in castles, the princess's parents, the king and the queen, live apart, and they both vie for her affection by trying to give her what she wants. On seeing a rainbow, the princess wonders how beautiful the experience would be if both her parents were able to enjoy its picturesque presence together. However, the king deems this impossible, saying that the queen may speak to him again only if the rainbow has eight colors. The princess then ventures out of the palace and approaches the rainbow, seeing it gradually develop its seven hues. Then a miracle happens.

> In the sky, the seven colors of the rainbow become more perceptible. Now its body is not only filled with colors, but there is also some fragrance. This is mysterious and strangely beautiful. The little princess blinks, and tears flow from her eyes blissfully. She realizes why she came here but becomes speechless in the pool of time that almost comes to a standstill. The rainbow turns around and casts a glance amid leaves and grass. Its eyes meet the little princess's, which sparkle like twinkles in the night sky. The rainbow smiles warmly. Needless to say, it stoops to kiss the tears on her cheeks.
>
> There are shouts and hails. The eighth color of the rainbow is the pink hue of the cheeks of the princess. (Binla Sankalakhiri 2003, 83–84; translation mine)

Binla's beautiful prose ties in well with the fairy tale mode of storytelling. Despite their light, jovial appearance, his stories deal with messages that are relevant to the contemporary world. In "The Eighth Color of the Rainbow," for instance, he shows how the family is important in the upbringing of children and how difficult it is to retain family values in a modern society in which more and more parents are either divorced or living apart. Happy endings still abound in Binla's short narratives, but they no longer signal happiness in the traditional sense, with the whole family reunited or a dragon slain.

His happy endings are related to a shift in perspective: his main characters need to understand and accept things as they really are. The princess in this story finally learns to accept the separation of the king and the queen, yet she realizes that she is still the apple of their eyes all the same.

"The Musical Chair," another story in the same collection, also deals with a contemporary issue despite its fairy tale veneer. The story centers around a chair that does not like to take part in the game of musical chairs. He finds the whole activity dehumanizing.

> Every evening, time after time, day after day, he needs to go out as a musical chair ... the chair of honor ... the chair of victory ... he is the last chair that everyone needs to compete for.
>
> Whenever he closes his eyes, he only sees the picture of competition, the bottoms of those competitors trying to obstruct other bottoms, and the full weight that bumps directly on him. Each day his ears are filled with laughter. Even though he can hear, he does not feel like listening to any music. (Binla Sankalakhiri 2003, 61; translation mine)

The musical chair becomes enraged and resists being used by the competitors, resulting in its premature abandonment in a field. With its looks no longer dignified, the chair is finally used by a little girl who has always been the first to lose in the musical chairs battle. And it is in the small house of the little girl that the chair finds true happiness. Like "The Eighth Color of the Rainbow," the happy ending of "The Musical Chair" does not entail the chair's pride at being the most important one in the game but its insightful recognition of its true purpose. This purposeful escape from competition can be interpreted as a poignant criticism of contemporary dog-eat-dog society under the impact of capitalism. Compared to other writers of the same generation, Binla has carved his own niche and found an alternative literary form through which to present his ideas. Due to this creativity and freshness, *The Princess* earned him the S.E.A. Write Award and has become a best seller enjoyed by adults and children alike.

Conclusion

Contemporary Thai short fiction is distinguished by its variety of style and content. In the past three decades, many writers have continued with the realist tradition of literary representation and many have experimented with alternative genres and formal elements. The rise of magical realism, as popularized by Kanokphong Songsomphan, testifies to the relevance of the genre to the social milieu of Thailand, where the discrepancy between the rural and the urban is inherent in the ways the two groups see the world. In addition, formal experimentation, as pioneered by Win Lyovarin, is another alternative that liberates writers from traditional realist representation, which enshrines the straightforward correspondence between the text and the world outside. Prabda Yoon tried his hand at this formal play by using quirky situations and characters to represent another facet of life, one that might be ignored by most people but still conveys the deep essence of being and existence.

The issue of gender is also touched on, especially by women writers who perpetuate a strong female literary tradition. From Sridaoruang to Duenwad Pimwana, one can perceive the persistent drive to reflect on the disparity between women and men and how it underlies the ideological structure of Thai society. While issues such as economic hardship and social injustice are still dominant, more and more writers are exploring other themes that are more philosophical and not directly related to day-to-day survival. Many issues that have emerged in a great number of works produced in this period are related to globalization and transnational capitalism, especially those of consumer culture, urbanism, and cultural clashes between the old and the new. The attitudes also vary: while some writers of the earlier generation voice concern over the superstitious worldview of rural people, who may resist modernization, some of the later generation question this position, nostalgically portraying the rural as an idyllic space that is gradually disappearing and the urban as a space where allure and corruption are rife.

This essay is by no means exhaustive. Several promising authors, such as Rewat Panpipat, Watchara Sujjasarasin, Ratanachai Manabut, and Sitangsupa, who have also written short stories of high literary merit should have been discussed, along with some writers of the latest generation such as Uthen Promdaeng, Phanu Traiwet, and Mud Sudphathai. However, to a certain degree, this essay may give the reader some ideas about the vibrant and diverse contemporary Thai literary scene. It may be said that, even though the Thai literary world may face a slump as the output of literary works may be rather small, various writers still soldier on and offer readers a wide variety of works that touch on contemporary issues by way of both traditional realism and alternative genres. There is an atmosphere of intellectual vivacity in the air as authors have emerged from various ethnic, class, and gender orientations. These authorial discrepancies are beneficial as it means the readership is wider and more eclectic; readers can choose to read the writers they identify with or those that expand their worldview. These discrepancies inherent in the choices of contemporary Thai short fiction are on the increase; hopefully they will continue well into the future.

References

In English

Anderson, Benedict R. O'G., and Ruchira Mendiones, eds. 1985. *In the Mirror: Literature and Politics in Siam in the American Era.* Bangkok: Duang Kamol.

Mattani Mojdara Rutnin. 1988. *Modern Thai Literature: The Process of Modernization and the Transformation of Values.* Bangkok: Thammasat University Press.

Nitaya Masavisut and Matthew Grose, eds. 1996. *The S.E.A. Write Anthology of Thai Short Stories and Poems.* Chiang Mai: Silkworm Books.

Phaitoon Thanya. 2001. *Paradise Waves.* Translated by Tom Glass. Bangkok: Nakorn.

Srisurang Poolthupya, ed. 2001. *ASEAN Short Stories and Poems by S.E.A. Write Awardees 1999.* Bangkok: P.E.N. Thai Center.

Ussiri Dhammachoti. [1978] 1987. *Kunthong, You Will Return at Dawn.* Translated by Chamnongsri L. Rutnin. 3rd ed. Bangkok: Ko Kai.

Yamada, Teri Shaffer, ed. 2002 *Virtual Lotus: Modern Fiction of Southeast Asia.* Ann Arbor: University of Michigan Press.

In Thai

Anchan. 1990. *Jewels of Life.* Bangkok: Polpan.

———. 1996. *The Wind Watcher.* New York: Phu Pha.

———. 1999. *The Invisible Hand.* New York: Phu Pha.

———. 2002. *Reading the Wide World.* New York: Phu Pha.

Binla Sankalakhiri. 2003. *The Princess.* Bangkok: Matichon.

Chamlong Fangcholachit. 1980. *The Caravan.* Bangkok: Ton Mak.

———. 1986. *The Prime Minister's Visit to the Bank.* Bangkok: Khon Wanakam.

———. 1988a. *Dog Color.* Bangkok: Kampaeng.

———. 1988b. *Homespun Silk Cloth.* Bangkok: Kampaeng.

———. [1988] 2000. *Man and Child.* Bangkok: Praew.

———. [1993] 2004. *Sarakan.* Bangkok: Siam Interbooks.

———. [1996] 2006. *The Gentleman with a Lighter.* Bangkok: Nakorn.

———. 1999. *The Pleasant City.* Bangkok: Praew.

———. [2000] 2004. *Car Boot Sale.* Bangkok: Samit.

———. 2002. *There Is Still Hospitality.* Bangkok: Praew.

———. 2005. *Ligor, They Have Changed.* Bangkok: Praew.

Chart Kobchitti. 1981. *The Judgement.* Bangkok: Tonmak.

———. 1984. *The Personal Knife.* Bangkok: Khon Wanakam.

———. 1989. *The OK City.* Bangkok: Khon Wanakam.

———. 1993. *Time.* Bangkok: Hon.

———. 2005. *Facial Massage Service.* Bangkok: Hon.

Chusak Patarakulwanich. 2002. "The Next Decade of the Thai Novel." In *Reading against the Grain*, edited by Chusak Patarakulwanich, 21–28. Bangkok: Kobfai.

Duenwad Pimwana. [1995] 2004. *The Second Book.* Bangkok: Samanchon.

———. 2006. *Relations.* Bangkok: Samanchon.

Ingorn Supanvanit. 2005a. *An Introduction to the Thai Short Story.* Bangkok: Active Print.

Ingorn Supanvanit. 2005b. *An Analysis of the S.E.A. Write Award Winning Short Stories.* Bangkok: Active Print.

Jiraphat Angsumali. 1996. *Sunlight Fog.* Bangkok: Kampaeng.

———. 2002. *Perversion.* Bangkok: Wali.

———. 2005. *Shadow Play.* Bangkok: Matichon.

Kanokphong Songsomphan. [1991] 2000. *The Broken Bridge.* Bangkok: Nakorn.

———. [1996] 1997. *The Other Land.* Bangkok: Nakorn.

———. 2004. *The World That Turns around Itself.* Bangkok: Nakorn.

———. 2005a. *Around Our Own House.* Bangkok: Nakorn.

———. 2005b. *National Tales.* Bangkok: Nakorn.

———. 2005c. *The Poet's Death.* Bangkok: Nakorn.

Paritas Hutangkul. 2002. *The Witch in the Building.* Bangkok: Rubchan.

———. 2005. *Digital Sloka.* Bangkok: Praew.

Phaitoon Thanya. [1986] 2005. *Building Sand Piles.* Bangkok: Nakorn.

———. 1994. *October.* Bangkok: Nakorn.

Prabda Yoon. 2000. *City of Right Angles.* Bangkok: Kai Marut.

———. 2001. *The Parts That Move.* Bangkok: Kai Marut.

———. [2000] 2002. *Probability.* Bangkok: Sut Supda.

———. [2001] 2002. *Flood in the Eyes.* Bangkok: Sut Supda.

———. 2002. *This Story Really Happened.* Bangkok: Openbooks.

———. 2004. *Rubbing Shoulders with Giants.* Bangkok: Rawang Bunthat.

———. 2005a. *Cleaning the Dead.* Bangkok: Sut Supda.

———. 2005b. *Rain at all Times.* Bangkok: Typhoonbooks.

———. 2006: *Sleep under the Cold Mist.* Bangkok: Typhoonbooks.

Prachakom Lunachai. [1996] 2003. *A Spare Glassball.* Bangkok: Matichon.

———. 1997. *The Moonlit Shore.* Bangkok: Sahakan Khon Wanakam.

———. 1998. *Outmoded Characters.* Bangkok: Sahakan Khon Wanakam.

———. 1999. *Drama of Life.* Bangkok: Sahakan Khon Wanakam.

———. [2000] 2002a. *The Underground City.* Bangkok: Sahakan Khon Wanakam.

———. [2000] 2002b. *Desirous Pollen.* Bangkok: Matichon.

———. 2002. *A Flower in the City.* Bangkok: Matichon.

———. 2003a. *The Pentagonal World.* Bangkok: Matichon.

———. 2003b. *In Deep Sea.* Bangkok: Matichon.

———. 2005a. *Moonlight Tales.* Bangkok: Matichon.

———. 2005b. *Writing Dreams.* Bangkok: Matichon.

Sila Khomchai. 1993. *Mid-Road Family.* Bangkok: Ming Mit.

Siriworn Kaewkan. [2001] 2004. *The Shattered World.* Bangkok: Siam Interbooks.

———. 2003. *Tales from Bangkok.* Bangkok: Ngai Ngam.

———. 2006. *The Story of Lost Ariya and Other Stories.* Bangkok Phachonphai.

Sridaoruang. 1983. *A Drop of Glass.* Bangkok: Met Sai.

———. 1984. *The Identity Card.* Bangkok: Met Sai.

———. 1994. "Matsi," In *The Woman That I Am,* 127–31. Bangkok: Thai Writers Association.

Vanich Charoongkij-anant. [1983] 1984. *Down the Same Lane.* Bangkok: Upimpeka.

Win Lyovarin. [1994] 1995a. *The Black Notebook and Red Leaves.* Bangkok: Dokya.

———. [1994] 1995b. *Lament of the Omen.* Bangkok: Dokya.

———. [1996] 2000. *Starry Moonlit Sky.* Bangkok: 113.

———. 1999. *A Creature Called Human.* Bangkok: Double Nine.

———. 2001. *Life in a Day.* Bangkok: 113.

———. 2003. *Truth or Dare?* Bangkok: 113.

———. 2004. *The First of the Remaining Days.* Bangkok: 113.

———. 2005. *Galaxial Lights.* Bangkok: 113.

———. 2006. *The Side of the Earth That Turns against the Sun.* Bangkok: 113.

Yurachat Boonsanit. 2004. "The S.E.A. Write Award Winning Short Stories: The Reflections of Failures or Truths of Postmodern Literature." In *25 Years of the S.E.A. Write Award*, edited by Wiput Sophawong, Ruenruthai Sujjapan and Dhanate Vespada, 97–118. Bangkok: P.E.N. Thai Center.

3

The Short Story and Contemporary Lao Literature
Peter Koret

A study of twentieth-century Lao fiction illustrates the extent to which a literature's form, content, and social role are dependent on the political conditions in which it is produced. Whereas the ethnic Lao have had a tradition of literature for several centuries, modern Lao fiction is a foreign implant of recent origin. Its development is a product of the same forces of modernization that have brought about the demise of traditional literature. Contemporary Lao fiction owes its origins to the introduction of print technology, the Western-oriented education of the elite both at home and abroad, and the rise of a literate segment of the population with the time, education, and resources necessary to regard literature as a source of entertainment.

Literature in Traditional Lao Society

The known history of the ethnic Lao began in the fourteenth century when King Fa Ngum united the territory that comprises contemporary Laos and parts of Northeast Thailand into the kingdom of Lan Xang. The earliest evidence that we have of a literary tradition in Lan Xang dates from two centuries afterward. The literature of Lan Xang was heavily influenced by both the Buddhist literary tradition of the neighboring kingdom of Lanna, centered in Chiang Mai, and what would appear to be an already well established, probably oral tradition of local origin.

Lao literature remained the major intellectual and artistic tradition of the Lao until the first half of the twentieth century. As in ancient societies throughout Southeast Asia, the link between art and religion was inseparable. In Lao society, the cultural center has traditionally been the temple. In the past, most Lao men spent a considerable amount of their teenage years as novices in temples, where they gained literacy and received their general education. The ability to read, perform, or compose Lao literature was based on skills that were learned in the temple. In the eyes of the Lao, both literature and the process of learning itself have therefore become intimately associated with the Buddhist religion. Works of Lao literature, whatever their origins or contents happen to be, are by and large presented as religious teachings.

This both legitimizes them in the eyes of their sponsors and affords them the high respect with which they are viewed by the Lao public, not merely as entertainment but as teachings of the Buddha. At the same time, whereas the stories are given status by their association with Buddhism, the popularity of the stories makes them a useful vehicle with which to spread Buddhist teachings among the Lao.

Due to internal rivalries, Lan Xang split into three separate kingdoms at the end of the seventeenth century: Luang Prabang, Vientiane, and Champhasak. This split and the weakness that followed had a great effect on the future of Lao literature, language, and culture in general. Lao fortunes vacillated with the power of its two neighbors, Siam to the west and Vietnam to the east. By the nineteenth century, most of Laos was either a vassal of Siam or Vietnam or of both at the same time. In 1829, the Siamese army razed Vientiane following a revolt by the Lao king Chao Anu and further consolidated its control over Lao-speaking territories. In 1893 the French annexed the territory that comprises present-day Laos, and the Siamese retained only the area that is now northeastern Thailand, a small percentage of what they formerly controlled. The division of regions inhabited by the Lao based on political rather than ethnic considerations has resulted in a situation in which over ten million Lao at present live within the boundaries of Thailand whereas approximately two million live inside of Laos.

Despite the lack of official sponsorship, the Lao people under French and Siamese control continued to preserve their tradition of transcribing, performing, and composing works of literature. There is evidence to suggest that a large percentage, and perhaps even the majority, of Lao poetic works were composed during this period. From the early twentieth century onward, however, traditional literature in Lao society has gone through a period of rapid transformation and decline, which is largely explainable as a result of the increased political and cultural contact between the Lao and foreign powers. First, secular government schooling has come to replace the traditional religious education in which literary skills were customarily taught together with the Buddhist worldview that informed its content. Second, the introduction of print technology has rendered obsolete the medium in which literary works were recorded and correspondingly decreased the relevance of the poetic style of its composition.[1] Third, entertainment forms of foreign origin, often spread with the aid of Western technology, have further served to decrease the popularity of traditional literature among a modern audience. Finally, it is impossible to estimate the exact amount of damage, both to culture and to human life, that was caused by the extended civil war in Laos in which 2.1 million tons of bombs were dropped within a single decade.

Lao Literature during the Period of French Colonization (1893-1954)

The slow pace of development in Laos during the French colonial period helped to ensure the continued survival of traditional cultural practices such as the composition and performance of literature, which were to decline at a markedly slower rate than in much of the rest of mainland Southeast Asia.[2] As late as three decades after the initial colonization of Laos, a greater number of students in the country were being educated in Buddhist temples than in government schools (Gunn 1990, 38).[3] As a result, traditional literature continued to flourish, and certain temples during the French period were renowned as centers of Lao versification in which monks were actively engaged not only in the recopying of traditional works onto palm leaves, but also in the creation of new tales that followed traditional conventions of composition.[4]

Although opportunities for education in government schools were extremely limited for the majority of the population, French schooling was influential in that it helped to shape the worldview of the members of Lao elite, who studied in French schools in the nation's capital and aspired to higher education abroad.[5] The origins of modern Lao literature can be traced to the imitation of French literary styles that were taught in French schools.

The slow development of a modern literature in Laos is attributable not only to the late establishment of modern schooling but also the lack of printing technology, which was introduced into Laos later than in most of the nations of Southeast Asia. This resulted in the unusual situation in which printed versions of Lao literature that were transcribed from palm leaves and published by small presses in Northeast Thailand were brought into Laos, where they were recopied back onto palm leaves, the only available means of circulation at the time. Although official announcements were published in Laos in the 1930s, the first Lao newspaper, *Lao Nyai,* was established in 1941 (Gunn 1990, 39). The earliest known Lao novel, *Phaphutahup Saksit* (The Sacred Buddha Image), by Somjin Nginn, was published shortly afterward in 1944. In this pioneering work of Lao fiction, the author tells the story of a clever detective who successfully investigates the disappearance of a Buddha image from Si Saket temple in Vientiane. *Phaphutahup Saksit* reflects the culturally hybrid nature of twentieth-century Lao literature not only in its imitation of Western detective fiction but also in the very identity of its hero—the son of a Frenchman and a Lao woman. The extent of French cultural influence on its author can be seen in the statement that is placed on the cover of his Lao-language publications: "Composed in easy to understand

Lao." The author's original compositions of French poetry included no similar disclaimer concerning his use of the French language, although French was presumably more difficult to understand for a Lao audience.[6] As in other Southeast Asian nations, modern fiction also developed from the translation of European works of literature. The early novel *Naung Phi Phet* (The Swamp of the Hungry Ghosts) by Thao Ken, advertised as a translation of *La Mare au Diable* by George Sand, included both Lao characters and Lao geographical settings.

As modern fiction was slowly beginning to emerge in Laos, traditional literature also began to undergo some revival.[7] Following a pattern that has continued to the present day, literary works of pre-twentieth-century origin became increasingly removed from the traditional context of their oral performance. They were given a new type of significance, largely political in nature, as a cultural artifact with which to construct a picture of the past in order to provide a particular meaning to the present.[8] Prior to World War II, both French and Siamese authorities made use of traditional Lao culture as a means through which to sway the allegiance of the country's people. When the Siamese government initiated an expansionist policy toward Laos on the basis of shared cultural and historical ties, the French responded through the official promotion of Lao culture, inclusive of literature, in an attempt to cultivate a Lao identity distinct from that of its neighbors.[9] At the same time that French officials made use of literature to strengthen their colonial rule, the Lao literary tradition became a vehicle through which Lao nationalists attempted to create a portrayal of the Lao as an ancient and highly civilized people deserving of independence from the French and membership in the community of nations. One of the major proponents of this movement, Maha Sila Viravong, a pioneer in the study of Lao history and culture, was also to become a pivotal figure in the promotion of modern literature in the pursuit of similar goals.

Lao Literature from the Period of Independence to the Communist Victory (1954-1975)

During the final years of French colonization preceding World War II, a Lao nationalist movement known as Free Lao (Lao Issara) was established under the patronage of several members of the Lao royalty. In 1945, when the Japanese took control of Laos, the country was declared an independent state under the leadership of the Free Lao. With the defeat of the Japanese, the French returned in 1946 and easily defeated the Lao resistance. The leaders of the Free Lao fled to Bangkok, where they set up a government in exile. When the French offered Laos partial independence within the French Union in 1949, the Free Lao was dissolved and more moderate members, such as Prince Suvanna Phuma, returned to Vientiane to work toward independence in cooperation with the French. Others, however, were not so easily satisfied.

Phuma's half brother, Prince Suphannuvong, traveled to Vietnam in 1949, where he worked with the Viet Minh to forge a Lao resistance movement that came to be known as the Lao Patriotic Front (Naew Lao Hak Sat). When the French granted complete independence to Laos in 1954, Prince Suvanna Phuma, who led the newly formed royal Lao government, found himself in conflict with his half brother Suphannuvong. At the same time, the country of Laos found itself facing the prospects of a major civil war. Two important provinces in the northeast, Sam Neua and Phongsali, were already under the control of the Lao Patriotic Front, and much of the rest of the country would fall into its hands in the years that followed. During the first two decades after independence, there were several unsuccessful attempts to form coalition governments and solve the country's problems in a peaceful fashion. Unfortunately for the Lao, the country was too weak to avoid being drawn into the larger Vietnam War, in which major superpowers supported each of the opposing sides. The civil war in Laos lasted the length of the United States' involvement in Vietnam. Subsequent to the ceasefire declared in Vietnam in the mid-1970s, the United States withdrew its financial and military support from Laos. The royal Lao government collapsed shortly afterward, and in 1975 the Lao Patriotic Front took control of the country.

During the civil war, from the early 1950s to the communist victory in 1975, there were two separate literatures in Laos, the objectives and content of which differed as a result of the political conditions under which they were produced. These two literatures, as described below, consist of the writing that was composed in the regions of the country controlled by the royal Lao government and in the "liberated zones" governed by the Lao Patriotic Front.

Lao Literature under the Royal Lao Government (Early 1954 to 1975)

This type of literature was mostly created and circulated in Vientiane. In 1951, prior to independence, an official Committee of Literature (Khana Kammakan Vannakhadi) was established, which published a monthly magazine, *Vannakhadi San,* devoted to traditional literature and culture.[10] In addition, a few other magazines that included some literary content also appeared. By the mid-1960s, short stories appeared regularly in a variety of newspapers and magazines, and collections of fiction began to be published in book form. Four of the major writers of fiction belonged to the family of the above-mentioned

Maha Sila Viravong, including his three children, Pa Nai (Pakiat), Duang Champa (Dara), and Dauk Ket (Duangdeuan), and a son-in-law, Outhine Bounyavong.

Although literature did not play a particularly prominent role in Lao society, there were a number of talented writers who devoted considerable effort in both the composition and circulation of their works. According to Outhine Bounyavong, a book-length collection of fiction could be expected to sell a total of one thousand copies. Such a sale, however, generally required both the author's personal financial investment in his own publication and the fortitude necessary to walk the streets of Vientiane hawking one's own writing.

Hao Hak Kan Dai
(How Can We Possibly Love Each Other?)
by Outhine Bounyavong
Courtesy of Dokked Publishing

Throughout the 1960s, there were a total of two bookstores in Vientiane, one of which sold books in Thai and the other in French. Not surprisingly, the literature in these two languages was the major influence on the fiction that was composed in Laos at the time. Whereas Lao people continued to learn enough French to read French literary works, the Thai language is similar enough to Lao to be understood without great difficulty. By the early 1970s, there was a large enough audience to support the existence of a popular magazine devoted solely to literature. In 1970, the literary magazine *Pheuan Kaew* was established after it ceased publication in 1972, it was followed by *Phai Nam,* which lasted until two months after the revolution. Maha Sila Viravong founded *Phai Nam*, and the editorial board consisted largely of his prolific children. The magazine was sold in Vientiane and also regularly sent out for distribution in other provinces.[11]

Lao literature in the 1960s and early 1970s served both as entertainment and a vehicle for social and political commentary. Stories that appeared in the magazine *Phai Nam* could be quite critical of corruption, the negative effects of capitalism, and the deterioration of values in Lao society. Romance was also popular, frequently influenced by Thai fiction. From the content of literature produced during this period, it is evident that the royal Lao Government allowed a greater level of freedom of expression than the government of Laos does at present.

An important source of funding for Lao books published in Laos prior to 1975 (including both traditional literature and, to a lesser extent, modern works) was foreign aid from the United States. The significance of such publications can be understood more as a gesture of official goodwill from the United States toward the Lao people than the promotion of reading. This is illustrated by the fact that hundreds or even thousands of copies of individual works produced during this period can still be found in storage at the National Library (if not, perhaps, in the best condition) through the present day. I was told that once a work was published the job was essentially considered finished and "less emphasis" was placed on its circulation.

Lao Revolutionary Literature (1945-1975)

Contemporary Lao literature originated in the revolutionary struggle of the Lao Patriotic Front and its literary movement in the years following World War II. As the Buddhist temple was the traditional patron of Lao literature and had great influence on both its form and its content, the Lao Patriotic Front has played a similar role in the development of modern Lao literature. From its origin in the early 1950s to the communist victory in 1975, the form and content of the literature were dictated by the needs of the revolution.

According to official Lao sources, there is a bridge between the ancient Lao literary tradition and modern revolutionary literature. Whereas the Lao Patriotic Front rejected many of the major works of traditional literature as "tools of the feudalists in their exploitation of the masses," certain stories, and particularly genres of poetic expression, were held in high regard as an example of art of the masses (Bua Kaew Chaleunsi [1972] 1993, 18–19).

According to an important official work of literary criticism, *Vannakhadi Lao* (Lao Literature), revolutionary literature originated in the popular expression of discontent with feudal rule and foreign domination. In an early study published shortly after the revolution (printed four times as of 1997), *Leup Phasun*, a traditional Lao poem composed during the early nineteenth century, was interpreted as coded resistance to Thai invaders and compared to the valiant struggle of the Lao Patriotic Front to liberate the country from the American imperialists (S. Desa 1993). Despite the popularity of such an analysis (which continues to be taught in Lao classrooms to the present day), *Leup Phasun* is understood very differently both in the traditional context of its performance, in which it is generally made use of as courtship poetry, and in the scholarship of neighboring Thailand, where it tends to be analyzed as a work of religious philosophy.[12]

According to *Vannakhadi Lao*, several other compositions were produced as anonymous protests to the French presence in Laos and performed by monks in Buddhist temples. In the manuscript *In Tok*, for example (the existence of which I have never been able to verify), the author declares himself to be the Lord Indra and states that even celestial beings in heaven know of the crimes committed against the Lao by the debased French colonists (Bau Saeng Kham Vongdala et al 1987, 298).

However, regardless of the extent to which political sentiment against the Siamese and French may have previously been expressed independently by the Lao in traditional form, literature during this period (and consequently contemporary literature) has developed according to the directives of the Lao revolutionary movement. Literary criticism by official Lao sources, therefore, serves as an important source of information on the role that literature is intended to play in Lao society and the expectations placed on authors as to how they can properly fulfill this role.

For readers familiar with the Western tradition of literary criticism, the Lao counterpart offers some interesting paradoxes. With over three hundred pages of literary criticism currently in print, Laos may have one of the highest ratios of criticism to actual literature in the world. Many of the composers of the literary criticism are not only writers in the Lao revolutionary movement but also authors of the very works they analyze. The importance given to literary criticism by Lao authorities is due to the fact that its ultimate objective is not to analyze individual stories but rather to collectively make use of stories created under government control to present an official analysis of Lao history, society, and culture. Stories are arranged to serve as part of larger explanations of specific problems in Lao society and/or the successes of the revolution in solving these problems. In traditional Lao Buddhist literature, works were thought of collectively as religious teachings, and individual stories were rarely attributed to an author. In a similar fashion, in Lao literary criticism, literature is perceived as a method of teaching political theory, and individual works (particularly from the pre-1975 period) are frequently cited with no credit given to their composer.

According to *Kan Patiwat Lao Lae Vannakhadi Patiwat* (The Lao Revolution and Revolutionary Literature), an official work of literary criticism published in 1972 (Bua Kaew Chaleunsi [1972] 1993), the "special attribute (of Lao literature) lies in its service to the revolution, resistance, the direction and policy of the Lao Patriotic Front, and the common people." Writers of the literature "have grown up amid the reverberant sound of gunfire that is annihilating the enemy in sharp bursts throughout the country" and have come to the realization that literature serves as a "pointed weapon" (25, 26). According to Prince Suphannuvong, in a speech delivered at a conference devoted to art and literature in 1971, the objectives of revolutionary literature include: 1) to illustrate contemporary problems and provide the appropriate remedy, 2) to accurately show the greatness of the revolution, and 3) to boost the morale of those who dedicate their lives to revolutionary service (Bau Saeng Kham Vongdala et al. 1987, 345–46). Other important goals that can be observed from literary content include the creation of role models to be emulated by people of different gender and ethnic identities, the portrayal of the heroism of the revolutionary struggle; political, cultural, and economic progress in the liberated zones; and the decadence of the enemy.

Whereas the topics treated in revolutionary works differed considerably from the standard fare of Lao literature in the past, writers continued to make extensive use of traditional art forms in their treatment of those topics. During the two decades that followed World War II, revolutionary literature was primarily composed in traditional poetic style. Even now, a significant percentage of the literature that is published in Laos consists of collections of poetry based on verse forms of ancient origin. The success of these literary forms as a medium with which to convey the political message of the Lao Patriotic Front is testimony to the integral role that traditional literature (particularly in oral form) continued to play throughout rural Laos in the mid–twentieth century. Literary forms of pre-twentieth-century origin have provided an ideal medium with which to spread a political message (and information in general) because of the abundance of 1) composers skilled in traditional forms, in which literacy is not a necessary prerequisite for composition, 2) performers skilled in rendering the traditional poetic forms before an audience, 3) occasions on which Lao traditional poetry is customarily performed, and 4) an audience appreciative of performances of traditional poetry and as such receptive to the message that it conveys.

In contrast to traditional poetry, the form of prose fiction was foreign to Laos. As a result, there was a lack of people experienced or skilled in its composition and severe limitations in the facilities through which it could be produced and circulated. It was without cultural precedent (with the small exception of a handful of foreign translations or foreign-influenced works that circulated by the elite in Vientiane), and had limited potential for appreciation by a Lao audience. Therefore, to understand the development of revolutionary prose fiction in Laos one must ask the question: Why did a form of literature so seemingly ill-equipped to take root in Laos (and particularly in the rural areas in which the revolution was based) come to be promoted by the Lao revolutionary movement as a vehicle with which to serve its political ends?

A fundamental reason behind the decision to produce short stories and novels by the Lao Patriotic Front was the cultural influence of communist allies, such as the Soviet Union, in which the prose genre of social realism was an established tradition. As the Lao revolutionaries saw themselves as part of a larger, worldwide movement, Lao revolutionary prose was intended to serve as part of a progressive tradition of art that transcended national boundaries. According to *Kan Patiwat Lao Lae Vannakhadi Patiwat* (The Lao Revolution and Revolutionary Literature), "Lao revolutionary literature adapts the best of both traditional Lao literature and progressive literature throughout the world. The literature is not only well received by intellectuals throughout the country, but it is also supported by a readership overseas" (Bua Kaew Chaleunsi [1972] 1993, 26). Works of Lao revolutionary literature have been translated into the Russian, Chinese, Vietnamese, and English languages. Inside of Laos itself, the literature was intended for an audience not only in the liberated zones but also in the areas controlled by the royal Lao government, where it was apparently circulated with little difficulty.

One could argue, however, that, despite the claims that revolutionary literature was intended for a readership throughout Laos and indeed the entire world, the true significance of the writing had nothing to do with the number of people who actually did (or did not) open its pages but rather with the fact that it existed as a body of works that symbolized the contribution of Laos to the worldwide revolutionary movement. Certainly the literature was taught in classrooms in the liberated zones, and, according to some accounts, it was also read by revolutionary soldiers during their spare time. One observer (himself a prolific contributor to the body of progressive Lao revolutionary art) states that much of the writing was ultimately intended to serve as termite food in the caves of Sam Neua.

According to official Lao sources, revolutionary literature originated in the early 1950s. However, until the mid-1960s, prose narrative consisted of articles, reports, and an occasional story by staff and soldiers of the Lao Patriotic Front in their newspaper *Lao Issara* (Bua Kaew Chaleunsi [1972] 1993, 27). Articles in *Lao Issara* typically consisted of true-life accounts of Lao men and women of various ethnic origins who were exemplary in the way in which they sacrificed personal interest for the cause of the revolution. Idealized life portrayals of revolutionary heroes and heroines are the predecessor of Lao fictional works and have served as the model for the composition of many subsequent stories.

By 1965, short stories of the Lao Patriotic Front both appeared in their official newspaper and were published as collections. Fiction was originally composed "in the style of a report" (Bau Saeng Kham Vongdala et al. 1987,

389). According to the account of literary development provided by the authors of *Vannakhadi Lao*, stories were gradually to show the distinctive traits of individual authors. "Phasa Mae" (Mother Tongue), a short story by Bua Kaew Chaleunsi, is an example of how the revolutionary movement made use of nationalist sentiment to draw people to their cause (398–400). The story's hero, Thaung Di, is a bright and idealistic student of high school age in Vientiane. He has the opportunity to further his education, marry a beautiful girl from a well-off family, and make a comfortable living in the future. However, he sees through the "rotten culture of the West that with each day is increasingly penetrating Lao society" and is aware that the "reactionaries," in their contempt for Lao traditions, are "turning Lao society into a bastardized version of American culture." He concludes with disgust that the phoniness of civilized society in Vientiane, with its "whorehouses and dance halls" . . . [has] "tarnished the national monument, That Luang, which once shone so brightly, and muddied the waters of the Mekong, which once flowed so cool and clear." In stark contrast to the corrupted Westernized values of Vientiane, the protagonist Thaung Di has heard about the ideal Lao society that is being created in the liberated zones. Rejecting a prosperous future serving "reactionary traitors," in the following passage he implores his girlfriend, Dara, to follow him and join the communist revolution.

> Thaung Di spoke: "Dara, have you seen? In the liberated zone there are high schools and junior highs where the teaching is conducted entirely in Lao. Now wouldn't we enjoy that?" Lifting his shirtsleeve to wipe back his tears, he continued: "As for us, we are forced to study in French from an early age. How can we help but feel pained in our hearts? . . . The Lao Patriotic Front has sent students to study further at universities in Vietnam, the Soviet Union, and other civilized countries so that they can return to apply their knowledge in the building of our nation" (400).

Much of Lao literature from this period is written in a similar vein.

Lao Literature from 1975 through the Late 1980s

In the first decade following the Communist victory in 1975, Lao revolutionary literature largely remained a tool of the party to propagate its political ends. However, as the needs of the party changed from military struggle to consolidation and legitimization of its rule, the role of literature changed accordingly.

As the center of control of the Lao Patriotic Front moved from the province of Sam Neua to the nation's capital, facilities for the distribution of revolutionary literature were greatly improved. *Vannakhadi Lao* states that among the many achievements of the early years of communist rule was the expansion of existing publishing facilities, the introduction of modern printing technology, and the training of a publishing staff abroad (Bau Saeng Kham Vongdala et al. 1987, 449). With the cost of paper and printing subsidized by the Lao government and the Soviet Union, books were distributed free or at minimal cost, and individual print runs ran into the tens of thousands. This should not be taken to mean that tens of thousands of people actually read the works.

Lao authors dating from this period to the present can be divided into three basic categories. The first consists of writers who originally served the revolutionary cause in the liberated zones prior to the communist victory, including, for example, Chanthi Deuansavan, Khamliang Phonsena, and Suvanthaun Bupphanuvong. The second category consists of established authors from the old regime who have continued to make use of their literary skills in the service of the new Lao society. Authors of this type include members of Maha Sila Viravong's family (namely, Outhine Bounyavong, Duang Champa, and Dauk Ket) and writers such as Seliphap, Pian Julamunti, and so on. The third category consists of a younger generation of authors who started their literary careers in the years immediately preceding the revolution or afterward. Prominent writers include Bunthanong Somsaiphon, Saisuvan Phaengphong, Viset Savaengseuksa, Dawviang Butnakho, Niti Saiyasaeng, Somsuk Suksavat, and Bunseun Saengmani. Several authors in this group, such as Bunthanong Somsaiphon and Saisuvan Phaengphong, were actively involved in some form of resistance to the former regime, as they have documented in their writing. By the mid-1980s, authors in this latter category had become the most active.[13]

From 1975 to the present, Lao writers have generally supported themselves as civil servants. In the first decade after the revolution, many authors worked for the State Printing House, translating communist literature into Lao in addition to producing their own works. In the early years of the new regime, writers in Vientiane were sent to interview soldiers in the liberated zones, and put their life histories into writing. A major result of this project is *Siang Kaung Khaung Latthi Vilason Pativat* (The Echoing Sound of the Doctrine of Revolutionary Heroes, 1982), by Outhine Bounyavong and others. Lao authors under the communist regime have generally worked as reporters for government newspapers and magazines in which the writing of fiction serves as one part of their overall duty. The editors of the various newspapers and magazines come under the supervision of the Ministry of Information and Culture, which is responsible for the review of its content.

From the time of the revolution, writers' associations have played an important role in the development of Lao literature. Their stated objectives are to bring writers together, produce magazines that serve as an outlet for an author's work, arrange for translations of socialist literature, and organize meetings with foreign writers. On a deeper level, they serve to regulate individual authors and foster the concept that a writer's duty is to produce literature as a worker of the state. A significant characteristic of literature composed during the first decade after the revolution (which persists to a lesser extent in the present) is that frequently published collections of stories are not by an individual author but rather by writers belonging to government sponsored organizations such as the Women's Union (Mae Nying Lao) or the Society of Young Lao Writers (Samakhom Num Lao).

As traditional Buddhist literature was frequently composed to be performed on specific religious occasions, many works of literature from 1975 to the present have been created for commemorative reasons, with the intent to honor events significant in the official history of the communist revolution. Authors are asked to write stories to be published on officially sanctified dates such as Armed Forces Day, the date of the communist victory, or an important national meeting of the Communist Party.

The official position on the role of literature during this period can be seen in an analysis of the function of literary competitions by the authors of the official work of Lao literary criticism, *Vannakhadi Lao*. According to this study, the quality of Lao short stories improved in the 1980s as a result of open competition between Lao writers. Lest this statement be rashly interpreted as having broader implications concerning freedom of ideas, literary improvement is attributed immediately afterward to the opportunity for authors to listen to literary criticism, defined as "proper guidance and direction from the authorities above [which allows them] to see clearly their duties and the [proper] direction for their writing." Nonetheless, the fiction composed during the decade following the communist victory should not be entirely dismissed as works of propaganda motivated by a sense of duty enforced from above. It should also be understood as at times representative of an idealistic belief that the new government would genuinely uplift Lao society and as an expression of anger at the United States for the great devastation that the American military inflicted on the Lao countryside.

"Poi Nok" (Freeing Birds), a short story composed in the mid-1970s by Bunthanong Somsaiphon, reflects this sense of idealism, and optimism for the future. The two main characters are intended as role models to be emulated by young men and women. Kavao is the beautiful young daughter of a village headman, and her lover, Phukhao, is a young man who becomes a soldier of the Lao Patriotic Front. The story begins with a depiction of the happiness of the two lovers as youths in the Lao countryside. Each year, during the Lao New Year's Festival Phukhao and Kavao engage in the customary practice of freeing birds from cages, an act that is believed to generate good merit and ensure a positive future. Kavao wishes that "the two birds will fly into the sky of love under the sunlight of hope" and that she and her lover will eventually marry. Alas, the fate of the young woman takes a sudden turn for the worse with the arrival of a military man from Vientiane by the name of Captain Phuangkham, who comes to her village with a lucrative business proposition for her father. The captain soon establishes a lumber mill, as a result of which the local forests are devastated and the headman and his family are showered with gifts.

One gift that the headman does not expect, however, is a grandchild; the captain has drugged and raped Kavao after convincing her to take a ride alone in his expensive car. Shamed by her pregnancy, Kavao leaves the village for Vientiane, where she lives a melancholy existence as the minor wife of the captain. Every year during the New Year's Festival, the young mother takes her child to free birds at a local temple and thinks regretfully of her old lover, who is now fighting for the destruction of the regime that allows people such as Captain Phuangkham to shamelessly exploit the people of Laos. Ultimately Kavao is spared from her fate as a minor wife and reunited with her childhood lover as a result of the communist liberation of her country. In the final days before the communist victory, Kavao leads the workers at her husband's mill in a great strike in which all of her husband's timber is seized. Captain Phuangkham flees across the Mekong River into Thailand shortly afterward, and with great patriotic spirit Kavao donates her husband's mill and all of its timber to the Lao state. As Phukhao is later to tell her with the utmost admiration, "By such an action, you have made merit in the greatest possible fashion." After Kavao and Phukhao are united in the dramatic final scene, once again they free a pair of birds and look forward to living under "the sky of love under the sunlight of hope" as their country enters a new age with the inauguration of the new regime.

In "Poi Nok," the communist liberation of Laos is symbolically compared to a religious act of great merit, and a citizen's self-sacrifice for the good of the state also takes on a religious significance. However ambivalent the communist leadership may have been concerning the value (and dangers) of organized religion, the transforming and liberating qualities of the communist takeover of Laos are placed within a traditional Buddhist framework, an advertising tool with a proven track record in promoting a moral message to a Lao audience.

The influence of the socialist literary genre of social realism on Lao literature during the fifteen years that followed the revolution should not be underestimated. As recently as the early 1990s, shelves of the few existing bookstores in Vientiane were largely filled not with Lao compositions but rather with translations of communist, primarily Soviet works, including political theory, fiction, and children's tales.

Lao Literature: Late 1980s through the Mid-1990s

In the late 1980s, following Mikhail Gorbachev's policy of glasnost and the collapse of the Soviet Union, the Lao government initiated a series of economic and social reforms known collectively as New Imagination (Chintanakan Mai). The perception that these measures would result in an increased liberalization of Lao society had a significant affect on Lao literature. Initially, Lao authors were officially informed that in future writings they should address in a constructive fashion both the strengths and weaknesses of the modern regime along with the areas in need of improvement. Taking advantage of this new freedom, Lao authors increasingly began to provide a constructively critical view of Lao society.[14] Certain authors wrote and published works of social and political criticism in the early 1990s with a degree of openness that has been unmatched. Within the course of a few years, however, Lao authors came to realize that, regardless of a policy outlined on a sheet of paper, there were limits to what was acceptable for publication.[15] By the mid-1990s, although literature continued to offer certain critical observations on the state of Lao society and values, it tended to avoid overt political analysis.

Lao Literature as Political Expression

The role of literature as a vehicle for social and political criticism during the early 1990s is reflected in three stories, "Khwai Doisan" (Passenger Buffalo), "Khon Yang Lung Dam" (A Man Such as Uncle Dam), and "Niyay Nai Haung Nam" (Novel in the Toilet). These stories were composed by the generation of authors who began to write in the years immediately surrounding the revolution.

"Khwai Doisan" was written by Saisuvan Phaengphong, an important writer of the post-1975 period, who makes use of satire to critically comment on the state of Lao society. Originally trained as a pilot, he has published short stories, novels, and poetry.[16] One of the most outspoken Lao writers during the New Imagination period, he now lives and writes in the United States. In "Khwai Doisan," published in 1990, Saisuvan describes the tribulations of a government pilot who has been given the task of transporting buffaloes to Vientiane from the distant province of Attapheu. The reasoning behind the order is that buffaloes in Attapheu are not only bigger and fatter than their counterparts in Vientiane but also cost substantially less. The pilot flies into Attapheu in the midst of heavy rains and is immediately faced with the task of loading eight unwieldy buffaloes onto a very small plane. He is concerned that if the buffaloes are free to move about during the flight the balance of the aircraft could be seriously disturbed. Therefore, it is decided that each of the buffaloes must first be wrestled to the ground, bound with rope, and then carried onto the plane. The completion of this job not only takes several hours but also requires the assistance of a total of fifty people.

Once the buffaloes have been boarded, the pilot is in a great hurry to make the journey, fearful that if he cannot arrive in Vientiane on the same day he will be faced with the unhappy prospect of having to unload the buffaloes for the night, and then reboard them the following morning. The plane takes off from Attapheu in bad weather, with the pilot and copilot, eight buffaloes, and a few squeamish nurses, who in dismay are forced to sit at close quarters with the animals. The buffaloes wreak havoc throughout the flight. Eventually, one of them manages to destroy a hydraulic pipe that controls the landing gear, and the pilots are forced to make an emergency landing at the Vientiane airport. At the end of the story, the author notes that a hospital car is waiting at the airport not to receive the nurses on their arrival but rather to collect the wounded and the dead. Whereas the story may appear to be nothing more than a tall tale designed to make people laugh, in a humorous manner it pokes fun at improper decision making by officials in Vientiane, who have little understanding of the effect of their decisions on the people who have to carry them out.

The second story, "Khon Yang Lung Dam" (A Man Such as Uncle Dam), was composed by Viset Savaengseuksa, a talented writer who is a member of the Lao National Parliament. In his tale, a typist at a government import/export office has a miscarriage and lies in critical condition in the hospital.[17] Unfortunately, the hospital lacks the blood that is needed to perform an operation. Therefore, the typist's husband appeals to the woman's colleagues at the government office for assistance. Throughout the story, the problem of the woman's health becomes a topic of heated debate in meetings of various committees at her place of work. "Of course we could help her with a donation of blood," states one high-ranking official, whose words are echoed throughout the tale, "but we wish rather to suggest that the problem of responsibility is the primary issue."

As the woman lays dying, the Women's Section, the Youth Committee, and the Worker's Union each in turn deny their responsibility in the matter and leave it up to others for further consultation. Ultimately the woman is spared only through the generosity of Uncle Dam, a janitor who has been given the responsibility of relaying messages between the various committees. Taking pity on the dying woman, he brings his family and relatives to the hospital to make a donation of blood of sufficient quantity for the operation to be performed. When the doctor asks the reason behind the old man's generosity, Uncle Dam's explanation is a summary of traditional Lao religious philosophy. He declares, "I believe that one is rewarded for one's good deeds and punished for one's evil. I donated blood today as a result of my compassion and pity for the life of a fellow human being. I did not come here in an official capacity."

When Uncle Dam returns to work, he overhears a meeting of the Worker's Union. Unaware of the old man's donation, the members state that the woman's health problem remains "a critical issue that must be attended to with the greatest of urgency" once the "issue of responsibility" is officially resolved. In comparison with Bunthanong's "Poi Nok," in which the liberation of Laos is seen as a religious act of great merit, the author's use of Buddhism in this tale suggests that traditional Buddhist values are showing signs of greater resilience than faith in the transforming and liberating qualities of the communist regime.

The third story, "Niyay Nai Haung Nam" (Novel in the Toilet), stands in sharp contrast to the sentiments expressed by the identical author in "Poi Nok," which was composed a decade earlier.[18] Bunthanong describes the different levels of bathrooms at an unnamed ministry that are allotted for the use of government officials of various ranks. In the bathrooms for ministers, where there is a constant supply of soap, towels, toilet paper, and deodorizers, the doors need to be opened with a key. In contrast, the doors to the bathrooms for civil servants, "whose salaries could be paid for with half a bag of rice, three kilos of meat, and ten cans of milk," are left unlocked because there is nothing inside that anyone might possibly steal. In the course of the story, the narrator, fed up with the unsanitary conditions in the lower-level bathrooms, secretly arranges to make a private copy of the key to a more luxurious toilet. This sets the stage for the climax of the tale, in which the narrator opens the bathroom door to witness a young secretary, naked and in a compromising position, with an elderly man he is "not quite certain is a minister or head of the cabinet." It is not surprising that Bunthanong was to find himself in trouble as a result of such writing, and by the late 1990s he was working not as a writer but as the owner of West Wind, a bar and restaurant with a cowboy decor.

Freedom of Expression in Lao Society: The Career of Bunthanong Somsaiphon

Government control of the printed word is a central issue in any discussion of Lao literature. The extent of freedom of expression in Lao society can be seen in the career of Bunthanong Somsaiphon. Bunthanong is a writer who, more than any other contemporary Lao author, has tested the limits of what is acceptable in literary content. He states that his stories are intended to serve as open letters to government officials to inform them of the problems and concerns of the common people of Laos.[19] The critical content of his work has caused him complications since he began his career during the final years of the old regime. In the post-1975 period, Bunthanong was a prominent writer whose stories were taught in schools; he served for a number of years as the head of the Young Writer's Association (Samosaun Nakkhian Num) and as the editor of its literary newspaper, *Sao Num*.

After receiving political training in the New Imagination policy, Bunthanong wrote a series of articles for a Lao newspaper in 1991 describing various social problems in Luang Prabang. This caused enough displeasure to force his departure as the head of the Young Writer's Association and as the editor of its newspaper. With his resignation, the association and its newspaper abruptly came to an end. Shortly afterward, Bunthanong was one of ten writers who established the Lao Writer's Association under the auspices of the Ministry of Information and Culture. He played an important role in the association, writing its regulations and helping to organize three seminars in conjunction with Thai authors in Laos and Northeast Thailand. However, his connections with Thai writers and his critical speeches at the seminars on the state of Lao literature and society further damaged him in the eyes of the authorities, particularly when Thai newspapers gave him the label "Fighter of the System."

In a repeat of the past, Bunthanong resigned under pressure from his position in the Lao Writer's Association in 1991, and five other like-minded writers followed him. After Bunthanong left the association, the regulations that he had written, which emphasized the rights of authors and their honored role in Lao society, were changed to stress the duties and obligations of writers as workers of the state. In 1991, Bunthanong published "Niyay Nai Haung Nam" in a Lao newspaper, causing him further complications and near arrest.

Ironically, however, after this incident officials asked editors of Lao newspapers to include stories or articles by Bunthanong because the Lao public saw him as a barometer of freedom of expression in Laos. Officials believed that, if his stories continued to appear in print the impression would be that there was an adequate amount of freedom of expression in the country. As a result of strict editing of his writing, however, Bunthanong has contributed few stories to Lao newspapers during the past decade. Instead, he has sent his fiction to Thai newspapers and magazines. Although a Lao audience would have enough knowledge of the Thai language to read these publications, they are not available in Lao bookstores. Bunthanong's first book-length collection of short stories to be printed in Thailand, *Kaduk American* (American Bones) was published in 1991, and a second work has been completed, the publication date of which remains uncertain.[20] Although Bunthanong originally composed his works in Lao to be translated by a Thai author, in several of his more recent writings he has bypassed the Lao language altogether. It is unlikely that the Lao government would take pride in the fact that, as a direct result of its policy toward literary expression, one of the most foremost writers in Laos has taken to composing Lao literature in the Thai language.

Lao Literature: Mid-1990s to the Present

From the mid 1990s to the present, Lao authors have struggled with a number of serious obstacles that have threatened to undermine the growth—and even the very survival—of a meaningful tradition of literature in Laos. In order to understand the content and context of contemporary Lao literature, therefore, one needs to appreciate the nature of these obstacles and their effect on Lao writing.

First, the great amount of poverty in Laos, the limited spread of education (and literacy), and the lack of a widespread culture of reading continue to provide formidable obstacles to the growth of literature, especially outside of Vientiane.

Second, the political situation in the country does not permit the degree of freedom of expression that is necessary to allow literature to flourish. From independence onward, the popularity that literature has enjoyed is largely attributable to the role that it has played as a forum for the expression of social and political commentary in Lao society, a trait that is particularly evident in works produced both during the early 1990s following the New Imagination policy and during the late 1960s and early 1970s under the former regime. Unfortunately, the social and political role of literature that motivated authors to write and inspired an audience to read is a role that literature currently is not permitted to fulfill—unless one writes in Thai for a Thai audience.

Third, one cannot overestimate the effect of the Lao economy on the growth—or stagnation—of literature. The Asian economic crash of the late 1990s had a devastating effect on Lao writing. Lao authors, no longer subsidized by the government, are struggling to meet the increasingly high cost of publishing. For the first time in recent Lao history, the success or failure of literary works is dependent on their ability to attract an audience or sponsor. As during the old regime, foreign sources have proved an important source of funding for Lao publications. However, with a few notable exceptions, contemporary literature does not benefit from this type of funding. In attracting an audience, a formidable obstacle that faces Lao authors at present is the competition of written material from neighboring Thailand, which increasingly can be found in Lao shops. In addition to benefiting from a greater freedom of expression, Thai publications are typically more slickly produced and more fashionable and up-to-date in the eyes of a Lao audience.[21]

As a result of these obstacles, the immediate future of literature in Laos does not appear particularly positive. The number of book-length collections of fiction is approximately ten per year, with an average print run of two thousand copies. This is an incredibly low figure not only in comparison with other nations in Southeast Asia, with the exception of Cambodia, but also in comparison to the amount of literature that was produced in Laos only a decade ago. In addition, short stories are commonly found in newspapers and magazines. The most significant literary forum is *Vannasin*, a magazine founded in 1979, which includes an average of two stories per issue and a notably more substantial amount of verse.

As time grows increasingly distant from the revolution that brought the communist regime into power, there is an observable tendency to make use of literature as a means through which to revitalize important events in communist Lao history in order to convey their significance to the present generation. This is achieved both through the reprinting of works by the older generation of revolutionary authors and, to a lesser extent, through the composition of new works that attempt to breathe life into the past through its dramatic representation in literature.

In 1997, Laos was invited to become a member of the Association of Southeast Asian Nations (ASEAN). Many people have expressed the hope that a broader participation in regional affairs will result in a greater liberalization of Lao political and economic affairs. As part of its membership, Laos takes part in a number of cultural events, including S.E.A. Write, an annual literary competition in which authors from each of the member states are granted awards and public recognition for the composition of outstanding works of new literature. In contrast to most of the nations in the region, the winning Lao author is not chosen by a panel of literary experts based on the quality of annual submissions but rather is appointed by the government controlled literary association as a result of seniority and influence. In some cases, the winning authors receive awards for works produced decades earlier. Needless to say, this practice—and the government approach to literature that it reflects—does little to encourage literary creativity among the present generation of Lao.

Recurring Themes in Contemporary Lao Literature

From the 1980s to the present, there are a number of recurring themes that can be found in Lao fiction. One important theme is the poverty of the country's inhabitants and the ingenuity that is required simply to survive. In "Thuay Feu Nai Laup Phi" (A Yearly Bowl of Noodle Soup), by Dawviang Butnakho (1992), for example, the main character, Kham Ko, is the son of a rickshaw driver who is forced to leave school at an early age as the result of a fire that has destroyed his family's already limited fortunes. In the opening scene, he is pictured as gazing longingly at a bowl of noodle soup for sale in a local shop. It is not that Kham Ko lacks the money to buy the soup but rather that he considers it too much of a luxury. In the course of the tale, Kham Ko improves his financial state through the collection and sale of scrap metal, much of which is left over from the Lao civil war, an unintentional form of foreign aid from the United States. By the end of the story, Kham Ko has lifted himself to the point that he can enter a noodle shop with great confidence and order what he refers to as his "yearly bowl of soup and coffee with milk."

Related themes that are commonly found in literature are the indignities of being poor, discrepancies in wealth, and the contemptuous attitude of the rich toward poor. In "Khoi Bau Maen Khau Than" (I Am Not a Beggar), by Bunseun Saengmani (1995), a soldier of the Lao Patriotic Front is blinded during the revolutionary war and marries the nurse who treats him in the hospital. Decades afterward, the now elderly couple travels to Vientiane for the first time in many years. The wife leads her blind husband through the Morning Market, where they plan to buy a tape cassette. As they stop to choose the tape, a stranger walks over to them and places some spare change in their hands, mistaking them for beggars. Speaking politely, he tells them to step aside and get out of the way of the people who are actually shopping. Rather than being appreciated for the sacrifices that they have made in the liberation of their country, the story shows how the rural poor who served as the foot soldiers of the Lao revolution have ultimately come to be treated by the present generation of Lao city dwellers in the same contemptuous matter that one might speculate led them to join the revolution in the first place.

Self-sacrifice for the greater good also remains a prominent theme in Lao literature, although it is no longer narrowly defined in terms of the fulfillment of the political goals of the government. In "Chak Vanni Chon Kwa Cha Leum" (From Today until I Forget), by Bunseun Saengmani (1997), for example, a sixteen-year-old boy is praised for his willingness to give up his education in order to take care of his sick mother and younger brothers after his father dies. In "Haeng Chai Chak Theung Phudoi" (Motivation from the Mountain), by Hom Phothaung (1997), a young woman who has been educated as a teacher in Vientiane joins the staff of a school in a remote Hmong village in the mountains despite the pleadings of her boyfriend, who wishes for her to live a more comfortable and less idealistic life.

Nationalism and pride in being Lao is also a theme that is found in many Lao works. In "Hak Kham Khaup Fa" (Love That Crosses the Sky), by Bunseun Saengmani (1997), the narrator is a Lao refugee who lives in the United States. Traveling to Laos, he meets and falls in love with a young woman named Phetsomphu. At the end of his vacation, he promises to return to Laos within a year and take the woman to attend the annual That Luang Festival. When a year passes by and he returns, however, his beloved is nowhere to be seen. He attends the festival alone and is shocked to find Phetsomphu walking with another man, pretending not to notice him. In the climactic final scene, the narrator is handed a letter in the airport as he prepares to return home, alone and brokenhearted. In the letter, he is informed by Phetsomphu that after much consideration she has decided to marry another man, one who is "Lao, just like she is," so that she will "have the opportunity to stay in Laos until she grows old." In the final paragraph of the story, the narrator takes a deep breath and reflects with resignation and a new found wisdom.

> "I knew then that she was correct in her decision", he thinks to himself, "because the man that she will marry is a Lao man, and 100 percent Lao. Being a foreigner, I thought that in this day and age my money would be enough to win over the heart of a Lao woman. Alas, I was taught a lesson that I will remember until the end of my days."

The nationalistic sentiment of the author reflects, albeit inversely, the increasing tendency of Lao women to seek out foreign spouses (including quite frequently Lao men living overseas) in the hopes of migrating to a more developed and wealthier nation.

Modern Lao literature also frequently discusses the roles and responsibilities of women, presenting an interesting mixture between advocacy for greater freedom and fairness for women in Lao society and insistence on the continual applicability of traditional restrictions regarding their behavior. "Kaun Cha Theung Van Ni" (Before Having Reached This Day), by Duang Champa

(1983), illustrates the difficulties of a poor woman named Kaew Mani who is engaged to be married to a young man from a wealthier family. As a condition of the marriage, Kaew Mani's future mother-in-law insists that she give up her lifelong passion for traditional Lao dance, which is perhaps considered an unsuitable activity for a young woman of a respectable family. As Kaew Mani's fiancé does not intervene on her behalf, she breaks off the engagement and eventually marries a more supportive man. In the final scene, Kaew Mani is performing at an important event attended by foreigners, while her husband watches proudly in the audience. Her former suitor from the wealthier family, who has also come to watch her dance, remains single and is presumably quite miserable.

In "Meua Haut Thi Jua" (When It Comes the Turn of the Buddhist Novice),[22] by Viset Savaengseuksa (2000), a man named Kalaum blames his wife for her failure to give birth to a child, which he insists is because of a black birthmark on her stomach. He then takes a second wife, but she also fails to produce a child. Upon seeking a third wife, Kalaum is stopped by the village headman, who insists that he visit a local hospital, which can determine through modern scientific methods the reason for his family's lack of offspring. After reluctantly entering the hospital, Kalaum is teased by the doctors, who tell him, "In order to be fair, your wives should have the opportunity to sleep with other men to see if they can give birth, as you yourself have had the chance to sleep with two different women." When Kalaum cries out that such a practice would "go against the spirits," he is forced to sign a written agreement that the spouse of whoever is proved to be sterile will have the legal right to obtain a divorce and remarry. Shortly afterward, the tests disprove Kalaum's notion that a birthmark could cause infertility, and, to make matters worse, Kalaum is declared to have "weak sperm." Devastated, he returns home with one of his wives, who terrifies him by stating that she will seek a divorce in the morning. Once he has been sufficiently frightened, however, Kalaum's wife tears up their agreement and, playing the role of a proper Lao woman, reassures him that she will remain his devoted wife forever.

In "Kham Khau Thot Thi Bau Yaum Hai Aphai" (An Unaccepted Apology), by Phuangphet Buaphachan (1996), a young wife is punished for her unfaithfulness. Manivan is separated from her husband for a period of several years as he works overseas. During their separation, she has an affair with a friend of her husband, which she breaks off shortly before his return, recognizing the mistake she has made. Alas, her recognition comes far too late. When her husband learns of her affair, she admits her indiscretion and begs his forgiveness. The indiscretion is too great to be forgiven, however, as she realizes sadly when he immediately leaves her and her children.

In "Bua Khaem Beung" (Lotus at the Edge of the Swamp), a story by the same author (1997), a young woman named Phaunvilay supports herself by selling beer and whiskey at a small outdoor stand. Two male customers flirt with her, assuming that because she is poor she will be willing to sleep with them for one hundred thousand kip. "I am a rural girl of little knowledge," she lectures them. "I have had no chance to get a good education. However, Lao women have high moral standards, regardless of whether they have attended school or not. As for myself, I have had my parents and elders to teach me." The two men, shamed, depart in a great hurry, leaving behind a pair of dark glasses. Phaunvilay has no intention of returning the glasses (despite her high level of morality), concluding that what she has taught the "two men who think that women are nothing more than toys" is worth far more than what they have lost. Whereas this story is clearly a critique of the behavior of Lao men toward Lao women, it also serves as a statement concerning clearly defined boundaries of proper behavior for Lao women of high moral standards who have been "taught by their parents and elders." It is worth noting that, with the exception of "Meua Haut Thi Jua," all of the above stories concerning women were composed by female authors.

Finally, romance is a common theme in Lao literature, as reflected in the fiction of Duangsai Luangphasi, who both writes literary accounts of the heroic glory of centuries of Lao revolutionary warfare and works with such titles as *Ba Chiang Niyay Hak Aummata* (Ba Chiang: An Eternal Novel of Love), *Hak Lae Phukphan* (Love and Ties), and *Chao Sao Bang Bot* (The Bride with a Secret). In *Hak Lae Phukphan*, a typical work of romantic fiction by the author, the front cover is decorated with drawings of red and yellow roses. Between the roses is a photograph of a beautiful young woman wearing lipstick and mascara whose name (Nang Maninut), age (twenty-three), and neighborhood (Ban Khua

Sai Leuat Diao Kan
(Our Blood Courses through the Same Vein)
by Duangsai Luangphasi
Courtesy of Dokked Publishing

Luang) are listed on the first page. The relationship of this woman to the story itself is never satisfactorily explained. The novel is an account of a young man who is separated from his lover when she is obliged by her parents to become engaged to a young man from a wealthier family. However, fate intervenes, and when she is diagnosed with a serious illness she is quickly abandoned by her fiancé, leaving her free to happily rejoin her true love. Alas, such happiness is short-lived, as is the woman herself, as the cause of her freedom is also shortly afterward the cause of her death. Whereas the level of popularity of such a work is open to question, its author has the distinction in recent years of consistently having the greatest quantity of works on the Lao market.

Conclusion

In order to give a proper perspective to contemporary literature in Laos, Lao writing must be compared to both the modern literary traditions of neighboring Southeast Asian nations and traditional Lao literature. On one level, there are significant similarities between the old and new traditions of Lao literature. Both literatures draw greatly from foreign sources. Both have been patronized by powerful social institutions, traditionally the Buddhist temple and in the twentieth century the Lao government and Communist Party, which have made use of literature as a vehicle to encourage or enforce a particular worldview or policy. A major difference between the ancient and modern literary traditions, however, is the extent to which each has been incorporated into Lao consciousness and culture. Whereas Western influence on Laos in the twentieth century has largely been successful in destroying the traditional Lao system of education and many of its cultural traditions, it has not been similarly successful in providing a replacement that is effective in its communication of knowledge to the Lao people, regardless of geographical location or social class. This is illustrated by the fact that the modern Lao script, despite its simplified system of spelling, is probably not as widely known among the ethnic Lao of the present day (particularly in rural areas of the country) as were the more complex traditional scripts of the past.

If one accepts, however, that modern fiction is composed and consumed by a small group of people in Laos, largely in the nation's capital, one can appreciate its development from the colonial period to the present. A large body of writing has been created in Laos during the past half century with a form and content radically different from anything that existed in the past. In the midst of great social change, the transformation of Lao society is being recorded by Lao writers in a form that is a very part of that change.

Notes

[1] For a detailed look at how traditional literature was affected by the change in medium, see Koret 1994a.

[2] Note that the performance of traditional literature in the ethnically Lao areas of neighboring Northeast Thailand came to an end at a considerably earlier date.

[3] The first junior secondary school in Laos was not established until 1921 (Evans 2002, 49).

[4] Naung Lam Chan Temple in Suvannakhet Province is a good example of this type of temple.

[5] After independence in 1954, although Lao officially became the national language, in practice French remained prominent in the spheres of government and higher education. The consistent implementation of Lao as a national language began only with the communist victory in 1975. Note that even a historical figure as important as Prince Suvanna Phuma, who served as prime minister of Laos for two decades, preferred to speak French rather than his native Lao.

[6] In *Vannakhadi Lao*.

[7] For a succinct overview of the development of literature in the twentieth century, see Compton 1988.

[8] For a more detailed discussion, see Koret 1999.

[9] Ironically, the French, for a similar reason also attempted to separate the Lao from their own traditions. Prior to World War II, plans were made to replace Lao script with the Roman alphabet. As the Lao and Thai scripts are closely related, its replacement would have increased the difficulty of communication between people in both countries.

[10] The Committee of Literature was originally organized in 1949 under the name Bureau of Literature (Kaung Vannakhadi); see Koret 1994a, 294, 326.

[11] In the mid-90s, the two daughters of Maha Sila Viravong, Dara and Duangdeuan (Duangdeuane), acquired a printing press. They resurrected the name *Phai Nam* and published for several years the nicest-looking and best-produced literary publications in Laos.

[12] The poem has also been used by Lao refugees in the United States as an ode of resistance to the communist regime. For further information, see Koret 2003.

[13] Authors who produced revolutionary literature in the liberated zones prior to 1975 are prominently represented in contemporary writers' organizations; some of their major works are occasionally reprinted. Note, however, that only two decades after the establishment of a communist regime in Laos, many of the novels and short stories that *Vannakhadi Lao* (Lao Literature) describes as classics of the revolution are unavailable at the National Library; they are exceedingly difficult to locate. There is also little new fiction by writers in this category. This is probably due to their advancing age and the current literary taste of Lao readers.

[14] If one makes a comparison of short stories composed by an identical author in Laos during the 1980s and 1990s, there is typically a considerable difference in their content. See, for example, the works of Viset Savaengseuksa and Bunthanong Somsaiphon.

[15] Bau Saeng Kham Vongdala et al. (1987, 453).

[16] The story "Khwai Doisan" was published in a collection of Saisuvan's short stories and poetry entitled *Lao Thevada*. (Note that Lao authors are commonly referred to in this article by their first names following Lao custom.)

[17] This story was published in *Lam Se Saeun*, a collection of short fiction by Viset.

[18] The change in Bunthanong's political orientation can also be seen quite clearly in "A Bar at the Edge of a Cemetery" (Koret 2002, 108–15).

[19] As stated in a personal interview.

[20] The short story "Ran Khai Lao Rim Placha" (A Bar at the Edge of a Cemetery), that is translated in *Virtual Lotus*, is taken from this collection.

[21] In many ways, the state of songwriting in Laos is similar to that of literature. Lyrics have to be submitted to the government before they can be published or performed. The strict censorship does little to enhance the popularity of Lao music, and locally produced songs can hardly compete with more risqué—and popular—Thai hits that would never pass the Lao censors. The government attempts to promote local music through the enforcement of a legally required percentage of Lao songs per night that people are forced to dance to in Lao discos.

[22] The title is based on an expression that refers to occasions when people with little power or rank in society gain the upper hand. Novices at a temple normally defer to monks.

References

Western Language Sources

Bounyavong, Outhine. 1999. *Mother's Beloved: Stories from Laos.* Seattle: University of Washington Press.

Bunthanong Somsaiphon. 2002. "A Bar at the Edge of a Cemetery." Translated by Peter Koret. In *Virtual Lotus: Modern Fiction of Southeast Asia*, edited by Teri Shaffer Yamada, 108–15. Ann Arbor: University of Michigan Press.

Compton, Carol. 1988. "Lao Literature." In *Far Eastern Literature in the Twentieth Century: A Guide*, edited by Leonard S. Klein, 143–45. Harpenden, Herts: Oldcastle Books.

Evans, Grant, ed. 1999. *Laos: Culture and Society.* Chaing Mai: Silkworm Books.

———. 2002. *A Short History of Laos: The Land in Between.* Chiang Mai: Silkworm Books.

Goscha, Christopher E., and Søren Ivarsson, eds. 2003. *Contesting Visions of the Lao Past: Lao Historiography at the Crossroads.* NIAS Studies on Asian Topics, no. 32. Copenhagen: Nordic Institute of Asian Studies Press.

Gunn, Geoffrey C. 1990. *Rebellion in Laos.* Boulder: Westview.

Koret, Peter. 1994a. "Whispered So Softly It Resounds through the Forest, Spoken So Loudly It Can Hardly Be Heard: The Art of Parallelism in Traditional Lao Literature." PhD thesis, School of Oriental and African Studies, University of London.

———. 1994b. "Laos." In *Traveller's Literary Companion to South-East Asia*, edited by Alastair Dingwall, 120–53. Brighton: In Print.

———. 1996. "Understanding the History and Social Use of Lao Traditional Literature in Relationship to the Literary Tradition of the Tai Yuan." Paper presented at the Sixth International Conference on Thai Studies, Chiang Mai.

———. 1999a. "Books of Search: The Invention of Traditional Lao Literature as a Subject of Study." In *Laos: Culture and Society,* edited by Grant Evans, 226–57. Chiang Mai: Silkworm Books.

———. 1999b. "Contemporary Lao Literature." In *Texts and Contexts: Interactions between Literature and Culture in Southeast Asia,* edited by Luisa J. Mallari-Hall and Lilly Tope, 77–103. Quezon City: University of the Philippines Press.

———. 2003. "Leup Phasun: Romance, Religion, and Politics in the Interpretation of a Traditional Lao Poem." In *Contesting Visions of the Lao Past: Lao Historiography at the Crossroads,* edited by Christopher E. Goscha and Søren Ivarsson, 181–208. NIAS Studies in Asian Topics no. 32. Copenhagen: Nordic Institute of Asian Studies Press.

Koret, Peter, trans. 2002. "A Bar at the Edge of a Cemetery" by Bunthanoung Somsaiphon. In *Virtual Lotus: Modern Fiction of Southeast Asia,* edited by Teri Shaffer Yamada, 108–15. Ann Arbor: University of Michigan Press.

LaFont, P. B. 1989. "Laos." In *Southeast Asia: Languages and Literatures: A Select Guide,* edited by Patricia Herbert and Anthony Milner, 67–76. Arran, Scotland: Kiscadale Publications.

Peltier, Anatole R. 1988. *Le Roman Classique Lao.* Paris: École Française D'Extrême Orient.

Lao Language Sources

Bau Saeng Kham Vongdala et al. 1987. *Vannakhadi Lao.* Vientiane: Social Science Research Institute.

Bua Kaew Chaleunsi. [1972] 1993. *Kan Pativat Lao Lae Vannakhadi Pativat.* Vientiane: Seuksa Printing House.

Bunseun Saengmani. 1995. *Khoi Bau Maen Khau Than* (I Am Not a Beggar) in *Peum Bantheuk Si Fa* (Blue Colored Notebook). Vientiane: Seuksa Publishing House.

Bunthanong Somsaiphon [Burengnong]. 1974. *Khang Chaeng Nai Khwam Meut.* Vientiane: Pak Pasak Press.

———. 1983. *Peun Lae Dauk Mai.* Vientiane: Office of the Num Lao Newspaper.

———. 1989. *Long Su Thanon Lan Sang.* Vientiane: Samosaun Nakkhian Num.

———. 2002. *Khon Khai Khon.* Vientiane: International Labor Organization.

Bunyong Saipanya et al. 1985. *Hom Leuang San: Saw Num Kaung Lamlieng.* Vientiane: State Publishers and Distributors.

Dawviang Butnakho. 1992. *Khaung Fak.* Vientiane: State Publishers and Distributors.

———. 2000. *Pratsaya Hang Ing.* Vientiane: Education Department Printing House.

Duang Champa. 2002. *Kaun Cha Theung Vanni* (Before Having Reached This Day) in Fa Pin. Vientiane: Daukket (Dokked) Publishing Company.

———. "Ran Khai Lao Rim Placha." Manuscript.

Duangdeuane Bounyavong et al. 2001. *Kheut Haut Outhine Bounyavong*. Vientiane: Manthatulat Press.

Khana Kammakan Vitthayasat Sangkhom. 1990. *Maha Sila Viravong: Sivit Lae Phon Ngam*. Vientiane: State Printing House.

Ministry of Information and Culture. 1975–. *Vannasin* (Vientiane), various issues.

Outhine Bounyavong. 1995. *Meua Mae Jak Pai*. Translated by Jintray. Bangkok: Kham Phang Press.

Outhine Bounyavong et al. Nangseu Phim Siang Pasason (The Voice of the People Newspaper). 1982. *Siang Kaung Khaung Latthi Vilason Pativat*. Vientiane: State Printing House.

Phuangphet Buaphachan. 2003. *Buakhaem Beung* (Lotus at the Edge of a Swamp, 1997) in *Hom Reuang San Wannakam Ruam Samay* (A Collection of Modern Stories). Vannasin Magazine, ed. Vientiane: Vannasin.

S. Desa. 1993. *Pheuy San Leup Bau Sun*. Vientiane: State Publishers and Distributors.

Saisuvan Phaengphong. 1990. *Lao Thevada*. Vientiane: Young Writers' Association.

Viset Savaengseuksa. 1995. *Lam Se Saeun*. Vientiane: State Publishers and Distributors.

———. 2000. *Meua Haut Thi Chua* (When It Comes the Turn of the Buddhist Novice) in Nok Iang Khi Ta Khwai. Vientiane: Num Lao Publishing House.

———. 2000. *Nok Iang Khi Ta Khway*. Vientiane: Num Lao Publishing House.

———. 2001. *Chok Hua Chai Ma Haung Khian*. Vientiane: Num Lao Publishing House.

Thai Language Sources

Bunthanong Somsaiphon. 1991. *Kraduk Amerikan*. Bangkok: Ban Nangseu Publishing House.

Jarubut Reuangsuwan. 1977. *Khaung Di Isan*. Bangkok: Kan Sasana Publishing House.

Thanya Sangkhaphanthanon [Phaitoon Thanya]. 1995. "Chom Na Reuang San Ruam Samay Khaung Lao." In *Prakotkan Haeng Wannakam,* Bangkok: Nakhaun Publishing House.

Thawat Punnothok. 1979. *Wannakam Isan.* Bangkok: Odeon Store.

Wanalak Piyakamol, trans. 1991. *Pai Tam Jotmai.* Bangkok: Ya Daung Publishing House. A collection of short stories by Lao authors.

Wiraphong Misathan, ed.. 2005. *Phlik Phaendin Plin Phaen Fa Wannakam Lao Rangwak SEAWRITE.* Bangkok: Matichon Press.

"Kulap Pailin" (The Rose of Pailin, 1943) by Nhok Them is one one of Cambodia's most famous, early modern novellas (pralomlok).

4

Modern Short Fiction in Cambodia: A History of Persistence
Teri Shaffer Yamada

During the twentieth century, modern short fiction in Cambodia encountered significant political and cultural barriers that either prevented or restrained its popularity and development.[1] Consequently, the short story in Cambodia remains a minor literature compared to the narrative sophistication of contemporary short fiction published in other Southeast Asian nations such as Myanmar, Indonesia, Vietnam, and Thailand.[2]

A synergy of factors has contributed to this unique situation. To a significant degree, the comparative underdevelopment of all genres of modern Cambodian literature is due to a "conservative" cultural aesthetic whose formation can be traced to the early twentieth century (Edwards 2007).[3] This conservatism formed as a synthesis of the French colonial objective to preserve the "traditional" as a means of reifying an "authentic" Cambodian cultural/national identity *and* the reaction to French domination. Colored with an anti-intellectual overtone, this conservative aesthetic has become unconsciously and deeply interwoven into the fabric of public culture and discourse during the modern period.[4] It is currently being contested by popular youth culture in terms of nontraditional behaviors, musical tastes, and dress styles (Weinberger and Sam 2003; Ollier and Winter 2006).

There are still other contingent factors that have contributed to the short story's literary underdevelopment in Cambodia. One is the comparatively delayed transfer of print technology. Due to different political conditions, the training of Cambodians in publishing and journalism took place in the 1930s compared to the early 1800s in Thailand. The first Thai-language newspapers and journals, actually published by Thais, appeared in 1875 and 1876, compared to the mid-1930s in Cambodia when Cambodians controlled the publication process (Bee et al. 1989, 30). The popularity of the serialized modern novella and translations of Western and Chinese literature, which were published in Cambodian newspapers then, led to the novella (*pralomlok*) being the preferred form of modern entertainment literature in Cambodia, as it is today.[5]

Yet another factor in short fiction's literary underdevelopment is the state and self-censorship. Formal censorship in Cambodia includes state policies regarding the content of literary production during the post-independence period (1953–74), which is a continuation of French colonial policy;[6] the near extinction of modern writers and their literature during the Pol Pot era (1975–79); the enforcement of socialist realism and state control of literary production during the People's Republic of Kampuchea (1979–89); and, finally, the continuing shadow of potential state censorship and violence since the 1990s, which suppresses unfettered creative expression.

Another very important factor facilitating the underdevelopment of modern literature in Cambodia, following the period when the country was under the jurisdiction of the United Nations Transitional Authority in Cambodia (UNTAC, 1992–93) until today, is the rapid emergence of a consumer culture enamored with visual and aural entertainment devices (video and compact disc players, MP3 downloads, cell phones, the "ring tone" phenomenon etc.). This new consumer culture, with its desire for relatively expensive commodity goods, encounters an economy that requires the "typical" Cambodian to work several jobs in order to afford luxury goods on top of ordinary expenses. Middle-class professionals often work in various capacities at three or four different locations as part of their multiple-job employment strategy. This means there is less time and incentive to read for entertainment even if it were enjoyable.[7]

The wholesale pirating of writers' works, which occurs in Cambodia irrespective of the 2003 copyright law, also serves as a disincentive to writers, who already receive little monetary compensation for their creative work (Ryman 2006).[8] All of these factors, covering a span of more than one hundred years, form a silent conspiracy of literary underdevelopment, which will be further explored in this essay.

Traditional Influences

Cambodia's modern literature, like those of its neighbors, has been shaped partly by premodern literary traditions. The earliest written literature in Khmer dates from 611 CE in the form of inscriptions. Judith Jacob describes the early Sanskrit inscriptions (613 CE) found in Cambodia as "poetical," and certainly the many forms of Khmer verse that developed over subsequent centuries show the influence of Sanskrit metrics (1996, 2). Inscriptions and bas-reliefs from the pre-Angkor period of the two important Hindu epics, *Ramayana* and *Mahabharata*, reveal the importance of those texts in the future development of Cambodian literary and artistic traditions (Amratisha 1998, 32).[9]

After the Angkor period (800–1431 CE) Cambodia's cultural traditions fade into the "Middle Period" (1432–1887).[10] Its surviving literature, mostly in verse form, would later be regarded as the "Cambodian classics." This corpus of work appears to date from the sixteenth or seventeenth century. It includes manuscripts of the Cambodian versions of the *Ramayana* (*Ramakerti*); the early Royal Chronicles; Buddha birth stories in Pali (*jatakas*) and the apocryphal collection of fifty *jatakas*; various Codes of Conduct (*chbap*) whose dates are still disputed; and poetic texts such as "The Poem of Angkor Wat" (Jacob 1996, 2–4; Amratisha 1998, 35; Khing Hoc-Dy 1990). The very popular verse novel *Tum Teav*, a tragic romance, was composed in the waning days of the Middle Period (Chigas 2005). From the 1930s on, researchers at the Buddhist Institute collected oral folktales of unknown antiquity, and published them in the institute's literary and cultural journal *Kambuja Suriya* (Edwards 2005).[11] In 1982, Judith Jacob opined that the folktale remained Cambodia's "short story." One certainly can see its influence in the current popularity of the modern fable among some short fiction writers.[12]

Transitioning to the "Modern"

The date 1863 signifies the symbolic transition from the Middle Period to the modern. In this year, King Norodom signed a treaty with France, making Cambodia a French Protectorate to preserve its borders from encroaching neighbors Thailand and Vietnam (Dommen 2001, 7). In 1884 a new treaty provided France full and complete control over Cambodia.

While experiencing unanticipated challenges with their policies in Vietnam, the French colonial administrators were also perplexed by the "underdevelopment" they encountered in Cambodia, particularly regarding the temple school system (Amratisha 1998, 50–63). These schools essentially taught young boys how to read—or rather chant—Buddhist scriptures, inadequate training for employment in a French colonial bureaucracy. In response to its own needs, the French Protectorate (1863–1953) utilized Vietnamese civil servants in Cambodia. While slowly establishing several "modern" schools (with instruction only in French) for the education of future Cambodian civil servants, the colonial bureaucrats attempted to reform the temple school system (Dy and Ninomiya 2003; Amratisha 1998, 54-57). They also failed to train Cambodians (and Laotians) in print technology and journalism. These are crucial skills underlying the emergence of modern literature in other Southeast Asian nations.[13]

Although French officials found the Cambodian peasants "childlike or naive," they fostered a type of cultural conservatism that reinforced resistance to the very changes they wished to produce. The past was glorified—specifically in the symbolic form of the archaeological remains of Angkor Wat and classical texts—cultural relics that could be ideologically exploited for colonial ends (Edwards 2004, 2007; Nepote and Khing 1981, 57).[14] The French fixation on Cambodia's *past* brilliance, combined with their mission to save the remnants of it's culture and identity, seemed to overshadow any encouragement to develop a modern literature.[15]

After Khmer-owned presses were finally established later in the 1930s, the French enforced strict censorship on newspaper content.[16] Perhaps they feared anticolonial repercussions fostered by an independent media similar to those they were experiencing in Vietnam.[17] By the end of 1941, anti-French sentiment had increased in Cambodia. The advocacy of French language in the schools and newspapers had exacerbated public resistance to modernization.

This reaction intensified between 1943 and 1945 when French officials attempted to impose a romanized script for the Khmer language, as they had done in Vietnam with *quoc ngu* after overcoming much resistance there (Chandler 1991, 15; Amratisha 1998, 89).[18] The Buddhist clergy in Cambodia was especially incensed with the French ordinance proscribing the use of traditional Khmer script, a regulation that profoundly affected education at the temple schools. For many centuries the clergy and the public had considered both monks and Khmer script as sacred[19] (Nepote and Khing 1981, 62). The imposition of a roman orthography to replace this sacred script—symbolic of colonial hubris—was finally abandoned by the French, but this failed experiment further impeded the progress of literacy in a country already trailing most other Southeast Asian nations (Sharma 1994, 147; Nepote and Khing 1981; Paterson 1996, 46).

One other point regarding the politics of romanized Khmer script is how the resistance to its implementation also reflected a conservative cultural response to a secular written literature. Reading for pleasure was not a common practice in Cambodia with the exception of a very small middle class. Ironically, the reverence for Khmer script as sacred impeded its use for the production of modern, secular literature while simultaneously serving as a form of resistance to colonial authority and hubris. The French, having abandoned their policy to preserve the traditional by forcing a Westernized script, found their previous position used against them. This kind of antimodern, anticolonial nationalism would inform Pol Pot's ideology during the 1970s. The conflation of colonial authority with forced modernization contributed to the difficulty of developing a respected modern literature in Cambodia.

Early modern writers in Cambodia in the 1930s were able to overcome these cultural and colonial obstacles. They emerged from three groups: (1) princes, who did not become authors but were the first to be fascinated by the "Sino-Vietnamese world" and later by Western ideas (they would popularize the notion of modernization); (2) non-Buddhist Cambodians, either Catholic descendants of the Portuguese or Malaysian Muslims; and (3) "other marginal Cambodians who were Buddhists" such as French-influenced Cambodians from Cochin China (Nepote and Khing 1981, 60). Many who belonged to this small cohort of young male writers were graduates of the kingdom's first high school, the Lycée Sisowath, with its instruction in French.[20] They probably read the pro-Cambodian newspaper *Nagara Vatta*, the first Khmer language newspaper to cover international events, and worked in the lower ranks of the civil service (Chandler 2000, 163–4).[21] Among them, Rin Kin experimented with the short-story by revising several folktales (Nepote and Khing 2001, 1–2).[22] The creative effort of these new writers was a nationalist reaction to their French education with its dismissive attitude towards Khmer literature and an urban marketplace saturated with modern Vietnamese and Chinese novels (Amratisha 1998, 57, 67–8; Nepote and Khing 1987).[23]

The Buddhist Institute's journal, *Kambuja Suriya,* served as a forum during the 1930s for a discussion between French and Cambodian intellectuals about Khmer literature.[24] Several of the young writers worked at the Buddhist Institute. In 1939 it assisted their efforts with the serialization of Kim Hak's *Tik Tonlesap* (Waters of the Tonlesap). French disdain for Khmer literature had encouraged Kim Hak to write the novella. He explains his intent in its preface, indicating that his reason for writing it was "to end the talk of those who represent the country, who only know our Khmer language slightly and say the Khmer don't have any books or stories that are easy to read." (Chigas 2005, 153; Paterson 1996, 27–28). He also uses two important new terms in the preface: *pralomlok*—a story that is written to seduce the hearts of human beings—for "novel/novella," and *aksar sastr* for "literature."

Although *Kambuja Suriya* was instrumental in legitimizing this new innovative literature through its publication of Kim Hak's novella, its conservatism favored traditional literature. The new literary and cultural weekly newspapers that became popular from the mid-1930s on were the ones that published "modern" stories. The novelist Rim Kin had some "short stories" published in the weekly literary supplement *Reatrei Thngai Sau* (Saturday Night*)*, which was founded in 1935 (Amratisha 1998, 75; Tauch 1998, 43). This Khmer-language literary supplement of the newspaper *L'Echo du Cambodge* became the most important venue for the publication of short fiction over the next several decades (Nepote and Khing 1987, 365; Amratisha 1998, 75). Unfortunately, nearly all copies of *Saturday Night, Neary* (Woman*),* *Roummitt* (Friends), and other early literary magazines have vanished, thus diminishing our ability to know how the short story developed over those years.[25] The 1940s and 1950s remain a mystery for the short story.

The research of Kho Tararith on the contents of the remaining copies of disintegrating and disappearing literary magazines from the 1950s found in the special collections section of the National Library in Phnom Penh has revealed several short stories by Nou Hach (1917–75).[26] His short fiction, typically one to five pages in length, was published in *Saturday Night, Neary,* and *Roummitt*.[27] Reflecting the socially critical sentiment of other new writers who criticized cultural belief in superstition and magic, his "Koun Krak" (Dried Embryos), published in *Roummitt* (1953), is a didactic reflection on the cultural practice of using

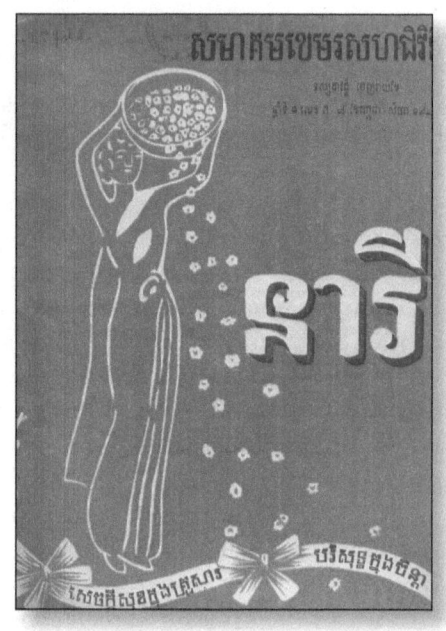

Neary (Woman), literary magazine

embryos for medicinal purposes. In contrast, his short story "Meathurueh Citt" (Sweet Thoughts) is more romantically sentimental, another popular theme of the new writers.[28] Since Nou Hach was just one of many talented writers during this period (late 1940s to 1950s), it is logical to assume that other authors were also publishing short fiction and expository essays in the literary newspapers and magazines of the time.[29] Tauch Chhuong describes scores of writers during this period as "famous and popular" authors and journalists who elevated the quality of the magazines and newspapers that published their work in an age of intellectual curiosity (1998, 44).

These innovative writers were concerned with both content and form. Their first attempts were largely socially critical, romantic novellas, which explored a modern Cambodian identity in terms of realistic human experience, partly in response to a "national identity crisis" caused by "a diminishing French influence" (Nepote and Khing 1981, 64). Their writing represents a "total break from traditional literature," not just in content but also in form, as they abandoned the verse novel to write in prose and colloquial dialogue (Jacob 1995, 160). This early period of the novel, from the late 1930s through Cambodian's independence in 1953, is perhaps the most freely creative and experimental era in the history of modern Cambodian literature (Vickery 1990; Bitard 1955).

After the French returned at the end of World War II, they allowed the formation of political parties, elections, and the development of a constitution. The 1947 Constitution guaranteed freedom of expression, which appears to have encouraged Khmer writers (Amratisha 1998, 91). Novels were now being serialized in the Khmer-language newspapers that flourished during this period, especially after 1949 when all educational institutions were transferred from French to Cambodian control and the Khmer language became more important. Journalism and publishing flourished, a literate readership grew as public education was strengthened, literary genres increased beyond young romance, and bookstores and bookstalls appeared on the city streets (Ueda and Okada 2006, 69).

Complete creative autonomy was short-lived, however. Most of the early experimental novelists stopped writing after independence from France in 1953 largely for political reasons (Amratisha 1998, 161–62). Total literary autonomy appears to have ended in 1955 with Prince Sihanouk's successful subversion of Cambodia's first prodemocracy movement, led by the Khmer Independence Party under the direction of newspaper publisher, journalist and creative writer Son Ngoc Thanh (Sharma 1994, 71).

In this age of nationalism, Cambodian intellectuals were still reacting strongly to the low opinion the French had expressed about Cambodian literature (Chigas 2005, 148). Khim Sam Or illustrates this sentiment in *The History of Cambodian Literature* (1961).

> Under the iron yoke of imperial colonialism of the last 100 years, our people have been far removed from our culture. The French colonialists made us study and use their language and swallow the culture of their corrupt imperialism. Thus, many of us became stricken by their contempt and forgot the legacy of work of the Khmer people who have always had their own literature. (148)

In fact, literary criticism began to develop more seriously in the mid-1950s. Discussions about the role of the writer in society became topical as more writers had their biographies produced along with their work, echoing an emerging nationalist pride in being Cambodian.

The Sihanouk era, which encouraged this nationalist sentiment, was symbolized by a new organization, the Sangkum Reastr Niyam (Popular Socialist Community, 1955–70). It advocated nationalism, loyalty to the monarch, and the struggle against injustice and corruption, while it also deflected criticism of a Cambodian Buddhist religion that accepted social inequalities as legitimate because of individual karma (Sharma 1994, 71).

Although Sangkum ideology advocated the struggle against injustice and corruption, Sihanouk's regime was noted for its "vanity, eccentricity, and intolerance to dissent;" it was riddled with "unbridled greed and corruption inspired by a foreign policy motivated by opportunism rather than a desire to preserve national independence" (1994, 70; see also Osborne 1994). Partly to control the output of writers, the government sponsored the establishment of the Khmer Writers' Association (KWA) in 1956. The Sangkum era was a time of serious restrictions on freedom of speech, as Sihanouk brooked no opposition even when his critics posed little political threat (Martin 1994; Mehta 1997; Chandler 2000; Amratisha 1998, 172).

Nevertheless, writers during this period were often actively associated with political parties. Their fiction was published in party newspapers, the major venue for short fiction and serialized novels. Mehta relates a 1960 incident involving Khieu Samphan, the founder of the newspaper *L'Observateur*: "Sihanouk could not tolerate gratuitous criticism from young French-educated political activists in their columns. As a result Samphan's humiliation began on April 13, 1960, when he was riding his motorcycle near the police headquarters in Phnom Penh. He was stopped and taunted by the police agents, stripped and photographed in the nude" (1997, 1).

Sihanouk was especially antagonistic to the Pracheachon Party since some members of the communist Khmer Peoples Revolutionary Party (KPRP) had become affiliated with it[30] (Sharma 1994, 89). At the same time he promoted literature that supported his agenda as a symbol of a modernizing nation and Cambodian cultural identity. He advanced literacy in the countryside and expanded educational opportunities for women (Amratisha 1998, 189). In order to maintain ideological control over writers, he became the patron of literature. Prince Sihanouk provided political, social, and financial support to members of the KWA and became the organization's honorary president (179). He presented some politicians who were KWA members with political positions in his government. He financed KWA's first literary contest, the Indradevi Literary Competition, which was held in the Royal Palace in 1961 (173). During his speech at this event, Sihanouk informed the writers that they must support government policy at every opportunity; if they described other political ideologies in their writings, their works would not be considered literature (174). Decoded this means "banned from publication." Irrespective of Sihanouk's political influence, the activities of the KWA were instrumental in promoting and popularizing literature during the 1960s, especially the apolitical social novel and the ideological or nationalistic historical novel.

According to Khing Hoc Dy, the Sangkum era was a period of full cultural development for the Khmer novel (1993, 27–30). Over a thousand novels were published. Authors were also influenced by a variety of literatures from Europe, America, Vietnam, Thailand, and China in the original or translation.[31]

Government policy during the Sangkum era fostered politically correct fiction in the form of the romantic historical novel. These historical novels, often set in the Angkor period, were frequently dedicated to Prince Sihanouk and often extolled the current monarchy's commitment to the betterment of Cambodia (Ueda and Okada 2006, 70). The reading public became accustomed to this type of nation-building literature, which reflected the glories of the Angkorean past (Amratisha 1998, 176). Essentially Sangkum policy indirectly reinforced an ideology of nationhood first established by the French. And writers were to support it.

After a new press law was passed in 1957, there were few political or socially critical novels and little creative experimentation in the areas of character development or narrative form.[32] The 1960s became the age of the detective and adventure novel (Nepote and Khing 1981, 65). Permission to publish any book had to be obtained from the Ministry of Information, which clearly approved only pro-Sihanouk literature. The few clandestinely published novels that were critical of the monarchy were banned and the writers arrested (Amratisha 1998, 180).

Soth Polin, who grew up during this era and became enamored with the new fiction he read in *Saturday Night*, was also influenced by the discourse on Buddhist philosophy and existentialism he found at the university (Stewart and May 2004, 11). He self-published his first socially critical novel, *Jivit It Nay* (*Jivit Ot Ney*, Life without Meaning, 1964), at the age of twenty-two. Including both sex and nihilism, it became one of the most severely criticized and popular novels of the late sixties. His next regnant novel, *Chamtet et Asor* (Love without Pity, 1967) was banned. After a year in France, Soth Polin returned in 1969 and self-published a collection of short stories, *Whatever You Order Me . . . I will Do It,* which he states didn't sell and was "completely, totally unsuccessful" (Stewart and May, 15). He does remark that a number of writers were publishing short fiction in *Saturday Night* at that time; perhaps *Whatever You Order Me...I will Do It* was one of the first collections of short fiction in Cambodia (11).[33] You Bo, a longtime associate of the KWA, mentions two of his short stories being serialized in three different newspapers in the mid-1960s (Sen Nith 2007).

Tomoko Okada has translated a number of stories from Soth Polin's collection into Japanese (2001a).[34] She describes them as typically about a young male protagonist, the narrator of the story, who is unable to express his feelings directly to the young woman he loves (237). Soth Polin's stories foreground an emotionally immature but philosophically complex, alienated protagonist unable to be honest with himself and others, as illustrated in "Communicate, They Say."

> It was unbearable. So unbearable that one day, to console myself, I bared my soul to Sary, a colleague in my office, a pretty girl, approachable and smiling. I had always been a little in love with her. Of course, I didn't dare tell her about the images swirling in my head. I made her pity my fate, telling her of my anxiety, my sadness, my apathy, my sickening lack of decisiveness. I told her I was unhappy, rudderless, alone, much too alone and alienated from others.
>
> She stared at me for a while. Intensely. Adorably. Then she said in a decisive tone, hammering every word, "You're suffering, sweet Vanna; but do you know why? I'll tell you why. You're suffering because you do not communicate!" . . . "We've been working together for two years and I've had time to observe you: you never talk; you never mix in with the others; you never make the least bit of effort; you're always in your corner, glum, invisible, indifferent to everything." (Stewart and May 2004, 2)

Finally, after an excursion with some office mates, the protagonist concludes, "I was in despair. So *this is communicating?* I asked myself. *It's nothing! It's empty? You communicate to avoid communication?*" (6).

Piat describes the popular literature of this period as an escapist, melodramatic literature, rarely portraying contemporary society and, if it is portrayed, done so only through stereotypical characters devoid of self-reflection or psychological depth (1975, 257, 259). Soth Polin's popularity among intellectuals may be due to his tendency to go against this trend. He writes of complex social subjects; his discourse is more philosophical and socially critical. He did, however, pay a price for this audacity. He was forced to flee the country in 1974, and his newspaper, *Nokor Thom* (Great Nation), was shut down by the government.

Irrespective of the state's concern with controlling the free speech of its creative writers and journalists, the early 1960s was a time of advancement in terms of literary criticism and the recognition of literature as part of the university curriculum.

> During the 1960s some literary history and criticism by Khmers began to appear. Dik-Keam, Leang-Hap An, and Ly-Theam Teng wrote lives of the poets (Sri Dhammaraja, Nong, Ang Duong, Mok, and Seth) and studies of texts (Reamker, *Hans Yant*). An anthology of parts of the Chronicles was published by Eng Soth. Saram Phan and others wrote in French (and even

English) in an effort to make their songs and stories more widely known. And as Khmer literature was now taught at the Université Royale des Beaux Arts of Phnom Penh, there appeared a course of Khmer literature on the radio, two or three books on literature in Khmer, and many editions of works for teaching. (Jacob 1996, 10)

Interest and respect for literature had advanced dramatically since the 1930s; four new novellas had been included in the high-school curriculum in 1958.[35] However, we see little discussion of the modern short story, which was so overshadowed by the new novella. The minor status of short fiction during the 1960s is reflected in the Khmer Writers' Association's Indradevi Literary Award for the genres of novel, poetry, and play but not for short story (Amratisha 1998, 209).[36]

The new generation of young writers from the late 1960s was more market oriented. Some produced sensationalist and sometimes sexually obscene fiction; others plagiarized Western or Chinese literature, thus lowering the public's respect for modern fiction (Amratisha 1998, 269). The older generation of writers was very critical of the quality of such work, considering modern Khmer literature to be superficial and underdeveloped (271). Educated Cambodians and other members of the upper classes disdained the new novel, directed to adolescents and women, as childish, vulgar, and unsophisticated. They preferred Western fiction (Nepote and Khing 1981, 69–70). Ultimately the public school system had failed to develop a discerning audience for serious fiction, thus hindering writers who were seduced by market forces to produce more sensational fiction. Political censorship and the book publishers, who selected less serious fiction to publish, also played a role in shaping the novel as sheer entertainment (Amratisha 1998, 277–81).

As the country descended into civil war in 1967 and 1968, the government implemented strict censorship measures against both communist and progressive thinkers. As all private newspapers were shut down, a number of writers stopped producing fiction in protest against such strictures (181).

The Suppression of Fiction in the 1970s

In 1970, while on a trip abroad, Sihanouk was deposed by a "quiet coup" under the direction of a U.S.-backed general, Lon Nol. State ideology was reshaped to support Lon Nol's new agenda. He worked to undo the socialist economic policies of Sihanouk, which he believed had impeded economic development (Sharma 1994, 76, 89). Yet Lon Nol's Republic had the reputation of being equally corrupt as it engaged in a disastrous full-blown civil war with the encroaching Khmer Rouge.

In a familiar pattern, writers under Lon Nol were encouraged to criticize the previous regime as corrupt and decadent. Tomoko Okada reports that during this period the writer Khun Srun "was imprisoned for half a year in 1971, because his integrity and honesty kept him from accepting a conciliatory gesture of the new government that needed him" (2001b). The state wanted the literary allegiance of a small number of popular writers and exerted pressure to assure it. Although publishing initially increased under Lon Nol, after a year in power his policy toward literature mimicked Sihanouk's repression of politically critical fiction (Amratisha 1998, 182). As his control over the Khmer Republic disintegrated, even paper had to be imported since the only paper factory in the country was now in an enemy zone. Martial law was declared in 1973, and all private newspapers were forced to suspend publication (184). Adventure, mystery and sentimental novels were popular with readers living in the midst of this emerging dystopia.

The appearance of largely adolescent, black-clad Khmer Rouge cadres in Phnom Penh on 17 April 1975 and the subsequent "liberation" and chaotic evacuation of the capital city signified the demise of the Khmer Republic (Kiernan 1996, 31–47; Short 2005, 266–85). The destruction wrought by this "new beginning" over the next several years defies description (Power 2002). Although the ideology of the Khmer Rouge under Pol Pot was to build socialism in Democratic Kampuchea, they produced new class distinctions as they purged the country of anyone who might be considered an enemy in terms of their inconsistently defined and capriciously implemented ideology (Kiernan 1996, 55–62; Sharma 1994, 91). Many Cambodians died, unable to endure the multiple relocations from cities and villages to work cooperatives, disease, and starvation, until 7 January 1979 when the Vietnamese drove the Khmer Rouge from Phnom Penh (Ponchaud 1989).

Democratic Kampuchea illustrates the success of State power in eliminating the right to be creative to the extent that nearly all literary activity was suppressed (Thion and Jarvis 1993). The Khmer Rouge's proposed policy for the future (1977–80) states that culture, literature and the arts "should be rid of all vestiges of imperialism, colonialism, feudalism and other former ruling classes" (Keyes 1994, 56). They valorized oral traditions and locution for the masses (Ponchaud 1989, 158). The range of literature under the Khmer Rouge was largely limited to the Organization's (Angkar's) approved revolutionary songs, poems, slogans and proverbs, forced confessions, and a few publications, such as *Revolutionary Flag*, intended only for the party elite, and *Revolutionary Youth* (Locard 2004; Chandler 1999; Khing 1994, 27–29). To establish their new Cambodia, Angkar executed thousands of teachers and set up new "schools" for children, where they were taught only the rudiments of reading, writing, and arithmetic. Essentially an entire generation of Khmer children remained illiterate (Sharma 1994, 93, 151; Vickery 1990, 49–52; Jarvis and Arfanis 2002, 1.2).

Although Khmer Rouge cadres would conspicuously display confiscated ballpoint pens in their shirt pockets as a symbol of power, they did not like creative writers, who were found mostly among the bourgeois "new people." Only a score of writers and intellectuals survived the experience of starvation, disease, torture, and execution.[37] When the Vietnamese finally overthrew the Pol Pot regime on 7 January 1979, many of the surviving writers, such as Pin Yathay, fled to France. Over the next several decades, they would develop a distinct Cambodian literary tradition in exile supported by the energies of the journalist Pech Sangwawann, who had left Cambodia prior to 1975. She was instrumental in organizing the Association des Écrivains Khmèrs à l'Étranger (AEKE) in 1989 and establishing the Literature of Peace Award for the genre of the novel.[38]

Cambodian refugees in Thai border camps also wrote short stories and poems and were able to have some textbooks published (Amratisha 1998, 313; Thompson 1993; Khing 1994, 30). A few writers eventually relocated to the United States from France or the border camps, such as Soth Polin and U Sam Oeur, but they would have difficulty publishing their works due to the limited number of literate Cambodians who had relocated there.[39] Women novelists such as Darina Siv would begin writing in the United States in the early 1980s; the novelist Duong Ratha emerged in the 1990s. Later in that decade, the exiled writer Keo Chambo would self-publish her novels and collections of short fiction and poetry and have them distributed in Cambodia due to its wider reading audience.[40]

Among writers of the Cambodian diaspora, literary development from 1980 until today is overshadowed by the testimonial memoir, especially among Cambodian Americans. Survivors of the Pol Pot era have written over twenty of these memoirs, mostly in English or French (Yamada 2005).[41] This type of testimony would mirror the anti Khmer-Rouge novels encouraged by the next government in Cambodia, the People's Republic of Kampuchea (PRK) during the 1980s (Khing 1994, 32). Khmer writers in France have also written novels and short stories about their exile experience, while those in America have focused on exploring exile through the memoir. Khing Hoc Dy notes in 1994 that writers outside of Cambodia are strongly influenced by Western literature and culture while literature within Cambodia "remains managed by the machinery of the Communist party and increasingly diverges from that of the diaspora" (34). That trend may be changing because Cambodian writers from France and the United States are now returning to Cambodia and conducting writers' workshops.

The remaining handful of well-known literary survivors within Cambodia during the 1980s, including Vandy Kaon and Kong Bunchoeun, became part of the new PRK government established by the Vietnamese (Khing 1994, 30–31).[42] One of the first actions of this government, under President Heng Samrin, was to sign a twenty-five-year Treaty of Peace, Friendship and Cooperation with Vietnam followed by agreements of cooperation in economic, cultural, educational, and other sectors. This ensured a different type of control over literary production.

The Struggle to Rebuild Modern Literature

Although Heng Samrin set out to restore social and economic stability, the intellectual capital of Cambodia had been nearly destroyed and the material infrastructure dismantled.[43] Most members of the surviving educated elite had fled the country, and the government had to expend energy combating oppositional factions, including Pol Pot's lingering influence along the Thai border.[44]

Although a number of surviving writers were enlisted as officials in the government and valiantly attempted to reestablish literature in the country, the new government's socialist agenda once again constrained the subject matter of literature in a politically correct mode through the ideology of socialist realism. Independent publishers had vanished. Now all published novels had to be approved by a state agency and produced through state publishing houses. Politically correct novels occupied the entire field of Cambodia's "official" literary production during the 1980s (Khing 1994, 32; Amratisha 2006, 151). One of the state's four official newspapers, the national weekly *Kambuchea,* regularly published morally appropriate short stories and serialized novels (Khing 1994, 30). The State Publishing House of the Ministry of Information and Culture was set up in 1985 and enjoined to publish short stories along with other literature (Amratisha 1998, 300). Literary awards for the novel were reestablished in the late 1980s. Most authors of socialist novellas were young members of the Communist Party. Among them were two women officials, Pal Vannarirak and Oum Suphany (Amratisha 2006).

Okada describes these socialist writers as technicians who wrote a formulaic literature extolling the behaviors of faultless protagonists whose heroic actions included self-sacrifice for the nation. Such protagonists were typically soldiers of the people's revolution, and women in stereotypical roles of self-sacrificing nurses and teachers. The content of these state-sponsored novellas contained laudatory comments praising the socialist revolution while condemning American and Thai imperialism (Ueda and Okada 2006, 71). It is questionable how popular they were; however, the new detective and sentimental novels surreptitiously produced and distributed appear to have been in high demand (UNICEF 1990, 149).

One exception to this socialist literary production was Vandy Kaon's *Kaoh Beysach* (Island of Evil Spirits). It is a cleverly disguised allegory of state corruption that managed to slip under the censor's gaze (Okada 1998). Although many state-sponsored novels were published during the 1980s, their formulaic content did not appeal to many readers eager for entertainment. To meet this demand, authors using pen names for political protection wrote romance and adventure novellas. These handwritten manuscripts were sold to underground rental book shops, sometimes located in private homes, part of a black market, book distribution system (Okada 2003). The shop owners hand copied these manuscripts for surreptitious distribution, unable to advertise the rental of this unofficial literature for fear of the authorities closing down their shops; yet readers knew of them through word-of-mouth. Underground novellas were circulated to the most remote provinces and as far as the Thai border camps (Ueda and Okada 2006, 71). The women officials Oum Suphany and Pal Vannarirak—the latter a young socialist writer who would later become one of the most celebrated authors in Cambodia—were among these underground novelists (Lon Nara 2002; Amratisha 2006, 151).

Toward the end of the 1980s, writers were less constrained by socialist ideology as the public demand for escapist literature increased. One of the most popular authors, the woman writer Mao Samnang, wrote sentimental romances on school notebooks of low-quality paper for underground distribution in the literary market, a common practice at the time (Amratisha 2006, 151). By 1989, with the formation of the State of Cambodia (SOC), censorship restrictions were somewhat mediated and new laws were promulgated to promote a more vibrant market economy. These changes brought back commercial bookshops and publishing (151). However, only a few novels were produced due to the high price of paper, the diminished purchasing power of the public, and the low rate of literacy. At the same time, television sets and videos were introduced to the public, and writers turned to the more lucrative production of "film and soap opera scripts for television and video companies," allowing a few of them to make a living through creative writing (151). Amratisha states that the introduction of new entertainment technology had a great impact on the decreasing relevance of modern literature in the 1990s as the social realist fiction of the 1980s was replaced with mysteries and sentimental novels (311).

An independent print media, which was encouraged after the arrival of UNTAC in November 1991, published ghost stories and serialized pornographic novels written by men.[45] This opening of cultural space for the publication of literature encouraged women writers as the short story became more popular in newspapers and women's magazines (Amratisha 2006, 251). In 1993, UNTAC held democratic elections, which facilitated the establishment of a new government, the People's Republic of Cambodia (Heder and Ledgerwood 1996). A new 1995 Press Law assured freedom of the press and granted the right to publish (Jarvis and Arfanis 2002, 2.7). The actual implementation of this law remains contingent on the politics of power.

A new generation of writers born after 1975, with little memory of the Khmer Rouge era, was successful in having their short fiction published in the scores of newspapers that began to flourish after 1995. This expanding opportunity to publish did more to promote the development of short fiction that any other factor. Tomoko Okada describes newspaper short fiction as often overlooked or ignored because such stories are not considered "significant for the canon," yet they are ethnographically and socially relevant. During the mid-1990s, the short story was popularized in newspapers and magazines, somewhat reminiscent of popular short fiction in the literary magazines of the 1950s and 1960s.

One unique example of this type of newspaper fiction is "Just a Human Being" (1993) by an anonymous writer (Marston 2002, 39–41). In the form of a short play, the dialogue takes place between two faceless bureaucrats, a chief and his assistant, and a voiceless "human being." It is a socially critical commentary on the lack of humanism found among officials in contemporary government bureaucracies. The Chief is interested in meeting this nameless human being only if he appears to have some social status or influence. Once the Chief finds out that the man is weeping out in the waiting room, he is summarily dismissed.

> Assistant: He's there, sir. But there's one matter which I thought I should come back and ask you about. He's weeping. . . .
> Chief: What? How do you mean, "He's weeping"?
> Assistant: In the usual miserable way, with tears pouring from his eyes like drops of rain.
> Chief: Is that so? Weeping. Then he must be just a human being after all. So then we try to. . . Ho, ho. Then everything is already quite in order. You can go kick his ass out of here, and you don't need to say anything to anybody. Tell the secretary

> that it's not necessary to make the coffee. As for the cognac, though . . . a stressful situation does strap one's energies. A human being, then . . . It's a problem we can handle by ourselves. (Marston 2002, 41)

By the late 1990s, the situation had changed for the publication of such serious, experimental fiction. There were fewer newspapers and magazines. Now, in the 2000s, authors often have to pay a fee to have their short fiction published.[46] The era of the newspaper short story of imagination and depth may have already faded, although women's magazines still publish sentimental short fiction, often by women writers.

Currently television, digital video discs (DVDs), and karaoke have superseded literature as popular entertainment in Cambodia. And writers are eager to produce screenplays for television production since these are much more lucrative than novellas, still the most popular form of fiction. Newspapers tend to publish more sensational short fiction with a penchant towards the pornographic (Lon Nara 2002). Although literacy rates have improved, most rapidly during the 1990s, they still significantly lag behind literacy rates in the rest of Southeast Asia with the exception of Laos.[47]

Contemporary Themes

One of the most popular writers in Cambodia today is Kong Bunchoeun (Kong Bun Chhoeun).[48] A prolific novelist, many of the over 130 "sentimental" novels he has written since the 1960s have socially critical themes (Bou and Kyne 2000). His 1999 *The Destiny of Tat Marina*, a fictionalized version of an actual acid-attack on his sixteen-year-old niece, Svay Sitha, the former mistress of the Council of Ministers' undersecretary of state, reflects a socially critical literary tradition with roots in Cambodia's traditional tales, which are known for their satire (Bitard 1951, 214). The *Phnom Penh Post* reported Kong Bunchoeun as saying:

> Cambodia is a society that has lost any sense of morality, riven by violence and injustice. . . . By highlighting the case of Tat Marina, we can hold up a mirror to the ills affecting Cambodian society. . . . The book is not a product of anger, but for the purpose of educating girls not to become involved with married men and to teach "first wives" not to use violence against "second wives." (Bou and Kyne 2000).

His comment harkens back to the socially critical novels of the 1940s and 1950s. It also reflects a common concern of many young women authors during the 1990s, who wrote about the status of women in a society undergoing tremendous economic change (Amratisha 2006; Okada 2001a).

One of them is Mey Son Sotheary, whose short story "My Sister" was published in the newspaper *Reasmey Kampuchea* in 1995 (Yamada 2002, 45). In it the protagonist, San, a young man with two sisters and no surviving parents, has moved from a rural area to Phnom Penh in order to attend the university. His older sister, Keo, unbeknownst to them, is working as a bar girl in order to support their college educations and future aspirations. When one night San surreptitiously spies Keo working as a prostitute on the street, he is deeply shamed. The next day he angrily banishes her from the family. After brutally sending Keo away, San realizes her self-sacrifice and berates himself: "I know self-forgiveness will be difficult. I just feel compelled to find her, to let her know she's a great person regardless of that profession. She is still noble, I still respect her. One day I hope to find Keo, to beg forgiveness for my cruelty" (Yamada 2002, 52). Changing gender roles, the economic struggle of women, and the stress of a rural to urban shift with its new complexities of life and seductions in the big city have become important themes in the new socially critical short stories of the 1990s and 2000s.[49]

In the early 2000s a number of authors were writing serious short fiction— urban or modern tales—possibly reflecting the deeply entrenched appreciation of the folktale genre in Cambodian culture. An example is Darina Siv's "Sokha and Apopeal," written in 1981, somewhat earlier than its publication in 2004 (Stewart and May 2004, 41–47, 215). Reflecting some of the sentiment of the testimonial memoir, it provides an alternative ending to the Khmer Rouge tragedy. The tale begins with the happy childhood of the six-year-old protagonist Sokha. He has a favorite cow that gives birth to a male calf called Apopeal. The mother cow unexpectedly dies, and Sokha has to feed and care for the calf. When the Khmer Rouge arrive in 1975 they take Apopeal, using him to pull a cart, much to the sorrow of Sokha. Though separated by the Khmer Rouge, Sokha and Apopeal continue to unexpectedly cross paths as they confront the struggles of existence under the Khmer Rouge. Ultimately they escape together into a deep forest, where they find a lake filled with lotus flowers, surrounded by a green pasture of lush grass. They befriend a rabbit and a family of otters in this natural paradise. After several years of refuge in the forest, Sokha and Apopeal miraculously encounter his brother and father walking in the forest. They joyfully proclaim, "Now, everything is fine again in our country. You can come back home without any danger" (47). The tale has a happy ending.

Sokha, Apopeal, the rabbit, and Sokha's father and brother all went back to his village. He returned to school, joining the other children. Every day, he rode Apopeal to school, the rabbit sitting on Apopeal's head.

From then on, Sokha and his family lived peacefully in their village. (47)

Like some traditional Cambodian folktales, harmony or social order may prevail in the end (Chandler 1996).

Another allegorical modern tale, a descent into dystopia with a "survivor" ending, is Nhem Sophath's "Lord of the Land" (2006). This story begins with a herd of wild oxen—divided by color into a black and a white group—peacefully sharing the same bountiful land. There is a pack of wolves in the northern part of their territory so they need to stay together for protection; to the south is a river full of hungry crocodiles, an area they also need to avoid. As the plot develops, the climate has changed and there is no rain; consequently, the oxens' supply of grass has dwindled. As the entire herd faces starvation, fighting breaks out among them over the scarce supply of food and safe water. It becomes easy for the wolves to prey on the oxen since they refuse to cooperate by protecting each other. Individualism has taken over. Then conflict breaks out between the two groups until all of the black oxen are dead. The remaining herd of white oxen, led by Laan, its leader, decides to cross the river despite the dangerous crocodiles. In the end only a few of them survive.

Laan is searching for his wife but he cannot find her. He knows clearly in his heart that she has not been able to cross the river. Tears stream down his face and he feels deep regret. He is very sad about everyone's loss of family. He is suffering about the loss of their land that has been taken over by wild dogs.

The twilight has a melancholic feel. There is the sound of wild dogs' happily howling and many corpses of the wild oxen can be seen floating on the river. Laan, the Lord of the white oxen, sadly gazes at his lost land and leads some of the surviving oxen in the twilight, leaving this land with deep regret . . . (Nou Hach translation group, unpublished translation)

Since 2002 the "Nou Hach Literary Journal" has published award-winning short fiction and some English translations.

This dystopic tale—a fall from grace with a limited restoration of "harmony"—shares a melancholy sadness seen in other contemporary tales. One is Pen Chhornn's "Destitute Pelican" (2005), which takes place in the "land of animals."[50] Its protagonist is an impoverished father pelican who desperately struggles and fails to obtain enough food to feed his sole surviving child. It allegorizes the struggle of many rural parents in contemporary Cambodia.

Another cautionary allegory, with people instead of animals as characters, is Kao Seiha's "A Boat" (2006). This story involves a fisherman's family adrift at sea in their boat due to a broken motor. At last they are discovered by a "foreign" boat, which refuses to help; it waits for them to sell their boat out of desperation. Instead of working together, the brothers fight over control of the boat as their father succumbs to illness. Without consulting anyone, the eldest son makes a deal with the foreign boat owner: he will sell his family's boat in exchange for a job as soon as their father dies. The family is then directed to a deserted island. The father dies, and the foreign owner quickly establishes his control with force. He makes the oldest son the overseer of his family's former boat on which the mother, daughter, and younger brother now work as slaves. Meanwhile the boat's name has been replaced with a foreign one as the story ends: "The boat is being improved, its name changed to a foreign name. It looks nothing like the original. The family is sad but they can do nothing. It will never be their property again. Now everything has changed" (Nou Hach translation group, *Nou Hach Literary Journal*, Vol. 5, 2008).

Ultimately "A Boat" is a story of multiple betrayals: the failure of trust and cooperation within the family lead to exploitation by "outsiders," who also cannot be trusted. There is treachery everywhere. Like "Lord of the Land," the inability of the group members to cooperate under duress leads to their destruction, an old theme in Cambodian folktales.

Another type of short story published since the early 2000s contains a coming-of-age theme somewhat reminiscent of the socially critical literature of the 1940s. In Pen Chhornn's humorous "Obscure Way" (2006), the adolescent protagonist, a university student recently arrived in the big city from the countryside, encounters a series of unfortunate events following an atypical evening of fun at a disco, casino, and karaoke bar. A recurrent theme in modern Khmer literature, our naïve rural lad gets taught a lesson in the big city. He has incurred a big hospital bill from being mugged on his only evening out. In order to repay this debt, he becomes a security guard at a wealthy politician's house. At this point the story devolves into a parody of corruption in contemporary Cambodia (Nissen 2006). Although our protagonist has lost his true love by the end of the story, he has gained a much deeper understanding of contemporary society and himself.[51] A similar theme occurs in Phy Runn's "An Orphan Cat" (2007). In this story a rural cat, befriended by a city cat, discovers that life is not so wonderful in Phnom Penh.

A coming-of-age theme, combined with the difficulties of a rural-to-urban transition also occurs in the Venerable Yoeun Saolee's "Thick Eyes' Residue" (2006), based on the author's understanding of problems encountered by rural Cambodians gained in his social work as a Buddhist monk. The story is a modern morality tale. It begins in Phnom Penh with a wealthy and successful man complaining to himself because every morning his unsophisticated wife from the countryside, acquired in an arranged marriage, rouses him from sleep. He is tired of hearing her voice. The plot then moves into his memories of the past. He, too, is from the countryside originally, from an impoverished, single-parent family. His mother's inability to provide him with many material things during his youth causes him to admire a wealthy boy, returned to the countryside by his worried father, who turns out to be a bad influence. Deciding that his life plan will be to get rich quickly, the impoverished boy grows up to become involved in the illegal but lucrative logging and forest animal trades as well as criminal drug activity. A wealthy man now, he moves to Phnom Penh where everything is "modern." There he becomes infatuated with the beautiful and seductive, modern city girls; ignoring his health, he indulges in a life of entertainment. In the meantime, his worried mother arranges for him to marry a village girl, who has become one of the many garment workers in Phnom Penh, the kind of unsophisticated woman he now despises. By the end of the story, the protagonist realizes that he is lucky to have this "traditional" wife from the countryside.

Finally, Phin Santel's example of expatriate writing, "The Revolver" (2006), is an English version of his Khmer short story "Katuoch" (2005). In it the writer-protagonist leaves an attractive French lover and a life of luxury in France to return to Cambodia, tired of reconstructing memories of his homeland from books and photographs. As a writer, he feels compelled to create a great love story, to expand Cambodian literature, as he is tired of seeing only grim testimonial memoirs in the French bookstores. He finds this love story through an unanticipated encounter with some shady characters. It is ironic that today Phin Santel represents so many Cambodians who still feel they have no modern literature of great worth, echoing the concern of writers from the late 1930s and 1940s.

Conclusion

There is no doubt that the years of censorship and historical trauma have impeded literary development in Cambodia. According to the critical reflections of the scholar Som Samuny, "The works of today's writers are not considerable. . . . I have seen nothing outstanding, and that is because they do not follow what they have in their hearts" (Lon Nara 2002).[52] Indeed, You Bo indicated in 2003 that only "fifty books of Khmer literature have been written since 1993" (Chea Chou 2003). The German journalist Susanne Mayer foregrounds this literary void in her 2006 article "Überleben statt Lesen" (Survive Instead of Read).

Many writers throughout Southeast Asia have overcome tremendous obstacles and prospered. Given the continuing repercussions of the Khmer Rouge era, Cambodia is still in recovery mode, making more progress in the educational and economic sectors.[53] Many writers would like to have their fiction and poetry published. Yet, without funds to self-publish, without an organized distribution system, and without significant public interest in the pleasure of reading serious literature, writers remain deeply frustrated (Jarvis and Arfanis 2002, 3.17–18). Pal Vannarirak expresses this frustration in her response to a question about the current situation of Cambodian writers.

> Oh, we have many problems. Cambodia is very poor, and not many people can read and write. Those who can don't have much time. And if they have time, they read about the subjects they are studying: medicine, law. Because they need to make a living, people with knowledge and skills do not want to become writers.
>
> I have a lot of work writing my books, but you can see my house is in very poor condition. Others live in places worse than mine. (May 2004c 171)[54]

The depressing situation Pal expresses in this newspaper interview has been slowly changing. Amratisha mentions the great strides made by women writers since 1979 and the increasing popularity of the short story during the 1990s (2006). A new generation of educated Cambodians is now graduating from a coterie of recently constructed private colleges, which augment the highly competitive and overcrowded public institutions that are unable to keep up with the demands of a population explosion.[55] Some young writers associated with the Khmer Writers' Association have published popular novels. One is Sam Suphearin, whose novel *Samnaok Anuksavarry* (Sorrow of Remembrance) has been well received by his peers. Other fiction writers have moved away from "literary language" and are experimenting with a more contemporary form of conversational prose in an attempt to broaden their reading audience.[56]

Rapid growth in the Cambodian economy has and will continue to improve the literacy rate, thus broadening the readership. Yet other factors will also need to change if literature is to develop further in Cambodia. A culture of reading serious literature for pleasure needs to be reinforced by the state at the public school level (Moriarty 2001). The state still largely finances most literary prizes and controls them by determining both the topics for the writers and the winners (Cameron 2005).[57] This constricts creative expression. The state also financially supports the Khmer Writers' Association, thus indirectly influencing its approach to literary criticism and pedagogy (Cameron 2005). Creative writing is not yet part of the university curriculum, so most writers' workshops have been sponsored by the Khmer Writers' Association until recently.

Newspapers, which in the 1950s were often purchased for the fiction or translations they published, are sometimes viewed with general disdain as mere political propaganda rags so writers may hesitate to publish in them.[58] The state still exerts substantial influence over the press through its control of the military and police and its influence over an underdeveloped judicial system. This casts a shadow over the practice of free speech and reinforces self-censorship (Hayes 2006).

Writers also face problems of publication costs and distribution, including the several thousand dollars it costs for self-publishing a run of a thousand copies in contrast to several hundred dollars a publisher may offer as a one-time payment for a novel. Once published, a writer faces the problem of pirated copies irrespective of the new copyright law, which prohibits this practice (Chea Chou 2003). State corruption remains an issue to be addressed (Barton 2006; Heng 2006). These are all discouraging factors.

Creative writers may also need to be more widely read. It would help if the great works of modern world literature, such as Franz Kafka's *Metamorphosis* or Chinua Achebe's *Things Fall Apart,* were translated to Khmer; the art of translation needs to be revived. Novelists must consider the quality of their work rather than the rapid production of similar novellas since "mass production" weakens the public's respect for literature as a serious endeavor. Piat referred to this practice in the late 1960s as "market literature" (1975, 253). It is not uncommon for some writers to have written several hundred novellas. A literary bulletin devoted to book reviews would improve this situation through the art of constructive criticism.[59]

Ultimately one may ask why it matters whether Cambodia ever develops a vibrant modern literature comparable in quality and creativity to the novels, novellas, and short stories one finds elsewhere in Southeast Asia. It has cell phones, DVDs, Internet cafes, and an important and thriving tourist industry promoting Angkor Wat. Why worry about the development of modern literature? My response is that literature fosters creative imagination in a way that the latest digital cell phone model does not. Creative writers, who are often also journalists, have always been at the forefront of socially critical, political discourse in Southeast Asia. The quality of our global commons suffers when writers are silenced.

Notes

[1] Cambodia is used to indicate the country and its citizens; Khmer is used to indicate the Cambodian language. There are numerous transliteration systems for Khmer. The transliteration of names and titles follows the precedent set by previous scholars in order to maintain some sort of consistency.

[2] For a more positive opinion regarding the status of the short story in Cambodia, see Amratisha 2006. I would argue that modern literature, especially the short story, is more fully developed in Laos, making Cambodia the Southeast Asian country with the least developed modern literature. See Peter Koret's essay, "The Short Story and Contemporary Lao Literature," in Chapter 3 of this collection.

[3] French policy in Cambodia emphasized the craft of reproduction rather than innovation in the arts and literature. Other comments about Cambodia as a conservative society "crushed by tradition" can be found in Martin 1994, 1–28.

[4] This becomes an unconscious cultural process; see Jameson 1996. As an example of how this aesthetic has become internalized, see Bernard-Thierry 1955.

[5] Currently, many Cambodian authors refer to *pralomlok* as "stories" or "novels." Typically they are quite short, one hundred pages or less, and are more like Western novellas, see Jacob 1974.

[6] Many independent nation-states in Southeast Asia incorporated some aspects of a colonial censorship policy into their own public policies. Some of the more extreme examples of this are Myanmar, Vietnam, and Indonesia. Ironically, writers in those three countries developed experimental narrative strategies, including escape into fantasy or romanticism, to deflect state censorship while continuing to develop the philosophical depth, social significance, and popularity of the short story. Cambodia's anti-intellectual aesthetic distinguishes it from these three countries, which also had longer and more developed traditions of secular writing.

[7] An Email communication with Hel Rithy (2003), who holds an MA in cultural studies from the Royal University of Phnom Penh, notes that reading for pleasure still is not a common practice in Cambodia.

[8] On the seriousness of copyright infringement and pirating in Cambodia, see International Intellectual Property Alliance, 2007. In 2007, the Nou Hach Literary Group found pirated copies of volume 1 of its journal and two CDs of its musical performances and radio programs being sold at various bookstalls and bookstores in Phnom Penh.

[9] For further information on this early period, see Khing and Mak 1989; and Jacob 1996.

[10] Dates for the Middle Period vary. Judith Jacob identifies the period as extending from the sixteenth to the nineteenth century (1996, 2). For further information, see Thompson 1997.

[11] This journal was founded in 1926 by the Royal Library of Cambodia, which was renamed the Buddhist Institute. It was one of the most important forums for the serious study of Khmer religion and literature. For further information, see Edwards 2007, 194–95; Chigas 2000; and Chigas 2005, 149–54).

[12] Several of these have been awarded literary prizes in the annual Nou Hach Literary Competition and are published in its journal: Pen Chhornn's "Destitute Pelican" (2005), Kao Seiha's "The Boat" (2006), and Phy Runn's "An Orphan Cat" (2007).

[13] For a more complete discussion of printing and the development of the press, see Khing and Mak 1989, 53–55; and Edwards 2007. The issue of technology transfer is important. The first Cambodian typewriter, invented by Keng Vansak in 1955, with the 120-plus elements of Cambodian script and punctuation marks, required a larger keyboard than the standard typewriter of 46 keys and 92 positions; see Tonkin 1962, 45.

[14] Khing Hoc Dy suggests that the French colonialists were first attracted to the collection and translation of Cambodian folktales and legends simply because they were relatively short and easy to understand (1998).

[15] For further information on the development of literary institutions in Cambodia, see Chigas 2000. He notes Joseph Guesdon's remarks that "all Khmer literature is only a sequence of poems about the life of the Buddha" (136). With the establishment of l'École Française d'Extrême-Orient in 1901, the investigation of classical texts began in earnest. This very traditional "academic" institution would not have been interested in the promotion of a modern literature.

[16] For more information on the history of the early press in Cambodia see Nepote and Khing 1981. They also remark on Cambodian resistance to the introduction of the press and journalism in three areas: technological, sociological, and religious (62). The appearance of several hundred westerners, who used print material as a means of obtaining information and entertainment, helped to initiate its appreciation. Some Cambodians were privately publishing in the early 1900s, and school texts in Cambodian were

printed and widely distributed in 1912 over the strong objections of the Cambodian traditionalists (63).

[17] The French, unlike in Vietnam, did not promote a large-scale program of public education reform in Cambodia but decided to import Vietnamese clerical workers, "leaving the majority of Khmers in their illiterate state." See Jarvis and Arfanis 2002, 2.1; Amratisha 1998, 77; Mehta 1997; and Paterson 1996, 43.

[18] On the importance of *quoc-ngu* in the development of modern literature in Vietnam, see Peter Zinoman's "The Modern Vietnamese Short Story" (chap. 9 in this volume) and O'Harrow 1973.

[19] For further information, see Dommen 2001, 55. This public opprobrium was fueled by the French arrest of the Venerable Hem Chieu in a manner that did not allow him to remove his Buddhist robes before being incarcerated.

[20] The school originally known as the French-Language School of the Protectorate was renamed Lycée Preah Sisowath in 1933. There is a nostalgia about this school and a sense of privilege among its surviving alumni even now.

[21] For further information, see Khing 1978, 799.

[22] Rim Kin finished his first novel, *Suphat*, in 1938. It was finally published in Vietnam in 1941 (Khing 1993, 33). Literary development was not confined to Phnom Penh; see Nepote and Khing for a geographical analysis of its development (1981).

[23] The influence of both traditional and modern Chinese literature on the development of Cambodian fiction has been generally overlooked with the exception of Nepote and Khing 1987 and Khing 1993. See also Amratisha 1996, 63–68; and Jarvis and Arfanis 2002, 3.2.

[24] For more information on the important role of the Buddhist Institute and its *Kambuja Suriya* in establishing literary institutions and a canon in Cambodia, see Chigas 2000.

[25] *Nagaravatt* was shut down by the French in July 1942; *Kambuja Suriya* took its place. It serialized Nou Hach's novel *Phka Srabon* in 1947.

[26] Kho Tararith, director of the Nou Hach Literary Project, has copied all of Nou Hach's short stories from these remaining magazines. "The Writer Nou Hach," an unpublished .pdf file, is available through the Nou Hach Literary Project (www.nouhachjournal.net).

[27] Ly Theam Teng mentions the dates 1953–56 as a period that saw increasing numbers of apolitical literary magazines, including *Vicitra, Supin Nimitt* (Good Dream), and *Mitt Sala Poali* (Friends of the Pali School) (1960, 207). The number of literary magazines was about forty between 1970 and 1974; although Judith Jacob considers this later time the key period in the formation of the short story, we should consider the possibility of the early 1940s and 1950s (Amratisha 1998, 201; Jacob 1982, 254).

[28] Jacob discusses the importance of the romantic theme in this early modern literature, speculating that it may be due to French romanticism and the influence of earlier verse novels with their tragic-romantic sensibility, such as *Tum Teav* (1988). Vandy Kaon also discusses French romanticism and its influence (1981, 48).

[29] According to Jacob, the first short story in Cambodia was published in 1962, with the term used to describe this new genre, "invented story" (*rioen pratist khli*), first noted in 1970 (Davidson 1982, 16). Jacob states that she knows of only two literary short stories, "Kim Phien" (1962) and "Rddhi" (1972) (Jacob 1982, 50). Davidson describes these as chiefly love stories, similar to those found in Khmer novels of the time but sometimes framed within political events. Davidson states that they may be "examples of literature condoned by the authorities, since evidence from other parts of Indochina suggests the possible existence of politically oriented short stories patterned on Vietnamese models," echoing Jacob's opinion about this possibility (Davidson 1982, 16; see also Jacob 1982, 50). Although Vietnamese models may have influenced the development of the short story in Laos during the 1960s and 1970s, it is difficult to prove a similar influence in Cambodia. Martine Piat does not even mention the "short story" in her article "Contemporary Cambodian Literature" (1975) in which she states that popular literature in Cambodia has only existed since the end of the 1960s. She defines popular literature by the criterion of low price. It includes filmstrips and historical novels. According to her, the print run was no more than a thousand copies, which typically took six years to sell, and there were no reprints. Piat reports that this literature is found for sale in bus stations, marketplaces, and itinerant fairs. Newspapers would also be sold at bus stations and marketplaces and would have been the major venue for the short story genre, which she does not mention.

[30] The Pracheachon Party, founded in 1954, openly opposed Sihanouk's Sangkum Reastr Niyam (Popular Socialist Community). It was finally driven underground by Sihanouk in the 1960s.

[31] These include *Romance of the Three Kingdoms* and *Dream of the Red Chamber* from China, as well as George Orwell's *Animal Farm*, Jean de la Fontaine's *Fables*, Gustave Flaubert's *Madam Bovary*, Bernardin de Saint Pierre's *Paul and Virgini*, Albert Camus's The Stranger, and William Shakespeare's *A Midsummer Night's Dream* and *Romeo and Juliet* (Ueda and Okada 2006, 70; Aveling and Yamada, 2008; Amratisha 1998, 62).

[32] This law replaced the more moderate 1951 press law (Steinberg 1959, 145).

[33] Soth Polin has resided in Southern California for many years and currently eschews creative writing. Ironically, You Bo reports that his novels, including *Jivit It Nay*, have been republished, are stocked on bookstore shelves, and have been selling well in Phnom Penh (Cameron 2005). These are pirated copies for which he receives no royalties. For more information about him and his works see Paterson 1996, 47–63.

[34] Other writers included in this collection are Khun Srun, Mao Samnang, and Sothea.

[35] These were *Suphat* (The Story of Sophat) by Rim Kin, *Kulap Pailin* (The Rose of Pailin) by Nhok Them, *Phka Srabon* (The Faded Flower) by Nou Hach, and *Mala Tuon Citt* (The Garland of the Heart) also by Nou Hach.

[36] The *Nou Hach Literary Journal* appears to have been the first organization in Cambodia to establish a literary award for short fiction and only since 2002.

[37] Sharon May gives an undocumented estimate as follows: "Out of approximately thirty-eight thousand Cambodian intellectuals, only three hundred survived—less than one percent" (2004b, 29). Amratisha reports that two-thirds—approximately two hundred people—of known writers were killed (2006, 152).

[38] The best information on this period is provided by Khing Hoc Dy (1994) and Amratisha (2006).

[39] Research assistant Kiry Poeun's March 2002 survey of the Long Beach Cambodian stores that sell Khmer books revealed only one novel published in the United States: *Khmer Oeuy Khmer* by Heng Sou Sieu. Ultimately Soth Polin, currently surviving as a taxicab driver in Long Beach, California, would give up writing completely (May 2004, 9–20; Beller 2006).

[40] For information on the emergence of women writers, see Amratisha 2006.

[41] This trend continues in the United States where Cambodian Americans are still only writing the testimonial memoir. For one of the latest examples in short essay form, see Pol-Paul Pat 2006.

[42] Both would eventually become exiles abroad. Vandy Kaon has resided in France for over twenty years; Soth Polin initially resided in France after fleeing in 1974, then relocated to Southern California.

[43] Heng Samrin and Hun Sen, who together led the government established after the Vietnamese invasion, were former Khmer Rouge officials who had defected to Vietnam in 1977. Hun Sen has maintained his political power up to the present.

[44] You Bo, president of the Khmer Writers' Association between 1993 and 2005 reports that two hundred of the three hundred postindependence writers were killed during the Khmer Rouge period; only 10 percent of all teachers and professors survived (Amratisha 1998, 287).

[45] For information on the media during this period, see Marston 1996, 208–42.

[46] Hel Rithy's research on current magazines in Phnom Penh (2003) indicates that charging an author's fee was a common practice for magazines. Journalists also expect a fee to write articles about various events for publication in their newspaper.

[47] Among 80 countries, the youth literacy rate for 2004 provided by UNESCO ranks Cambodia at 50 with a youth literacy rate of 80.3 percent and Laos at 53 with a rate of 78.5. In contrast, Myanmar is ranked at 34 with a 94.4 percent rate, the Philippines at 31 with a 95.1 percent rate, Malaysia at 22 with a 97.2 percent rate, Thailand at 17 with a 98 percent rate, and Singapore at 5 with a 99.5 percent rate. Literacy in this context is defined as "The percentage of people ages 15–24 who can, with understanding, both read and write a short, simple statement related to their everyday life." (www.unu.edu) For the year 1990, the youth literacy rate for Cambodia was 73.5 percent and for Laos, 70.1 percent. For 1985, the rate for Cambodia was 70 percent and for Laos 66.6 percent. Laos appears to have done somewhat better at improving this rate. "The Cambodia Socio-economic Survey, 2004," prepared by the National Institute of Statistics in the Ministry of Planning, gives the adult literacy rate, population aged 15 and older, at 60 percent for women and 80 percent for men. (www.nis.gov.kh on 30 July 2007) The gap between rural and urban literacy rates for women is about 20 percent lower for rural areas according to the 1998 Population Census of Cambodia.

[48] For further information on this writer, see Chigas 2004.

[49] Most of the prize-winning short stories published in the *Nou Hach Literary Journal* are socially critical in content. Many are available in pdf files from www.nouhachjounal.net, (accessed 18 May 2008).

[50] This story won the first-place prize for short story in the 2004 Nou Hach Literary Competition and was published in 2005.

[51] For an English translation of this story by the Nou Hach Literary Group see *Nou Hach Literary Journal* 3 (2006): 19-30.

[52] Som Somuny, a professor associated with the Royal Academy in Phnom Penh, has been working on a history of modern Khmer literature supported by the Toyota Foundation. A somewhat similar opinion is expressed in a 1999 report by Harrison and Okada.

[53] Some rural women are seriously lagging behind the gains others have received from this development. On this, see Rasheeda Bhagat 2000; and Derks 2006. For a Western journalist's perspective on current life in Cambodia see Coates 2005.

[54] During a 2004 radio interview, Geoff Ryman reported that Pal had written "one hundred short stories, forty novels, many screenplays, and eight verse collections and lyrics for popular songs." Her persistence and determination paid off in 1988 when her novel *The Starless Night Is Over* was translated and published in Japan. In 1989 she won a national competition for writers, and in 1995 she won first place in another national writing competition. In 2006 she won the prestigious S.E.A. Write award. The other writer is also a woman, Mao Samnang. For more information about her, see Cameron 2005; and May 2004c.

[55] These include Norton University, Regent College, Pannasastra University, the National Institute of Technology and Management, and the International Institute of Cambodia. These private institutes have largely developed since 1997 when the government first allowed the privatization of education. In 2001 there were ten state-run and six private institutions. (Jarvis and Arfanis 2002, 2.5). Vong Sokheng reports that "thirty or so private universities . . . have sprung up around Phnom Penh during the last decade" (2003). In the same article he reported that Chea Chamroeun, the rector of Chamroeun University of Polytechnology, stated that when he started his school in early 2002 there were only two universities in the country.

[56] This type of less embellished prose is seen in Phy Runn's "An Orphan Cat" and in the short stories of Keo Chambo and Pech Sangwawann (2004). For a comment on its importance see Jacob 1993.

[57] The state sponsors the following awards for novel writing and poetry through the Department of Books and Reading: (1) the Preah Suramarit Award for novels and poetry dealing with the theme "culture of peace" (2000, five prizes

for novels and five prizes for poetry were given); (2) Children's Picture Book (in 2001 five prizes); (3) Queen Indradevi Award, a novel and poetry competition based on a selected theme; and (4) Certificate of Recognition as Outstanding Achievers in the Arts (MOCFA). The writer Kong Buncheoun received the latter award in 2000. The state sponsors the Khmer Writers' Association and thus indirectly its literary awards. It gives two main awards in alternate years: (1) the Preah Sihanouk Reach Award for novels and poetry, the topic of which is national unification and peace; and (2) the 7 January Award for novels and poetry, which is organized around the theme of "national development." More information about these awards can be found at *Cambodian Culture Profile* (2005). It appears that the state has stopped sponsoring awards since 2004. This will have a negative impact on literary development, which is prize driven. Nonstate organized or funded awards are far fewer. In 2000 the Reyum Institute of Arts and Culture sponsored a children's book award. The AEKE (France) sponsored the Kram Ngouy Award. In 2000 it gave a Literature of Peace Award. On 21 June 2002, the Nou Hach Literary Project gave first, second, and third place literary awards for best poem, best short story, and best research. It continues to give the awards to poetry and short fiction. For information on some of these awards, see Jarvis and Arafanis 2002; and *Cambodian Culture Profile* 2005.

[58] Over the past four years, the newspaper *Koh Santepheap* has republished award-winning stories from the *Nou Hach Literary Journal*, often removing or altering their political content without the journal's consent. The *Rasmei Kampuchea Daily* has a section on arts and culture. The French-language *Cambodge Soir*, which ceased publication during the summer of 2007, had a page devoted to Cambodian literature.

[59] The French (and Khmer intellectuals writing in French) published reviews of Cambodian literature in French during the 1970s at least (Amratisha 1998, 201). Teri Yamada, under the auspices of the Nou Hach Literary Group, conducted a seminar on the mechanics of writing a book review to a young writers group in June 2007 and 2008 at the Buddhist Institute.

Bibliography

Amratisha, Klairung. 1998. "The Cambodian Novel: A Study of Its Emergence and Development." PhD Diss., School of Oriental and African Studies, University of London.

———. 2006. "The (Re-)emergence of Cambodian Women Writers at Home and Abroad." In *Expressions of Cambodia: The Politics of Tradition, Identity, and Change,* edited by Leakthina Chan-Pech Ollier and Tim Winter, 150–63. London: Routledge.

Aveling, Harry, and Teri Shaffer Yamada. 2008. "Southeast Asian Traditions." In *Routledge Encyclopedia of Translation Studies*, edited by Mona Baker and Gabriela Saldanha, 527–33. London: Routledge.

Barton, Cat. 2006. "Grim Picture Painted of All-Pervasive Corruption." *Phnom Penh Post*, Issue 15/26, 29 December 2006–11 January 2007.

Bee, P. J., I. Brown, Patricia Herbert, and Manas Chitakasem. 1989. "Thailand." In *South-East Asia: Languages and Literatures: A Select Guide,* edited by Patricia Herbert and Anthony Milner, 23–48. Honolulu: University of Hawai'i Press.

Beller, Thomas. 2006. "The Debris of the Visible: *In the Shadow of Angkor: Contemporary Writing from Cambodia.*" *Cambodia Daily*, 26 August.

Bernard-Thierry, Solange. 1955. "Imagerie populaire." *France-Asie* 12.114–15: 351–54.

Bhagat, Rasheeda. 2000. "Cambodian Women: Outnumbering the Men, but Sidelined." *Business Line*, Internet Edition (Friday, March 24). (http://www.blonnet.com/businessline/2000/03/24/stories/042444gj.htm)

Bitard, Pierre. 1951. "Essai sur la satire sociale dans la littérature du Cambodge." *Bulletin de la Société des Études Indochinoises* (Saigon), new ser., 26.2:189–218.

———.1955. "La Littérature Cambodgienne Moderne." *France-Asie* 12. 114–115, 467–79.

Bou Saroeun and Phelim Kyne, 2000. "Victim's Misery a Modern Morality Tale." *Phnom Penh Post*, Issue 9/13, 23 June–6 July.

Cambodian Culture Profile. 2005. www.culturalprofiles.net, accessed on 18 May 2008.

Cameron, Amy. 2005. "Pulp Fiction." *Phnom Penh Post*, Issue 14/04, 25 February–10 March.

Chandler, David. 1991. *The Tragedy of Cambodian History: Politics, War, and Revolution since 1945.* New Haven: Yale University Press.

———. 1996. "Songs at the Edge of the Forest: Perceptions of Order in Three Cambodian Texts." In *Facing the Cambodian Past*, edited by David Chandler, 76–99. Chiang Mai: Silkworm Books.

———. 1999. *Voices from S–21: Terror and History in Pol Pot's Secret Prison.* Berkeley: University of California Press.

———. 2000. *A History of Cambodia.* 3rd ed. Boulder: Westview Press.

Chea Chou. 2003. "Intellectual Property Laws Win Cautious Acclaim." *Phnom Penh Post* 24 September–October 9.

Chigas, George. 2000. "The Emergence of Twentieth Century Cambodian Literary Institutions: The Case of *Kambujasuriya*." In *The Canon in Southeast Asian Literatures*, edited by David Smyth, 135–46. Richmond, Surrey: Curzon.

———. 2004. "Social Criticism in Modern Cambodian Literature: The Case of Kong Bun Chhoeurn." Paper presented at the annual meeting of the Association for Asian Studies, San Diego, 5 March.

———. 2005. *Tum Teav: A Translation and Analysis of a Cambodian Literary Classic.* Cambodia: Documentation Center of Cambodia.

Coates, Karen J. 2005. *Cambodia Now: Life in the Wake of War.* Jefferson, NC: McFarland.

Davidson, Jeremy H. C. S. 1982. "The Modern Short Story in South East Asia: An Introduction." In *The Short Story in South East Asia: Aspects of a Genre*, edited by Jeremy H. C. S. Davidson and Helen Cordell, 1–28. London: School of Oriental and African Studies, University of London.

Derks, Annuska. 2006. "Khmer Women and Global Factories." In *Expressions of Cambodia: The Politics of Tradition, Identity, and Change*, edited by Leakthina Chau-Pech Ollier and Tim Winter, 193-204. London: Routledge.

Dingwall, Alastair, ed. 1995. *Traveller's Literary Companion: South-East Asia.* Lincolnwood, IL: Passport Books.

Dommen, Arthur J. 2001. *The Indochinese Experience of the French and the Americans: Nationalism and Communism in Cambodia, Laos, and Vietnam.* Bloomington: Indiana University Press.

Dy, Sedeth S., and Akira Ninomiya. 2003. "Basic Education in Cambodia: The Impact of UNESCO on Politics in the 1990s." *Educational Policy Analysis Archives* 11.48: 1–21.

Ebihara, May, Carol A. Mortland, and Judy Ledgerwood, eds. 1994. *Cambodian Culture since 1975: Homeland and Exile.* Ithaca: Cornell University Press.

Edwards, Penny. 2004. "Making a Religion of the Nation and Its Language: The French Protectorate (1863–1954) and the Dhammakay." In *History, Buddhism, and New Religious Movements in Cambodia,* edited by John Marston and Elizabeth Guthrie, 63–85. Honolulu: University of Hawai'i Press.

———. Trans. 2005. *The Buddhist Institute: A Short History.* Phnom Penh: Heinrich Boll Foundation.

———.2007. *Cambodge: The Cultivation of a Nation, 1860–1945.* Honolulu: University of Hawai'i Press.

Harrison, Rachel, and Tomoko Okada. 1999. "Report on the Literature Panel." Manuscript, Center for Khmer Studies, Phnom Penh.

Hayes, Michael. 2006. "Accident Feared Deliberate." *Phnom Penh Post,* 29 December 2006–11 January 2007.

Heder, Steve, and Judy Ledgerwood, eds. 1996. *Propaganda, Politics, and Violence in Cambodia: Democratic Transition under United Nations Peace-Keeping.* Armonk, NY: M. E. Sharpe.

Hel Rithy. 2003. E-mail communication, 4 August 2003.

Heng Sreang. 2006. "Justice in Cambodia: A Short Reflection on Some Obstacles to Implementing 'Justice' within the Context of the Law in Present-Day Cambodia." NIAS*nytt Asia Insights,* (December) 3: 20–22.

Herbert, Patricia, and Anthony Milner. 1989. *South-East Asia: Languages and Literatures: A Select Guide.* Honolulu: University of Hawaii Press.

International Intellectual Property Alliance. 2007. "International Intellectual Property Alliance 2007 Special 301 Report: Special Mention Cambodia." www.iipa.com, accessed on 30 July 2007.

Jacob, Judith M. 1974. "Pralom-Lok." In *Dictionary of Oriental Literatures,* edited by Jaroslav Prusek, 123. London: G. Allen and Unwin.

———. 1982. "The Short Stories of Cambodian Popular Tradition." In *The Short Story in South East Asia: Aspects of a Genre,* edited by Jeremy H. C. S. Davidson and Helen Cordell, 37–62. London: School of Oriental and African Studies, University of London.

———. 1986. "Cambodian Literature." In *Far Eastern Literatures in the Twentieth Century: A Guide,* edited by Leonard S. Klein, 10–11. New York: Ungar.

———. 1993a. "The Deliberate Use of Foreign Vocabulary by the Khmer: Changing Fashions, Methods, and Sources." In *Cambodian Linguistics, Literature and History: Collected Articles,* edited by David A. Smyth, 149–66. London: School of Oriental and African Studies, University of London.

———. 1993b. "Some Features of Modern Khmer Literary Style." In *Cambodian Linguistics, Literature and History: Collected Articles,* edited by David A. Smyth, 263–79. London: School of Oriental and African Studies, University of London.

———. 1995. "Cambodia (Kampuchea)." In *Traveller's Literary Companion: South-East Asia,* edited by Alastair Dingwall, 154–75. Lincolnwood, IL: Passport Books.

———. 1996. *The Traditional Literature of Cambodia: A Preliminary Guide* London: Oxford University Press.

Jameson, Fredric. 1996. *The Political Unconscious: Narrative as a Socially Symbolic Act.* London: Routledge.

Jarvis, Helen, and Peter Arfanis. 2002. *Publishing in Cambodia.* Phnom Penh: Center for Khmer Studies, Reyum Institute, the Toyota Foundation.

Kao Seiha. 2006. "A Boat." *Nou Hach Literary Journal* 3:31–39.

Keyes, Charles. 1994. "Communist Revolution and the Buddhist Past in Cambodia." In *Asian Visions of Authority: Religion and the Modern States of East and Southeast Asia,* edited by Charles F Keyes, Laurel Kendall, and Helen Hardacre, 43–73. Honolulu: University of Hawai'i Press.

Khim Sam Or. 1961. *The History of Cambodian Literature.* Phnom Penh: Yoveak Peanich.

Khing Hoc Dy. 1978. "Le Développement Économique et la Transformation Littéraire dans le Cambodge Moderne." *Mondes en développement* 28:793–801.

———. 1990. *Contribution a l'historie de la littérature Khmère.* Vol. 1: *L'Époque Classique XVe–XIXe siècle.* Paris: L'Harmattan.

———. 1993. *Écrivains et expressions littéraires du Cambodge au XXème siècle.* Paris: L'Harmattan.

———. 1994. "Khmer Literature since 1975." In *Cambodian Culture since 1975: Homeland and Exile*, edited by May Ebihara, Carol A. Mortland, Judy Ledgerwood, 27–38. Cornell Ithaca: University Press.

———. 1997. "Les Études sur la littérature khmère en France: Bilan et perspectives." 123–31. In *Bilan et perspectives des études Khmères (langue et culture)*. Actes du colloque de Phnom Penh, 29–30 novembre–1 décembre 1995 (Collection Recherches Asiatiques). Paris: L'Harmattan.

Khing Hoc Dy, and Mak Phoeun. 1989. "Cambodia." In *Southeast Asia: Languages and Literatures: A Select Guide*, edited by Patricia Herbert and Anthony Milner, 49–66. Honolulu: University of Hawai'i Press.

Kiernan, Ben. 1996. *The Pol Pot Regime: Race, Power, and Genocide in Cambodia under the Khmer Rouge, 1975–79.* New Haven: Yale University Press.

Locard, Henri. 2004. *Pol Pot's Little Red Book: The Sayings of Angkar.* Chiang Mai: Silkworm Books.

Lon Nara. 2002. "The Unlucrative State of the Khmer Novel." *Phnom Penh Post*, Issue 11/07, 29 March 29–11April.

Ly Theam Teng. 1960. *Aksarsastr Khmer* [Khmer Literature]. 2nd ed. Phnom Penh: Seng Nguon Huot.

Marston, John. 1996. "Cambodian News Media in the UNTAC Period and After." In *Propaganda, Politics, and Violence in Cambodia: Democratic Transition under United Nations Peace-Keeping,* edited by Steve Heder and Judy Ledgerwood 208–42. Armonk, NY: M. E. Sharpe.

———. trans. 2002. "Just a Human Being." In *Virtual Lotus: Modern Fiction of Southeast Asia,* edited by Teri Shaffer Yamada, 39–41. Ann Arbor: University of Michigan Press.

Martin, Alexandrine. 1994. *Cambodia: A Shattered Society*. Berkeley: University of California Press.

May, Sharon. 2004a. "Beyond Words: An Interview with Soth Polin." *Manoa* 16.1: 9–20.

———. 2004b. "In the Shadow of Angkor: A Search for Cambodian Literature." *Manoa* 16.1: 27–35.

———. 2004c. "Words from the Fire: Three Cambodian Women Writers." *Manoa* 16.1: 169–175.

Mayer, Susanne. 2006. "Überleben statt Lesen." *Die Zeit* (April 2005). www.zeit.de, accessed on July 30, 2007.

Mehta, Harish. 1997. *Cambodia Silenced: The Press under Six Regimes*. Bangkok: White Lotus Press.

Mey Son Sotheary. 2002. "My Sister." Translated by Tomoko Okada, Vuth Reth, and Teri Shaffer Yamada. In *Virtual Lotus: Modern Fiction of Southeast Asia*, edited by Teri Shaffer Yamada, 45–52. Ann Arbor: University of Michigan Press.

Moriarty, Erin. 2001. "Book-shy Cambodia Seeks Literary Culture Rebirth." *Phnom Penh Post*, Issue 10/15, 20 July–2 August.

Nepote, Jacques, and Khing Hoc Dy. 1981. "Literature and Society in Modern Cambodia." In *Essays on Literature and Society in Southeast Asia*, edited by Tham Seong Chee, 56–81. Singapore: Singapore University Press.

———. 1987. "Chinese Literary Influence on Cambodia in the Nineteenth and Twentieth Centuries." In the *Literary Migrations: Traditional Chinese Fiction in Asia (Seventeenth-Twentieth Centuries)*, edited by Claudine Salmon, 321–72. Beijing: International Culture Publishing Corporation.

Nepote, Jacques, and Khing Hoc Dy, trans. 2001. "Samapheavi par Rim Kin." *Péninsule* 32.43: 25–102.

Nhem Sophath. 2006. "Lord of the Land." *Nou Hach Literary Journal* 3:40–51.

Nissen, Christine. 2006. "Corruption Is 'Cool': Reflections on Bureaucratic Practices in Cambodia." *NIASnytt Asia Insights* (December) 3:18–19, 22.

O'Harrow, Stephen. 1973. "French Colonial Policy towards Vernacular Language Development and the Case of Pham Quynh in Viet-Nam." In *Aspects of Vernacular Languages in Asian and Pacific Societies*, compiled by Nguyen Dang Liem, 113–35. Southeast Asia Papers, no. 2. Honolulu: Southeast Asian Studies Program, University of Hawai'i.

Okada, Tomoko.1998. "Abutsu no Shima' ni Kansuru Ikkosatsu: Sakka Vandy Kaon no Mita Cambojia Gendaishi" [A Study on 'The Island of Evil Spirits': A Modern History of Cambodia through Vandy Kaon's View]. Tokyo University of Foreign Studies. *Southeast Asian Studies* 4:31–48.

———. 2001a. *Gendai Kambojia Tampenshu* [Modern Cambodian Short Stories]. Tokyo: Daido Life Foundation.

———. 2001b. "Modern Short Stories: People's Experiences and Memories Recorded by Novelists." *Siksacakr* 3.23 (July) 26–27.

———. 2003. Personal email communication "Hen Samrin Regime" (July 26).

Ollier, Leakthina Chau-Pech and Tim Winter. 2006. *Expressions of Cambodia: The Politics of Tradition, Identity, and Change*. London: Routledge.

Osborne, Milton. 1994. *Sihanouk: Prince of Light, Prince of Darkness*. Honolulu: University of Hawai'i Press.

Paterson, Lorraine Marion. 1996. "Re-placing 'Imitation': Cambodian Romantics and Post-independence Narratives." MA thesis, Cornell University.

Pech Sangwawann. 2004. *Mday Kmeek Tumloap* [La belle mère moderne]. France: Montigny les Cormeilles: Association des Écrivains Khmers à l'Étranger.

Pen Chhornn. 2005. "Destitute Pelican." *Nou Hach Literary Journal* 2:2–16.

———. 2006. "Obscure Way." *Nou Hach Literary Journal* 3:19–30.

Phin Santel. 2005. "Katuoch." *Nou Hach Literary Journal* 2:17–30.

———. 2006. "The Revolver." *Nou Hach Literary Journal* 3:60–67. In English.

Phy Runn. 2007. "An Orphan Cat." *Nou Hach Literary Journal* 4: 33–36.

Piat, Martine. 1975. "Contemporary Cambodian Literature." *The Journal of the Siam Society* 63.2: 251–59.

Pin Yathay with John Man. [1987] 2000. *Stay Alive, My Son*. Ithaca: Cornell University Press.

Pol-Paul Pat. 2006. "The Movement of Seals in the Temple of Two Suns." *Amerasia Journal* 32.3: 91–104.

Ponchaud, François. 1989. "Social Change in the Vortex of Revolution." In *Cambodia, 1975–1978: Rendezvous with Death*, edited by Karl D. Jackson, 151–77. Princeton: Princeton University Press.

Power, Sharon. 2002. "Cambodia: 'Helpless Giant.'" In *A Problem from Hell: America and the Age of Genocide*, 87–154. New York: Basic Books.

Ryman, Geoff. 2004. "Living Cambodia: A Look at Khmer Arts." Manuscript.

———. 2006. "Writing after the Slaughter: Geoff Ryman on Cambodian Writers." *Guardian*, 8 April.

Sen Nith. 2007. "For the Love of Words." *Cambodian Scene Magazine*, 29 (May–June).

Sharma, Sanjeev. 1994. *Cambodia: An Historical Overview.* Honolulu: Center for Southeast Asian Studies, School of Hawaiin, Asian and Pacific Studies. University of Hawai'i Press at Manoa.

Short, Philip. 2005. *Pol Pot: Anatomy of a Nightmare.* New York: Henry Holt.

Siv, Darina. 2004. "Sokha and Apopeal." *Manoa* 16.1: 41–47.

Smyth, David, ed. 2000. *The Canon in Southeast Asian Literatures: Literatures of Burma, Cambodia, Indonesia, Laos, Malaysia, the Philippines, Thailand, and Vietnam.* Richmond, Surrey: Curzon.

Steinberg, David J., 1959. *Cambodia: Its People, Its Society, Its Culture.* New Haven: HRAF Press.

Stewart, Frank, and Sharon May, eds. 2004. "In the Shadow of Angkor: Contemporary Writing from Cambodia." *Manoa* 16.1.

Tauch Chhuong. 1998. "Les Publications au Cambodge après 1980," 43-62. In *Bilan et perspectives des études Khmères (langue et culture).* Actes du colloque de Phnom Penh, 29–30 novembre–1 décembre 1995 (Collection Recherches Asiatiques). Paris: L'Harmattan.

Tham Seong Chee. 1981. *Essays on Literature and Society in Southeast Asia: Political and Sociological Perspectives.* Singapore: Singapore University Press.

Than Bunly. 2004. "The Status of Oral Folktale Narration in Contemporary Phreah Theat Thmor Da Village." MA thesis, Royal University of Phnom Penh.

Thion, Serge, and Helen Jarvis. 1993. "SASTRA: A Project for the Restoration of Cambodia's Written Heritage." *Library Automated Systems Information Exchange* 24. 2–3: 52–56.

Thompson, Ashley. 1993. "Oh Cambodia! Poems from the Border." *New Literary History* 24.3: 519–44.

———. 1997. "Changing Perspectives: Cambodia after Angkor." In *Sculpture of Angkor and Ancient Cambodia: Millennium of Glory*, edited by Helen Ibbitson Jessup and Thierry Zephir, 22–32. Washington, DC: National Gallery of Art.

Tonkin, Derek. 1962. *Modern Cambodian Writing.* Phnom Penh: Université Buddhique Preah Sihanouk Raj.

U Sam Oeur. 1998. *Sacred Vows: Poetry by U Sam Oeur.* Translated by Ken McCullough and U Sam Oeur. Minneapolis: Coffee House Press.

Ueda, Hiromi, and Tomoko Okada. 2006. *Kambojia o Shiru Tame No* [Understanding Cambodia]. Tokyo: Akashi.

UNICEF. 1990. *Cambodia: The Situation of Children and Women*. Phnom Penh: Office of the Special Representative, United Nations International Children's Emergency Fund.

Vandy Kaon [Kaonn]. 1981. *Réflexion sur la littérature Khmère*. Phnom Penh: Institut de Sociologie.

Vickery, Michael. 1990. "Cultural Survival in Cambodian Language and Literature." *Cultural Survival Quarterly* 14.3: 49–52.

Vong Sokheng. 2003. "Universities Fear Lower Fees, Lower Standards." *Phnom Penh Post*, 21 November–4 December.

Weinberger, Evan, and Sam Rith. 2003. "Phat Times in Phnom Penh: Khmer Hip-Hop Takes the Rap at La Casa." *Phnom Penh Post* 4–17 July.

Yamada, Teri Shaffer, ed. 2002. *Virtual Lotus: Modern Fiction of Southeast Asia*. Ann Arbor: University of Michigan Press.

Yamada, Teri Shaffer. 2005. "Cambodian American Autobiography: Testimonial Discourse." In *Form and Transformation in Asian American Literature*, edited by Zhou Xiaojing and Samina Najmi, 144–67. Seattle: University of Washington Press.

Yoeun Saolee. 2006. "Thick Eyes' Residue." *Nou Hach Literary Journal* 3:52–59.

5

The Short Story in Myanmar/Burma
Anna Allott

The small number of Burmese short stories that are available in English translation can in no way convey the quantity and variety of stories that are published today in Myanmar. It is the most popular and important literary genre. The stories first reach the reading public through the pages of numerous monthly magazines, privately owned publications catering to various special interests such as literature, poetry, films, sports, business, and religion, almost all of which also include several short stories. Later on, many of these stories will happily be preserved for posterity, and even for critical study, by being republished in collected volumes, some representing an individual author's choice of his own work, some as annual anthologies or selections of prize-winning new authors. An example of this important trend is the popular Readers' Choice (Khan-za-thu akyaik) series, which began in 1996.[1]

We can gain some idea of the number of stories involved from a 1999 publication by Aung Thin,[2] *My Favorite Short Story,* in which he collected the monthly contributions he had been writing between 1983 and 1985 for *Thabin* magazine (1999). Aung Thin had promised the editor, Chit U Nyo, of this newly established magazine that he would survey each month's output of short stories, choose his favorite, and write a reasoned appraisal in support of his choice. He commenced his first article in October 1983 by listing the fifteen magazines he had surveyed and revealing that out of 81 stories only some four or five seemed worthy of closer study.[3] He had excluded all translations. Two months later, Aung Thin had added three more magazines to his list, with a total of 90 stories to read.[4] By October 1985, when he finally gave up struggling to complete this most demanding monthly task, he was perusing twenty magazines and reading over 100 stories.

These numbers make two things clear: by the 1980s the short story was immensely popular in Myanmar; and the literary critic or historian, especially the nonnative one, has a vast field to survey and may well find that she or he fails to note some writer worthy of attention. This huge amount of short fiction also presents a problem to anyone wishing to select representative pieces for teaching material or translation.[5]

The Press Scrutiny Board (PSB) and Censorship

Before proceeding to survey a whole century of short story writing, it is important to point out that, from around 1964 authors began to face a major change in the publishing world with the military regime's establishment of a Press Scrutiny Board (PSB), which controlled and censored all printed matter.[6] In effect this has meant that for the last forty years Burmese writers have not had the freedom to write that is enjoyed in the majority of democracies.[7] To quote a Burmese author, "Every writer, every poet, every painter, every cartoonist works with the fear that his work will not escape censorship. Every freely created work of art can fall prey to the censor."[8]

For some, the challenge to get published can be the spur to greater creativity and ingenuity; for others, it may be too great a discouragement. Consequently, authors have come to terms with the restrictions and arbitrariness of the censors in different ways: by self-censorship and taking care to avoid impermissible subjects; by not writing original material but choosing instead to make large numbers of translations; by testing the limits of acceptability and being prepared to have stories banned; by recourse to satire, metaphor, allegory, and allusive "new style" (*han-thit*) writing; or by simply ceasing to write (Allott 1993; Smith 1991). However, as this survey shows, censorship has in no way caused the torrent of Burmese short stories to dry up, though it may have affected its nature.

Early Short Stories

The traditional literature of Myanmar is rich in tales and stories of all kinds. There are Buddhist birth tales (*jatakas*), the epic tale of the *Ramayana*, and the folktales of the *Hitopadesa*. There are also numerous folktales and legal tales frequently related to children by parents and elders as guides to conduct. Myanmar is especially rich in folktales as the various ethnic minorities each have their own traditions and stories, many of them made available in Burmese in the collections gathered by Ludu U Hla (Allott 1997). More recently, Gerry Abbott and his wife Khin Thant Han have published excellent new English translations of some hundred or so folktales from all parts of the Union of Myanmar (2000).

Throughout the period of the monarchy up to 1886, when Myanmar came under British rule, and into the beginning of the twentieth century, verse was the preferred medium for imaginative literature. Short stories did not develop until after the first novel had been published in 1904 and until vernacular newspapers and magazines were established around 1917 (Allott 1982). Among the earliest works of short fiction were detective stories chronicling the exploits of Maung San Sha, a Burmese Sherlock Holmes, the author remaining anonymous since fiction writing was not yet considered a respectable occupation. However, Detective Maung San Sha soon became as well known in Myanmar as his English original, and Shwe U-daung ceased to conceal his identity as the author. Modern Burmese prose literature owes a great debt to Shwe U-daung who, from 1917 until his death in 1973, adapted or translated many of the best-loved works of Western literature, suiting them with great skill to the taste of the Burmese reader.

By 1920 the short story had become firmly established as a popular form of fiction. In September of that year, the most influential prewar literary (monthly) magazine, *Dagon*, was founded and became a model for those that followed. In addition to short stories with illustrations, it had sections for films and books, household matters, current affairs, classical and modern poems, and in later issues for contributions by student writers from the University of Yangon. Owing to the prestige and influence of its editors—first Thakhin Kodaw Hmaing and later Leh-di Pandita U Maung Gyi—it attracted many keen young writers and became one of the leading vehicles of nationalist protest. It had to pay heavy fines several times for printing antigovernment items before it ceased publication in 1941.[9]

The Khit-san[10] Movement and the Modern Short Story

The year 1920 is remembered for another significant event, for it was the year of the founding of the University of Rangoon. Here, under the guidance of Professor Pe Maung Tin, the study of Pali, and for the first time of Burmese literature, was to lead by the 1930s to a new generation of writers, known as Khit-san, who began to look critically at the way Burmese fiction was developing.

In the meantime another writer, P. Monin (1883–1940), was experimenting with a new type of short story publication, small booklets selling for four annas or less consisting of a long short story or novelette. This type of work began to prove more popular with the reading public than the full-length novel, probably because it was cheaper. P. Monin was an original and independent thinker, critical of those aspects of Burmese tradition that held back economic progress. He also contributed greatly to a changed perspective in Burmese fiction. Educated by Catholics and a master of both Latin and English, he abandoned a seminary career and plunged back into a secular Burmese way of life, at times traveling with a troupe of actors, at other times idling and drinking or teaching, reading, and writing. He wrote numerous self-improvement works—called in Burmese *tet-kyan*—explaining how to get on in the world. These were still in print and on sale in bookstalls at the start of the twenty-first century. He was a gifted storyteller who began writing under the influence of contemporary Victorian novels but went on to develop more original Burmese themes in his short stories, many of which were first published in *Dagon* (Than Htut and Thaw Kaung 2003, 3).[11]

Although a large number of these early short stories were concerned with the vicissitudes of young love, many also expressed the frustrations of the rising generation of nationally conscious Burmans. By the end of the 1930s, popular love stories had begun to give way to two other types: success stories and nationalistic stories. The first were stories of rewarded effort, usually about a simple Upper Myanmar peasant who finds success and a rich wife in Lower Myanmar. These developed partly as a result of the writings of P. Monin and partly from a popular story by Yan Aung, entitled "Anya-tha-gale" (Young Lad from Up-Country), written in 1938. The second type, which developed alongside the success story, was more openly anticolonial and included stories written by Maha Swe. The mood of those nationalists who felt that independence from the British could only be achieved by violent means was reflected in stories about a patriotic brigand, Robber Thet-pyin, a Burmese Robin Hood who engaged in such exploits as robbing foreigners of the jewelry they were about to take out of the country. Such stories of adventure, in which bold patriotism was combined with a slight threat of terrorism, enjoyed great popular success from 1934 onward. The writing and reading of modern fiction was the younger generation's rebellious expression against authority and part of the national struggle against the country's colonial status.

However it is not these two types of popular stories that have been singled out for attention or translation in existing accounts of the development of Burmese literature. Far more importance has been attached to the works of the generation of young graduates in Burmese literature from Yangon University who began writing at the start of the 1930s and whose works were published first in *Gandalawka* (The World of Books) and then, in 1934, in a collection entitled *Khit-san Pon-byin-mya* (Experimental Tales) edited by their teacher, Professor Pe Maung Tin. J. S. Furnivall had founded the periodical with the name *The World of Books* in 1925; in 1928 a Burmese section was added, and in 1930 it appeared under its Burmese name. Even though it had only a small monthly printing of five hundred copies, it was very influential in the development of the modern short story. Under the influence of their university studies of Burmese and English literature, the young graduates became more aware of the techniques of writing; they wanted to break away from the more traditional, overly ornate language, to broaden the subject matter, to deepen the psychological content, and to work out a new style of creative writing.

It is possible to detect a slightly defensive note in Pe Maung Tin's foreword to the work of his students. He says (in Burmese) that he offers these examples of modern literature by his own pupils to readers as part of a search for a new direction in Burmese literature and in the belief that the stories will help it to flourish and develop. He also explains that he chose the phrase *khit-san* to describe these new-style stories and sketches because he wants to test them on, try them out on, the reading public to judge its reaction; they are a sort of experiment. And he calls them *pon-byin* to indicate that they are tales about ordinary, everyday events and to distinguish them from Buddhist stories based on *jatakas* and *vatthus*.[12] He continues with a stout defense of the academic qualifications of his five pupils, pointing out that each has an honors degree in Burmese and is at present studying for an MA. He observes that this means they have made a thorough study of Pali, Burmese, and English, as well as Burmese and Mon inscriptions, and that they have studied how language changes and the various ways to investigate this change. So, he wonders, is their new style of writing perhaps the result of studying other languages? Finally, Pe Maung Tin asks the reader to enjoy the best things in the book and to judge it benevolently. It is on record that a few scholars did raise objections to the new style, but most readers approved of the collection.

Even today there are only a few Burmese who have not read the "tales" of Theikpan Maung Wa (real name U Sein Tin, 1899–1942), humorously ironic sketches of a district officer's life working for the British administration in the Indian Civil Service from 1929 to 1941 that are based on the author's own experiences.[13] His simplified language style, detailed records of everyday life, and sympathetic interest in ordinary people have been taken as a model by many postwar authors. In the earlier pieces he describes the places where he is carrying out his administrative duties; after the twelfth sketch, he introduces the protagonist, Maung Lu Aye, a young unmarried subdivisional officer, easygoing and levelheaded, who observes events without becoming too involved. In most of the sketches (called *wuthtu hsaung-ba* in Burmese) the author describes village life and its social and economic problems, which become more pressing as the 1930s draw to a close. In a spare, rather dry style laced with gentle sarcasm, he paints a picture of a village in the back of beyond with its petty feuds and dishonesty, its dirt and lack of sanitation.[14] In "Le-lan-bweh" (The Auction), he makes fun of the boastful nature of certain villagers who try to outbid each other at the annual auction of fishponds, with the result that they will end up paying the colonial government far more than they can hope to earn while being well aware that their false pride will land them in debt.[15]

Two other stories from this period have achieved lasting fame, as have their authors. One story, by Minthuwun (1909–2004), a particular favorite, is "Ba-gyi Aung Nya-deh" (You Lied to Me, Uncle) about a young boy's disappointment when an adult fails to keep his promise to give him a beautiful little figurine. Fifty years later, this story has acquired a modern relevance; it was once banned from republication because the censors felt it might be interpreted as an allegory of the military government's failure to keep its promises.[16] Another story, "Thu Maya" (His Spouse), by Zaw-gyi, tells of a husband who suddenly decides to become a monk, not through religious conviction but as a way to avoid the duties and troubles of family life, leaving his wife and three children in great difficulties.[17] At first his wife begs him to come back.

> Three months had now passed, though Ko Hsin had said he would wear the robes for only a month. His wife's aunt who had come over to help look after the children began to yearn for her own in her own village.
> "When will you return to lay life, Upazin?" she had asked the monk one day.
> The monk had not replied, but had only quoted some sacred verses extolling the life of a monk.... Ma Paw too wanted her husband to return home. She had alluded to the matter once or twice only to be turned back with sermons. Now the month of Wazo was near when the monks would go into retreat for 3 months. And the aunt was nagging her. Not knowing what to do she conferred with a friend. After some talk they burst into laughter.
> (Milton and Clifford 1961; translation by Win Pe)

After seeing that he is adamant, she finally asks his permission to go back to her aunt's village to look for another husband who will assist her with the children. This is too much for him. Faced with the reality of his wife transferring her affections to another man, the monk leaves the order and returns home to secular life. The story combines a masterly critique of Burmese social relationships with a subtle understanding of human psychology.

Stories of Village Life: Maung Htin and Man Tin

Maung Htin and Man Tin are two writers in the same tradition as Theikpan Maung Wa: administrative officials who write stories about village life for a largely urban readership. Their stories from the 1930s to early 1950s were all reprinted in collected volumes in the 1960s–1970s. Maung Htin came from a small town in the Irrawaddy Delta, but, being from an affluent, partly Chinese family, he was able to go on to study at the University of Yangon. By 1933 he had become a township officer, and by 1936 he had completed his first short story, "Taw" (Jungle)[18]. In another series of stories he introduced a young peasant hero through whom he describes, with loving detail and gentle humor, the courting customs of a typical Lower Myanmar village. We also gain a picture of everyday village life through his stories: periods of hard work broken by lazing around and getting drunk, visits to the Chinese noodle shop, helping a friend to elope with a girl, or gambling at the local pagoda festival. Although Maung Htin left the administrative service in 1940, he continued to write stories based on his experiences during the war and the period leading up to independence (1948) right up to 1972. After the takeover by the military regime in 1962, he felt even less enthusiasm for politics than after 1948 and so continued to write only about this earlier period (Allott 1982, 108–9).[19]

Man Tin also describes life in the districts as seen through the eyes of a young township officer, this time Maung Pyon Cho (Master Sweet Smile), a character who first appeared in his short stories in 1937. In 1942 Man Tin fled from Yangon to a small delta town where for three years he served as a township officer under the Japanese. In 1946 he recorded his wartime experiences in one of the first collections of short stories published after the war. In 1968, thirty-four of his stories, written between 1942 and 1950, were reprinted in one volume at a time when the military government was urging writers to support the building of a revolutionary socialist society by writing more works about peasant life (1968a). In his introduction to *Collected Stories of Township Officer Maung Pyon Cho*, Man Tin feels the need to apologize: "Maung Pyon Cho was sometimes drawn as a true picture, sometimes like a cartoon, and cartoons often exaggerate. This was especially so in some of my earlier stories, which are not included in the collection" (1968b). We cannot now know if the exclusion of some stories was due to early pressure from the government's Press Scrutiny Board to reject portrayals of unflattering or undesirable aspects of Burmese society, a policy that came to greatly influence literary publishing in the last decades of the twentieth century.

After Independence, 1950-1960

After the war and during the 1950s, short stories began to increase in number and to develop freely into different types. More stories appeared about harsh peasant life such as those by Hsin-byu-gyun Aung Thein and Kyeh Ni's fictional accounts of the impoverished living conditions of Burmese fishermen. At the same time there were the popular tales of romantic love by Tint Teh, as well as numerous accounts of soldiers' lives, whether fighting the Japanese or Myanmar's own insurgents as in Min Shin's stories. In Min Shin's collection *Tahka-don-ga Do Yeh-haw* (We Were Comrades Once, 1963), we are given an insightful record of life in the Burmese army during a time of uncertainty.[20] It reflects the change from fighting Western colonialists and the occupying

Japanese to quelling communist and ethnic insurgencies in the civil war that erupted between 1948 and 1958.

Another very popular storyteller, Thaw-da Swe (Hswei), began writing in 1947. At first he wrote humorous stories and later powerfully moving reminiscences of his life as a pony cart driver and tea shop proprietor during the Japanese occupation (1943–45). He continued to write down-to-earth descriptions of village life and his own iconoclastic lifestyle until his death in 1995 (Allott 1982, 123–25).[21]

As mentioned at the start of this essay, it was then and still is the monthly literary magazines that first publish short stories. Some magazines have a long life; some appear and disappear quickly but are still very influential. One of these was the magazine *Ta-ya* (Star), which was published from December 1946 until 1950 edited by writer, poet, and literary critic Dagon Ta-ya. It initiated discussion on the role of literature and the writer in society and published articles on literary theory; it adopted the term *sa-pe thit* (new literature) and introduced Russian literature to the Burmese reading public. Dagon Ta-ya's demand for *sa-pe thit*, or "people's literature," as it was also called, was in effect a call for socialist realism of the Soviet type, which was to depict the struggles of the poor and expose the evils of capitalism. At the same time he displayed a love of poetic language and unusual word choice and favored a style of writing nearer to the patterns of colloquial speech (Allott 1982, 114–15).[22]

Shwe-amyu-tay magazine

One of the writers whose early stories were published in *Ta-ya* was Kyi Aye, a young doctor with a very individualist outlook who wrote openly about sexual matters and the unfair treatment of women in society at a time when such subjects were considered unsuitable for a woman writer. She is often described as an existentialist influenced by the writing of Jean-Paul Sartre and Albert Camus. Although she left in 1972 to live and work in America, her writings are still admired, and four collections of her short stories were published in Myanmar during the 1990s.

Thein Pe Myint, Htin Lin, and Maung Tha-ra

The Khit-san writers, though modern in outlook, were not committed to any particular political ideology, unlike some of their contemporaries such as Dagon Ta-ya or the writer-politician Thein Pe Myint, who, in 1932 was studying Burmese, English literature, and modern European history in Mandalay. Later Thein Pe Myint moved to Yangon where he joined the nationalist Do Bama Asi-ayon (We Burmans Party). In an early story in 1934 he has already showed his concern about an unjust society. His short story "Nga lin nga ngwe" (Her Husband or Her Money) is about a rich landowning widow who is punished for her greed by being robbed by the peasants to whom she has shown no sympathy.[23]

Thein Pe Myint's stories are unlike the majority of the country sketches mentioned earlier. They nearly all highlight some social injustice: peasant indebtedness, the poverty of oil field workers, the tragedies of the civil war, or the precarious lives of the urban poor who are forced to trade on the black market or are driven into prostitution in order to survive.[24] His short story "Oil" illustrates his ability to portray sexuality in fiction, for which he has been criticized.[25]

> There were five families altogether in the quarters where they lived. A newly married couple lived in the next room on the south side; ever since they were married, they hadn't dared to enjoy themselves happily in bed for fear of being overheard in the next room. The young wife pleaded with her husband to speak quietly, pointing out that everything could be heard next door . . .
>
> "Let's go to bed," said the young husband.
>
> "Wait a moment, they haven't gone to sleep yet next door." When the young man heard his wife's answer, he gave a sigh and retired abashed . . .
>
> Ko Lu Dok couldn't sleep. He kept thinking about his young son and how he could get some oil for the lamp so that the boy could read a book containing some proper Buddhist prayers and not just what he had been taught at the Burmah Oil Company school. "My son is learning all the wrong things. He hasn't even learnt to say our Buddhist prayers yet. It's a good thing he can read, but not when he has to read what is not true." The noise of the pump machinery resounded through the village with its dull roar. "I can't buy paraffin/kerosene oil so that my son can read. Even though I work as hard as I do, I shall never manage to get out of debt, and I shall never be free of the consequences of past sin, shall I?" As he muttered complainingly to himself, the sound of giggling, like the clucking of a house lizard, came loudly from the next room, and Ko Lu Dok's train of thought was broken for a moment (Thein Pe Myint 1973, translation by Patricia Milne).[26]

The demand for short story collections grew during the 1970s. Two skilled authors here deserve special mention. Htin Lin (1919–96) read widely in English literature and was at one time a tutor in the English Department of the University of Yangon. Several of his early stories from the 1950s and 1960s vividly re-create the student life of the time and are fondly remembered by today's academics. His writing is rich in carefully observed human relationships, especially those between parent and child in which it is often difficult to find the middle way between strictness and permissiveness (Allott 1982, 122).[27] He is a fine craftsman, skillful at describing a rural or urban setting, and a true master of an effective ending. A seemingly artless description of the departure of a diesel express train from Yangon Station turns out to be a fascinating study of the relationships among a young woman, three young men who adore her, and a new companion she meets as she boards the train. The crosscut conversations of the other passengers waiting overnight on the station platform skillfully hint at contemporary social concerns.

Maung Tha-ra (1930–) was active in student affairs during his youth. After a short period in jail in 1953, he took up writing as a career without graduating from college. In the early phase of his writing career, he was known for his rather mannered prose style; in later stories and novels, his characters and themes assumed greater importance, and he wrote in a more straightforward style. He often portrayed the hypocrisies and contradictions of urban middle-class life in a way that appealed greatly to the modern Burmese reader. Maung Tha-ra was also able to portray empathetically the difficulties faced by the inexperienced soldier administrators who took over the government in the 1960s; at the same time, he did not hesitate to draw attention to the faults and inefficiencies of the "socialist revolution." He was a careful craftsman, who often went out of his way to experience at firsthand the kind of life his characters were to live, thus giving his stories great authenticity.[28]

Prison Stories, Medical Stories

The range of subjects in fiction broadened as the number of short stories increased in the 1950s and 1960s. Two types in particular deserve mention: prison stories and medical stories. Ludu U Hla, who was already a journalist and publisher before the war, spent three years as a political prisoner in the early 1950s (Allott 1997, 85–6). He related the life stories of many of the criminals he met in prison in a series of books written soon after his release. *Hlaung-gyaing-dwin-hma hnet-ngeh-mya* (The Caged Ones, 1958) portrays the lives of young people who tell in their own words of the social pressures and impoverished circumstances that led them into a life of crime. The book won a UNESCO award in 1958 and was translated into English by Dr Sein Tu (Ludu U Hla 1986). Other prison stories arose out of the experiences of a prison officer and were written to show how often a prisoner comes out of incarceration determined to continue his life of crime because the prison system is not able to offer any significant help.[29]

Medical tales were even more numerous. These were usually serious, medically informative, and above all cautionary, warning of the dangers of sexually transmitted diseases (HIV/AIDS did not appear until the early 1990s), drug taking, and heroin addiction. The military government viewed such stories favorably, and several collections were awarded National Literary Prizes. They were also popular with readers, as evidenced by the fact that Maung Thin, who published his first collection of *Hsaya zat-lan-son* (Doctor's Casebook) in 1959, was able to issue in 1977 an omni edition of forty of these stories drawn from five preceding books.

Women Writers

From 1920 onward, and especially in the second half of the twentieth century, women have played a major part in establishing and maintaining the popularity of the short story. During the colonial period, Dagon Khin Khin Lay (1904–80), born in Mandalay and the granddaughter of a minister at court, was a widely read author and a defender of Burmese traditional values whose stories appealed to the nationalist feelings of her readers. As well as writing love stories, she was one of the first to describe (in *Dagon* magazine from 1920 on) the daily life of the ordinary peasant, especially the hard lot of the poor woman. After the war she wrote less but took a leading part in promoting writing for and by women as the owner and publisher of *Yu-wadi Gya-neh* (Young Woman) magazine.

One of Myanmar's most important postwar women writers Ma Ma Lay (1917–82), started writing before the war and began to make a name for herself with her first novel, *Thu-ma* (She), the story of a woman's courage and resolve in the face of adversity (1944). When for a time she was unable to contribute her usual stories to the *Gya-neh-gyaw* periodical, the demand from readers led to the publication of one of the country's first books of collected short stories (Ma Ma Lay1948).[30] Similar to Thein Pe Myint, but more movingly and from a woman's point of view, Ma Ma Lay depicts the major political crises and social problems of modern Myanmar in her writings. She always took an active interest in political and social matters; and having acquired a good knowledge of Western culture, she was greatly aware of the conflict between Burmese traditions and Western attitudes.[31] Ma Ma Lay does not spare women who forget their natural dignity in an attempt to imitate Western behavior or who are thoughtlessly cruel to their servants out of greed and petty ambition. Her stories are full of closely observed detail with characters drawn with sympathy and perception. As in "A Blade of Grass," they often portray the victims of urban poverty or exploitation by corrupt officials.

> Military officer's wife Khin Ma Ma wrinkled her nose in disgust as she looked at the young shaven-headed girl. Fifty kyats might well be too much to pay for her. There was good reason to think twice about the five ten-kyat notes she had in her hand. The money had been won after sitting through a whole day's back-aching session of poker. . . .
>
> Laughter mingled with post-mortem comments as the well-to-do wives of officials and business men ended their poker session. When a large woman with a protruding stomach entered the dining room, a sudden hush fell. The fat woman's swarthy face was roughly smudged with *thanakha* on both cheeks. Clutching at her skirt and clinging to her thigh was a thin small child, just about three foot high, with a clean-shaven head. The ladies in the room could see only the half of the child not hidden by the woman's thigh.
>
> Brown-complexioned and with wide bold eyes, Shaven Head was dressed in a brand new cotton chemise which was much too large for her pitifully bony body, and the shoulder straps of the chemise hung loosely against her thin arms. Her faded and dirty skirt looked more like a piece of old worn-out cloth with both ends stitched together. Her wide-open eyes were fixed somewhat insolently on the pink-cheeked, red-lipped, dressed-up ladies in the room.
>
> "This little female?" asked the District Commissioner's wife who was standing next to Khin Ma Ma. The fat woman answered coyly and ingratiatingly, "This young girl is not for hire but for sale. I have brought her along in case anyone is interested." "Certainly not," said the D.C.'s wife.
>
> The Secretary's wife remarked that such a small girl was useless; the rice miller's wife pointed out that it would be quite a burden to keep and feed such a girl till she grew up. The advocate's grey-haired wife lit a cigarette, leaned back against her chair and spoke weightily. "It's not every day that you get such a chance to own somebody who will work for you for life. The most you may have to wait is one or two years. By the time she is eight or nine years old she should be ready for washing plates, grinding *thanakha*, washing clothes and scrubbing floors. I have no young children. If I had I would buy her as a companion for them.
>
> Khin Ma Ma at once remembered her seven-year old son Michael and her daughter Lily, aged 10. Both were incorrigibly naughty and unbearably

spoilt. This young female was just the answer. (Translation by Zaw Myint Thein, *Working People's Daily* 1973).[32]

During the 1950s, Ma Ma Lay was actively involved in the World Peace Movement; under the military government after 1962, her outspoken pen earned her three years in prison. After her release in the late 1960s, she wrote mostly novels as well as pursuing her interest in studying and writing about indigenous Burmese medicine.

Another woman writer who became popular in the 1950s and 1960s was Khin Hnin Yu (1925–2003), who continued to enjoy respect and a wide readership until her death. A masterful storyteller, she writes easily and fluently with a talent for creating atmosphere and describing scenery. Many of her works, which are often autobiographical, show her concern with the position of women in society. And the ten years she spent as a secretary in the office of Prime Minister U Nu gave her insight into the attractions and dangers of political power.[33] A characteristic story is a long one called "Nwe-hnaung Ywet-kyan" (The Last Leaves of Summer, 1961), a sad love story about a young Shan woman, a doctor, who marries a Burman politician. He is ruined by drink and the machinations of fellow politicians; she, disillusioned by the politician's desire for self-aggrandizement, goes off to the Chin Hills to work and devote herself to spreading the idea of a united Myanmar. This story reminds its readers of the civil war, the internal insurgencies that have plagued Myanmar since independence, and the difficulty of building national unity on ethnic diversity.

Some consider a younger woman writer of this generation, Khin Swe U (1933-), the daughter of Maha Swe, a better writer than Khin Hnin Yu. She has written many short stories and novels, which were published in the leading magazines of the 1960s, and is still writing today.[34]

The Golden Age of the Short Story (1970s-1980s): Mo Mo (Inya) and Ma Sanda

As we move into the late 1970s and 1980s and reach what might reasonably be called the golden age of the Burmese short story, women writers become even more prominent. The two who are always the first to be named, and whose stories have been collected and frequently reprinted, are Mo Mo (Inya) (1944–90) and Ma Sanda (1947–), the daughter of Man Tin. Both take as their subject matter urban family life and intergenerational relations, the problems of a rapidly changing society, government employees trying to survive on inadequate salaries, and educated women trying to cope with family and career. Each, however, has a different approach. Mo Mo (Inya) often seems saddened and overwhelmed by life's disappointments and difficulties, whereas Ma Sanda writes with humor and not a little satire and nearly always finds a way to make the reader look on the more cheerful side of life, as in her short story "An Umbrella."[35] It is interesting that Mo Mo (Inya)'s stories found more favor with the judges of the National Literary Awards as she won awards for her short stories in both 1982 and 1986; Ma Sanda had to wait until 1999 to win one award. Maybe the judges were afraid that Ma Sanda's satire would be interpreted as criticism of the government.

Take, for example, Ma Sanda's story "The Tale of 80,000 Horns" (1988) on a theme that appears frequently in poems and cartoons and is a subject rarely far from the minds of Myanmar's citizens today—corruption. The necessity of offering a sweetener to almost every government official in order to get him to carry out his normal duties has become part of everyday life. Nevertheless, the majority, including the State Peace and Development Council (SPDC), feel this to be an undesirable state of affairs; letters to the papers, stories, and cartoons about official corruption are encouraged, as long as the net is not cast wide enough to catch the military. Similarly, investigations into corruption take place and arrests are made but only of junior officials because when it becomes apparent that the trail is leading to a more powerful individual the investigation tends to collapse. Ma Sanda must have delighted her readers with her updated "folktale" about a local boss who falls into his own trap and is revealed to be just as corrupt as the people he is hoping to catch. Using a clever narrative device, she avoids explicitly saying that the official concerned was guilty.

Corruption among high-level officials was a fact of life before the 1988 State Law and Restoration Council (SLORC) takeover and has continued since then. The opportunities for personal enrichment increased with the opening of the Burmese economy, particularly in Mandalay, and some may feel that Ma Sanda's story is even more apt today than when it was written in 1988. Along the way, she takes a swipe at those who brazenly steal government building materials or demand payment for allowing visitors to see patients in the hospital. In another story, "The Uninvited Guest" (1989) Ma Sanda indirectly criticizes consecutive governments for failing to develop the country in the forty or so years since independence. In her story, a house (Myanmar) has a leaky roof (literally, "leaks from the roof"), a common phrase used to describe corruption at the highest level, and it has been built and rebuilt using a mixture of good and bad materials (referring to different policies followed in the years since independence).[36]

Mo Mo (Inya) and Ma Sanda were by no means the only women writing interesting short stories at that time. The author Maung Tha-ra edited a small book containing twelve stories by twelve contemporary women writers (1985). Frustratingly for the student of literature, he provides no introduction or reasons for his choices, only some dates and the briefest details about the authors, three of whom are doctors. The following year Maung Tha-ra published a second selection of recent stories (1986), this time by twelve young doctors, four of whom were women and two of whom, Ju and Mya Hnaung Nyo, were included in the earlier collection. At this time Ma Sanda also brought out a second collection of her recent short stories (1985).

It is evident that the short story continued to be extremely popular. One reason for this is surely because for a nation of keen readers the government-controlled daily press, with its endless reports of ministers' visits to building projects and exhortations to the population at large to work harder, was boring and contained almost no human interest stories. Television, introduced in 1980 and not yet widespread, was broadcast for just a few hours in the evening. The monthly magazines, with their many realist short stories provided the same sort of reassuring commentary on the lives people were leading as we in the West receive from our daily press and in our radio and TV soap operas.

A detailed analysis of the writing by women represented in the three collections described above reveals something of their preoccupations and approaches to literature. So what are their stories about? None is a fantasy, a mystery, or a thriller; all are realistic and set in the present day; none is about war, fighting, politics, or the government; none is even gently erotic or about either adultery or prostitution; and only one is an innocent love story. Many present a true picture of the difficulties and shortcomings of urban life, but none contains anything directly critical of the government.

Perhaps these stories are realistic because women have written them. They are stories full of precise detail about the ordinary lives of poor and middle-class people struggling with everyday problems, quarrelling with relatives or grieving over their untimely deaths, recalling childhood memories, worrying about what to cook for the next meal or how to find the money to pay for a doctor's visit, wondering if they should marry, or bitterly regretting having taken this step. Many of the stories portray the suffering caused by poverty, especially that of young children; the unhappiness of young mothers burdened by successive pregnancies; or the dilemma of middle-aged women looking after aged parents as well as their young children. We meet women doctors, teachers, divorced women bringing up their children alone, women who resent their unhelpful husbands, and women who abandoned their education to marry young. I am not able to say if this type of story, with its authentic dialogue and local atmosphere, appeals equally to men and women readers.

However, only two or three of the monthly magazines in which they appeared are thought of as being for women, and I know for certain that men enjoy reading Ma Sanda because of her sense of humor.

The majority of stories in Maung Tha-ra's collections (1985 and 1986) provide us with a general commentary on modern Burmese society, particularly in the area of personal and family relationships. Some stories by Ma Sanda could be called openly didactic but are written with a skill and humor that places them far above the traditional moral tale. One, entitled "I Hate Pasteur," is written entirely from the point of view of a rabies virus, cleverly teaching the reader about rabies and the potential danger posed by all dogs, including nice, middle-class dogs, and about the need to go immediately for treatment if bitten. The image of the virus, first gloating as it multiplies in a poor boy's leg and then cringing as it faces the onslaught of injections, leaves a stronger impression on the reader than a straightforward warning.

Another story, "One Sesame Seed, One Star, One Drop of Ink," written originally for a government youth magazine in 1983, makes the point that the quality of life in society is determined by the sum of all our small, individual acts, however insignificant they may seem.[37] Three episodes are described, typical of life in Yangon then and now. A woman on her way home from shopping pauses after passing a huge stinking refuse pile at the corner of the street and becomes involved in a discussion with a neighbor about whether or not one should wrap up one's rubbish before tossing it on the pile. For hygiene's sake it should be wrapped, but the neighbor says he cannot afford to use newspaper that could be resold. Next it is early morning, and she is riding on a bus to visit her elderly mother before work when the bus breaks down. Most Yangon buses were, and still are, decrepit and desperately overcrowded. If the passengers are willing to get out and push the bus, it might start; but they don't, so they have to change to another bus and are late. When the woman finally reaches her office, she finds that thoughtless colleagues have left the fans on all night, wasting precious electricity—precious because Yangon suffers frequent power cuts, with some districts receiving electricity only two evenings a week. The story is told with humor, and the author does not labor the moral point.

From a story by a woman doctor, Win Win Lat, we learn a great deal about the state of health care in Myanmar.[38] In this story a young woman doctor trudges all over Yangon and its outskirts trying to find a place to open a small private surgery. Government posts in hospitals are scarce, the pay is meager, and there is no national health service. Finally, she sets herself up in a poor suburb. Early on she has to decline an offer of marriage from a patient by pretending that she is married to a soldier away at the front. This is a rare reference to the continuing civil war in Myanmar. She experiences enormous difficulties in getting medicines for her patients as the system is subject to chronic abuse and medicines are allocated from government centers. Older doctors can buy a week's or a month's allocation at a time; new doctors get only two days' supply each time they queue up. In order to supplement their meager incomes, young doctors take their full allocation of all types of medicines, retain what they must have for treating their poorest patients, and resell the rest on the black market. For the majority of people, medicine is available only at black market prices, so serious illness is a disaster for poor families, and likely to leave them permanently in the hands of the moneylender. The young doctor struggles with her conscience as she has grown up believing that it is a doctor's duty to serve her fellow human beings and not exploit them, and yet she herself must live on something. She works long hours, often going home by bus at midnight. The story is given a positive ending as the doctor wins the trust and affection of her patients and sticks to her principles.[39]

A well-loved story by Ma Sanda, entitled "TV Disease" (1982), carries a humorous warning about the disturbing effects of western consumer goods, in this case a 202 TV set purchased in Japan with money saved during a study visit. The owners are very proud of their television and eagerly welcome the neighbors in to watch it. But, like a royal white elephant, the set proves to be very expensive for the family to maintain because of all the cups of coffee and snacks they must serve to the neighbors who crowd in to watch it. The proud owner is reduced to a sleepless near invalid, fearing that he has contracted tuberculosis and wishing that he had never bought the wretched set.

The material conditions characteristic of the different social classes are clearly reflected in these stories, although there are almost no overt references to military rank or army families. The wealthy have houses with a telephone, a refrigerator and a TV. A large garden and a car mark them as even wealthier. The poorest families can cook only a stew of green leaves flavored with a little dried fish to eat with their rice and are often so much in debt that they have to pawn their family allocation book, which enables them to buy cheap rice and oil at the people's shop. In several stories we see the heavy economic burden that may fall upon the eldest daughter in a poor family as the need for her to earn money supersedes the importance of her education beyond the age of ten or eleven.

We learn a good deal about doctors and their patients since many doctors are also short story writers.[40] Patients expect doctors to cure them quickly; if not, they look for another doctor. This puts a young doctor under pressure to treat patients by giving them an injection. Burmese patients expect an injection for almost every ailment, and doctors usually provide them. There is a serious shortage of doctors in provincial hospitals since young graduates from Yangon and Mandalay are reluctant to take up these posts far from any kind of family support. In a disheartening story by Mo Mo (Inya) a young doctor's mother dies because she is sent to a hospital where there is no qualified doctor.[41] As a result he decides to go back to his native region to work in one of these country hospitals, and in doing so he comes to realize how differently fate has treated him, a country boy, compared to a young woman he has grown up with. She is now married and too poor to send her daughter to school in town even though he offers to pay for it.

In several of these stories we see that family ties are as strong as they have ever been. We see how much parents are respected and cared for in their old age; how four generations manage to live together in one house, humoring an ailing and cantankerous grandmother; and how older siblings feel it is their duty to give financial support to younger siblings and see them through their education.

These works by women writers are characteristic of much short story writing of the 1980s. They are strikingly realistic in their descriptions, for example, of mothers' feelings about being pregnant for the fourth or fifth time, tied down by small children, wondering why they bothered to work for a university education and wishing their husbands would take on more family duties.[42] Mo Mo (Inya) also writes about the unhappiness of well-off married women whose husbands have gone abroad to work. Although the husbands send back substantial sums of money and even cars, the wives have taken lovers. Before the 1980s, few Burmans went abroad to work, but with the failure of the Burmese economy to keep pace with surrounding countries, first seamen and later construction and other workers took jobs abroad, leaving their families behind.

Literary Criticism and Debate

Before the 1970s there was little published literary criticism and in-depth reviewing of new works. In the mid-1960s the military government had stipulated that literature must be *pye-thu akyo-byu* (beneficial to the people) and must assist in building socialism. The result was that the discussion of literature became highly politicized, and writers who were more interested in form, technique, and style were condemned as being in favor of "art for art's sake." However, in 1983 a newly established magazine, *Thabin* (Performance), asked Aung Thin, a leading critic of modern literature, to write a regular new feature entitled "My Favorite Short Story." He was to survey each month's total output of magazine short stories, choose his favorite, and write a reasoned appraisal in support of his choice. He carried out this task without a break for twenty-five months.

This series of articles aroused great interest among readers and probably helped to create a greater awareness of the value of a more critical and analytical approach to fiction writing. The two collections by Maung Tha-ra, (1985, 1986) were published shortly after the series in *Thabin* came to an end; three of the stories selected by Aung Thin were included by Maung Tha-ra, but as mentioned earlier, without any accompanying editorial comments. Surprisingly, one of the works chosen by Aung Thin in 1984, "Htamein-le tahteh" (One Little Sarong), is missing from his 1999 publication.[43]

"One Little Sarong" is a touching account of a young girl whose last wearable *htamein* (sarong) splits as she squats to cook the family's pitiful meal. Her mother had died the previous year, leaving her to care and find food for her three younger sisters. The story ends with an unforgettable scene in which the girl struggles to get a large fish caught in a fish trap out of the river. She succeeds in dragging the fish to the shore, but in her struggle to get the hook out her worn *htamein* comes loose and floats away without her noticing until she gets out of the water. Determined not to lose this prize meal, the girl clasps the fish to her body and bravely runs home naked through the village. Some Burmese considered this story to be in poor taste because it was so shocking. It was the first work of an as yet unknown writer, Nu Nu Yiy (Inwa), now a very successful author, and was not included in Aung Thin's 1999 publication because the Press Scrutiny Board banned its republication. Between the year it was written (1984) and 1999, there was great political upheaval in Myanmar. The prodemocracy demonstrations of 1988 had been followed by even stronger military control of the country; censorship of privately printed material had become even tighter and more arbitrary. Stories that were felt to present the country in a less than favorable light were often banned, and it seems that this picture of poverty did not project the desired image.

Literary Prizes

Nevertheless, whatever problems writers experienced with the Press Scrutiny Board, public interest in the literary aspects of short fiction had been aroused, as can be seen from the regular review articles and discussions that began to appear in many of the monthly magazines during the 1990s. When the writer Mo Mo (Inya) died tragically young in 1990, her husband and a group of writers set up an organization in her memory to arrange lectures and establish an annual prize for new short story writers. The competition was held for four years (1994–97), and in the first year attracted six hundred entries![44] A panel of four judges managed to select sixteen winners from this amazing number.[45]

Since 1963, the military government had been running a scheme of National Literary Awards for different genres of literature. Many consider these awards to be somewhat discredited because the criteria used to select the winners are primarily political and nationalistic. The effort by the independent writers to establish a private prize was a challenge to officialdom; not surprisingly, several of the stories selected as winners were banned by the censors from publication in the small books published after each competition. A story about a schoolteacher succumbing to great pressure to allow a pupil to cheat on exams, awarded second prize by the independents in 1995, was banned despite the well-known fact that teachers were regularly bribed. On the other hand, in 1996 Daung Ne Min's revealing true-to-life story, "Htaung win-za" (Prison Visiting), was chosen and published in spite of the fact that it gave an accurate picture of the prisoners and conditions in Insein prison.[46]

> My name is Sein Yun and I was born in prison. That's because my mother was heavily pregnant when she came in. She got a stiff sentence for dealing in drugs. Not long after I was born she fell ill and died. They didn't know who my father was, couldn't trace any relatives, in the end they sent me to a children's home. Luckily, one day, a person turned up who wanted to adopt me. My adoptive father was very good-natured and loved me very much, just like his own son. Because of him I learnt to read and write and never lacked for anything. But in time, blood will out. I just couldn't behave decently and kept running away from home . . . However much my father tried to set me on the right road it was no use. In the end he disowned me. I couldn't care less and by then I was just going in and out of prison without thinking twice about it (Anna Allott, trans.).

Another example of a controversial subject that passed the censors' scrutiny was the first-prize award in the 1994 competition, a harrowing story, "Bed No. D12," about a young man in a hospital dying of AIDS.

Nu Nu Yiy and Ju

Two young women writers who became popular during the 1980s were Nu Nu Yiy (Inwa), mentioned above, and Ju. Both are from Upper Myanmar, the former from a village (Inwa) near Mandalay, the latter from Yenan-gyaung, a town near the oil fields. Both had to study university subjects (mathematics and medicine) they were not interested in pursuing but they were finally able to take up writing as a full-time career. Nu Nu Yiy is deeply sympathetic toward the poor and oppressed in society and has written many stories that vividly, often in a somewhat dramatized manner, portray the hardships and suffering of those at the bottom of society.[47] She displays a special talent in her stories for conveying the feelings and attitudes of young people growing up in extreme poverty based on her personal observations and experiences traveling around the country and on interviews (Allott 1993, 30–36).

The writer Ju trained and qualified as a doctor but, as she says, only due to the insistence of her mother. Her first story was published in 1981; subsequently, she gave up working as a doctor and achieved a certain notoriety with her first short novel, *Ahmat-taya* (Remembrance, 1987), in which she wrote openly about an unmarried young couple living together. Her stories are completely different in style and content from those of Nu Nu Yiy, exploring intimate personal feelings, psychological states, and dreams, often with feminist themes. She has gained a wide and admiring readership. Interviewed in 2003, she pointed out that the Press Scrutiny Board is more fearful of the power and effect of the short story than of the novel. Both she and Nu Nu Yiy have had a considerable number of their short stories banned.

Mya Than Tint's Portraits

One of Myanmar's most prolific contemporary writers, Mya Than Tint (1928–98), a former communist who had begun writing for *Ta-ya* magazine in 1949 and spent a total of eleven years in prison, has left us a series of fascinating portraits based on interviews with ordinary people.[48] They first appeared in *Kalya* magazine between 1987 and 1991 and were then included in two volumes in 1993. One of them, "Miss Paleface," reveals the strength of Burmese women.

> Think about it, Saya. My father had gone away, my mother was suffering from clinical depression. I had four sisters younger than me. If I didn't assume responsibility for the family who would?
>
> That's when I tried to get the sawmill back into business again. I got in touch with the workers and machine operators. They used to look down on me for being a woman. Some of them even tried to tease me and touch me up. But I don't tolerate any of that and I lose my temper quickly. If any of them try it on too much they get a slap from me.
>
> Look at how I live now, Saya. This sawmill is about 3 miles from town. I have to come and go by bike. I have a quick breakfast of fried rice at 5.30 and then cycle over here to let the workers in. I have to manage them, tell them which logs to use for which jobs, what size of planks to cut and so on. Then I measure the output and calculate the tonnage. We take a short break for lunch and then carry on till half past four. Then I cycle home. That's what I do every day, in all seasons, riding my bike to work and back.
>
> How did I learn to run a sawmill? Experience, Saya, that's all. (Mya Than Tint 1996, translation by Ohnmar Khin)[49]

After his release from prison, Mya Than Tint began translating rather than writing fiction. As he says: "By 1972, the Press Scrutiny Board was already in existence and we could no longer write quite freely. Sometimes books were banned, sometimes passages were painted out by the censors. Strange to say, even some of my translations have been banned." Of his life stories of ordinary Burmese men and women, he says:

> My interviews are intended to let Burmese people know about the contemporary life of our country, the life of people from every class. Ours is a closed society, we don't understand enough about one another. We in Rangoon do not know how people suffer in the countryside, how hard they have to work because we have to rely on the official media which says nothing about this. And people in the country don't know about life in Rangoon, in the towns, for instance about how a karaoke machine works and so on. I am not writing for the outside world but for Burmese people. I think my interviews are popular with the readers, especially younger ones. (Mya Than Tint, 1996 p.11 and 12)

This statement goes a long way toward explaining the continuing importance and relevance of the realistic short story in Myanmar at the beginning of the twenty-first century. To the extent that the censors permit, it plays the role of the popular press and TV in the West.

Humor, Satire, and New-Style or Postmodern Writing

During the 1990s the popularity of the short story showed no sign of waning. Together with the realistic portrayals of contemporary life, two other types of story should be noted: the humorously satirical, and the "new-style" or "modern" (*han-thit* or *mau-dan*) writing of often-enigmatic musings. Interestingly, it is more often the latter type that is banned because the censors, being unable to work out what they mean, are afraid to let them pass.[50]

Two extremely popular writers of humorous and satirical short stories, who came to public notice in the 1980s and 1990s, are Win Pe and Ne Win Myint, both from Mandalay. Until 1995, when he left Myanmar to live in the United States, Win Pe divided his time between making video films, painting, and writing. His varied career has equipped him with experiences that give power and authenticity to his short stories; at the same time his artist's eye enables him to portray a vivid scene in just a few lines.[51] Many of his literary sketches are amusing tales of mostly male Burmese life, rich in dialogue and comic situations. They are often set in tea shops, the primary venue for what remains of political debate in Myanmar. The stories move rapidly, and often comically at first, but the mood can change suddenly. At the end of the story the reader may be left wondering if there is a deeper meaning to the events described. The short story "Clean, Clear Water" illustrates this talent.[52] In it the protagonist, Ba Gyi Kyaw, infatuated with modern scientific technology, instructs his large extended family to take better care of the toilets: "To his way of thinking, toilets are a person's world, the most important things in life. Time and again he says that a person's health, wealth, wisdom, and mental balance depend upon toilets more than anything else" (Yamada 2002, 13). Ba Gyi Kyaw has become an expert on all aspects of the subject and decides that his family will install a "new experimental toilet" one that produces filtered water suitable to drink. After its installation, he even invites a biochemistry professor over to test the filtered water's quality in front of his resistant family. The water passes the test, yet we are left to wonder at the end whether Ba Gyi Kyaw will really be able to drink it.

In Win Pe's second collection of stories (1992), the humor is still present, though more sardonic, while the theme of violence and violent death appears more frequently. Aung Thin said of him, "From his deceptively simple, often comic narratives there emerge powerful images of the greed, anger and stupidity of human life."[53]

Ne Win Myint, a younger writer than Win Pe, began writing in 1972 and by the 1990s was firmly established in the affection and respect of the reading public, having contributed nearly 100 articles and well over a 150 short stories to Myanmar's numerous monthly magazines. Many of his stories evoke the dry and dusty villages of the dry zone, the heartland of Upper Myanmar; others give a vivid picture of Yangon where he used to work as a government servant. His earlier work, usually very realistic, could be nostalgic, moving, and sad. Recently a playful note has appeared in many of his tales, sometimes satirical, sometimes ludicrous, humorously making fun of authority. If he intends the story to be critical of the current political situation, he skillfully avoids problems with the censors by setting it well back in time. He uses this device in "Thadun," an allegory of political corruption written in 1993, which begins, "This is a story about a small incident that happened during the days of the village chiefs. I should set the record straight because I fear some people will think that it happened just recently. It isn't a story about anything very out of the ordinary. It's just about five people who performed a small one-act play" (Yamada 2002, 4–5).[54] The "small one-act play" and the subsequent debacle of its production may be interpreted as illustrating the destructive tendency of self-serving leaders.[55]

In his 1990 story "The Advertising Wagon" there is a detailed and loving description of the old traveling cinema, now replaced in the villages by the video parlor.[56] However, the story could be interpreted as a comment on the failure of successive military governments to modernize the country. The difference between the pre-1988 "socialist" regime and the then SLORC regime was felt by many to be merely one of name.[57] Taking up where his father left off, the son in the story tours the villages making exaggerated claims in the same way the SLORC boasts about its (non)achievements.

The titles of several recent pieces included in a selection of Ne Win Myint's most popular stories give a hint of his style of mocking humor: "Nescafe,"[58] "Video," "Plutonium," "Remote Control," and "Body Lingo" (2000). He depicts the impact of new technology on a simple workman unable to comprehend it, the confusion caused in the mind of a well-meaning rural official by reading in old magazines about the uncontrolled spread of nuclear weapons, or the fatal effect of tasting Nescafe on a villager used to drinking only local-grown coffee. It seems that "Nescafe" (1990) became a great favorite and was often asked for by his audiences, perhaps because the ending is so grotesque that there is little agreement about its interpretation. In Burmese, Nescafe can sound like "Nat coffee," that is, the drink of the *nats* (gods), which is how it tasted to a poor villager, who turned against his usual coffee from the local tea shop and began to waste away for want of Nescafe. His wife managed to procure the remains of a jar for him, but when this was finished he began to pine again, clutching the empty jar tightly to his nose. Then he died. Twenty years later, a peasant plowing his field unearthed an arm still gripping a Nescafe jar that could not be prised away. By this time, of course, Nescafe and many other types of new-style drinks were readily available in the village coffee shop.

Ne Win Myint's stories appeal to the politically sophisticated reader, as well as to those who just like a rattling good yarn, to a generation that feels nostalgia for the old times so lovingly conjured up in his stories, as well as to those who admire his simple but effective style and mastery of language. His stories especially appeal to those who feel there is some deeper significance in the many farcical situations he describes. One of Ne Win Myint's published collections is entitled *Bazin Yin-gweh* (The Cicada and Other Stories, 1995). The Burmese word for cicada combines the words for "dragonfly" and "heartbreak": a beautiful flying insect that sings on and on as if its heart would break. The writer of the foreword to the collection wonders why this title was chosen but leaves it to the reader to decide. Maybe the author means he will simply keep on and on writing and drawing attention to the ludicrous things that are going on in the country until his heart breaks with the effort.

The 2000 collection also has a short introduction written by a fellow writer. The editor confesses that he planned to read a couple of stories and then write the introduction, but after reading the first one he could not put the book down. None of the terms used currently to characterize an author's work such as *true-to-life, modern, post-modern, symbolic,* and *magical* came to mind as he read; it was just the images and scenes conjured up by the stories that stuck in his mind. In fact, Ne Win Myint's chameleon-like talent means that among the 150 or so stories that he has already written there are many to which one could attach one of these various labels. This is why his work both delights today's readers and gives them cause to reflect.

Other authors have been developing various forms of experimental writing in a small but significant literary movement that is still controversial among Burmese intellectuals. The name New Style (*Han-thit*) is derived from an experimental literary magazine of that name, published since the late 1980s. It is frequently associated with a younger, post-1988 generation of authors and appears to be most popular with urban-dwelling high school and university youths. Jennifer Leehey has argued that New Style writing "is an indicator of current conditions for meaning-making in Burma today" (2005, 176). She analyzes its development as both a negative reaction to the literary style of realism, popular in Myanmar during the 1960s and 1970s, and as a reaction to the SLORC-SPDC regulatory and censorship system. Although New Style writing is often described as a literary expression of "art for art's sake," it can also be interpreted as a semiotic response to a coercive style of government control over public discourse, which consistently presents a "reality" that contradicts lived experience.

Influenced by western postmodernism, New Style or modern (*mau-dan*) writing generally privileges "textual form over content." It is subjectivist, a literary form that is often stream of consciousness as it explores internal experience, symbolically expressed in fantastic, enigmatic, or magical imagery, as in Zaw Zaw Aung's "Nameless Prose No. 12."

> Watering and cleaning the small lawn. I can't take on this responsibility, so I give it to my best friend, Miss Rose. She will handle it. If something is wrong, look to tomorrow. The present can be found there. Upon the lake, the moonlight establishes a castle of laughter. Don't let the wicked men come. (Leehey 2005, 194–95)

Multiple images in a shifting context of unstable meaning have led some Burmese intellectuals to consider this type of writing as evidence of a deterioration in contemporary intellectual life, a superficial, self-indulgent borrowing from Western postmodernism. Others find it exciting and innovative.

Contemporary Literary Developments

Along with the continuing popularity of the short story, monthly literary magazines from the 1980s onward began to carry more and more interviews with writers, discussions of their attitudes toward writing, and, at times, reviews of actual works.[59] The innovative series of articles by Aung Thin in 1984–85 on his favorite short stories seems to have encouraged other critics.[60] In 2000 a useful guide to ten contemporary short story writers was published. In addition to the writers mentioned in this essay, there are essays on the authors Win Si Thu, Pe Myint, Thaik Htun Thet, Maung Lun Kyin, Thitsa Ni, Myint Than, and Mo Nyein E, each followed by one of their most popular stories (Le Ko Tin 2000). Of this group, the first two deserve extra study, as does the Mandalay writer Nyi Pu Lay, who spent nine years in prison (1990–99). Unlike his father, Ludu U Hla, who was able to draw on and write freely about his experiences in prison during the 1950s, Nyi Pu Lay found that stories overtly reflecting his life in prison were not publishable, for example, "Country Boy" (2000), which tells of a young boy in prison being groomed by an old convict for rape.[61] As an ex-prisoner, Nyi Pu Lay's writing comes under special scrutiny and is more likely to be banned, but, he has been able to publish a considerable amount since his release.

Padaukpwinthit magazine, first published in 1991

It is impossible to do justice to all the talented authors writing short stories in present-day Myanmar. They are only one element in a strong and continuing literary tradition, which, side by side with poetry and the novel, continues to flourish in spite of political uncertainties, economic difficulties, and arbitrary government censorship. With the increasing interest being shown in literary developments in Myanmar, both by native scholars and by students of cultural and social history from abroad, there is now the prospect of more short Burmese fiction being made available in translation to a world readership.

Notes

[1] The Readers' Choice series *Myitkyina* (Northern Moon) originated in Upper Myanmar under the sponsorship of the entrepreneur U Htun Htun. Two volumes of selected stories from 1995 were published in 1996, then subsequently one volume per year has been published through 2003. The volumes contain twenty or more short stories written by both well-known and new writers, which are selected from a wide range of the previous year's monthly magazines. There is no editorial material, only the place and date of first publication. These small anthologies in paperback format appear regularly and sell out rapidly. It is certain that to be included in these annual volumes is a valued achievement, perhaps more highly valued than an official National Literary Award, even though it brings no financial reward. The first book of the series in 1996 cost one hundred kyat; the 2003 book cost eight hundred kyat, an indication of the disastrous inflation rate prevailing in Myanmar.

[2] U Aung Thin was formerly a lecturer in modern literature in the Myanma Sa (Literature) Department of Yangon University.

[3] The fifteen magazines were *Shu-mawa, Sa-pe Loktha, Mo-we, Ngwe-ta-yi, Mya-wadi, Sanda, Pe-hpu-hlwa, Sitpyan, Thaung-byaung htwe-la, Giti pade-tha, Yok-shin meggazin, Yokshin myet-hman, Thabye, Thwe-thauk,* and *Pan.*

[4] The three additional magazines were *Kalya, Cherry,* and *Dagon.*

[5] See the article by Saw Lu (U Saw Tun), currently Professor of Burmese at Northern Illinois University, DeKalb, who writes about this difficulty and the need for more translations (1993).

[6] For example, the informative account of Burmese short stories by Thaw Kaung and Than Htut (2003) makes no mention, not even in a footnote, of the establishment of the PSB and the introduction of censorship in the mid-1960s. And their list of reference works does not include the American PEN Center freedom to write report *Inked Over, Ripped Out: Burmese Storytellers and the Censors* (Allott 1993). It does include Anna Allott's article on the short story in Burma (1982).

[7] Censorship has also created numerous problems for scholars and academics writing in Myanmar, both in English and Burmese. From the 1970s onward, some people, including writers, have fallen out of favor with the military regime and have become, sometimes only temporarily, nonpersons. They may not be invited to chair an important seminar, their names may be blacked out in articles, their photographs may not be published, or some of their writings may be banned from reprinting. It must be stressed that the list of

those in disfavor can vary from time to time; the only person who may never be favorably referred to is Daw Aung San Suu Kyi. Similarly, the government considers the description of certain events and circumstances, even if well known, to be off limits because they do not present the country in a "correct" and favorable light.

[8] For example, a recent work in Burmese entitled *Hnahseh ya-zu Myanma Sa-ye-hsaya-mya-hnint sa-zu-sayin* (Myanmar Writers of the Twentieth Century and Their Works), prepared by a thirteen-member editorial committee from the Information and Public Communications Directorate, was published in April 2003. Several important twentieth-century writers are not included in this book, which does include several insignificant ones. The introduction makes no mention of the criteria used to select authors for inclusion in this seemingly official work; indeed, shortly after its publication, a very critical review by a former national librarian, Myint Kyaing, writing under his pen name Aung Mo Hsaung, appeared in the weekly journal *Mo-hsan-pan* (2003). He points out the compilers' failure to explain the basis of their selection and also notes numerous errors and omissions in their work. In particular, he shows how inadequately the compilers have researched the authors' different, and in some cases extremely numerous, pseudonyms. The reviewer does not actually ask why certain leading writers have been omitted such as P. Monin, Khin Swe U, and Htin Lin (who are mentioned in this survey); their omission looks like sheer incompetence. The absence of others can be explained for political reasons, for example, Minthuwun (1909–2004); Maung Tha-ra, and the poet Tin Moe (1933–2007), both were living in America; and San San Nweh, who served a long prison sentence after 1989. It is very possible that the reviewer was reticent about including the names of politically incorrect writers for fear of coming up against some blacklist held by the censors. This review provides a concrete example of the ongoing problems in the Burmese literary domain caused by the fear of censorship.

[9] An indication of *Dagon's* importance is the number of writers, such as Dagon Ta-ya and Dagon Khin Khin Lay, who chose pen names that contain the word *Dagon* because they first came to be known through its pages.

[10] *Khit-san* literally means "to test the age" or "experiment for the times."

[11] Many Burmese literary historians recognize a close resemblance to popular Victorian novels in the early novels of P. Monin and hence suggest that his short stories were also adapted from English. However, in view of the local settings of his short stories, in which he often showed how Burmans could be as commercially successful as the Indians and Chinese who had settled in the

country if only they would exert themselves, they would seem to be original rather than adaptations.

[12] *Jatakas* are narratives based on the Buddhist scriptures. *Vatthus* is the term for a narrative based upon the Buddhist scriptures. It is worth noting that *pon-byin* is also the Burmese word for folktale.

[13] These tales were published in *Khit-san pon-byin-mya*, vol. 1 (1934) and vol. 2 (1938).

[14] Dunn (1947) translates the title of this short story as "Limbo."

[15] This short story, translated by Yin Wyn, was published in The Working People's Daily's *One Thousand Hearts and Other Modern Burmese Short Stories* (1973, 129–36).

[16] "You Lied to Me, Uncle" was recently reprinted as the first story in *One Hundred Burmese Short Stories by One Hundred Authors of the Twentieth Century* (2005). This ambitious, 990-page collection was edited by the grandson of Gya-neh-gyaw (Ma Ma Lay). It reflects the continuing popularity and viability of the short story genre in Myanmar.

[17] This short story was translated by Win Pe and published in Milton and Clifford 1961, 138–42.

[18] For this story, see Maung Htin 1976.

[19] Maung Htin's skill and charm as a writer have stood him in good stead, and he has managed, without writing to their tune, to retain the respect of the military government. On 24 November 2003, Prime Minister Khin Nyunt presented him with a National Writer's Lifetime Award.

[20] This book was awarded a Sa-pe Beikman Prize for the best short story collection of 1963.

[21] Among his several collections, see *Bawa Hto Hto* (Life Here and There, 1961).

[22] Now in his eighties and unable to see, Dagon Ta-ya is still greatly loved and revered by all prodemocracy Burmese writers.

[23] This story is in his collection *Wuthtu-do baung-gyok* (Thein Pe Myint 1966). For translations of some of these stories and a critique, see Thein Pe Myint (1973, 1999).

[24] An example is "She Broke Her Oars While Rowing" in *Sweet and Sour* (Thein Pe Myint 1999, 117–38).

[25] One Burmese critic, Maung Swan Yi, has even said that some of Thein Pe Myint's work reads like soft porn (1976).

[26] This was first published in 1938.

[27] For example see the story "Diesel" in *Saung-gyo tin-thi thachin-than* [Too Harsh a Note], Htin Lin, 1977.

[28] In the foreword to the 1969 collection *Nyi-ako mathi tathi* (A Confusing Time), the editor writes: "Maung Tha-ra is a person who supports the naturally progressive aspects of Burmese society but who at the same time courageously exposes its unnatural and contradictory aspects. . . . Some people of immature judgment may form the wrong impression of Maung Tha-ra's socialist realism and may feel wrongly that he is attacking the Burmese Way to Socialism. On the contrary, to this day, things are happening just as he portrays them; the present time really is a time of confusion, a time of revolutionary change"(Maung Tha-ra 1969). These lines were written when the military government had been in power for about seven years, and they reveal that some members were beginning to feel that too much realistic criticism in literature was not helpful to their cause. By the 1990s, Maung Tha-ra had left Myanmar to live in Thailand. This may explain why his name does not appear in a government publication *Myanmar Writers of the Twentieth Century and Their Works*, compiled by the Department of Information in April 2003.

[29] Stories by Yan Aung Maung Maung are discussed in Aung Mun 1973.

[30] As with several other early short story collections, the foreword explains why stories that have already appeared were being republished: "Readers are demanding to know why she has stopped writing. In the West, authors who are as well known and popular as Ma Ma Lay usually have their stories published in a collected edition, so we are venturing to do the same."

[31] This is the theme of her perceptive and tragic novel, *Mon-ywe mahu* (Not Out of Hate), which was awarded a Sarpay Beikman prize in 1955 and is available in an English translation by Margaret Aung-Thwin (Ma Ma Lay 1991). Her novel *Blood Bond* was also published in an English translation (Ma Ma Lay 2004).

[32] From the collection *Twei dazeint-zeint* (Reverie: Collected Short Stories, 1963). It was translated by Zaw Myint Thein in *One Thousand Hearts and Other Modern Burmese Short Stories* (*Working People's Daily* 1973).

[33] For example, in a story called "Khan Pwint" (1955), quoted in Than Htut and Thaw Kaung 2003, we are shown a village girl who marries a young politician who has just become a parliamentary secretary to the government;

she had helped him in the fight to gain independence, but she is not happy in the new society in which her husband now moves, as he learns to play tennis, dines frequently at foreign embassy functions, and mixes with Westernized town girls. The story ends with the wife, ignored by her husband, returning to her village greatly disillusioned. Another story, written about the same time, portrays the life of pagoda slaves, the lowest class of Burmese society, who, although they were officially freed at independence, continue to be socially stigmatized and despised.

[34] These magazines included *Shu-mawa*, *Thwe-thauk*, *Ngwe Ta-yi*, and *Mya-wadi*.

[35] "An Umbrella," was first published in *Sandar* magazine in July 1990. It was translated into English by Than Than Win (2002).

[36] This story was eventually published in a government-sponsored magazine, *Sitpyan* (Veteran), because several editors of privately owned magazines had interpreted the story as being hostile to Daw Aung San Suu Kyi and for a while refused to publish Ma Sanda's work.

[37] The title of the story reflects a Burmese proverb included at the end of the story: "One sesame seed won't make oil," meaning that only a significant number of acts will facilitate change. This story is interesting because it humorously reveals contemporary economic problems.

[38] The title of this story, "Trying to Keep the Rain Off with a Coconut Palm Leaf," (1982) refers to the act of carrying out an impossible task with inadequate resources.

[39] The story, "Salu-ywet hpyu-let-weh kaing mo-lo" is collected in Maung Tha-ra (1985, 61–125).

[40] This is the result of a state system of higher education that automatically channels students with the highest marks in the tenth standard exit exam into medical studies. Many who might otherwise have followed an arts career find themselves studying to become doctors.

[41] The story "Ma Nyo Pya Kaw-li-ya chaung-nabe-hma ne thi" (Ma Nyo Pya Lives by the Creek) is collected in Maung Tha-ra (1985, 187–246).

[42] In Burmese this sub genre is called *bawa thayok hpaw* (portraying real life) or *thayok-hman sa-pe* (true to life).

[43] See my introductory comments on pages 157–58 above.

[44] The seventh volume of this independent literary prize appeared in 2004.

[45] The judges were Aung Thin, Maung Swan Yi, Daw Khin Swe U, and Sa O (a pen name).

[46] These two stories have been translated by Anna Allott but are not yet published. The first-prize winner for 1995, "An Unanswerable Question," is included in Yamada (2002, 25–36).

[47] This sensibility is shown in her "One Little Sarong," discussed previously.

[48] For the cool dry months of December and January, popular writers are invited by local organizations and literary groups to come and speak at open air gatherings. Mya Than Tint used to interview local people from all walks of life on these journeys. He then wrote about them and their lives in *Kalya* magazine. (Mya Than Tint 1993 and 1996)

[49] This interview was first published in 1989. (Mya Than Tint, 1996, 99)

[50] In this connection see a most perceptive essay by Jennifer Leehey (2005, 175–205). She writes, "The *han-thit* [new-style] movement is both an expression of disillusion with the literary realism of the 1960s and 1970s and a response to the Byzantine workings of the press regulatory and censorship system" (176).

[51] For translations of three of his stories from his 1991 collection, see Allott (1993, 37–53).

[52] The story was published in *Dhana* in November 1992. It was translated by Robert Vore and published in Yamada 2002, 11–17.

[53] Aung Thin, personal communications, 1993.

[54] "Thadun" was first published in *Ba-zinyin-gweh and Other Short Stories* (Ne Win Myint 1995). It was translated by Patrick A. McCormick and published in Yamada 2002, 4–10.

[55] Thaw Kaung makes the following comment on this story: "He makes gentle fun of the Burmese desire always to be the main actor, the leader and not to play a minor part, in the story about a failed village theatrical performance of the life of the Buddha; all want to take the role of the future Buddha, none to take the lesser parts." (Than Htut and Thaw Kaung 2003)

[56] This story has been translated by Allott (1993, 21–36).

[57] The State Law and Order Restoration Council (SLORC) changed its name to the State Peace and Development Council (SPDC) in 1997.

[58] For four translated stories, including "Nescafe," see Ne Win Myint 2002.

[59] The writer Ma Thida (Sangyaung) in 1990 interviewed some thirty authors about their reasons for writing short stories and published a series of articles in *Pe-hpu-hlwa* magazine. She was able to edit these into a book after having served five years of a twenty-five-year prison sentence; it was published under her pen name, Le Net (2001).

[60] See note 1.

[61] "Country Boy" was translated in Allott and Khin Thant Han 2002.

Bibliography

Abbott, Gerry and Khin Thant Han. 2000. *The Folk-Tales of Burma: An Introduction*. Handbuch der Orientalistik, Dritte Abteilung, Südöstasien; 11.Bd. Leiden: Brill.

Allott, Anna J. 1981. "Prose Writing and Publishing in Burma: Government Policy and Private Practice." In *Essays on Literature and Society in Southeast Asia*, edited by Tham Seong Chee, 1–35. Singapore: Singapore University Press.

———. 1982. "The Short Story in Burma: With Special Reference to Its Social and Political Significance." In *The Short Story in South East Asia: Aspects of a Genre*, edited by Jeremy H. C. S. Davidson and Helen Cordell, 101–38. London: School of Oriental and African Studies, University of London.

———. 1993. *Inked Over, Ripped Out: Burmese Storytellers and the Censors*. New York: PEN American Center.

———. 1996. "The Study of Burmese Literature: A General Survey." In *Southeast Asian Languages and Literatures: A Bibliographical Guide to Burmese, Cambodian, Indonesian, Javanese, Malay, Minangkabau, Thai, and Vietnamese*. edited by E. Ulrich Kratz, 7–56. London and New York: I. B. Tauris. Includes an annotated list (up to 1996) of translations of Burmese literature into English, French, German, and Russian.

———. 1997. "Half a Century of Publishing in Mandalay: The Ludu Kyibwa-yay Press." *The Journal of Burma Studies* 1:83–106.

———. 2000. " Nu Nu Yiy: Portraying life in Burma." *Persimmon: Asian Literature, Arts, and Culture* 1.2 (summer): 34–35.

Aung Mo Hsaung (U Myint Kyaing) 2003. "Sa-ye-hsaya-hnint sa-zu sayin" (Writers and Their Works). *Mo Hsan Pan* 1.40:17–18.

Aung Mun. 1973. "*Sit-pi-hkit myanma wut-htu-do-mya.*" (Postwar Burmese Short Stories) *Sa-ok Sa-pe* 1:148-78.

Aung Thin (U Aung Thin). 1999. *Aung Thin-i akyaik-hson wuthtu-do-mya-hnin thon-that-gyet-mya* (My Favorite Short Stories with Appraisals), Vols. 1–2. Yangon: Mo-min sa-pe.

Myanmar Writers of the Twentieth Century. 2003. *Myanmar Writers of the Twentieth Century and Their Works* (in Burmese). Rangoon: Government Department of Information

Dunn, C. W. 1947. "Country-Life in Burmese Literature." *Bulletin of the School of Oriental and African Studies* 12.3–4: 703–712.

Htin Lin. 1977. *Saung-gyo tin-thi thachin-than* [Too Harsh a Note]. Rangoon: Pa-rami sa-pe.

Khit-san pon-byin-mya [Experimental Tales], vol. 1 (1934) and vol. 2 (1938).

Le Ko Tin. 2000. *Myanma wut-htu-do hsaya-mya* [Burmese Short Story writers]. Yangon: N.p.

Le Net (Ma Thida) 2001. *Yaung-zin-mya-ye izarta* [A Spectrum of Questions]. Rangoon: Pe-hpu-hlwa

Leehey, Jennifer. 2005. "'Writing in a Crazy Way': Literary Life in Contemporary Urban Burma." In *Burma at the Turn of the Twenty-First Century*, edited by M. Skidmore, 175–205. Honolulu: University of Hawai'i Press.

Ma Ma Lay (Gya-neh-gyaw). 1944. *Thu-ma* (She). Rangoon: Gya-neh-gyaw Press.

———. 1948. *Shu-manyi* (Most Beautiful). Rangoon: Gya-neh-gyaw Press.

———. 1963. *Twei dazeint-zeint* (Reverie: Collected Short Stories). Rangoon: Gya-neh-gyaw Press.

Ma Sanda. 1985. *Ma Sanda-i wuthtu-do-mya* [Short Stories of Ma Sanda]. Yangon: Sa-pe Law-ka.

———. 1997-2002. *Ma Sanda-i wuthtu-do-mya* [Short Stories of Ma Sanda]. Rangoon: Parami. Seven small books.

Man Tin. 1968a. *Ko Hpo Lon*. No 148 of Pagan Press. Rangoon: Pagan Press.

———. 1968b. *Myo-baing Maung Pyon Cho baung-gyok* [Collected Stories of Township Officer Maung Pyon Cho]. Pagan Books, no. 159. Rangoon: Pagan Press.

Maung Htin. 1976. *Myo-ok pon-byin* [Burmese Short Stories of Today]. Rangoon: Sa-thabin.

Maung Swan Yi. 1976. "Bama Sa-pe Ba-leh Bel-leh?" [What is and Whither Burmese Literature]. Mandalay: Upper Burma Writers' Association.

Maung Tha-ra (ya). 1969. *Nyi-ako mathi tathi* [A Confusing Time]. Rangoon: Mo-hiyan.

———. ed. 1985. *Yane Myanma wut-htu-do-mya*. Yangon: Sa-pe Law-ka.

———. ed. 1986. *Na-kyat-ko hsaung kalaung-go kaing-sweh* [Carrying a Stethoscope, Holding a Pen: Real Life Stories by Twelve Young Doctors]. Yangon: Sa-pe Law-ka.

Maung Thin. 1977. *Hsaya zat-lan-son* [Doctor's Casebook]. Rangoon: Shumawa.

Min Shin. 1963. *Tahka-don-ga Do Yeh-baw* [We Were Comrades Once]. Rangoon: Mya Sa-pe Taik.

Mo Mo (Inya). 1982. *Mo Mo (Inya)-i wuthtu-do-mya-1* (Short Stories by Mo Mo Inya-1). Yangon: Sa-pe Law-ka.

———. 1986. *Mo Mo (Inya) –i wuthtu-do-mya-2* (Short Stories by Mo Mo Inya -2) Yangon: Sa-pe Law-ka.

———. 1993. *Mo Mo (Inya)-i wuthtu-do-mya-3* (Short Stories by Mo Mo Inya-3). Yangon: Sa-pe Law-ka.

———. 1994. *Hsu-ya wuthtu-do-mya* (Prize-winning Stories in Memory of Mo Mo (Inya). Yangon: Sa-pe Law-ka.

———. 1995. *Hsu-ya wuthtu-do-mya-2* (Prize-winning Stories in Memory of Mo Mo (Inya) – 2). Yangon: Sa-pe Law-ka.

———. 1997. *Hsu-ya wuthtu-do-mya-3* (Prize-winning Stories in Memory of Mo Mo (Inya) – 3). Yangon: Sa-pe Law-ka.

———. 1999. *Hsu-ya wuthtu-do-mya-4* (Prize-winning Stories in Memory of Mo Mo (Inya) – 4). Yangon: Sa-pe Law-ka.

———. 2004.. *Hsu-ya wuthtu-do-mya-7* (Prize-winning Stories in Memory of Mo Mo (Inya) – 7). Yangon: Sa-pe Law-ka.

Mya Than Tint.1999. *Khit-pyaing Yok-pon-hlwa-mya* [Contemporary Profiles]. Yangon: Quality Publishing House.

Ne Win Myint. 1995. *Bazin Yin-gweh* [The Cicada and Other Stories]. Yangon: Today Media Group.

———. 2000. *Let-ywe-sin wuthtu-do-mya, 1990–99* (Selected Short Stories, 1990–99). Yangon: Ottara La-min.

Nu Nu Yiy. 1996. *Nu Nu Yiy (Inwa) Let-ywe-sin Myanma wuthtu-do baung-gyok* (Selected Burmese Short Stories of Nu Nu Yiy (Inwa). Yangon: Wa-mo-aung.

Nyi Pu Lay. 1990. *Hkale lu-gyi kyaik-pi chit-kya-ba-deh* (Short Stories for Children and Grownups). Mandalay: Kyi-bwa-yay.

———. 2003. *Lu-a eip-met wuthtu-do-mya* (Dream of a Dumb Man—Short Stories). Mandalay: Kyi-bwa-yay.

———. 2006. *Nyein-thet tami-nit-hnin acha wuthtu-do-mya* (A Quiet Moment and other Short Stories). Yangon: Seit-ku Cho-gyo.

Saw Lu [U Saw Tun]. 1993. "Kaba-hnin Myanma" [Myanmar and the World]. *Mahe-thi* magazine (May), 172–6.

Than Htut and Thaw Kaung. 2003. "Mirrored in Short Stories: Some Glimpses of Myanmar Life and Society in the Twentieth Century." Paper read at the Traditions of Knowledge conference, Yangon, December.

Thaw-da Swe (Hswei). 1961. *Bawa Hto Hto* (Life Here and There). Rangoon: Kyi Win Press.

Thein Pe Myint. 1966. *Wuthtu-do baung-gyok* [Collected Short Stories]. Yangon: Pagan Press.

Win Nyein. 2006. *Ahmat-taya shwe-60.* (60 Short Stories from Shwe Amyute Magazine). Yangon: Kangaw Wutyiy.

Win Pe (U Win Pe). 1991. *Wuthtu-do-baung-gyok* [Collected Short Stories]. Rangoon: Ah-man-thit.

———. 1992. *Let-ywe-zin wuthtu-do-mya* [Selected Short Stories]. Rangoon: Ah-man-thit.

Translations

Allott, Anna, and Khin Thant Han, trans. 2002. "Country Boy," by Nyi Pu Lay. *Kenyon College Review*. 24.3–4: 80–89.

Esche, Annemarie, trans. 1968. *Der Markt von Pagan: Prosa aus Burma* [Pagan Market: Prose from Burmese]. Berlin:Verlag Volk und Welt. (Twenty stories translated into German).

Bernot, Denise, trans. 2003. *Le rire de la terre: Anthologie de nouvelles birmanes*. Paris: Langues et Mondes, L'Asiathèque. Seven stories, bilingual texts in Burmese and French.

Lulu U Hla. 1986. *The Caged Ones*, Translated by Sein Tu. Bangkok: Tamarind Press. Life stories of sixteen young prisoners published in 1958 as *Hlaung-gyaing-dwin-hma hnget-ngeh-mya*.

Ma Ma Lay. 1991. *Not Out of Hate: A Novel of Burma*. Edited by William H. Frederick. Translated by Margaret Aung-Thwin. Introduced by Anna Allott with an afterword by Robert E. Vore. Monographs in International

Studies, Southeast Asia Series, no. 88. Athens, OH: Ohio University Center for International Studies.

———. 2004. *Blood Bond*. Translated by Than Than Win. Honolulu: Center for Southeast Asian Studies, University of Hawai'i.

Milne, Patricia M., trans. with intro. and com. 1973. *Selected Short Stores of Thein Pe Myint*. Ithaca: Southeast Asia Program, Cornell University.

Milton, Daniel L., and William Clifford, eds. 1961. *A Treasury of Modern Asian Stories*. New York: New American Library.

Mya Than Tint. 1996. *On the Road to Mandalay: Tales of Ordinary People*. Translated by Ohnmar Khin and Sein Kyaw Hlaing. Bangkok: White Orchid Press.

Ne Win Myint. 2002. "Nescafe" and "Three other Stories." Translated by Vicky Bowman. Special issue on Burma and Vietnam. *Tenggara* 45-46: 1-23.

Nyi Pu Lay. 2002. "Country Boy." Translated by Anna Allott and Khin Thant Han. *Kenyon College Review* 24.3–4: 80–89.

———. 2001. "Moe Hlaing Settles the Score." Translated by Anna Allott. *Tenggara* 43:1–9.

Than Than Win, trans. 2002. "An Umbrella" by Ma Sanda. In *Virtual Lotus: Modern Fiction of Southeast Asia,* edited by Teri Shaffer Yamada, 18–24. Ann Arbor: University of Michigan Press.

Thein Pe Myint. 1973. *Selected Short Stories of Thein Pe Myint*. Translated by Patricia M. Milne. Data Paper, No. 91. Ithaca: Cornell University Southeast Asia Program.

———. 1999. *Sweet and Sour: Burmese Short Stories*. Translated by Usha Narayanan. New Delhi: Sterling.

Working People's Daily. 1973. *One Thousand Hearts and Other Modern Burmese Short Stories*. Rangoon: Sarpay Beikman Press.

Yamada, Teri Shaffer, ed. 2002. *Virtual Lotus: Modern Fiction of Southeast Asia*. 1–36, (four Burmese stories). Ann Arbor: University of Michigan Press.

Yin Wyn, trans. 1973. "Le-lan-bwe" [The Auction] by Theikpan Maung Wa. In *One Thousand Hearts and Other Modern Burmese Short Stories*. Rangoon: Working People's Daily, 129–136.

Censorship

Allott, Anna J. 2000. "Continuity and Change in the Burmese Literary Canon." In *The Canon in Southeast Asian Literatures*, edited by David Smyth, 21–40. Richmond, Surrey: Curzon.

Smith, Martin. 1991. *State of Fear: Censorship in Burma (Myanmar)*. London: Article 19.

Tin Maung Than. 1996. "Journalism in Burma." Paper presented at Carleton University, Ottawa. November.

6

Storytelling across Boundaries: Malaysian Short Stories

Shirley Geok-Lin Lim and Wong Soak Koon

While the short story is celebrated in many national literatures, particularly in the twentieth century, it has received less critical interest in Malaysia, where much of the focus has been on the genres of drama, poetry, and the novel.[1] This may be because relatively few individually authored collections of short stories (with the exception of those featuring Malay writers) have been published in comparison to novels, collections of poetry, and dramatic performances. Yet the short story continues to be popular in the newspapers and literary journals that sprang up after Malaysia achieved independence in 1957, and individually authored volumes have been appearing with some regularity since 1980.

Tales, legends, and stories formed a major part of the *Malay Annals,* first gathered in the early part of the seventeenth century and later translated by British scholars during the colonial period.[2] Literary works like the *Sejarah Melayu, Hikayat Abdullah,* and *Pelayaran Abdullah* contain a rich lode of stories still to be mined. Similarly, many folktales from the indigenous oral traditions of East Malaysia have been transcribed into English and published, especially through the Borneo Literature Bureau in the 1960s. The existence of these tales in print, taken from the Murut and Dayaks, and from other indigenous tribes in Sabah and Sarawak, testifies to the attempt by anthropologists and ethnographers to preserve the cultures of native people, yet they also point to the ambiguous relationship between native cultures and Western or Western-trained transcribers. Indeed, these published tales suggest the tricky nature of linguistic and cultural translation, for they share elements drawn from Western narratives as well as from folk oral traditions.

The best of these collections, Walter Skeat's *Fables and Folk-Tales from an Eastern Forest* (1901), illustrates the inevitable "corruption" or transmutation of the original folktales into narratives recognizable to a British imagination. Malay-, Chinese-, and Tamil-language stories draw on the rich literary traditions associated with these languages. Still, the modern short story as a literary form owes as much to its Western inception as to these traditions or the oral folktales popular in the indigenous traditions. In the face of the multiplicity of language traditions and written languages in Malaysia, this essay will attempt only a partial introduction to the short story genre, focusing on the short story in the national language, Bahasa Malaysia, here presented in translation in English, the language now perceived as the language of globalization and one shared by all Malaysians as much as Bahasa Malaysia.

Historical and Linguistic Context

The short stories that compose the opus of twentieth-century Malaysian literature show the influence of swift social and cultural changes in the country and exhibit themes that illuminate the major crisis of modernity in territories where traditional belief systems and forms of behavior persist. Malaysia was and continues to be a nation of many faiths, ethnic communities, languages, and cultures.[3] The first Indianized kingdom in Malaysia is said to date from the second century BCE and Indianized settlements as early as the fourth century have been found in the north of the peninsula. In 1403, Chinese records show contact between Malacca and China. Hinduism and Buddhism preceded Islam, but an increasingly powerful sultanate in Malacca helped spread Islam throughout the region. Christianity appeared together with the Portuguese, Dutch, and English colonialists. Thus, many of the short stories take a profound resonance in the context of instabilities set up by the incongruous convergence of Malay, Indian, Chinese,[4] and European cultures and an encroaching secular and material history.[5]

Right up to 1957, when Malaysia (then known as Malaya) celebrated its independence from the British Empire, much of the published short fiction in English was by British colonial administrators such as Sir Hugh Clifford and Sir Frank Swettenham and visiting authors such as Joseph Conrad, Isabella Bird, and Somerset Maugham. These fictions offered a colonialist vision of the place, with white British protagonists struggling against alien, exotic, and dangerous customs and inhabitants. While these stories possess historical interest, they did not and could not represent the interior lives of Malaysians. The attempt to voice a "local habitation and a name" through the short story in English began in earnest when Malaysians, in response to nationalist sentiment and rapid social change, found avenues for publishing and produced works that reflected, critiqued, and constructed these new ways of being. In this way, British English has been appropriated and shaped as one of the new "Englishes" of the world.

Development of the *Cerpen*

Prior to 1957, stories from the Malay, Chinese, and Indian Malaysian communities seldom crossed the translation barrier and were not noticed outside their immediate language audiences. Yet, before World War II, Malay writers were already formulating a didactic definition of the short story, the *cerita pendek* or *cerpen,* whose purpose was to teach Malays "to know themselves in order to make them aware of their national identity and to incite them to come out of their torpor" (Zaini-Lajoubert 1982, 185).[6] This period of "submerged creation" in the early twentieth century carried the seeds of the emergence of the modern Malay short story. The development of the Malay short story is closely linked to the development of printing and the proliferation of newspapers in the 1930s, which serialized the works of pioneers such as Abdul Rahim Kajai, Ishak Hj. Muhammad, and Shamsuddin Salleh. Besides a didactic concern with religious observances and moral behavior, an embryonic nationalism may be discerned in the intense interest in the correct usage of the Malay language, which was felt to have been grossly neglected under the British administration. With the exception of Abdul Rahim Kajai and Ishak, the artistic merit of this spate of early stories is arguable. More concerned with instruction than artistic value, most of these early writers produced black and white characters that have hardly any inner conflict. Some of these characteristics, such as stereotyping and a lack of interior psychological landscapes in favor of externals, are carryovers from the oral tradition, whose influence on traditional and modern Malay literature has been perceptively noted by Amin Sweeney.

According to Sweeney, "Western print technology did not suddenly replace the old radically oral manuscript culture" (1987, 70). In Malay oral society the preservation and retrieval of knowledge was possible through modes of stylized discourse, which included the use of strong rhythms, mnemonic patterning, parallelisms, and other formulaic devices that enabled the encapsulation of "large chunks of knowledge for storage and recall" (83). This concern with wholes and types contributed to the recurrent appearance of stock characters in these early Malay stories, a feature that persists in the stories of the 1990s. Sweeney also elaborates on the problematic positioning of the self as "I" in Malay society. The individual in Malay society often feels himself to be so much a part of his community that "he is unable to extricate the center of that situation—himself—for the purpose of introspective examination of that self" (158). If much of Western literature is predicated on a subjectivity that emerges from the interface of individual integrity and public discourse, and moral exploration is preferred over prescription, then one can see the grappling that early Malay short story writers experienced in reconciling a Western narrative form and the legacies of Malay oral traditions. Rather than concluding that the modern Malay short story was little influenced by the imitation of Western techniques (Zaini-Lajoubert 1982, 187), one may more profitably discern an ambivalent mix of fascination and hesitation in the face of this Western influence, which may even result in unique creativity.

Certainly the case of Ishak Hj. Muhammad (English educated) who wrote with a strong anticolonial bent, reveals a sensibility critical of received ideas, both Western and traditional Malay. He boldly critiqued not only British colonialists but the Malay aristocrats who collaborated with them through a reworking of old motifs, for example, in the novel *Putera Gunung Ledang* (The Prince of Mount Ledang). Using gender inversions and other devices, he indicts cultural hegemony, not only in the case of the colonizers but also in the case of the colonized, and chastises those who profit from Malay backwardness.

Ishak's concern for social justice and the fate of the Malay peasantry, in particular, was taken up by other Malay writers during the Japanese Occupation and after the war. In Indonesia, as well as in Malaysia, the Japanese Occupation saw the elevation of the Malay language as the power of the European colonialists was challenged. A new self-awareness among writers was accentuated by a rising nationalism, which climaxed in the opposition to the Malayan Union (Allen 1967).[7] The heroes in the Malay short stories of this period were patriots ready to sacrifice personal happiness for race and country. Leading writers of the 1950s, many members of the Angkatan Sasterawan 50 (Literary Generation of 1950), such as Usman Awang and Keris Mas, did imbibe Western social criticism in their own ways so as to awaken the Malay reader to social injustices such as poverty, corruption in politics, and the backwardness of the Malays in comparison with the perceived prosperity of other races in the country.[8] Among lesser writers a shrill critique of perceived injustice led to stereotyping and cardboard characters so that social criticism degenerated into propaganda. Keris Mas's call to writers to use simple, clear language produced clichés, and his advice to them to provide some kind of solution to societal problems sometimes resulted in contrived endings and weak closures, characteristics that can still be found in many Malay short stories today. And yet it cannot be denied that the Angkatan Sasterawan 50, whose slogan was "art for the people" (*seni untuk masyarakat*), introduced more serious themes and made more emphatic the social, anticolonial nature of the Malay short story.

Similarly, Chinese Malaysian authors had been producing an abundance of literature, unknown to the West, although Han Suyin noted in 1964 that "in Malaysia, it is not only known, but has always had an extensive readership"

(Allen 1967, 2). By 1965, when Singapore merged briefly with Malaysia, "95 percent of the active functioning writers of Chinese stock" were locally born, and, according to Ly Singko, from 1945 to the end of 1960 these writers published "at least 137 novels and collections of short stories, twenty books of poems, sixteen books of plays, and fifty-six books of essays and prose" (26). Like Malay writing, Chinese Malaysian literature, with the short story as "the main output" (Han 1967,17), was "strongly anti-colonial, . . . revolutionary, and therefore open to suppression by the colonial authorities" (8).

Language and Identity

After independence, English continued to be the language of education and administration, but language differences, together with other political-economic tensions, became major sources of conflict among Malaysian citizens. The government took a strict line on the adoption of Bahasa Malaysia as the national language only after the 13 May 1969 riots[9]; English was reduced to second-language status, and Chinese and Tamil were reserved as sectarian languages serving the minority communities. These language debates, however, did not result in the complete cessation of writing and publishing in English, the literary language for many Malaysians who came to political maturity at the time of national independence. Indeed, according to K. S. Maniam, "The Malaysian writer in English began to function as a genuine literary artist [only] from the early 1960s onwards" (Dingwall 1994, 212).

At the same time, the language debates and the subsequent primacy of Bahasa Malaysia as the national language further revitalized Malay literature, which had been neglected through much of British rule.[10] Malay writers participating in the historical move toward decolonization generally rejected modernization, which was frequently associated with Westernization and urbanization, and constructed instead an idealized vision of a communal, rural, village (*kampong*) society as the alternative to colonial subjection. In the 1960s, short story writers such as Shahnon Ahmad, Kassim Ahmad, S. Othman Kelantan and women writers such as Adibah Amin and Anis Sabirin began to write with an interest in technique and psychological realism. But in the 1970s, despite some interest in experimental forms, a number of Malay short story writers returned to Islamic ethics to shape their social vision.

Shahnon Ahmad's *The Third Notch and Other Stories* (1980) is usually taken as an exemplar of such Islamic-based didacticism.[11] "The Third Notch" is an epistolary narrative, in which the letter writer sets out a series of tasks presented as religious and social rituals for his sister to follow ensuring a proper Muslim burial for their sick mother to whom the sister is ministering (94–102). Yet it is altogether possible to read the story not as an Islamic tract but as a complex and layered representation of traditional Malay psychology. Two major attitudes are voiced repeatedly in the letter: a religious piety that shades into fatalism and a concern for communal social relations. While both attitudes appear to appeal to positive value systems that place religion and community first, the narrator/protagonist's obsessive listing of rituals, attention to petty details, and concern with social appearances begin to intimate an authorial perspective that perceives the narrator/protagonist as narrow, self-absorbed, and self-defeating. Against the surface religious tenor of the discourse runs a counterdiscourse of money. The villagers live in rural poverty without easy access to medical care. The protagonist does not have enough money to visit his dying mother or to send her to Mecca, yet he advises his sister that she "will need money on hand all the time" in order to fulfill the expensive rituals of prayers and feasting. "The Third Notch" suddenly stands the discourse of religion on its head as the authorial voice inserts through narrative irony the dissonance between religious and material fatalism: "If we have to pawn everything and go into debt, it doesn't matter. Sell whatever you need to for the feasts. Our economic destiny is in God's hands. . . . We should give thanks to God for our generations of poverty" (1980, 102). Shahnon Ahmad's subtle conjunction of the religious and the material spheres in this short story makes it a masterpiece of poetic irony.

Short story collection by various Malay writers, courtesy of Harry Aveling.

The layerings and subtle ironies in Shahnon Ahmad's story are also evident in the tales of the 1980s by prominent writers such as S. Othman Kelantan and Anwar Ridhwan, although the didactic bent inherited from oral tradition remains dominant in S. Othman Kelantan's oeuvre knitted to a carefully constructed traditionalism and Islamic conservatism. In one of his 1980s stories, "The Voice of the Waves," the mystical sea voyage, a traditional motif of the spiritual journey in Malay literature, acquires fresh resonance as two brothers share this quest (Aveling 1991, 47–61). The erotic imagery even hints at incest and homosexuality.[12] Whether the author intended such a reading or not, clearly the Malay story of the 1980s, such as S. Othman Kelantan's, opens up a postmodern dimension in making use of both the traditional cultural past of the society and the greater freedom offered by psychology to be in touch with the subconscious roots of contemporary life (Aveling 1991, x). In Anwar Ridhwan's narratives that deal with the world of the urban Malay intellectual, a broadening concern with global issues, rather than communal matters, results in a story such as "Tick! Tick! Tick!" which employs absurdist elements as the narrative of a woman pregnant with a bomb unfolds (Anwar Ridhwan 1991, 121–28).[13]

The Emergence of Women Writers

A burgeoning of stories by Malay women writers in the 1970s and 1980s, which continued into the 1990s points to the wider educational opportunities that opened to Malay women after independence.[14] Among the best-known of Malay woman short-story writers of these decades are Siti Zainon Ismail, Fatimah Busu, Zaharah Nawawi, and Khadtijah Hashim. Siti Zainon Ismail's "The Fable of Tiny Siti" narrates with gentle irony the sufferings of women, but it is not written as a strident protest against the status quo, which marks out a domestic sphere for women and a public sphere for men (Aveling 1991, 97–110). Mak, or "Mother," in the story recollects past events that flood back through waves of pain as she awaits the birth of a child from her second marriage. It would be easy, but quite unprofitable, to read this tale as yet another in the collection of tales of the Asian woman as "victim." Within the brutalizing circumstances of custom and tradition (Mak is married off to her first husband at thirteen), she retains a will to survive. Mak is the "artist" of everyday activities, embroidering and sewing so as to earn her own money. She creates, out of wax and cotton, "fruits," which she then sells. Siti Zainon paints vividly the violence of a world where men are often unquestioned authority figures, but against this she evokes a sphere of mutual help among women. Mak is soothed by older women who come to minister to her as she suffers the pangs of birth; they present her with gifts when the child is born, and they listen to and speak to her pain. The reference to a figure from folktales, the wily Mousedeer (Sang Kancil), who outwits the stronger beasts of the jungle, in describing Mak's strategies emphasizes Siti Zainon's desire to portray Mak as more than a mere victim. Although some readers may dismiss Mak's strategies as weapons of the weak, others (more aware of cultural specificities) will read her life empathetically.[15]

Crossing Language Borders

Although the Malay short story has generally found a Malay ethnic audience, in the decades after 1969, when Bahasa Malaysia had become the medium of instruction in schools, its readership became more multiethnic. In fact, in recent years many non-Malay writers have won prizes for their short stories in Malay; among them are Jong Chian Li, a Chinese from East Malaysia, and Uthaya Sankar, an Indian from peninsular Malaysia. The same is true of poetry.

English-language fiction has been able to reach across ethnic boundaries and to a wider international readership even more successfully as seen in the reviews and scholarly reception accorded it. Malaysian anglophone short stories appeared first in the University of Malaya literary magazines in the 1950s, some of which were included in *Bunga Emas: An Anthology of Contemporary Malaysian Literature, 1930–1963* (Wignesan 1964). *Tumasek* was published briefly in 1964, and *Tenggara,* the longest-lived Malaysian literary journal, began publishing in 1968. Both journals carried stories written originally in English and also in bilingual text, in Malay and English translation, and published writers who went on to write novels and short story collections, among them Lee Kok Liang, Usman Awang and Keris Mas. In 1968 also, Lloyd Fernando edited the first anthology of English-language short stories, *Twenty-two Malaysian Stories*,[16] which gathered stories first published in literary magazines and included stories by Lee Kok Liang, whose collection, *The Mutes in the Sun* ([1964] 1974), was the first individually authored volume of English-language short stories to come out of Malaysia.

In *The Mutes in the Sun* and his second collection of stories, *Death Is a Ceremony: and Other Short Stories* (1992), Lee records the harsh world of material struggle for the immigrant Chinese. Lee's stories compose disturbing psychological fragments of a Malaysian world whose violence, disorder, and moral corruption are vividly imagined through a supple narrative style that exploits a full range of local idioms and conversational registers. In "Dumb, Dumb, Stung by a Bee," the funeral of a wealthy Chinese businessman, Tze Tai Yuen, offers Lee rich satiric and ironic opportunities to critique the self-seeking and concern with appearances of newly powerful Chinese community leaders after independence (145–63). This company of "notables" is sorely challenged by the police, who have canceled the permit for a funeral route, earlier determined to be the best for feng shui and the prosperity of the heirs. That Chinese customs and philosophy have degenerated into avenues for self-importance is seen in Chee Beng, a character whose knowledge of these issues is clearly superficial. The Honorable Mr. Kung (newly appointed to guard Chinese political rights under the consociational politics of multiethnicity after independence was achieved) and the lawyer Hin Too (representing the new Chinese professionals) are merely concerned with their public images. All claim to have special powers to make the police change their minds about the funeral route. Hovering near, like a painful and unwelcome reminder of the spuriousness of their effort, is a dumb, hunchbacked boy whose unflinching stare invokes the decay of all organic matter and of mortality. Lee's stories, which are often infused with Buddhist teachings, place the ephemeral nature of human effort against the frantic acquisitiveness of postindependence Malaysia.

According to K. S. Maniam, the stories that appear in *Twenty-two Malaysian Stories* (Fernando 1968), spanning about a decade, "represent a period of rapid change. . . . [that] produced a disturbing process of national and self-questioning" (Dingwall 1994, 212). Maniam's several collections of his own short stories contain many narratives treating the core issue of multiracialism in a divided society. The stories thematize the question of communal identity and individual dignity in a society where "race" is politicized. The place of non-Malay citizens in a Malay-dominant realpolitik, for example, forms the theme of "Arriving," the title story of one of his collected volumes (1995). Maniam argues, "In a multiracial country, the chances are that the ignored realities remain ignored if the writer does not probe deeper into its culture and the interfaces of cultures" (1996, xi). Maniam's remarks may well strike a chord with Malay short story writers, too, since self-censorship operates heavily when, on rare occasions, multiracialism is thematized and non-Malay characters are portrayed in their narratives.[17]

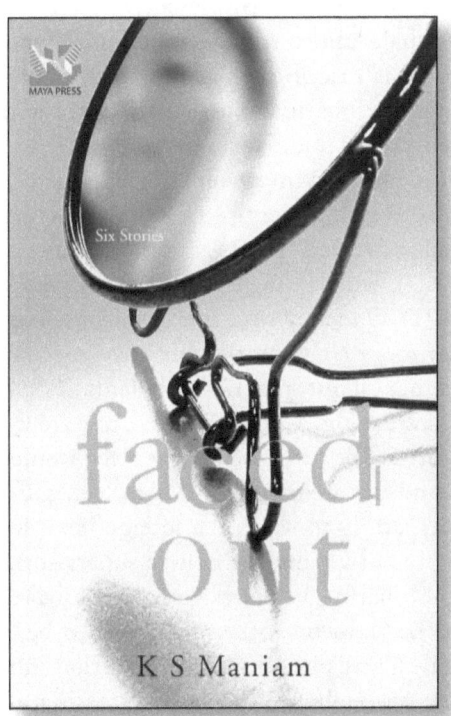

Courtesy of Maya Press

While pessimism pervades Maniam's sharp depiction of psychologically paralyzed characters in a grasping world, the stories also suggest the perspective of a spiritual locus from which to critique these characters.

Like Lee Kok Liang, but referring to an individual reading of Hinduism rather than Lee's Buddhist perspective, Maniam subtly works in a spiritual dimension. In "The Dream of Vasantha," the young protagonist, Ganesh, understands anew the meaning of loss for both his widowed, washerwoman mother, Vasantha, and himself when his friend, Chan, dies of typhoid (1996, 190–210). The story gestures to the possibility of cross-ethnic, cross-class bonds even as it portrays an intolerant society in which a young boy's innocence must be broken as he enters manhood.

Indian women, such as Vasantha, feature prominently in Maniam's stories. In "The Kling-Kling Woman," a four-generational perspective on women's positions within communal constructs emerges as one character Sumathi, reviews her mother's and great-grandmother's lives (Yamada 2002, 119–130). Into the domestic communal tale of the great-grandmother's strategies for self-preservation as she works on railroad-building sites, Maniam weaves an indictment of the colonialist's ruthless treatment of migrant Indian workers, male and female alike. At the same time, the labor of Indian women railroad builders is inscribed as a vital part of the country's history rescued from the relative obscurity to which historians have consigned their contribution even in postcolonial research.

The great-grandmother (who is the "kling-kling woman" of the title) organizes the other woman workers, suggesting the use of anklet bells as protection against the men's brutal sexual advances. Yet she stubbornly insists on wearing a sari ("I was born in a sari!"), which enhances her "comely and full-bosomed" figure (Yamada 2000, 121). One may read this as unconscious irony on Maniam's part. But, perhaps more consistently, one may see the great-grandmother as bravely not caring about the obscene fantasies of others in vindicating her own ethnic costuming. Clearly, to read the great-grandmother's story simply through latter-day feminist perspectives would be to forget her strong sense of the traditional. In spite of her clear, self-assertive acts (in running away from her family to work in a foreign land, in standing up to the Chinese shopkeeper, in outwitting the British supervisor), she sees the trajectory of her life as culminating in marriage to "a husband she could respect" so that "she would be the woman she was born to be." Maniam's woman figures are often ambivalently placed between tradition and fresh assertions of subjectivity, and the writer himself sometimes oscillates ambiguously between biology as destiny and bold, new alternatives.

"The Kling-Kling Woman" critiques the nostalgic and uncritical absorption of family stories that seduce but do not empower. As Sumathi notes, the bells (once powerful "amulets") are ironically transformed into flippant toys of sexual exchange at communal courtship rituals by great-grandmother's heirs: "Some of the older girls put on anklets with bells and ran about noisily, pursued by those young male relatives who would be reaching or had already reached marriageable age" (Yamada 2002,120).

Among woman short story writers in English, such as Siew-Yue Killingley, Pretam Kaur, Cynthia Anthony and Maureen Ten, Shirley Lim is the most prolific and also one of the few Malaysian writers to have achieved an international reputation. Besides literary criticism, poetry, and a memoir, she has published several collections of her stories.[18] Lim's "Hunger" (1997) like Maniam's "The Dream of Vasantha," thematizes innocent childhood and loss played out in the context of postcolonial multiracial, multicultural locations. Like Ganesh, the girl runs wild, outside the authority of narrow social rules, but here the mother is the missing figure. Moments of plotted intensity in this tale suggest a different development for the protagonist, as seen in the concluding image of her triumphant solitude, a turning away from the role of victim. Whereas Maniam's young boy settles into a working-class role, there is no such closure for the girl child in "Hunger," only a point of illuminated sensibility, a narrative epiphany.

The Short Story in the 1990s

In the 1990s, the short story in English pioneered by writers such as Lee Kok Liang, K. S. Maniam, and the Shirley Lim acquired new resonances from the dialogic voices and fragmentation that undercut the government's universalistic vision of modernity.[19] Against a backdrop of accelerated economic growth and a restructuring of the economy, as well as the emergence of authoritarian structures, "contemporary Malaysia is characterized by a very fragmented vision" (Kahn and Loh 1992, 3). Economic transformation has "contributed to the emergence of a more differentiated society" not only in gender relations but in "the composition, delineation and dominant symbols of the major ethnic groupings; in the circumstances of minority groups such as the Orang Asli and the indigenous people of East Malaysia; in the religious life, for example, the rise of a new Muslim fundamentalism (also in non-Muslim religious changes), in national and local cultural life" (2). Some of these differentiated dialogic voices, which undercut the unitary language of governmental rhetoric, influenced the short story in English of the 1990s. A younger generation of writers, such as Karim Raslan, Dina Zaman, and Che Husna Azhari, critiqued the results of the project of modernity using English rather than Malay as the language medium.

Karim Raslan, born thirty years after Shahnon Ahmad, reveals in his stories a new generation of ideological concerns for Malay writers. In contrast to the antipathy to other races and the call to religious piety that form major themes in Malay short stories up to the 1970s, Karim Raslan's stories mock communalist narrowness and satirize the hypocrisy and bigotry of religious zealots. His wider experiences in the West represent those of a younger generation of urban Malays, some of mixed ethnic identity, who have studied and lived extensively in Western societies and construct selves through bricolage and technological and multilingual cultural hybridity. The stories in Karim Raslan's second book, *Heroes and Other Stories* (1996), are immediately transgressive, especially to an Islamic conservative audience, with their portrayals of homosexual erotic scenes and criticism of upper-class Malay corruption, greed, and mendacity.

Karim Raslan's "The Inheritance," read against Shahnon Ahmad's "The Third Notch," demonstrates the vast social distance traveled by the Malay community within a generation. In this story, even as the Islamic rituals are being carried out, the sons-in-law are scheming as to how the millions left by the dead man are to be shared among the five daughters. The narrative slyly constructs a covert competition between Mahmud and Tajuddeen, with the two initially cast in the stereotypical roles of decadent villain and pious son-in-law. As the plot progresses, Tajuddeen's character is gradually shaded with self-righteousness, hypocrisy, and greed, and the appearance of five sons from a hitherto secret second marriage reverses his fortunes in a comic conclusion. Like "The Third Notch," the story's major interest lies in the obsessive details offered of the society in which the funeral is being staged, except here the rituals occur among the "princely residences" of Kuala Lumpur, the capital city, and the Malay characters

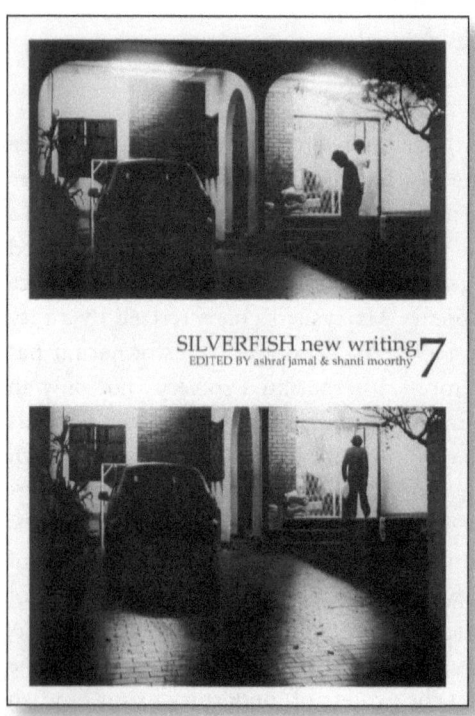

This collection of new fiction from Silverfish Books (2008) reveals contemporary Malaysian writing in a trans-local and transnational world.
Courtesy of Silverfish Books

are "rich men" who acquire "company directorships, cars, land and greater responsibility." Karim Raslan's characters, no longer the humble villagers victimized by loan sharks of another ethnicity, engage in the modern world as scheming capitalists who have abandoned social customs and community bonds for profit.

The stories in this essay map out some of the major configurations of the short story genre in Malaysia: its different deployments, reflecting the different ethnic, class, and cultural communities from which the authors speak; and the historical trajectory of themes that treat resistance to colonialism, the rise of nationalism, and the crisis of modernity in a developing nation. Ranging widely in themes, these stories explore rural poverty, religious extremism, and class inequities; the threat of deracination, anomie, and social injustice; and the development of the individual as a conscious agent in a confusing yet richly tapestried multicultural society.

Notes

[1] For some critical work on the short story in Malaysia, see Monique Zaini-Lajoubert 1982, and Ungku Maimunah Mohd. Tahir 2000.

[2] The *Malay Annals (Sejarah Melayu)* is often considered the seminal classical prose text of traditional Malay literature. It charts over six hundred years of the Malaccan sultanate in a collection of stories and legends about court life and history. Although some scholars believe it was written prior to 1536, tradition holds that it was commissioned by Sultan 'Ala'u-d-din Ri'ayat Shah of Johor and its editor, Tun Seri Lanang, started work on the *Annals* in 1612. It is known for its well-written prose and characterization of personalities.

[3] For information on the Malay short story before World War II, see Hashim Awang 1988.

[4] For information on Straits Chinese literature, see Clammer 1981.

[5] For a succinct overview of the premodern period, see Tham Seong Chee 1981b. An extremely important overview is Jones et al. 1989.

[6] For further information on the politics of literary development, see Tham Seong Chee 1981c.

[7] The Malayan Union was proposed by the British in 1946 to turn the Federated and Unfederated Malay States, plus Penangard Malacca (but not in Singapore) into one uniting state with common Malayan citizenship regardless of race.

[8] An example of their writing in English translation may be found in Muhammad Haji Salleh 1988, 3–14, 127–39. [Ed.]

[9] Also known as the "May 13 Incident," it refers to the Sino-Malay race riots in Kuala Lumpur which began on May 13, 1969. These riots lasted for many months, leading the government to declare a state of emergency and suspend Parliament until 1971.

[10] See Loh's and Yamada's essay in this collection (Chap.7) for a related discussion on language debates in Singapore. [Ed.]

[11] For more information on this from a writer's perspective, see Shahnon Ahmad 1988. [Ed.]

[12] For further information on Shahnon Ahmad, see Harry Aveling 2000.

[13] For an English translation of one of his short story collections, see Anwar Ridhwan 1991. [Ed.]

[14] On women writers and a feminist criticism that emerged in the 1980s, see Littrup 2000.

[15] For more of Siti Zainon Ismail's short stories, and modern Melayu language literature, see a recent collection *Rindu pala muda* 2005.

[16] Mohammad Haji Salleh (1988) edited a collection of modern Malay literature in English translation that contains a short story section. The short story translations are taken largely from the journal *Tenggara*. [Ed.]

[17] On a writer's life in Malaysia, see Maniam 2006. [Ed.]

[18] For some of her short story collections, see Lim 1982, 1995, 1997.

[19] Unlike the other authors mentioned in this essay, Shirley Lim could be considered a writer of the Singaporean diaspora, as she is currently based at the University of California, Santa Barbara. Besides her writing career, in her role as a university professor she has been active in the academic development of critical theory on Asian American literature, specifically gender studies. [Ed.]

References

Allen, James de V. 1967. *The Malayan Union*, New Haven: Council on Southeast Asian Studies, Yale University, 1967.

Anwar Ridhwan. 1991. "Tick! Tick! Tick!". In his *After the War and Other Stories*. Translated by Adibah Amin, 121–28. Kuala Lumpur: Dewan Bahasa dan Pustaka, Ministry of Education. Also translated by Harry Aveling as "Tik, Tik, Tik," in *Fables of Eve* (1991), 65–72.

Aveling, Harry, trans. 1991. *Fables of Eve*. Kuala Lumpur: Dewan Bahasa dan Pustaka.

Aveling, Harry. 2000. *Shahnon Ahmad: Islam, Power, and Gender*. Bangi: Penerbit Universiti Kebangsaan Malaysia.

Bigar Anak Deboi. 1956. "Rang Dungo: A Murut Story of Creation." *Sarawak Museum Journal*, new ser. 7.7: 205–7.

Brown, C. C., trans. 1966. *The Malay Annals*. Kuala Lumpur: Oxford University Press.

Clammer, John R. 1981. "Straits Chinese Literature: A Minority Literature as a Vehicle of Identity." In *Essays on Literature and Society in Southeast Asia*, edited by Tham Seong Chee, 287–302. Singapore: Singapore University Press.

Dewan Bahasa dan Pustaka. 1983. *Modern Malaysian Stories II*. Kuala Lumpur: Dewan Bahasa dan Pustaka.

Dingwall, Alstair, ed. 1994. *Traveller's Literary Companion: South-East Asia*. Brighton, U.K.: In Print.

Fernando, Lloyd, ed. 1968. *Twenty-two Malaysian Stories: An Anthology of Writing in English Selected and Edited by Lloyd Fernando*. Singapore: Heinemann Educational Books (Asia).

―――, ed. 1981. *Malaysian Short Stories*. Kuala Lumpur: Heinemann Asia.

Han Suyin, 1967. Foreword to *Modern Malaysian Chinese Stories*, edited and translated by Ly Singko, 1–21. Hong Kong: Heinemann Educational Books (Asia).

Hashim Awang. 1988. "The Malay Short Story before the Second World War: A General Observation." In *An Anthology of Contemporary Malaysian Literature*, edited by Muhammad Haji Salleh, 345–53. Kuala Lumpur: Dewan Bahasa dan Pustaka.

Herbert, Patricia, and Anthony Milner, eds. 1989. *South-East Asia: Languages and Literatures: A Select Guide*. Honolulu: University of Hawaii.

Jones, R. A., Ibrahim bin Ismail, E. U. Kratz, A. C. Milner, N. G. Phillips. 1989. "Malaysia." In *South-East Asia: Languages and Literatures: A Select Guide*, edited by Patricia Herbert and Anthony Milner, 99–122. Honolulu: University of Hawai'i Press.

Kahn, Joel S. and Francis Kok-Wah Loh, eds. 1992. *Fragmented Vision: Culture and Politics in Contemporary Malaysia*. Sydney: Allen and Unwin.

Karim Raslan. 1996. "The Inheritance." In his *Heroes and Other Stories*, 73–79. Singapore: Times Editions.

Lee Kok Liang. [1964] 1974. *The Mutes in the Sun, and Other Stories*. Hong Kong: Heinemann Educational Books (Asia).

———. 1992. *Death Is a Ceremony: And Other Short Stories*. Singapore: Federal Publications.

Lee Su Kim. 1991. "Malaysian Literature In English: The Use of English by Writers of Fiction." *Journal of Language Teaching, Linguistics, and Literature* 1:28–37.

Lim, Shirley Geok-Lin. 1982. *Another Country and Other Stories*. Singapore: Times Books International.

———. 1994. *Writing S.E./Asia in English: Against the Grain, Focus on English-Language Literature*. London: Skoob Books.

———. 1995. *Life's Mysteries: The Best of Shirley Lim*. Singapore: Times Books International.

———. 1997. "Hunger." In *Two Dreams: New and Selected Stories*, 3–12. New York: Feminist Press.

Littrup, Lisbeth. 2000. "Development in Malay Criticism." In *The Canon in Southeast Asian Literatures; Literatures of Burma, Cambodia, Indonesia, Laos, Malaysia, the Philippines, Thailand, and Vietnam*, 76–87. Richmond, Surrey: Curzon.

Ly Singko, ed. and trans. 1967. *An Anthology of Modern Malaysian Chinese Stories*. Hong Kong: Heinemann Educational Books (Asia).

Maniam, K. S. 1989. *Plot; The Aborting; Parablames and Other Stories*. Kuala Lumpur: AMK Interaksi.

———. 1994. "Malaysia." In *Traveller's Literary Companion: South-East Asia*, 204–51, edited by Alastair Dingwall. Brighton: In Print.

———. 1995. "Arriving." In *Arriving–and Other Stories*, 7–20. Singapore: Times Books International.

———. 1996. "The Dream of Vasantha." In *Haunting the Tiger*, 190–210. London: Skoob Books.

———. 2001. *The Loved Flaw*. New Delhi: Indialog Publications.

———. 2006. "The 2006 Nou Hach Conference Address." *Nou Hach Literary Journal* 3:123–126.

Maugham, Somerset. 1969. *Maugham's Malaysian Stories*. London and Singapore: Heinemann Educational Books.

Muhammad Haji Salleh, ed. 1988. *An Anthology of Contemporary Malaysian Literature*. Kuala Lumpur: Dewan Bahasa dan Pustaka, Ministry of Education.

Nyandoh, R. 1956. "The Story of Kumang Ruwai." *Sarawak Museum Journal*, new Ser. 7.7: 208–20.

Platt, John, and Heidi Weber. 1980. *English in Singapore and Malaysia: Status, Features, Functions*. Kuala Lumpur: Oxford University Press.

S. Othman Kelantan. 1991. "The Voice of the Waves." In *Fables of Eve*, translated by Harry Aveling, 47–61. Kuala Lumpur: Dewan Bahasa dan Pustaka.

Shahnon Ahmad. 1980. *The Third Notch and Other Stories*. Translated by Harry Aveling. Kuala Lumpur: Heinemann Educational Books (Asia).

———. 1988. "Literary Activity as Religious Duty." In *An Anthology of Contemporary Malaysian Literature*, edited by Muhammad Haji Salleh, 391–98. Kuala Lumpur: Dewan Bahasa dan Pustaka.

Siti Zainon Ismail. 1991. "The Fable of Tiny Siti." In *Fables of Eve*, translated by Harry Aveling, 97–110. Kuala Lumpur: Dewan Bahasa dan Pustaka.

———. 2005. *Rindu pala muda*. Kuala Lumpur: Dewan Bahasa dan Pustaka.

Skeat, Walter W., trans. 1901. *Fables and Folk-Tales from an Eastern Forest: Collected and Translated*. Cambridge: Cambridge University Press.

Smyth, David, ed. 2000. *The Canon in Southeast Asian Literatures: Literatures of Burma, Cambodia, Indonesia, Laos, Malaysia, the Philippines, Thailand, and Vietnam*. Richmond, Surrey: Curzon.

Sweeney, Amin. 1987. *A Full Hearing: Orality and Literacy in the Malay World*. Berkeley: University of California Press.

Swettenham, Frank. 1984. *Malay Sketches*. First published in 1895. Singapore: Graham Brash.

Tham Seong Chee, ed. 1981a. *Essays on Literature and Society in Southeast Asia*. Singapore: Singapore University Press.

———. 1981b. "Literary Response and the Social Process: An Analysis of Cultural and Political Beliefs among Malay Writers." In *Essays on Literature and Society in Southeast Asia*, edited by Tham Seong Chee, 253–86. Singapore: Singapore University Press.

———.1981c. "The Politics of Literary Development in Malaysia." In *Essays on Literature and Society in Southeast Asia*, edited by Tham Seong Chee, 216–52. Singapore: Singapore University Press.

Ungku Maimunah Mohd. Tahir. 2000. "The Construction and Institutionalisation of Abdullah bin Abdul Kadir Munsyi as the Father of Modern Malay Literature: The Role of Westerners." In *The Canon in Southeast Asian Literatures: Literatures of Burma, Cambodia, Indonesia, Laos, Malaysia, the Philippines, Thailand, and Vietnam*, edited by David Smyth, 99–113. Richmond, Surrey: Curzon.

Wignesan, T., ed. 1964. *Bunga Emas: An Anthology of Contemporary Malaysian Literature (1930–1963)*. London: Anthony Blond and Rayirath (Raybooks) Publications, Malaysia.

Wong, Irene F. H. 1986. "The Search for Localized Idiom in Malaysian English Literature." *ACLALS Bulletin*, 7th ser., 6:97–110.

Yamada, Teri Shaffer, ed. 2002. *Virtual Lotus: Modern Fiction of Southeast Asia*. Ann Arbor: University of Michigan Press.

Yeo, Robert, ed. 1981. *ASEAN Short Stories*. Singapore: Heinemann Educational Books (Asia).

Zaini-Lajoubert, Monique. 1982. "The Evolution of the Malay Short Story: From Its Origins to the Present Day." In *The Short Story in South East Asia: Aspects of a Genre*, edited by Jeremy Davidson and Helen Cordell, 185–201. London: School of Oriental and African Studies, University of London.

7

Conflict and Change: The Singapore Short Story
Mary Loh and Teri Shaffer Yamada

The history of modern Singaporean literature is closely connected with the country's own independent development as a nation. Autonomy—first from the British colonial masters and then from the Federation of Malaysia in 1965—gave rise to the urgent necessity to find a separate and distinct national identity, one that clearly could be called Singaporean. It is this process of national identity formation that can be traced in the development of Singapore's modern short story as a literary genre.

After 1965, Singapore's new government used English to construct a more homogeneous national identity from a multilingual, multicultural population.[1] Authors of every ethnic group experimented with English to express their experience of life in Singapore. Although the government framed English as a neutral language, it still had an emotional resonance colored by its British colonial past. This emotional baggage led to disputes over how "English" could represent the "real" Singaporean experience. Thus, our discussion of the modern short story and Singaporean identity will begin with a short overview of the language politics that confronted the new nation and its writers of different ethnicities.

The Politics of Language

From Singapore's inception, the multiethnic intellectuals in charge of developing the new nation-state selected English as the language of government, law, and social discourse. At the same time they established a bilingual public education policy that included four languages: English, Malay, Mandarin, and Tamil (S. Lim 1989, 532). This pragmatic policy, which privileged Mandarin, the official dialect of China, over other Chinese dialects, added an extra burden for Singaporean Chinese speakers, most of whom spoke Hakka, Hainanese, Teochew, and other dialects but not Mandarin.[2] Consequently, the government's choice of Mandarin unintentionally influenced the younger generation of Chinese Singaporeans (the post-1965 generation) to study English, not Mandarin, as their dominant language since they were already speaking a Chinese dialect at home. This is ironic since English is the only language of the official four considered to be limited in its semantic ability to foster and express non-Western values and ethnic identities. The government's language policy had an unintended consequence: the social construction of a cultural identity paradox. Shirley Lim explains this dilemma for writers.

> In choosing to write in the English language and, more importantly, in accepting the standards, form, and traditions of British and American literature, the English-language writers, especially those in the first tradition, are exhibiting a certain colonialist and/or cosmopolitan mentality, not always consonant with nationalist or indigenous identity and values. (539)

Writers who chose English, with its suspect colonial resonance, as their medium of expression were initially condemned to a marginal status as literary artists, whereas, authors who preferred writing in Tamil, Malay, or Chinese faced an increasing decline in their readership since the government privileged English as its lingua franca.

The issue of English as an adequate literary medium to represent the new Singapore was addressed at the International Chinese Writer's Forum in 1983. Professor Edwin Thumboo, then Dean of the Faculty of Arts and Social Sciences at the National University of Singapore, postulated that the inability of local writers to create "real" characters could be attributed to their writing in a language that was not their own: English. His contention was that, unlike writers of Tamil, Chinese and Malay literature, the English-language writer and his or her creation were not one with the linguistic community. While they were rooted in the local culture, such writers employed a language that carried with it a completely different cultural and historical tradition. This problematic is described by Yong Pow Ang as follows.

> Because it lacks a base of a community, sizeable, complete and rooted here, those who use the English language creatively for literary purposes at least, enter a kind of hinterland, an auxiliary area in which we function for professional and other practical purposes. (1983, 5)[3]

Yet it is a fact that most Singaporean English-language writers are actually monolingual. In 1966 A. L. Macleod recognized that "the generation who acquired their university education in the 1950s . . . generally regarded English as their first language" (S. Lim 1989, 313). Ong Teong Hean pointed out in 1975 that, since such writers were educated in the colonial period between 1935 and 1959, they were "monolingual" in English (1975, 64). And Simon Tay, speaking of writers of the 1980s, notes that English-language writers "have little choice . . . a generation, my generation is emerging of which many have little or no knowledge of another language" (1984, 57). Despite the early controversy, which continues to surround the legitimacy of a Singaporean literature in English, Shirley Lim noted that it is precisely this group of writers that has "emerged to flourish in Singapore's exciting, energetic, and dynamic last twenty years" (1989, 532). Their success is apparent in the twenty-first century.

The Language Mix

Singaporean writers of English were naturally influenced by their heritage—Tamil, Chinese, and Malay—even though they wrote in English. Initially poets experimented with bilingual or trilingual fusion (EngMalChin), but several short-story writers also wrote in "Singlish" as the "language" that most authentically represented modern multiethnic Singapore.[4] Shirley Lim considers the three types of Singlish, based on Chinese, Malay, and Indian idiolects and code mixing, to be used "often with an emphasis on local colour, social observations, and socio-political comments or criticisms" (1989, 534).

One of the earliest and perhaps best-known examples of Singlish in short fiction is Catherine Lim's "The Taximan's Story," for example, in the dialogue: "Yes, Madam, can make a living. So so. What to do. Must work hard if wants to success in Singapore" (Yeo 1978b, 1). Yeo believes that the most successful use of Singlish since the 1980s has been in experimental theater, not in prose (1983, 117).

Suchen Christine Lim's short story "Two Brothers" provides a satirical view of English as a vehicle for attaining wealth and power among the Straits Chinese, although Chinese writers also wrote in a creole Malay (Yamada 2002, 130–36). Local short stories concerned with Peranakan (Straits Chinese) culture and identity were published in the *Straits Chinese Magazine* (1897–1907), legitimizing the practice of writing in English.[5]

While some Straits Chinese writers were experimenting with English, others still preferred to write in their heritage language or patois. As they developed modern stories with local flavor, these Straits Chinese writers had a long history of three thousand years of Chinese literature to draw on for inspiration, especially the swashbuckling stories found in *Romance of the Three Kingdoms* and *The Water Margin*. Thumboo believes that the "variety of themes and situations in Chinese fiction is far greater than that in either Malay or Tamil" (1993, xv). As modern literature developed in China, local writers in Singapore were influenced by the new naturalism popularized by the innovative May Fourth movement during the 1920s and the modern literature that emerged from Hong Kong and Taiwan after 1949.[6] According to Wong Meng Voon, local Singapore short story writers in Chinese have been prolific; many anthologies were published prior to 1965, and a significant number of young Chinese short story writers have emerged since then (1993, 254, 260). Some of the best were able to incorporate dialects and colloquialisms in a skillful and aesthetic manner—including Chinese dialects with English.[7] Due to the demands of newspapers and literary supplements and the tastes of readers, a type of Singaporean Chinese mini-story become popular and has been anthologized in various collections (260).

Singaporeans writing in the Tamil, Chinese, and Malay languages, who wanted to reach a broader audience, must have appreciated English as it grew in cultural importance. During the 1980s, Wong Yoon Wah reported that the readership of Chinese literature was very small. At the same time, the "once active Malay Writers' Association" had dwindled to fifty members and was reduced to publishing its own works (S. Lim 1989, 532). Some writers attempted to solve this limited readership problem by writing in English as well as their heritage language. Wong Meng Voon revised a number of his Chinese-language short stories and translated them into English for a collection entitled *Glimpses of the Past* (1981).[8] Although his short stories reveal socially critical themes that often focus on the Chinese community, they also share a similar penchant for realism favored by the early Singaporean English short story writers. Themes include the failure to make good in the city and the consequences of gender disparity (Thumboo 1993, xvi–ii).

Writers in Tamil also chose to publish in one or more languages. They were influenced by an oral storytelling tradition based on two Hindu epics, the *Mahabharata* and the *Ramayana*. These were passed down orally from generation to generation and transplanted to the alien soil of Singapore both by merchants who traveled to the region in the fourteenth century and by migrant workers who arrived in the nineteenth and twentieth centuries.

Naa Govindasamy traces the Singapore Tamil short story—the most popular and well-developed genre among Singapore Tamil writers—back to 1887 with the publication of Makadoom Saiboo's short stories in the Tamil newspaper *Singai Nesan*. This important newspaper provided the early impetus for the development of the modern Singapore short story in Tamil (1993, 619). Saiboo's "A Dialogue between a Singaporean and an Indian" contains a humorous conversation about languages in Singapore (620).[9]

Indian: I came to earn a living in Singapore. I like to know about the lifestyle and trade here.

Singaporean: Well... the languages spoken here are Malay, Javanese, Bugis, Boyan, Chinese, Tamil, Hindustani, Bengali, Gujerathi, Kannadam, Telengu, Marathi, Arabic, Portuguese, Dutch, Turkish, French, Spanish, Italian and English.

Indian: Oh! Oh! I would need at least three years to memorize these names. How am I going to learn the languages to do business here? (638)

The local Tamil writers were also influenced by reforms in India during the 1930s and 1940s, a period during which the quality of their lives improved in Singapore. In the 1950s, the newspaper *Tamil Murasu* ran a monthly short story competition and later published a literature column, which fostered an important debate about the qualities of a good short story (Govindasamy 1993, 628). In 1953 this newspaper introduced a separate column to encourage the literary productivity of younger creative writers. These activities helped to foster a large number of new fiction writers whose short stories often expressed socially critical themes, drawing on immigrant and gender issues within the Tamil community in Singapore.

After the disruption of World War II and the changes caused by independence, a new generation of bilingual Singaporean Tamil writers emerged in the 1970s during a period when Tamil literary organizations, the press, and radio, encouraged the development of short fiction. In 1976 a group of ten Singaporean writers established the Singapore Literary Circle (Ilakkiya Kalam), which "read, gathered and selected short stories published in various periodicals in Singapore and Malaysia for every two months and sent them to established literary critics/academicians in the region and in Tamil Nadu for their critical evaluation" (Govindasamy 1993, 634). These evaluations were published and subsequently inspired other writers to create short stories. One of the first collections of Tamil short stories to emerge through this critical process was published in 1981 and included five stories by Singaporean writers.[10]

English-Tamil bilingual expertise may have been short-lived, however, as reflected in Rama Kannabiran's 1977 story "Gypsies." Here the protagonist comments about Tamil language loss while observing a birthday party in progress: "One could make out from the conversation that the predominant language used here was English, not Tamil. The topics were Western politics, economics and films. Only a handful of girls spoke in Tamil. Even then, they spoke it with difficulty" (Govindasamy 1993, 668). The historical conditions for this contemporary scene are then related.

> Under the encouragement of the British Raj, many Tamils had migrated from India to Singapore. Many sank roots and had been here for two or three generations. He thought there were basically two social groups among the Tamils, divergent in their outlook and aspirations. One group still identified with their Tamil and Indian origins. The other placed self-fulfillment above group identity. Dhanapal belonged to the latter group, which was smaller in number. Parthiban belonged to the other group.
>
> Like Dhanapal, many Tamils had acquired education, entered the professions but had alienated themselves, lost their mother-tongue and forgotten their culture and customs and imbibed Western ways of thought. It was about this alienated group of Tamils that Parthiban was now reflecting upon so sadly and deeply. (669)

The experience of self-fulfillment associated with English-language acquisition and the concomitant loss of traditional values has been a recurrent theme in Tamil fiction since the 1970s. All ethnic groups in Singapore have experienced a gradual shift toward English monolingualism. During the 1980s, interest in the Tamil short story appears to have waned somewhat, although an excellent selection of Tamil short fiction is included in Edwin Thumboo's *The Fiction of Singapore* (1993).[11]

Malay writers had a similar language choice—English and/or Malay—yet Thumboo indicates that they may have felt less "language" stress compared to their Chinese and Tamil counterparts since "Malay society and tradition, including the literary, were indigenous, complete" (1993, ii). Malay writers could draw on a long tradition of didactic storytelling, which reflected Islamic sensibilities, and their own "nativized" *Mahabharata* and *Ramayana*. Their love for the land and its seasons and their acceptance of life are recurrent themes in their modern fiction; yet as Singapore became more modernized and "detribalized," new themes emerged: conflict due to economic and social changes, resistance to change, and a critique of materialism (ix).

Singapore's English Short Story: A History of Paradox

Singaporean writers of English during the late 1950s and 1960s—whether Tamil, Malay, or Chinese—just like their heritage-language counterparts, typically wrote about local customs in a form of ethnographic realism or naturalism (Koh Tai Ann 1981, 167). Robert Yeo describes them as "realists, interested in people, interested in portraying people directly in actual, verifiable contexts" (1983, 114). The tension that developed between English and heritage-language writers would be less over language and tradition than over the purpose and form of "good" literature.[12]

The modern Singaporean short story in English, with its tight focus, plot, and unexpected ending, apparently had its inception at the University of Singapore, formerly the University of Malaya, founded in 1949. There, influenced by courses in Edgar Allan Poe, O. Henry, and Guy de Maupassant, the first generations educated in English at the tertiary level began to experiment with the short story form. During the 1950s and 1960s, many of the published short stories were by undergraduates in various university-supported student publications, including the *The Cauldron*, *Span*, *Focus,* and *Compact* (de Souza and Yap 1993, 765). Independent student publications such as *Saya* and *Write* were popular in the late 1950s, and independent writers began to produce their own journals—*Monsoon*, *Tumasek*, and *Impression*— in the early 1960s. Several collections of short stories were edited and published during this early period, including Herman Hochstadt's *The Compact* (1959) and Lloyd Fernando's *Twenty-Two Malaysian Stories* (1977), who selected the material from publications produced by the University of Malaya and the University of Singapore. [13] Writers in English attempted to distinguish themselves from other local writers at the Malayan Writers' Conference in 1962 by declaring that "art comes first, everything else is second," thus distancing themselves from a literature of social responsibility (Koh Tai Ann 1981, 165).

In the 1960s, the first decade of the English-language short story, there was growing apprehension about what it meant to be Singaporean and the yet unresolved tensions between culture and change irrespective of the art for art's sake aesthetic. Stories during this period still closely adhered to traditional themes as opposed to exploration and experimentation, even though writers at the 1962 Malayan Writers' Conference had declared that a writer's responsibility was "to explore new forms, themes, and methods of expression" (Koh Tai Ann 1981, 165). Shirley Lim defines the aesthetic tone of the 1960s.

> The dominant tone of this Singapore English-language writing is that of an international English-language variety, often in relation to more "universal" themes of individualism, love, disillusionment, personal conflicts, and so on, and in less identifiable, more metropolitan settings. (1989, 534)

Perhaps the greatest achievement of Singapore literature as it developed during the 1970s is its "documentation" of the growth of a national Singaporean identity. The English-language short story served to strengthen the consciousness of a national identity as the individual merged with the national. Two collections published in 1976 also may have provided a certain impetus for the construction of this Singaporean identity: Chandran Nair and Theo Luzuka's *Short Stories from Africa and Asia* (1976) and Geraldine Heng's *The Sun in Her Eyes: Stories* (1976).[14] Both collections include a variety of authors whose intent is to use the short story as a means to reveal authentic Singapore life and locales (Minjoot 1984). As author and literary critic Robert Yeo observed:

> If the published output of short stories is compared to that of poetry in English in the same period, it will be seen that there are fewer writers of short fiction than there are poets. Nearly a dozen individual collections have been published but no book of short stories by a single author has appeared. All the same, in the course of assembling this selection, I have been considerably encouraged by the increasing number who are practicing this difficult craft and doing so in a serious and sustained way. I expect that it will not be too long before we are reading a first book of short stories by a Singapore author. (1978a, vii)

Yeo's premonitions were realized later that year when a modest volume of short stories made its mark on the local literary scene. *Little Ironies: Stories of Singapore* by Catherine Lim, sold three thousand copies on the local market within six months (Ban Kah Choon 1979). Soon other writers, including Goh Sin Tub, Lim Thean Soo, and Gopal Baratham, formed the wave of writers issuing collections of their works.[15]

From the 1970s through the 1980s, many English-language writers shared a number of themes as they achieved a greater sense of "craftsmanship" and "surer use of language" in handling the short story form (de Souza and Yap 1993, 767). One was the will to succeed through wealth, a legacy inherited from their migrant forefathers who sailed the seas to Singapore in order to escape extreme poverty in the homeland. We are reminded of this time and again. In Wong Swee Hoon's short story "The Devil and the Kungfu Man," the narrator Weiji sees the parallel between his father, who came to Singapore as a cloth peddler, and the kungfu man who demonstrates the strength of his medicinal wares by staging pugilistic demonstrations (1984, 44–55). Both came to Singapore to make money. The kungfu man represents the old traditional system, and Weiji's father, with his entrepreneurial skills, represents a modern man in the making. One man succeeds while the other fails. The arrest of the kungfu man can be seen as a rejection of the old, failed traditions as changes in society are instituted.

Characters in the short stories are often driven to achieve through greed or just to survive. Obsession with wealth causes women to choose a marriage partner according to the size of his bank account rather than the depth of their relationship. In Catherine Lim's "The Marriage," Helen marries the old and decrepit Ling Aw Siak, admittedly for his money (1978, 58–62). Pearl, in "Love" in the same collection, considers the financial standing of the man she is supposed to be in love with before she finally decides to marry him (49–54). Equally foolish is the desire to obtain wealth by get-rich-quick means such as gambling. In "Lottery" (27–30), Ah Boh is a compulsive gambler who waits "patiently for the realization of her dream of overnight wealth. In the meantime, her old mother sometimes went hungry and Ah Boh went about in clothes and slippers worn thin" (28). Mrs. Alice Wee, a teacher who is also a compulsive gambler, steals school funds and blames an intellectually challenged student in Ho Kin San's short story "Tze Yong" (1986, 66–71). In these short stories values such as integrity and humanity, which marked an older and gentler society, are sacrificed in the "quest for wealth."

Wealth is but one facet of treasure. To scale the social ladder is the larger objective of human endeavor according to the Singapore short story. In "A Change of Heart," Catherine Lim paints a picture of the protagonist Michael's keen political ambitions, which overrule his marital discontent (1987, 1–35).[16] He experiences a sudden change of heart when he realizes that it would destroy his future political opportunities if he were to divorce his wife and marry his mistress. Such stories mirror an author's concern with the driven mentality of most Singaporeans, who are dedicated to the pursuit of wealth and position simply because they think it will provide a better material life and greater happiness.

The different objectives pursued—whether wealth, love, perfection, or happiness—can be collectively deemed the great Singapore dream, a nirvanic state of being to which all Singaporeans aspire. This is not unlike the American dream with its fundamental beliefs about the right to an individual pursuit of happiness. However, there is always disillusionment with such pursuits. Characters in search of their identity and self-fulfillment always find that reality has a bitter aftertaste. In Wong Swee Hoon's short story "The Landlord," the protagonist Boon Keng, leaves his wife and old mother to chase his dream of becoming an illustrator (1984, 1–22). Instead of achieving fulfillment, he realizes the emptiness of his dream and returns home in disgrace.

> Boon Keng learnt that his wife left home a month ago.
> "What do you expect?" his mother screamed at him acrimoniously.
> "You fool, she ran away with your best friend, Seng!" (21)

As "The Landlord" indicates, human relationships have been one casualty of Singapore's rapidly developing society. Urbanization has increased a sense of individuality and isolation. To break out of these silences, people strive even harder to establish relationships. The search for love forms the thematic basis for a number of short stories in Singapore. Characters, lonely and alienated from the rest of society, spend time futilely chasing illusions of love. Chan in S. Kon's "The Ships in the Harbour, the Cars on the Street" is trapped in a world circumscribed by routine; his life is one long, drawn-out yawn from which there is no escape other than romantic fantasies (Heng 1976, 4–8).

Marriages are not a solution to the problem of loneliness. Rebecca Chua also does not hesitate to criticize the hypermaterialism of the modern Singapore professional wife in stories such as "The Newspaper Editor" (1981, 1–11). At the heart of the problem are the intrinsic differences between men and women and the lack of communication between them. In "What My Wife Reads in the Newspapers and What I Read Are Two Different Things," Chua suggests that the problems are fundamental (62–66). The half-frustrated tone of the husbands, complaining that their wives do not understand them, satirizes the traditional expectation that wives are to serve their men submissively and consequently the women are not required to be terribly intelligent. This reflects a conservative view of women held by a traditional society.

In contrast, large numbers of women who have entered the workforce are facing rapid change. Women have greater access to higher education. They compete on an almost equal footing with men for jobs and have the privilege to choose whether to marry or have children. Yet women have found it difficult to come to terms with these changes because they have been tied to the yoke of tradition for so long. Consequently, most of the women portrayed in short stories are either domesticated, subservient slaves to their family's needs or characterized as brash or loud. The modern woman is often satirized. In Gopal Baratham's "Gretchen's Choice," the protagonist is a swinging single who flaunts her sexual liberty (1988b, 1–13).

> The sexual revolution of the sixties reached Singapore late and it wasn't until the early seventies that the island's women began to swing. The swingers included the brilliant and the benighted, the committed and the confused, the arrogant and the asinine and several so mixed up they defied classification. The various and contradictory assortment of individuals had one feature in common: a total lack of insight. Gretchen was typical of the group. (1)

The tension between the modern and the traditional perception of women is also enacted through the strife that is depicted between women and their mothers-in-law. In many of Catherine Lim's short stories, for example, the presence of the mother-in-law is a threat, and the daughter-in-law resents her interfering ways. At the same time, one recognizes that "duty" to others defines the ideal traditional woman while her modern counterpart is more concerned with personal fulfillment. The fact that the modern woman often is painted in an unflattering light indicates that society has yet to come to terms with the changing role of women.

Some stories, however, represent successful professional women in a culturally subversive, positive light, perhaps in anticipation of a social change that will open up more possibilities for talented women. Mary Loh's "Sex, Size, and Ginseng" is a humorous tale about the sad fate of a typical Chinese patriarch who is unable to produce male offspring irrespective of his having several wives (Yamada 2002, 178–82). Out of desperation, he consumes large quantities of ginseng in hopes of boosting his virility and allows a matchmaker to provide him with an unattractive but fertilely promising young woman whom he reluctantly embraces as Wife Number Three; the result is another pair of twin daughters. We find out, however, as the tale nears its conclusion, that all of his daughters have married well and provided him with many grandsons. By the end of the story only one unmarried daughter remains.

> I did not marry. I did not bear him a grandson. I live in his house and every night, when Ah Lan brews his ginseng tea, she brews me mine. It doesn't do him much good. I know from my science degree that it is a matter of genetics and chromosomes. It doesn't matter, of course. It is a special quality of ginseng. The Cantonese describe its unique flavor as being like *kum*— gold and glinting in a transparent glass. It is the color of pale gold; the best ginseng, of course. I should know because I own the ginseng farm and the best roots come from it. After all, someone must maintain the duty of managing the family business empire. (182)

Here the modern daughter—a single woman, highly educated and competent—runs the family empire.

Another persistent theme in the Singaporean short story is psychological or physical entrapment due to social and economic pressures. In Wong Swee Hoon's "The Phoenix," a young girl is sold into slavery in a brothel because of extreme poverty (1985, 1–23). The protagonist, Ming Fong, becomes a cabaret girl and dreams of a "normal" life—a husband, a home, children. She sews a phoenix with rainbow sequins on her red, ankle-length cheongsam. "As the legendary phoenix rose from the ashes reincarnated, Ming Fong hoped that she too would be able to rise from her abyss of humiliation, despair and misery" (8). She marries a poor hawker, and for a brief moment she is happy until her husband dies suddenly, leaving her to care for their daughter.

After discovering that her daughter has grown up to become a cabaret girl, immersing herself in the very lifestyle that she had denounced, Ming Fong sees the phoenix "transfixed in a nest of dull flames, with its wings lifted as if in a last gesture before dying. In fact, the phoenix appeared dead, with tongues of flame licking at its body" (23). The image of the phoenix without its accompanying association of resurrection captures her sense of despair and ruined hope.

Similarly, in Ong Choo Suat's "The Crooked Shrine" and "The Glass Cage" characters live in socially defined, confined spaces almost like prison cells (Yeo 1978b, 55–65, 66–80). Like Chan in S. Kon's "Ships in the Harbour, Cars in the Street" and Helen in Catherine Lim's "The Marriage," the search for escape is futile. Materialism is one reason for the change in traditional value systems, and it is suggested that entrapment results from materialism and greed.

Further Issues Regarding a Literary Aesthetic

Two separate strains—serious and sensationalist fiction—emerged from a single literary root planted in the 1960s. What is common to both is the importance of the universal over the local. Unlike the anthologies of the 1960s, which sought to locate the Singaporean within the context of his or her local community, the new anthologies attempted to establish the Singaporean as part of a larger world community. As a result, one of the key concerns was the need to confront change.

The first strain, that of serious fiction, was essentially a continuation of the mainstream style established in the 1960s, the first decade of published Singaporean literature. Woo Keng Thye, Lim Thean Soo, and Philip Jeyaretnam have continued to produce anthologies of serious short fiction. For example, "Painting the Eye," part of Jeyaretnam's Ah Leong cycle of short stories, reflects a melancholy mood of alienation in a globalized Singapore, echoing an existential angst shared by many young, successful professionals bound up in urban capitalism (Yamada 2002, 183–89). A sense of cultural and relational alienation is reflected in the opening thoughts of Ah Leong, a somewhat successful insurance salesman.

> Now that Song Jiang was abroad doing his doctoral thesis on some obscure branch of Chinese literature, Ah Leong suddenly felt his absence keenly. They had not really been together for a long time, eight or nine years, and especially once Song Jiang had entered the National University of Singapore, they had seen one another not more than once a month. Yet Song Jiang's being overseas, almost on the other side of the world at Harvard University, seemed to create a hole in Ah Leong's picture of his nation. He wondered

why it was necessary for Song Jiang to disappear across half the world in order to study something that ought to be at the center of our lives, right here, and yet wasn't. He wondered whether all these scholars, streaming outwards from Singapore, brought more back when they returned than they took when they departed. (183)

Ah Leong's consternation also illustrates the increasingly common experience of geographic displacement among Singaporean professionals caught up in the globalization of the world economy, including the translational flow of intellectual capital. Finally, Ah Leong's inability to prevent a client from committing suicide propels him to withdraw from the world of insurance and escape into the world of art.

Through Ah Leong and the other characters, Jeyaretnam explores what it means to live in Singapore at a particular time and place. Each story in his collection *First Loves* (1987) is complete in itself yet related to a larger whole. The main characters recur in different stories and have tenuous connections to one another. Along with a sense of community, however, there is also a feeling of fragmentation and alienation, which runs through the collection and expresses the social milieu of the 1980s and 1990s.

The significance of Jeyaretnam's achievement and those of his fellow writers marks a change in the perception of the value of Singaporean literature. Previously local writing had attracted a less than popular following due to prejudices regarding its styles and standards. Now the rising volume of sales of short story collections is the best indicator of an increasing acceptance of literary works locally written and published. Jeyaretnam's *First Loves* broke records on the "Top Sellers" list. This was a breakthrough since "for the first time in Singapore, a book written by a Singaporean, in English, topped the charts" for many weeks, causing quite a "buzz" (Singh 1998, xiii).

Nalla Tan, whose short stories appeared in the anthologies *The Sun in Her Eyes* (Heng 1976) and *Singapore Short Stories* (Yeo 1978a), produced a substantial collection of short stories entitled *Hearts and Crosses* (1989). Singapore's most prolific short story writer, Catherine Lim, brought out two collections in quick succession: *Deadline for Love: and Other Stories* (1992) and *The Woman's Book of Superlatives* (1993). Both women exploit the familiar language and narrative structure of their earlier stories as they explore the fragile relationships between men and women. Both raise the problems of women who must rapidly adapt to a modern environment but remain trapped within the social confines of their traditions and culture. Their stories reflect the ongoing dilemma of the modern woman in Asia, where the society has changed dramatically but her own situation has not changed quickly enough.

They also reflect a deep realism and a humanism that transcends cultural idiom.

Nalla Tan's short story "What you Asked," awarded a literary prize in the 1985 *Asiaweek* Short Story Competition, reflects this dilemma (1989, 96–115). The story is narrated from the perspective of the protagonist, Anne, the wife of an only son in a Chinese family, whose father has suffered a severe stroke from which he never fully recovers. The old man tragically lingers for years with limited mental capacity; when his death finally comes, it is sadly a relief. Anne, whose life had been defined through her role as devoted wife, must then bear the sudden death of her beloved husband from an unanticipated heart attack. The story, though grounded in a gendered experience within the ethnic confines of Singaporean expectations, also transcends cultural differences. Anne's thoughtful meditation on the deep yet ephemeral nature of their marital happiness is grounded in a reflection on traditional Chinese beliefs.

> The day had started with promise. My thoughts went back to that morning; the wet grass and the raw brown earth and the bougainvillea. Yet it had ended this way without warning, without goodbye, with a telephone call from someone else. Life, I supposed, brought the unexpected. Perhaps you and I had been too happy in terms of giving to each other, sharing, understanding each other's little idiosyncrasies and enjoying the common interests we shared. Some people would say it was not a good thing, being too happy. The gods did not like it. All mortals must suffer in some way. Happiness needed to be diluted with pain. (113)

In the context of this story Tan interweaves a universal, humanist perspective (love and death) with a particular Chinese cultural overtone, a blend that signifies the distinctive characteristics of mature short fiction in Singapore.

During the 1980s and 1990s, a number of new writers of serious short fiction emerged, adding to the collections by established writers, published works that emphasized brevity, a tight plot and a surprise ending. One is *Fascist Rock: Stories of Rebellion* (1990), the debut collection of the young Singaporean author Claire Tham. The common theme that runs through these stories is the rigidity of society's demands and her protagonists' fight in various ways against these established systems.

Tham's protagonists are essentially social misfits. She shows a clear understanding of the teenage mind, perhaps because she wrote most of these stories at age seventeen. She shows an admirable command of the written language, a quality that immediately brought her to the attention of the judges of the National Short Story Competition in 1984. Dr. Kirpal Singh, then senior lecturer in the National University of Singapore, spoke of Tham's talent and potential.

> I was struck by her vigour; a sense of life comes powerfully across. . . . She is obviously well read and has a good command of the language. . . . But the dialogues tend to sound false because of the formality of the expressions. It is as if she is afraid to record true conversations for fear of breaking grammatical rules. For example, there are no Singaporeanisms. (Ooi 1985, 4).

It is significant that Singh takes issue with the "formality of the expression" and the lack of Singaporeanisms. Rather than a negative, this reflects Tham's confidence in her linguistic range and an expressive ability that borders on the poetic. Tham's use of language is her strongest asset in this collection. *Fascist Rock* was a promising debut for this young Singaporean writer.[17] It was followed by *Saving the Rainforest and Other Stories* (1995) and *The Gunpowder Trail and Other Stories* (2003) in which she continued to explore themes of the conflict between the individual and conventional society. In these subsequent collections, her characters continue to be quirky and rebellious, though more adult.

Another young writer, Terence Chua, plumbs the depths of the imagination in his debut anthology *The Nightmare Factory* (1991). This collection of short stories is hard to categorize. There are elements of fantasy, science fiction, and the modern fairy tale cleverly interwoven in the narratives. The presence of these universal elements gives his stories a sense of timelessness and placelessness, yet, there is an accompanying sense of familiarity about each protagonist's experiences. The book received less attention than it deserved given Chua's ability to locate the Singaporean experience in the universal.

What is also encouraging about new writers such as Tham and Chua is the fact that they began writing at a fairly early age. They are not afraid of experimentation and are very familiar with craft and technique. Hence, the limited creativity that marked the first decade has been broadened. Moreover, their vision has a wider scope and addresses larger issues. Concern for deeper issues such as morality, justice, and equality finds greater expression in the stories of the second generation. One is also able to perceive a greater confidence and outspokenness about the younger writers, which is affirmative of the growth of the Singapore short story.

This second wave of books has been the source of some concern in literary circles, however, as it is aimed at general readers in the mass market. It includes collections of ghost stories and books that have sensational themes such as sexual deviance and crime.

At the 1989 Singapore Book Fair, *The Almost Complete Volume of True Singapore Ghost Stories*, by the phantom writer Russell Lee and his team of "ghost writers" (Lee 1989), garnered the title "Top Selling Book."[18] In the following year, another book of ghost stories, *Book of Souls*, vol. 1 (Ramesh 1990), achieved the same honor. This led to the issuing of more volumes, in the series *The Almost Complete Collection of True Singapore Ghost Stories*[19] and *Souls: True Ghost Stories* (Ramesh 1991).[20] Regarding the popularity of gothic themes among the post-1965 generation, Singh suggests, "There must be some deep cultural explanation as to why a whole generation turns to such writings to whet its appetite for the gruesome and horrible" (1998, xiv). Although written in the context of adolescent rebellion, Anne Brewster's critique of "bad boy" Colin Cheong's novel *The Stolen Child* may provide some further insight into this psychological dynamic in the sense that "fantasy narrative" stages "both a desire to escape or transgress the discipline of the polis nation and the anxiety occasioned by the impossibility/prohibition of such a desire" (1998, 83).

What is particularly interesting about the gothic books is the consistent attempt to present the stories as true and factual records of inexplicable and supernatural events and not works of the imagination. An example is K. Ramesh's *The Book of Souls* (1990) and *Souls: True Ghost Stories* (1991) Contained in the preface to both volumes is the assertion that the accounts are excerpts from the files of an independent research team. They claim to feature transcripts of personal accounts based on actual occurrences and advise readers that, although parts have been changed for rhetorical purposes, the stories must be regarded essentially as fact. This is also the case for Lee's *All New True Singapore Ghost Stories*.

Perhaps the only way to account for the popularity of the horror genre is to argue that it is an extension of the gothic mode in Singaporean literature. It may be true to say that, just as the gothic genre was a reaction to the strictures of Victorian society, the perception of entrapment fostered the growth of Singaporean gothic. The opposite of materialism is a strong belief in a spirit world, the world of the uncanny and inexplicable, the source of all superstition.

Two collections by the serious fiction writer Nicky Moey in the 1980s, *Sing a Song of Suspense* (1988) and *Let's Play Games* (1986), strongly feature elements of the gothic in their explorations of the irrational and supernatural. Catherine Lim's *They Do Return* (1983) also features stories in which the dead return to plague the living. The gothic not only conveys a sense of mankind's lack of restraint but also a sense of helplessness about humanity. There are circumstances beyond man's control, and he can only succumb to them. Despite its modern outlook, Singaporean culture is still embedded in folk superstitions and folklore. Whether he or she subscribes to an Eastern or a Judeo-Christian system of beliefs, the average Singaporean is not entirely skeptical about the existence of a spirit world. It is a comforting thought that should one fail to escape from the strictures of modern living there is the afterlife, and spirit possession becomes an excuse for the occasional aberration in behavior.

Another interpretation of gothic's current popularity is its ability to express the tension between the practical, material world and the spiritual, nonmaterial one. As in paranormal experience, the stories dispense with cause and effect. Hence, there is no plot, no explication, and no character development. There is some entertainment value only because some of the situations are so ludicrous as to appear comic. One finds the editors' attempts to authenticate these anthologies quite laughable. In real terms, books such as *All New True Singapore Ghost Stories* and *Book of Souls* have very little literary merit. Furthermore, standards of writing and editing have been sacrificed for the greater interest in capitalizing on the Singaporean's love of the macabre, and this has become an issue of concern.

Another source of concern is books that are sensational in nature. In *Sisterhood: The Untold Story* (1990), Joash Moo deals with the controversial issue of transsexualism and transvestism. Each story is told either by a person who would be considered a social outcast, a prostitute or sexually ambivalent person. Moo states that the objective of the book is "not to hurt anyone but to tell the story of a small minority, their struggles, their pains, their sorrows." Moo hopes that "readers will approach this anthology with a view to understand and not to judge" (iii). The intention, if true, is fair. However, its execution in this case leaves something to be desired. Rather than presenting the characters sympathetically, Moo tends to flaunt particular characteristics; they are promiscuous, vain, aggressive, and deviant troublemakers, and they do not elicit any sympathy from the reader.

One might rationalize that with the modernization of Singapore, it is now possible to discuss themes such as sexual deviance openly. The crucial issue that must be addressed, however, concerns the value of such works to Singaporean society. In terms of literary merit, none of these collections has the depth of insight that can nourish the soul and mind with perspectives and insights into the human condition or enlarge one's sympathies for humankind. Having only momentary entertainment value, these books are at best transitory. Although there is nothing inherently wrong with works of this quality, there is a growing fear that readers will perceive these publications as representative of the entire scope of contemporary Singaporean literature.

There have been attempts to turn the tide in favor of the first strain of literature. The most notable is the publication of *Stand Alone* (1991), the first collection of prose writing from the Singaporean poet Simon Tay. The twelve stories in the book are well crafted in terms of plot, theme, and character. In "A History of Tea," Tay plays on his own surname, which sounds like the Hokkien word for tea (133–52). Just as the taste of madeleines evokes memories for Swann in Marcel Proust's *À la recherche du temps perdu*, a hot mug of tea taken on a quiet afternoon with his family friend Beverly evokes Tay's memories. The story examines the subtle complexity of human relationships through different generations all held together by a common surname.

Tay's skill at characterization is seen clearly in his sensitive portrayal of women. In "Catherine Listening to the Rain," a young wife recalls her mother on other rainy days (1991, 95–114). In "Iris's Rice Bowl," Iris grows increasingly resentful of her brother as she slowly realizes that her family has the subtle means to enforce unequal treatment (201–08). Girls have been told that they should not eat the last piece of food on the table because they will end up as spinsters. Iris's belief is that they have been so told because mothers want to reserve the last pieces of food for their sons. The truth is tested when at lunch Iris's chopsticks are poised above the plate where the last piece of chicken sits. In this little fragment of time, Tay shows that, though mentally we dissent, we have been conditioned to believe what our mothers tell us.

Tay's sense of confidence is reflected in his use of language. In a small note before the preface, he states without apology, "Some of the words, usages and syntax in this book do not conform to standard English. There are words borrowed from Chinese dialect and Malay and some of which are neologised from the vernacular. These words are not italicized to further reflect the flavour of Singapore English" (1991). Tay draws from personal experience to craft his characters, an experience that is identifiably Singaporean and yet possesses a vision of the universal. Such is the quality of writing that made his anthology extremely popular on the mass market even without sex or horror.

Conclusion

It is now many decades since the beginning of a consciousness of what a Singapore short story might be. Anne Brewster describes the gradual emergence of a collective group identity.

> Although as a British colonial trading post its divergent social and racial groups shared little sense of unity or cultural coherence, during the twenty years since Independence, Singapore has indubitably developed a sense of collective group identity (even though, like many post-colonial nations, it is obsessed with the conviction that this identity is illusive, inchoate and fragile). (1998, 85)

Themes in the short fiction of the 1990s certainly include a sense of alienation, a deracinated self described as "the over-determined product of post-industrial consumerism, affluence and geopolitical and post-colonial cultural specificities, constituted at the intersection of global flows and a pedagogic nationalism" (86). Is it this alienated "illusive, inchoate and fragile" identity that actually informs contemporary Singaporean literature?

While there have been positive signs of growth, development, and greater confidence in writing today, fewer published writers are producing their own collections of short stories. While there is no longer the National Book Development Council's National Short Story competition, there is the biannual Golden Point Award and the biannual Singapore Literature Prize for short fiction. Regrettably, these have had a less than enthusiastic response, although there seems to be more interest in writing in general. Part of the problem may be ascribed to the perception that a short story is less important than a novel, and writers are now in pursuit of writing the "Great Singaporean Novel." Many of the established short story writers have in recent years graduated to writing exclusively novels and other prose works. These include Catherine Lim, Gopal Baratham, Philip Jeyaretnam, and Simon Tay.

Today the acceptance of the Singapore English short story as a unique genre is unquestioned. *Little Ironies* (C. Lim 1978) has sold well over forty-five thousand copies and undergone ten reprints.[21] Demand for collections of locally written short stories has also led to the reissue of collections. Early anthologies by Gopal Baratham, Goh Sin Tub and Nicky Moey have been reprinted under new titles.[22] Wong Swee Hoon's *The Landlord*, first published in 1984, was reissued in 1991 under the title *A Dying Breed* and included three new stories. Angelia Poon and Sim Wai Chew's anthology *Island Voices: A Collection of Short Stories from Singapore* (2007), continues to extend the literary significance of the Singaporean short story. And the gothic genre is still experiencing unparalleled sales. This popularity echoes the growth in achievement of the Singaporean short story since the 1950s and the emergence of English as the foremost language of its expression.

What does the future hold for the Singaporean short story? More experimental forms of short fiction in English are being published online at literary Web sites curated by Alvin Pang and other writers, which focus on experimental or language poetry and prose.[23] The importance of imagery, reflected in much of this new writing, is illustrated by the following selections from Alvin Pang's "Se7en."

> The secret behind the subtle, remarkable hues in each of Wu Ji's fifty-seven acclaimed self-portraits—one, famously, for every year of her life—was

finally revealed, when the celebrated artist collapsed while deriving another batch of paint from her own blood.

The sky was the exact shade of unopened irises when Ai felt her heart break. It shattered on the terrazzo-tiled kitchen floor with a soft crystal tinkle, as "Mood Indigo" played on her stereo like a soundtrack to her shame. She didn't have to count days to realize—although the man she loved must never know—she was pregnant again (2003).

This emphasis on the experimental can be traced to the 1962 Malayan Writers' Conference where Singaporean English-language writers enjoined their colleagues to be more innovative. Currently more experimental narrative forms have become popular among a small audience of younger writers, encouraged by literary Web sites that make publication and public accessibility more available through the Internet. This PoMo, or postmodern experimental writing, often expresses the frenetic social pace now experienced by many young Singaporeans as the country strives to maintain its economic edge in a highly competitive, globalizing economy. In an age of limited free time for reading, Web-based experimental fiction may be the next wave of literary change for the short story in Singapore; perhaps a new form is now emerging from the shadows between poetry and prose.

Alvin Pang's *City of Rain*
Courtesy of Pagesetters Services Pte. Ltd.

Notes

[1] For further information on this complex issue, see Siddique 1989; and Willmott 1989.

[2] There are more than twenty Chinese dialect groups in Singapore, most of which are dying out. On this issue see, http://singaporedialects.tripod.com/id1.html, accessed on May 16, 2008.

[3] Koh Tai Ann also comments on this paradox (1981, 163).

[4] On some Singaporean poet's use of Singlish, see Means 1993, 75; and Koh Tai Ann 1981, 160. By the 1970s, Singaporean poets had developed a third wave of innovation. By the 1980s poets such as Lee Tzu Pheng echoed the discontent of fiction writers who still struggle with a comfortable sense of urban Singapore, while others, such as Arthur Yap, have moved on to technology and urbanization as an integral part of Singaporean life for better or worse. By the 1990s they also reflected the contradiction of the modern Singaporean identity, which is still supposed to draw "core meaning and social values" from rapidly fading ethnic traditions. Older values have been replaced with such new core values as "individual achievement, utility, communication, fluidity of movement and material award" (Means 1993, 82). By this time many young Singaporean writers could only write fluently in English.

[5] Kirpal Singh suggests that these early Chinese writers of English still need much research. He mentions that the literary writings of two men—Lim Thean Soo and N. I. Loo—could yield fruitful information (1998, xiii–xiv). An excellent article on Straits Chinese literature and culture is Clammer 1981.

[6] Wong Meng Voon divides Singapore Chinese literature into three periods: 1919–45, 1945–65, and 1965 to the present (1993, 250–61). There was a debate at the end of 1947 about the independence of Malayan Chinese literature from mainland Chinese influence (253).

[7] For further information on this, see ibid. Thumboo's *The Fiction of Singapore* (1993).

[8] Wong's 1981 collection *Glimpses of the Past: Stories from Singapore and Malaysia* is culled from two earlier Chinese-language collections of his work published in 1969 and 1970. The preface indicates that Wong undertook serious revision of the short stories during their English translation, including slight alterations in the plots (i).

⁹ Govindasamy relates that Saiboo's second published story, "A Dialogue between a Singaporean and an Indian," is significant because it is both beautifully written and experiments with a conversational style (1993, 620–21). A translation of this story is found in Thumboo's *The Fiction of Singapore* (1993, 638–45).

¹⁰ Govindasamy mentions that five Singaporean Tamil writers identified in the 1977 collection include Ma Ilangkannan, Rama Kannabiran, Naa Govindasamy, Elangovan, and Uthuman Ghani. Three of them are anthologized in the final 1981 collection, which was edited by the critic T. K. Sivasankaran in Tamil Nadu (Govindasamy 1993, 635).

¹¹ This volume is based on the English originals and English translations from sections of a three-volume work, *Fiction of Singapore: Anthology of ASEAN Literatures* (Thumboo 1990). The abridged volume was copyrighted as 1990 but apparently not published until 1993 (Thumboo 1993).

¹² For further information, see S. Lim 1989; and Koh Tai Ann 1981.

¹³ Nair describes *The Compact* as "about the only collection during the period 1950–1963 when prose writing has been negligible" (1977, 3). *The Compact* contains fifteen short stories written between 1953 and 1959.

¹⁴ These were essentially collections of short stories by various writers rather than collections by a single writer. While there was no dearth of writing, there was no established short story writer as such at that point in time. A brief overview of this period is found in de Souza and Yap 1993.

¹⁵ It is interesting to note that Goh Sin Tub has also written short stories in Malay and poetry in English (Yeo 1978a, viii).

¹⁶ The anthology in which this story is included, *The Shadow of a Shadow of a Dream* (C. Lim 1987), was a winner of the 1999 S.E.A. Write Award. It was reprinted in 1999.

¹⁷ *Fascist Rock* received an award of commendation from the National Book Development Council in 1992.

¹⁸ It has been established that Russell Lee is the fictitious name of the group of writers who put the anthology together.

¹⁹ The latest work of Russell Lee ghost tales was published in 2002.

²⁰ The third volume of this trilogy (Ramesh 1992) was launched at the 1992 Singapore Book Fair.

[21] It has been accepted by the Cambridge Examinations Syndicate as the text for the General Certificate of Education, Ordinary Level Examinations. Catherine Lim has published seven collections of short stories to date. Her second book, *Or Else, The Lightning God and Other Stories* (1980) is studied in schools, and her other books have found their way onto required reading lists.

[22] Baratham's *Figment of Experience and Other Stories* was reissued as *Love Letter, and Other Stories* (1988a), and Nicky Moey's *Sing a Song of Suspense* was reissued under the title *Pontianak: 13 Chilling Tales*. Goh Sin Tub's *Honour and Other Stories* (1987a) was originally entitled *The Battle of the Bands, and Other Stories*.

[23] These include "Poetry Billboard" (www.poetrybillboard.com) and "Verbosity" (www.verbosity.net/index2/html). Accessed on May 16, 2008.

References

Primary Sources

Baratham, Gopal. 1988a. *Love Letter, and Other Stories*. Singapore: Times Books International.

Cheong, Colin. 1991. *The Stolen Child: A First Novel*. Singapore: Times Books International.

Chua, Rebecca. 1981. *The Newspaper Editor and Other Stories*. Singapore: Heinemann Asia.

Chua, Terence. 1991. *The Nightmare Factory*. Singapore: Landmark Books.

———. 1988b. *People Make You Cry and Other Stories*. Singapore: Times Books International.

Fernandez, George, ed. 1983. *Stories from Singapore: Twenty-four Short Stories by Eighteen Authors*. Singapore: Society of Singapore Writers.

Goh Sin Tub. 1987a. *Honour and Other Stories*. Singapore: Heinemann Asia.

———. 1987b. *The Ghost Lover of Emerald Hill and Other Stories*. Singapore: Heinemann Asia.

———. 2005. *The Angel of Changi and Other Short Stories*. Singapore: Angsana Books.

Heng, Geraldine, ed. 1976. *The Sun in Her Eyes: Stories by Singapore Women*. Singapore: Woodrose Publications.

Ho Mingfong, Poh Fun Ho, Thean Soo Lim, and Kin San Ho. 1986. *Tanjong Rhu And Other Stories*. Singapore: Federal Publications.

Ho Kin San. 1986. "Tze Yong." In *Tanjong Rhu and Other Stories*, 66–71. Singapore Federal Publications.

Jeyaretnam, Philip. 1987. *First Loves*. Singapore: Times Books International.

———. 2002. "Painting the Eye." In *Virtual Lotus: Modern Fiction of Southeast Asia,* edited by Teri Shaffer Yamada, 182–89. Ann Arbor: University of Michigan Press.

———. 2004. *Tigers in Paradise: The Collected Works of Philip Jeyaretnam*. Singapore: Times Editions.

Lee, Russell. 1989. *The Almost Complete Collection of True Singapore Ghost Stories*. Singapore: Flame of the Forest.

———. 1992. *The Almost Complete Collection of True Singapore Ghost Stories*, Vol. 2. Singapore: Angsana Books.

———. 2002. *All New True Singapore Ghost Stories 3*. Singapore: Native Communications.

Lim, Catherine. 1978. *Little Ironies: Stories of Singapore*. Singapore: Heinemann Educational Books (Asia).

———. 1980. *Or Else, The Lightning God and Other Stories*. Singapore: Heinemann Educational Books (Asia).

———. 1983. *They Do Return*. Singapore: Times Books International.

———. 1987. *The Shadow of a Shadow of a Dream: Love Stories of Singapore*. Singapore: Heinemann Asia. Reprinted in 1999 by Horizon Books.

———. 1989. *O, Singapore!: Stories in Celebration*. Singapore: Times Books International.

———. 1992. *Deadline for Love: and Other Stories*. Singapore: Heinemann Asia.

———. 1993. *The Woman's Book of Superlatives*. Singapore: Times Books International.

Lim Thean Soo. 1979. *Fourteen Short Stories*. Singapore: Pan Pacific Book Distributors.

———. 1980. *Bits of Paper and Other Short Stories*. Singapore: Pan Pacific Book Distributors.

———. 1981. *The Parting Gift and Other Stories*. Singapore: Sri Kesava.

———. 1985. *Blues and Carnations*. Singapore: Federal Publications.

Moey, Nicky. 1986. *Let's Play Games*. Singapore: Times Books International.

———. 1988. *Sing a Song of Suspense*. Singapore: Times Books International.

Moo, Joash. 1990. *Sisterhood: The Untold Story*. Singapore: Times Books International.

Nair, Chandran, ed. 1977. *Singapore Writing*. Singapore, Woodrose Publications, for the Society of Singapore Writers.

Nair, Chandran, and Theo Luzuka, eds. 1976. *Short Stories from Africa and Asia*. Singapore: Woodrose Publications.

Poon, Angelia, and Sim Wai Chew, eds. 2007. *Island Voices: A Collection of Short Stories from Singapore*. Singapore: Learners Publishing.

Ramesh, K., ed. 1990. *Book of Souls: True Ghost Stories*. Singapore: Knightsbridge Communications.

———. 1991. *Souls: True Ghost Stories*. Singapore: Knightsbridge Communications.

———. 1992. *Souls: True Ghost Stories*. Book 3. Singapore: Knightsbridge Communications.

Sim, Desmond, et al. 1990. *Tales of the Living: Tales of the Dead*. Singapore: Landmark Books.

Sim, Desmond, Ovidia Yu, and Kwuan Loh. 1990. *Mistress, and Other Creative Takeoffs!* Singapore: Landmark Books.

Tan, Nalla. 1989. *Hearts and Crosses*. Singapore: Heinemann Asia.

Tay, Simon. 1991. *Stand Alone*. Singapore: Landmark Books.

Tham, Claire. 1990. *Fascist Rock: Stories of Rebellion*. Singapore: Times Books International.

———. 1995. *Saving the Rainforest and Other Stories*. Singapore: Times Books International.

———. 2003. *The Gunpowder Trail and Other Stories*. Singapore: Times Editions.

Wong Meng Voon (Huang Mengwen). 1981. *Glimpses of the Past: Stories from Singapore and Malaysia*. Singapore: Heinemann Asia.

Wong Swee Hoon. 1984. *The Landlord*. Singapore: Federal Publications.

———. 1985. *The Phoenix and Other Stories*. Singapore: Heinemann Asia.

———. 1991. *A Dying Breed*. Singapore: Heinemann Asia.

Woo Keng Thye. 1989. *Encounter and Other Stories*. Singapore: Heinemann Asia.

Yamada, Teri Shaffer, ed. 2002. *Virtual Lotus: Modern Fiction of Southeast Asia*. Ann Arbor: University of Michigan Press.

Yeo, Robert, ed. 1978a. *Singapore Short Stories*. Vol. 1. Singapore: Heinemann Educational Books (Asia).

———. 1978b. *Singapore Short Stories*. Vol. 2. Singapore: Heinemann Educational Books (Asia).

———. 1993. *Singular Stories: Tales from Singapore*: Vol. 1. Singapore, Yang Publishers.

Works Cited

Ban Kah Choon. 1979. "Review of Creative Writing in Singapore." *Commentary: Singapore New Issue*, 3.3 (March).

Bonheim, Helmut. 1982. *The Narrative Modes: Techniques of the Short Story*. Cambridge: D. S. Brewer.

Brewster, Anne. 1998. "The Perplexity of Living: Adolescence and Nationalism in Colin Cheong's *The Stolen Child*." In *Interlogue: Studies in Singapore Literature*. Vol 1: *Fiction*, edited by Kirpal Singh, 83–92. Singapore: Ethos Books.

Clammer, John R. 1981. "Straits Chinese Literature: A Minority Literature as a Vehicle of Identity." In *Essays on Literature and Society in Southeast Asia: Political and Sociological Perspectives,* edited by Tham Seong Chee, 287–302. Singapore: Singapore University Press.

Current-Garcia, Eugene, and Walton R. Patrick. 1961. *What Is the Short Story? Case Studies in the Development of a Literary Form*. Chicago: Scott Foresman.

de Souza, Dudley, and Arthur Yap. 1993. "English Fiction." In *The Fiction of Singapore,* edited by Edwin Thumboo, 765–770. Singapore: Unipress.

Evans, Oliver, and Harry Finestone, eds. 1971. *The World of the Short Story: Archetypes in Action.* New York: Knopf.

Fernando, Lloyd, ed. 1977. *Twenty-two Malaysian Stories: An Anthology of Writing in English*. Singapore: Heinemann Educational Books (Asia).

Govindasamy, Naa. 1993. "Introduction to the Singapore Tamil Short Story." In *The Fiction of Singapore,* edited by Edwin Thumboo, 616–27. Singapore: Unipress.

Hochstadt, Herman, ed. 1959. *The Compact: A Selection of University of Malaya Short Stories, 1953-1959*. Singapore: Raffles Society, University of Malaya in Singapore.

Koh Buck Song. 1992a. "Book Bang." *Straits Times,* 24 January.

———. 1992b. "Singapore Literature: Taking Stock." *Arts on Campus* 1.4 (March).

Koh Tai Ann. 1981. "Singapore Writing in English: The Literary Tradition and Cultural Identity." In *Essays on Literature and Society in Southeast Asia: Political and Sociological Perspectives*, edited by Tham Seong Chee, 160–86. Singapore: Singapore University Press.

Lim, Shirley Geok-Lin. 1989. "The English-Language Writer in Singapore." In *Management of Success: The Moulding of Modern Singapore,* edited by Kernial Singh Sandhu and Syed Hussein Alatas, 523–51. Singapore: Institute of Southeast Asian Studies.

Lohafer, Susan. 1983. *Coming to Terms with the Short Story.* Baton Rouge: Louisiana State University Press.

Lohafer, Susan, and Jo Ellyn Clarey, eds. 1989. *Short Story Theory at a Crossroads.* Baton Rouge: Louisiana State University Press.

Means, Laurel. 1993. "Responses to Urbanization in the Poetics of Malaysia and Singapore." In *Cultural Environments in Contemporary Southeast Asia,* edited by Laurel Means, 67–87. Research Monographs, no. 4. Vancouver: Institute of Asian Research.

Minjoot, Veronica. 1984. "The Singapore Short Story: A Thematic Study," Academic Exercise, National University of Singapore.

O'Connor, Frank. 1965. *The Lonely Voice: A Study of the Short Story.* London: Macmillan.

Ong Teong Hean. 1975. "A Story of Singapore Poetry." *Prospect* 7.5: 64–65.

Ooi, Suzanne. 1985. "A Teenager in Her Own Write: Budding Writer Claire Tham Pens about Youth's Conflicts with Society and Authority." *Straits Times,* 29 December.

Shaw, Valerie. 1983. *The Short Story, A Critical Introduction.* New York: Longman.

Siddique, Sharon. 1989. "Singaporean Identity." In *Management of Success: The Moulding of Modern Singapore,* edited by Kernial Singh Sandhu and Syed Hussein Alatas, 563–77. Singapore: Institute of Southeast Asian Studies.

Singh, Kirpal. 1998. "Introduction." In *Interlogue: Studies in Singapore Literature.* Vol. 1: Fiction, edited by Kirpal Singh, xi–xv. Singapore: Ethos Books.

Tan, Nalla, and Chandran Nair, eds. 1977. *The Proceedings of the Seminar on Developing Creative Writing in Singapore, Aug. 6–7, 1976.* Singapore: Woodrose Publications.

Tay, Simon. 1984. "The Writer as a Person." *Solidarity* 99: 56–59.

Thumboo, Edwin, ed. 1990. *The Fiction of Singapore: Anthology of ASEAN Literatures,* Vols. 1–3. Singapore: ASEAN Committee on Culture and Information.

———. 1993. "General Introduction." In *The Fiction of Singapore*, edited by Edwin Thumboo, i–xv. Singapore: Unipress.

Wicks, Peter. 1991. *Literary Perspectives on Southeast Asia: Collected Essays*. Toowoomba: USQ Press.

Willmott. W. E. 1989. "The Emergence of Nationalism." In *Management of Success: The Moulding of Modern Singapore,* edited by Kernial Singh Sandhu and Syed Hussein Alatas, 578–98. Singapore: Institute of Southeast Asian Studies.

Wong Meng Voon. 1993. "Chinese Fiction." In *The Fiction of Singapore*. edited by Edwin Thumboo, 250-261. Singapore: Unipress.

Yeo, Robert. 1978. "Introduction." In *Singapore Short Stories*, edited by Robert Yeo, 1:vii–xvi. Singapore: Heinemann Educational Books (Asia).

———. 1983. "The Singapore Short Story." *Tenggara* 26: 114–19.

———. 1993. "Introduction." In *Singular Stories: Tales from Singapore,* selected by Robert Yeo, 1: 1–8. Singapore: Yang Publishers.

Yong Pow Ang. 1983. "Local Writers Can't Find 'Real' Characters. Says Prof. Edwin Thumboo." *Singapore Monitor*, 17 January.

8

Some Landmarks in the Development of the Indonesian Short Story

Harry Aveling

The contemporary Republic of Indonesia represents the political union of over 350 regional cultures and 250 distinct languages, within a geographically diverse archipelago (H. Geertz 1963, 24).[1] Proclaimed a nation-state in 1945, after three centuries of Dutch colonial rule, Indonesia today maintains both a "modern" culture in the "national language," Indonesian,[2] and a range of more traditional regional cultures in regional languages such as the Sundanese (West Java), Javanese (Central and East Java), Balinese (Bali), Minangkabau (West Sumatra), and so on.[3] The national culture is largely urban in origin. It is attached to the government, the schools, the mass media, and a range of commercial publishing and production houses and includes literature, film and theater, as well as music and art. The national culture is open to contemporary international forms and ideas, particularly those that are popular among young people. The regional cultures are oral (and sometimes print based), familiar—even intimate—and more subject to the religious and moral codes of those local cultures.[4]

A recognizably modern literature in the national language is commonly considered to have begun about 1920 and was primarily sponsored by the Dutch government publishing house, Balai Pustaka.[5] Established in 1908, Balai Pustaka first sought to provide cheap reading materials and textbooks in various local languages, including Malay, for a society that was rapidly being inducted into basic literacy. Later it also published a number of major novels that were critical of traditional ways and sympathetic to the problems of the newly emerging middle-class elite. These novels were written in a grammatically proper form of Malay (called Indonesian after 1928) and were, of course, devoid of obvious political and religious content. The novels published by Balai Pustaka arose from a context not unlike that which created new literary traditions in other developing societies. W. J. Harvey, in *Character and the Novel,* has noted that "the growth of the bourgeoisie in a modern capitalist system" encourages "an acknowledgement of the plenitude, diversity and individuality of human beings in society, together with the belief that such characteristics are good as ends in themselves" (1965, 24). At its best, modern literature, in Indonesia as elsewhere, is an attempt to record, and evaluate, this plenitude of new social situations and personalities.[6]

An earlier study of the Indonesian short story by E. U. Kratz asserts that, based on the sheer numbers of stories written in comparison with other genres, "Indonesian literature is a literature of short stories" (1982, 139). Today most major newspapers in Indonesia include a short story in their Sunday edition. If there are twenty major papers, this suggests an output of 80 stories a month and 960 in a single year. Many magazines also carry stories, further increasing the figure. It would be impossible to deal in detail here with this mass of material, some of which has aesthetic merit but much of which is written for the immediate amusement of the reader. Although in this chapter I want to provide a brief outline survey of the development of the short story during the twentieth century in Indonesia, in order to focus my discussion I will deal in most detail with a small number of works that have had major significance. It is these works that may be considered the "landmarks" within the development of Indonesian literature.

The First "Pre-Indonesian" Short Stories

Few volumes of short stories were published in Indonesia before World War II. A recent catalogue of Indonesian literature lists only five titles from this whole period. Muhammad Kasim is credited with three volumes of humorous stories, *Bertengkar Berbisik* (Fighting and Whispering, 1929), *Buah di Kedai Kopi* (Fruit in the Coffee Shop, 1930), and *Teman Duduk* (A Friend to Sit With, 1936); Soeman Hs. with one, *Kawan Bergelut* (Argumentative Companions, 1938); and Saadah Alim with one *Taman Penghibur Hati* (Garden of Consolation, 1941) (Pamasuk 2001, 3).[7]

This impression of poverty is misleading, however.[8] The establishment of printing presses in the Dutch East Indies during the latter part of the nineteenth century made it possible to publish a vast range of cheap material, including pocket books and newspapers, which could provide the public with stories of various types on an ongoing basis. The first authors of nontraditional fiction, written in a popular colloquial form of the Malay language, were of mixed Chinese or Eurasian descent, and they produced both original and translated literature.[9] Narrative works in the Malay poetic form, *syair*, date from 1871. The first work published was a description of the visit of the king of Thailand to Batavia in that year; the second was a romantic and didactic work called *Mengimpi dan syair burung* (Dreaming and the Poem of a Bird).[10] A third metrical work, a legendary romance set in India, the *Syair Tjerita Siti*

Akbari (Poem of Siti Akbari) by Lie Kim Hok (1853–1912), was published in 1884 (Quinn 1988, 62). This work has recently been shown to have been adapted from an earlier poem in Malay, the *Syair Abdul Muluk* (Poem of Abdul Muluk), composed by Zaleha, the sister of Raja Ali Haji of Riau (9, 37).[11]

The first novel translated from Chinese into Low Malay appeared in 1882. It was a version of a tale about Hai Rui (1513–87), a Ming dynasty politician famous for his incorruptibility whose subsequent dismissal from office has long been a staple diet of Chinese stories and dramas.[12] Stories from *The Romance of the Three Kingdoms* were very popular and extremely widely translated both in the form of books and as serials in newspapers (Suryadinata 1996, 8). Kung fu fighting stories were equally popular. Original narratives in prose soon followed these pioneering experiments. Two prose novels appeared in 1903: *Lo Fen Koei*, by Gouw Peng Liang (1868–1928), described as "a true story, which really happened in Java," and *Cerita Oey Se*, also "a beautiful and amusing story which really happened in Central Java", by Thio Tjin Boen (1885–1940?) (10).

Short stories assumed an important place in newspapers and magazines from the latter part of the nineteenth century onward. The 19 December 1904 issue of the business paper *Perniagaan*, for example, consisted of a single sheet with four pages of print. Page 1 included the story "Sajiman dan Katijah" (Sajiman and Katijah are two names, the story itself had "just happened in Java"); a feuilleton, or serial story, presumably a translation, "Roger Laroque," retold by "the Assistant" (assistant editor?); and "News from the Indies and Other Places." Page 2 carried other news: from China, from the local reformist association Tjong Hoa Hwee Koan, and that received by cable. Pages 3 and 4 were filled with advertisements.

The May 4, 1914, issue of *Sin Po* consisted of two sheets. Page 1 of the second sheet included the feuilleton "Jadi Korban Dari Kawan Pedagang Manusia" (Becoming the Victim of a Comrade Who Trades in Humanity), retold by R. Soepadmo. There were also four sides of advertising in this particular issue. Fourteen years later, the issue of *Sin Po* published on 4 September 1928 consisted of two and a half sheets, twelve pages, with advertisements integrated into the text of six pages, and included two serials: "Kang Ouw Kie Hiap" (a name) by Kwo Lay Yen, and "Pernikahan Ajaib" (Miraculous Wedding) by the same author. *Sin Tit Po* of 22 October 1932 included six sheets with two serials, "Dibuang Seumur Hidup" (Exiled for Life) and "Kuburan" (Grave), and what may have been two more stories, "Cerita Annemarie Lesser" (The History of Annemarie Lesser) and a piece simply entitled "Cerita Pendek" (Short Story). Of the twenty-four pages, five were fully given over to advertisements, while three others also included advertisements (the serials filled in the space left on two of these pages). As Leo Suryadinata, whose summary we are following here, has written: "Most of the peranakan Chinese newspapers lived off their advertisements, while they included serials as a way of capturing their reader's interest" (1996, 67).[13]

Although these early Sino-Malay short stories are, by their nature, obviously difficult to find today, fortunately Indonesian writers and scholars are beginning to collect anthologies of stories from these original sources. These new volumes confirm that the prehistory of Indonesian literature reaches back well before 1920. Following some scholarly discussion on this matter during the 1970s,[14] the major Indonesian prose writer Pramoedya Ananta Toer made available a pioneering anthology of seven "pre-Indonesian" works, *Tempo Doeloe: Antologi Sastra Pra-Indonesia* (Times Past: An Anthology of Pre-Indonesian Literature, [1982] 2003). The book is mainly based on works published between 1896 and 1910. Five of these works use the word *cerita*, "story," in their titles, but because of their length—only two are shorter than twenty pages—the book also reminds us that the novelette in Indonesian is simply a long short story made possible (in most cases) by the advent of the newspaper serial.

The stories in *Tempo Doeloe* are notable for their local settings, most commonly Java. Many date from early in the nineteenth century, suggesting that the printed versions are the end product of a long process of retelling these narratives. The stories are notable for their combination of strong romantic interests and morbid violence. The shortest tale in the collection is "Cerita Nyi Paina" (The Story of Nyi Paina), subtitled "A Girl Who Was Very Virtuous and Faithful" (Kommer 1982, 315–29). It is set around a sugar plantation in Purwo in East Java. We are first introduced to Niti Atmojo, a clerk in the factory, and a fortunate man with a good salary and two beautiful daughters. When the ownership of the factory changes hands, Atmojo has a much less sympathetic boss, Tuan Briot, who accuses him of theft but agrees to drop the charges if Atmojo will surrender one of his daughters, Nyi Paina, to him. Out of sympathy for her father, Nyi Paina agrees to go to Briot and become his concubine. Before she leaves, however, she deliberately contracts smallpox from members of a nearby village. Ten days later, Briot manifests the signs of the disease and forty days later he dies. In the last paragraph of the story, Atmojo receives a new and more sympathetic boss, while Nyi Paina not only recovers but also marries a wealthy Javanese and lives with him happily until her very old age.[15]

A second and slightly later anthology of stories from the "Beginning Period," *Antologi Cerpen Periode Awal*, was published by the Ministry of Education, Jakarta, in 2000. It includes thirty-one short stories (*cerita pendek* or *cerpen*) from nineteen magazines or newspapers, the first stories from 1890 and the last from 1929 (Mujiningsih et al. 2000). Of these stories, seven use the term "*cerita*" in their title (two from 1890, one from 1924, three from 1925, one from 1928), and two of these seven do indeed describe themselves literally as "short stories": "Ceritaan Pendek-pendek" by Samarindaan (1924), and "Cerita Pendek" by M. Saleh Oemar (1928).

The five authors in *Tempo Doeloe* include only one Chinese writer and four Eurasians. Twelve of the thirty-one authors included in the *Antologi Cerpen Periode Awal* had names that are clearly Chinese, four used European names that may have contained Chinese elements (Que, Touchstone, Juvenle Kuo, and Bruine Boonen), six used pen names based on Malay words, one used the name of a region (Wangke, Tanselama, which also suggests a Chinese origin), six were anonymous, and only one used a name (M. Saleh Oemar) that is clearly Malay. The volume probably reflects the common distribution of the ethnic origins of the authors of short stories early in the twentieth century, as shown by our earlier discussion of the use of short stories in the popular press.

The stories in the *Antologi Cerpen Periode Awal* are more varied than those in Toer's anthology. Some appear to be translations of originally Chinese or European stories. "Batoe jang Berhikajat" (The Stone with a Story), (Anonim [1926] 2000), published in 1926, tells of a police inspector, Webs, who buys a stone from a merchant that once allegedly belonged to a Chinese emperor and has the ability to forecast danger. One night, Webs's servant, Martha, presents him with his evening cup of coffee, then retires. The stone turns blood red, and, by accident, the officer spills the coffee. Martha returns, eager to watch him die. She has poisoned the coffee in revenge for Webs's action in imprisoning her son, Breemd, a thief. Webs, of course, does not die, but Breemd's mother goes mad and spends the rest of her life in a mental hospital. In the last paragraph of this story, we are led back into a scientific, non-superstitious world when we find out that the change in color in the stone was due to the spilling of a bottle of red ink during a strong gust of wind. The story is obviously a translation, but the connection with China is interesting.[16]

"Papa, Mama Kemana" (Daddy, Where Is Mummy? [1929] 2000), by Bruine Boonen, uses an Indonesian Chinese setting. The story is set in a prosperous agricultural region near Bogor in West Java. Eng Hok is a graduate of the Agricultural School in Sukabumi. He has the care of a large estate and also of his daughter Lily. Although it is New Year's Day (the Chinese New Year, in fact), Lily's mother, Hiang Nio, is absent. According to the gossip, Hiang Nio has run away with a young employee in the subdistrict. The girl's only visitor is Nora, a Malay woman by name, with whom Eng Hok had once been in love, although his parents insisted he marry Hiang Nio, whose parents were far wealthier than Nora's. At the end of the story, which is just over four pages long, everything is resolved. Hiang Nio has a heart attack and dies in a hospital. Her lover is imprisoned for fraud. Nora becomes Lily's honorary "mama," with the clear likelihood of her impending marriage to Eng Hok.[17]

The Beginning of an "Indonesian" Tradition

The final move from "pre-Indonesian" to Indonesian literature is to be found in a another anthology, which was issued by the Department of Education and Culture in 1994 and entitled *Tiga Puluh Cerita Pendek Indonesia Modern: Tahun 1920-1940* (thirty Modern Indonesian Short Stories, 1920-1940).[18] The anthology provides a variety of short stories drawn from the magazine *Panji Pustaka*, published by Balai Pustaka. The selection covers the period from 1928 to 1939. All of the authors in the *Panji Pustaka* collection appear to have been indigenous Indonesians.

The stories taken from *Tiga Puluh Cerita Pendek Indonesia Modern* are, on the whole, quite different from those in the preceding anthologies. The settings are obviously Indonesian, the characters are Indonesian, and many of the stories selected involve the celebrations that mark the end of the Muslim fasting month, Ramadan. "Surat dari Ibu" (A Letter from Mother, 1932), by the well-known Sumatran writer Or. Mandank, describes the return of a son, the narrator, to his village on this occasion (Mandank 1994). The motive for his return is a letter describing the serious illness of his mother. The core of the story, however, is his childhood recollections about a young girl playmate Dalima. When he again meets Dalima, their relationship has changed: "Now she is a young woman. And I am . . . a young man." Although at the end of the story the narrator must return "overseas" (to Java) to complete his studies, he has promised his mother and his kin that he will be back again in six months. His future marriage to Dalima (who in fact wrote the original letter on his mother's behalf, urging him to come home) is suggested but not explicitly stated.[19]

"Kalau Ibu Meninggal . . ." (If Mother Dies, 1934), by another well-known author, A. Dt. Madjoindo, was also published in an issue of *Panji Pustaka,* marking the end of the fasting month. The story describes a series of Lebaran nights. On the first, Alidin and Alimah are looking forward to the birth of their first child and imagining the pleasures of celebrating the holy day as a family. On the second, the husband is disappointed: the child, Nuraini is teething, and they must stay home with her. On the third, his wife is sick, and to console himself Alidin goes to a nearby coffee shop to play dominoes. Year by year the situation worsens. Finally, Alimah falls sick and is close to death. Nuraini, knowing her father's habits, encourages him to go to the coffee shop and enjoy himself as he always does. Stricken by conscience and remorse, Alidin instead goes to his workshop and resolves to change his ways. His wife recovers, and the story ends: "[T]hen husband and wife were at peace on that day of peace" (Djati and Syam 1994, 91).

The Japanese Occupation of Indonesia, 1942-45

With the stories in *Panji Pustaka*, we have clearly moved from the preliminary phase of an "amorphous and contradictory" mestizo literature to one of full participation in a growing national consciousness (Sykorsky 1980, 498). The tranquil world of small-scale, local, domestic dramas was shattered by the invasion of the Dutch East Indies by Japanese military and naval forces in early 1942. The Japanese were not slow to harness the Indonesian short story to their wartime economic and ideological efforts.

We are again fortunate that Indonesian scholars have prepared an anthology of twenty-one modern Indonesian short stories written during World War II and drawn from the thirty-two stories that were published in *Panji Pustaka* (Djati 1995). The majority of the stories relate to the Japanese desire to co-opt Indonesians to the support of their military aims and most particularly the encouragement of young men to enlist as soldiers in order to fight the Allies.

Matu Mona's "Gegap Gempita di Medan Perang Timur" (Thunder on an Asian Battlefield, 1942), for example, provides a detailed description of the various battles of the war, from the bombing of Pearl Harbor to the assault on Singapore (Mona [1942] 1995). The story is loosely linked by the figure of Lieutenant Ikeda, a pilot, who is shot down over the Straits of Johor but survives and manages to sabotage the largest British artillery gun protecting Singapore with his own life. The story concludes in a very un-islamic manner: "His body had been completely smashed. He had sacrificed himself for the glory of the Emperor and the greatness of his people! His hopes had been fulfilled, his wish granted. His soul flew to heaven, where all the holy spirits are enthroned, according to the teachings of Buddhism" (Djati 1995, 19).[20]

Another story, "Menuntut Bela" (Defense, 1945), by N. Asia, tells of a son, Iskandar, who is leaving his mother in order to fight the enemy on the front line "to defend the motherland from the attacks of Western imperialism which want to oppress and conquer Asian peoples" (N. Asia [1945[1995). His mother supports him in this, describing how his father had been killed by the Dutch twenty years before for taking part in a strike while he was sick. Iskandar's fiancée, Hatijah, too, encourages him to "serve the nation" and vows to "look after and defend the back lines. We will both fight," she tells him, "for the glory of our land and people, for ourselves, for our descendants"

(Djati 1995, 148–51).[21]

Only nine of the stories published during this time deal with more domestic, family situations, and these are all included in the anthology. The themes are similar to those used in stories before the war: young love oppressed by the traditional parental choice of a marriage partner, the pathetic story of a young orphan, the dreams of a young painter, the difficult life of a zealous physician, and such.

Although the personal risk was considerable, not all writers submitted to the demands of the censors. The radical pioneer of "the generation of 1945," Idrus, wrote strongly satirical "underground sketches" about the poverty, hypocrisy, and cruelty experienced throughout the Japanese Occupation.[22] Davidson has suggested that a sketch is "intercultural; it depicts some aspect of one culture for the benefit of another in a relaxed, informal style." Further, "It is factual, journalistic, primarily written, more analytic or descriptive than the tale . . . [and] by nature is *suggestive,* incomplete" (1982, 2). Idrus's sketches meet these criteria and provide brief cynical depictions of a corrupt, unheroic society brutally oppressed by Japanese rapacity.

The stories do not have a plot or even clearly defined characters. The title of one, "Kota Harmoni," literally suggests a "city of harmony" (Idrus [1948] 1990, 79–84). In fact, the work describes a tram ride from one part of Jakarta, namely Kota, to another, Harmoni, and the events are far from harmonious. The passengers on the tram include an arrogant Dutch Eurasian woman; a Chinese man, "as fat as Churchill"; an old woman who is no longer able to afford to travel in the first-class compartment and makes monkey faces at the conductor; a cowardly Indonesian young man; a quisling; and assorted Japanese soldiers. The people quarrel and bicker, the young do not respect the old, men do not honor women, and the Japanese, with one exception, are bullies. The cowardly young man comments under his breath that the Japanese treat all Indonesians equally, which sounds grand until he adds, "like animals" (80). As the passengers complain about the various items that have been taken by the army, it is clear that the idea of the Asian "Co-Prosperity Sphere," in which all the peoples of Southeast Asia were intended to share, would provide wealth for only one community, the Japanese themselves.

The 1945-49 Revolution

Idrus's work successfully put an end to the romanticism of both the prewar Indonesian novel and the short story. He continued to write his cynical, mocking sketches during the Indonesian Revolution against the Dutch (1945 to 1949), beginning with the Battle of Surabaya in November 1945 when the Allies tried to reestablish the groundwork for the return of Dutch colonial authority.[23] The same brutality, hypocrisy, and cynicism occur as in his earlier writing. Idrus's style of writing was not, however, followed by other authors (perhaps it was too distinct). Instead, he was subsequently overshadowed by the major figure of the literary "generation of 1945," Pramoedya Ananta Toer, commonly considered Indonesia's major prose writer of the twentieth century.[24]

Toer was a realist writer; he depicted the world as he saw it without sentiment or philosophical justification. His short stories, in particular, deal with his own childhood during the 1920s and 1930s, the war, and the Revolution. The outstanding collection *Cerita dari Blora* ("Stories from Blora," Toer's birthplace, first published in 1952),[25] opens with a first-person narrative, "Yang Sudah Hilang" (Things That Are Gone),[26] told from the perspective of a child aged perhaps three or four. Much of the surface material concerns the child's various nursemaids and how they appear and disappear in his life. At a more complex level is the story of the child's parents.

We know from other stories by Toer that the relationship between his nationalist, indulgent father and his strict Muslim mother was often tense and difficult. Following the frustration of his hopes for the independent school he had founded, the father spent long periods away from home, gambling. In this story, the child knows that his father is often absent but not the reasons behind his absence. Without understanding what is happening, the child nevertheless describes the collapse of the marriage and the mother's entrapment within the family. Following an implied quarrel between the parents, the pathos of the whole tale is caught in a few simple sentences: "She lifted me, swung me, then put me on her hip, remaining dumb the whole time. When we reached her bed, she hid her face against me. And father didn't come" (Aveling 1975, 20). Throughout the story there runs a "chorus" describing the River Lusi, which surrounds the town of Blora and in its blindness destroys the banks that are intended to protect it.

Courtesy of Penguin Group (Australia)

The young protagonist of "Yang Sudah Hilang" leads a protected existence; many other children in *Cerita dari Blora* are not as fortunate. Inem, for example (in the story of the same name), is the daughter of poor villagers, who is married off at eight, for the small dowry she will bring her parents. The marriage is short-lived, and the child is left to lead a life of brutality and suffering at the hands of members of her own family.[27] Ahyat, in "Anak Haram" (The Bastard), is the son of a traitor, a man who supported the Dutch during the Revolution. Despite the boy's sensitivity and undoubted intelligence, he is mocked by his classmates and his teacher and is (somewhat melodramatically) eventually sent to a reform school so he will learn more respect for his teachers.[28]

The longest story in *Cerita dari Blora* is "Dia Yang Menyerah" (The One Who Surrendered).[29] Like Idrus's sketches, the story tells of the destructive effects of the Japanese Occupation, and then of the Revolution, but focuses this suffering on a single family. The story begins with the arrival of the Japanese in Blora, "two trucks of fully armed soldiers," followed by four truckloads of dead soldiers. This inauspicious group signifies the end of some 350 years of Dutch rule over the East Indies. Within a few months, two of the brothers in the family leave home to become *romusha*, "conscript laborers," who were praised by the short story writers approved by the Japanese authorities. Toer's comment on the future of these laborers is brief: "Within a week or three, they would have to die." The oldest sister, Is, takes a job as a typist in a government office. One of the youngest sisters, Sri, barely eleven, is forced to leave school and look after the house. For the first, but not the last, time in her life, Sri surrenders to her fate.

The joy aroused by the eventual proclamation of independence does not last long. The family is caught between various warring factions during the subsequent Revolution: nationalist, communist, and Muslim, as well as the Dutch. Each faction brings violence to the town and takes away other members of the family, including the nationalist father, none of whom (except for Sri) ever return again. The story ends with the final implementation of independence but also with tremendous disappointment.

> While the government lived proudly in a castle in the sky somewhere above our small, unimportant town, Sri and her family lived in a cardboard shack. The word "development" was everywhere, but they had not begun their slow climb back up. They had neither the strength nor the capital to develop anything from the fragments of their lives. Their only option is to abstain from the national affirmation signified by "the mass rallies in the city square" (Aveling 1975, 105).

The Fifties

Like Toer, many others were disappointed by the apparent failure of the Revolution to bring widespread democratic procedures and economic prosperity to Indonesia. The short story "Usaha Samad" (Samad's Businesses), by Utuy Tatang Sontani, caught this mood in an effective if rather crude way.[30] Samad is a young man who has come from the countryside to earn a living in Jakarta. He first attempts to sell religious tracts written by his teacher. This is a massive failure, and he curses the city for its evil ways. Next he tries to sell pictures of the president. This brings better results but still far less than he had hoped for. Finally, he is successful beyond his wildest dreams—selling pictures of naked young women! His aunt, with whom he is staying, covers the shocked expression on her face with one hand but accepts the money he brings with the other. The chaos produced by the dislocation of almost a decade of war is very evident in the story.

During the 1950s authors explored a number of new settings for their writing. Writers who were still interested in using regional settings often consciously saw the countryside from the perspective of the city rather than on its own terms. In the case of Sitor Situmorang, this return to the village of his childhood was marked by a strong sense of alienation influenced by the French philosophy of existentialism, which he had experienced firsthand overseas.[31] The story "Ibu pergi ke sorga" (Mother Goes to Heaven) is reminiscent in its emotional attitudes to Camus' *Outsider* (1942). It describes the death of the narrator's mother in a distant mountain village. The narrator feels out of place in that poor, backward setting and utterly out of sympathy with his mother's Christian beliefs. Her death has no impact on him; the local pastor's reassurance that she is now in heaven strikes him as hollow and meaningless.

As a response to the increasing instability felt in Indonesia after the mid-1950s, President Sukarno introduced after 1957 a political system that he called Guided Democracy. The new system placed the president at the center of the political system and forced him to continually balance his actions between the power of the army and the extremist popular nationalism of the Indonesian Communist Party. Ideologically, the system was expressed through the term Manipol USDEK. It incorporated Sukarno's "Political Manifesto" speech of August 1959, the five principles of the 1945 Constitution, Indonesian socialism, Guided Democracy, Guided Economy, and the Indonesian identity.[32] This left-ward swing was felt in literature, too. As Goenawan Mohamad later wrote, both those sympathetic to the Communist Institute for the People's Art, Lekra,[33] and those opposed to it,[34] increasingly wrote on the same topics: the suffering and heroism of the masses, the inevitability of history, truth, and justice (1969, 42–43).

The story "Si Sapar" was an outcome of Sontani's increasing commitment to socialist causes (2002, 175–208). The story deals with two working-class figures, commonly sentimentalized in postwar Indonesian writing: a trishaw driver, Sapar; and a prostitute, Onih. The plot moves through a number of distinct scenes, beginning with Sapar's finding a job as a trishaw driver, his meeting with Onih, and his gradually becoming her regular means for meeting her customers. The counterbalance to these two working-class figures is an unnamed, stout, forty-year-old man who holds a lucrative position running a government enterprise. The climax of the story is motivated by Sapar's desire to have Onih for himself and his killing her when she refuses him. Sontani is conscious of the literary nature of the tale. When Sapar first meets Onih, she is fleeing from the police, but he fantasizes that he is a prince in an old legend saving the princess from some ravaging demon. The phrase "you may believe this or not" is used regularly throughout the story (as if Sontani himself probably did not believe it). But the real climax of the story is political: the punishment of the corrupt government official. This occurs when the official meets Onih for a second time and gradually realizes that he is riding in a ghost trishaw next to a corpse. The man is dreaming, of course, but the crude horror—and the strong element of didactic class conflict—remains.

The Beginning of the "New Order": After 1966

President Sukarno began to transfer his power to Major General Suharto in early 1966 and Suharto was finally sworn in as the Second President of Indonesia in 1968. At first, the realism of the previous period continued to dominate the short story genre. Soon social realism was abandoned, and a new literary élan slowly made itself felt.[35]

An outstanding indication of the use of formal realism can be found in the works of Umar Kayam,[36] which provided a balanced reflection on the dissolution of what quickly became known as the Old Order. Kayam wrote four long stories on the violent clashes between the army and communists that marked the end of 1965. "Bawuk" is the story of a daughter in an aristocratic (*priyayi*) Javanese family (Aveling 1976, 135–62). Her brothers and her sisters' spouses hold important positions within the government, the military, and the academic world. She, however, has deliberately turned her back on this type of success in marrying Hasan, a communist. As Bawuk tries to explain to her family:

> He dreamt that people could be important regardless of their position and qualifications. He was a fool. He thought he understood the society he lived in. He didn't understand it at all. He should have finished high school, gone to

university, at home or abroad, tried for a good position with the government, worked his way up to section head, hoped to be a manager or a director-general. Instead he left school, became a Marxist, studied politics, plotted, dreamed and then plotted again, dreamed and finally revolted. (159)

The story is divided into three sections. In the first, Bawuk's mother, Madam Suryo, remembers Bawuk's childhood and most especially the girl's sensitivity when Madam Suryo was suffering because of her husband's behavior but unable to say anything as befits a properly submissive Javanese wife. In the second part, Bawuk brings her two children for her mother to look after. Madam Suryo has called the whole family together for this occasion, and Bawuk explains to them that she has been trying to find Hasan now that the party has gone underground and is engaging in armed resistance against the army. At the end of the night, and of her explanation—which no one has heard but her mother—Bawuk again leaves to search for her husband. In the very short third part, Madam Suryo reads of the death of a number of communists in a battle with the army. Hasan is dead. She does not know what has happened to Bawuk.

Despite its contemporary setting, the story has deep roots in Javanese culture. The two women share the common experience of being faithful to their husbands despite the men's shortcomings. Bawuk's brothers and sisters offer her protection if she will stay with them. She refuses. In remaining faithful to Hasan, and therefore potentially associating herself with the outlawed Communist Party and its inevitable destruction, Bawuk aligns herself with one of the great Javanese *wayang* (puppet theatre) characters, Karno. In the great battle of the *Mahabharata*, Karno pledged himself to fight alongside his adopted benefactor, the evil Kurawa, and he remained faithful to that vow even though he eventually learned that he was in fact born among the virtuous and ultimately victorious Pandawa. Karno's tragic loyalty has earned the admiration of audiences for at least a thousand years. Bawuk's commitment to finding Hasan is similarly admirable despite its turning to the dark side.

The unexpectedly radical experiments that took place after 1967-68, in all areas of writing—prose, poetry, and theatre—were characterized by a turning toward what came to called "surrealism": fantasy writing based on the images and illogic of the subconscious. An outstanding advocate of this new freedom in fiction writing was Danarto.[37]

Like Kayam, Danarto made deliberate use of images drawn from Javanese *wayang* theater. "Nostalgia" retells one of the incidents of the war between the Pandawa and the Kurawa, the death of Abimanyu, Arjuna's son (1987, 90–105). Danarto does not use the incident for its own sake or seek to bring a contemporary political relevance to it. Instead, he turns Abimanyu's death into a profound meditation on the unity of creation, and the dissolution of the self into God in a way that has many resonances with the classical Hindu scripture, the *Bhagavad Gita*.

Some of Danarto's main characters in his first book, *Godlob* (The Love of God, English translation *Abracadabra* [Aveling (1978) 2001] are like figures from folktales, but they are nevertheless his own creations. There are Rintrik, a crazy old woman who spends her days burying unwanted babies, and Bekakrakan, a fiendishly handsome, ghostly male figure who appears to seduce both a young girl and her mother. And there are the more recognizable Salome, determined to provoke God into revealing Himself to her through her indecent behavior, and Hamlet, who reports back to his friend Horatio on the dazzling and paradoxical experiences he undergoes in the afterlife.

The End of the New Order: The Early 1990s

As the Suharto era progressed, there were increasingly tight controls over the public expression of personal opinions. Within the field of prose writing, as the Dutch critic Hendrik Maier has argued, "Suharto and his administrative apparatus have castrated a generation of writers, robbing them of their generative power, the power of being historical witnesses who could tell others about what is happening before their very eyes" (1999, 258).[38] A number of representative anthologies in English present the short stories from this later period; most of the works are more important for their entertainment value than their profound questioning of the human condition.[39]

The use of fantasy and symbolism could, nevertheless, still provide important literary strategies for finding ways of still speaking about the contemporary situation in Indonesian society. One of the clearest examples of this is to be found in the work *Saksi Mata* (Eyewitness 1994) by Seno Gumira Ajidarma.[40]

Sepotong Senja Untuk Pacarku
(A Slice of Twilight for My Sweetheart)
by Seno Gumira Ajidarma.
Cover art by Mansyur Mas'ud.

The title story "Eyewitness," begins: "The eyewitness came. He had no eyes" ([1994] 2002, 1–12). [41] Blood pours from his sockets, wetting his clothes and slowly covering the floor of the courtroom where he is to give testimony. After the judge has quietened the uproar that greets this appearance, he tries to find out what has happened to the witness's eyes. The man explains that they were taken by men in uniforms, Ninjas. He is, nevertheless, prepared to testify "for the sake of truth and justice." In the further uproar, the judge breaks the gavel by pounding it too hard on the bench in front of him. As he drives home, the judge is impressed by the witness's honesty and thinks that he should be prepared to sacrifice more for the public good—before promptly falling asleep. That night, the eyeless witness prays that goodness may rule throughout the world; then, while he sleeps, five Ninjas come and pull out his tongue.

Ajidarma was a journalist and the editor of an important glossy magazine, *Jakarta Jakarta*. Although the stories in *Eyewitness* are set in an imaginary Latin America state, the realities to which they refer were much closer to home. In order to forestall the possibility of a radical socialist state on its doorstep, the Indonesian Armed Forces invaded East Timor in December 1975 and declared it a province of Indonesia. Over the next two decades, many acts of violence were committed against the Timorese people by both official and unofficial militia groups. (The unofficial groups were, in fact, commonly known as "ninjas," because of the black clothing they wore during their stealthy operations.) Perhaps the most blatant, but also the most widely reported internationally, was the Dili Massacre of 12 December 1991.[42] Seno reported the invasion in his magazine and was, as a consequence, suspended from his duties for several months afterward. The stories in *Eyewitness* were his way of describing what had happened in Dili and how the wider Indonesian state had colluded to ignore the legal and moral issues arising from that incident.[43]

Contemporary Developments: Oka Rusmini

Suharto was forced to resign as president of Indonesia in May 1998. His downfall was followed by a widespread call for greater freedom of speech in public and through the press. There was an outpouring of new writing of all types—novels, poetry and short stories— particularly by women, many of whom represent a younger generation of experimental writers.

In the last part of this chapter, I want to concentrate on one contemporary woman writer, Oka Rusmini.[44] Oka writes consistently about Balinese society. In one way, this is an indication of the move away from Jakarta in many areas of life and the decentralization of writing in Indonesia that has been taking place since the mid-1980s. Oka was born into the highest caste, Balinese society being the last part of the archipelago to retain the Hindu religion and culture in the face of the conversion of most of the archipelago to Islam that began some eight centuries ago. On the other hand, Oka also writes at a distance removed from Balinese culture and is highly critical of it. (She was born and raised in Jakarta, and lost her caste position when she married a Muslim.)

"Cenana" is the story of two women, Cenana herself and her mother-in-law Ida Ayu Putu Siwi (2001, 169–200). When arranged in a linear manner, the story tells of Siwi's inability to have children; the death of her husband; her adoption of a young boy, Puja; her expulsion from her noble family group and subsequent extraordinary business success; Puja's rape of a village dancer, Cenana, whom he subsequently marries; and Cenana's pregnancy. In fact, the story is not written in a chronological sequence but moves back and forth among these various events.

Behind the story is another story; that story of Ken Angrok, a peasant bandit who eventually took the throne of Daha, East Java, in 1222 CE, and in the process kidnapped and married Ken Dedes, the former wife of the governor of Tumapel. Siwi identifies herself with Ken Dedes and Puja with Ken Angrok.[45]

"Cenana" as a whole indicates the powerful ways in which Balinese society can oppress women, particularly through the use of religious sanctions related to marriage, but it also suggests the power that is available to women who are prepared to step beyond its boundaries and define their lives in terms of modern commercial society. By becoming

The Lontar Foundation has been instrumental in promoting the publication of English translations of the best Indonesian writers in their "Menagerie" series. Cover painting: *Labyrinth* (Original title: *Labirin*) by Dede Eri Supria, 1990.
Courtesy of the Lontar Foundation.

rich and commercially powerful, Siwi is able to attain a higher status than her family would previously have allowed her. Puja, as her child (and, illegitimate though he may be, that of her husband) is also conceded a high standing, which his birth to a low-caste woman would not have allowed. "Cenana" is a feminist tale which is at once very modern yet also deeply traditional.

Beyond the Horizon

In his 1975 "Speech Accepting an Award of Honour from the Jakarta Academy," the distinguished Indonesian dramatist and poet (and sometime short story writer) Rendra insisted that "intellectuals, religious leaders and artists" should attempt to adopt an ascetic and analytical position toward their society, which would allow them "to guard spiritual values" and provide "inspiration and vitality" (Lane 1979, 75–87). I have suggested that the short story is ubiquitous in Indonesia and fulfills many functions. Most often, it soothes and comforts existing perceptions of a routinized and increasingly technocratic society. Occasionally, it can also challenge these perceptions and "defamiliarize" the world in such a way that readers are forced to reconsider their relationship to "those things which have become habitual or automatic" (Erlich 1965, 76). The landmarks described in this chapter have fulfilled this crucial function.

Notes

[1] A useful basic reference is Koentjaraningrat 1975.

[2] For a history of this language, see Robson 2002.

[3] Literatures in regional languages are beyond the scope of this essay. [Ed.]

[4] An early discussion of the "national art" complex can be found in (Clifford Geertz 1960, 302–3).

[5] See, for example, Teeuw 1967, 13–15. A critical study is Jedamski 1992.

[6] A. H. Johns has noted "that agonizing sense of doubt, that questioning and criticism of the bases of social life, and the analysis and presentation of the predicaments of individuals" that characterize a "modern literature" (1963, 411).

[7] Ajip Rosidi discusses the short stories of M. Kasim and Soeman Hs. in his pioneering work *Tjerita pendek Indonesia* (1959; 3–6, 25–31). Rosidi has modernized the spelling of these titles, in accordance with the reforms of 1973. In this chapter, I will follow his example within my main text, giving the original spelling, where available, in the notes.

[8] Note that the first story in volume 1 of Satyagraha Hoerip's valuable four-volume series *Cerita pendek Indonesia* (1979), for example, was published in December 1949. He also edited a collection of short stories in English translation (1991).

[9] Salmon (1981, 10) notes that over 3,000 works by Indonesian Chinese authors were published between 1870 and 1966. These included 73 plays, 183 long poems (*syair*), 233 translations of Western works (particularly stories of Sherlock Holmes, Fu Manchu, Tarzan, the Three Musketeers, and the works of Rider Haggard and Jules Verne), 759 translations of Chinese works, and 1,398 novels and short stories.

[10] *Sair Kadatangan Sri Maharadja Siam di Betawin pada tanggal 27 Maart 1871.* See Salmon (1992, 6, n. 9).

[11] For further information, see Zaini-Lajoubert 1988, 277–321.

[12] For details, see Salmon 1987, 402.

[13] Suryadinata's summary is found in Surjomihardjo 2002, 65–70.

[14] Some major studies include Nio 1962; Watson 1971; Sykorsky 1980; and Salmon 1981.

[15] Pramoedya incorporated this story into the second volume of his famous Buru quartet, *Anak Semua Bangsa* (Child of All Nations, 1990).

[16] This story by Anonim (anonymous), "Batu yang Berhikayat" was originally published in *Warna Warta* 1.22, 29 May 1926, and reprinted in Mujiningsih, et al (2000, 12-18).

[17] This story was originally published in *Keng Po*, 9 February 1929, see Mujiningsih, et al. (2000, 57–62).

[18] Widodo Djati and Suryati Syam edited this collection (Djati and Syam 1994).

[19] "Surat dari Ibu" was first published in *Panji Pustaka*, Lebaran, 1932, and reprinted in ibid 62–67.

[20] This story was first published in *Panji Pustaka* 20.20–22 (August 1942): 66–64; 21:735–36 and reprinted in Djati 1995.

[21] This story was first published in *Panji Pustaka* 23.3–1 (February 1945): 81–82 and reprinted in ibid.

[22] Idrus was born on 21 September 1921 in Padang and died on 18 May 1979 in Kampung Tanah, Padang. He was educated in various Dutch-language schools until 1943 when he became an editor with Balai Pustaka. He was head of the Education Section of GIA from 1950 to 1952. Subsequently he worked as an editor at the literary periodicals *Indonesia* and *Kisah*. He resided in Kuala Lumpur, Malaysia, from 1960 to 1964; and taught at Monash University, Melbourne, Australia, from 1965 to 1979, from which he received a master of arts degree in 1974. His earliest published works were dramas: *Dokter Bisma* (1945), *Aceh* (1945), and *Keluarga Surono* (1948). Idrus is best known for the collection *Dari Ave Maria ke Jalan Lain ke Roma* ([1948] 1990), but he also wrote novels: *Aki* (1949), *Perempuan dan Kebangsaan* (1949), *Hati Nurani Manusia* (1963), and *Hikayat Puteri Penelope* (1973).

[23] See the short story "Surabaya" in Aveling 1976, 1–28.

[24] Pramoedya Ananta Toer was born on 6 February 1925 in Blora, Central Java. He was educated at Blora Elementary School, Radio Technicians School Surabaya (1940–41), Taman Siswa (1942–43), Stenography School (1944–45), and Jakarta Muslim College (1945). He first worked as a typist at the Japanese News Agency, Domei (1942–45), then became a second lieutenant in the Sixth Regiment of the Siliwangi Division (1946). Later he became an editor at Balai Pustaka (1950–51), then head of the "Literary and Features Agency Duta" (1951–54). He was subsequently involved in various literary and cultural organizations. He was imprisoned by the Dutch between 1947 and 1949, by Sukarno in 1960, and by the Soeharto regime from 1965 to 1979. He is the author of many novels, including *Perburuan* (The Fugitive,

1950) and the "Buru Quartet" (*Bumi Manusia* [This Earth of Mankind], *Anak Semua Bangsa* [Child of All Nations], *Jejak Langkah* [Footsteps] and *Rumah Kaca* [House of Glass]). The best essays on Toer's work include Johns [1963] 1979, and Foulcher 1993a, 1993b.

[25] See Toer 2004 for a recent English translation of this collection.

[26] An English translation, "Lonely Paradise," is also found in Aveling 1975, 1–24.

[27] An English translation, "Inem," is found in Aveling 1976, 29–40.

[28] An English translation, "The Bastard," is found in Aveling 1976, 41–8.

[29] An English translation, "The Vanquished," is found in Aveling 1975, 45–15.

[30] Utuy Tatang Sontani was born in Cianjur, West Java, in May 1920. His short stories were first published in the collection *Orang-orang Sial* (The Unfortunates) in 1951. He is best known for his plays, which he wrote in story format. Sontani was a member of the left-wing Institute for Mass Culture and died in exile in Russia in 1979. "Usaha Samad" is reprinted in Rosidi 2002, 141–46.

[31] Sitor Situmorang was born in Samosir, North Sumatra, in 1923. He spent 1952–53 in Paris and 1956–57 in the United States. He was chairman of the Sukarnoist Lembaga Kebudayaan Nasional (National Cultural Institute) during the period of Guided Democracy and subsequently spent the years 1967–75 in detention. Although best known as a poet, Sitor published two volumes of short stories: *Pertempuran dan Saldju di Paris* (Battle and Snow in Paris, 1956) and *Pangeran* (Prince, 1963).

[32] A major reference is Feith 1963.

[33] For further information see Foulcher 1986.

[34] See Foulcher 1969 for an account of one attempt to oppose the prevailing literary ideology. This opposition had no real significant literary consequences.

[35] A number of left-wing authors, supporters of Sukarno, were imprisoned for varying lengths of time under the New Order regime of President Suharto, and many books were banned. For more details on this see Sen and Hill 2000, 37.

[36] Umar Kayam was born in Ngawi, East Java, in 1932. He studied in America, earning a master's degree from New York University and a doctorate from Cornell

University. After returning to Indonesia in the mid-1960s he worked as the head of the Indonesian Radio and Television Corporation, then of the Jakarta Arts Centre, and throughout most of his life as an academic. He died 2002.

[37] Danarto was born in 1940 in Sragen, Central Java. He trained at the Arts Academy, Yogyakarta, and worked in Jakarta as an artist, designer and cultural figure. Since his first book *Godlob* (1975), he has published three more collections of short stories: *Adam Ma'rifat* (1982), *Berhala* (1987), *Gergasi* (1993), as well as the novel *Asmaraloka* (1999). An important critical study is Prihatmi (1989).

[38] As I indicate in my *Secrets Need Words: Indonesian Poetry, 1966–1998* (2001, xiii), I do not believe that this statement holds in the field of Indonesian poetry.

[39] These anthologies include Allen 1995, Hill 1998, Lingard 1995, and Roskies 1997.

[40] Born in Boston in the United States in 1958, Ajidarma later studied in the Department of Cinematography, Jakarta Academy of the Arts. He was a journalist and editor of *Sinema Indonesia* (1980), *Zaman* (1983–84), and *Jakarta Jakarta* (since 1985). He has published various volumes of poetry: *Granit dan Dinamit* (Granades and Dynamite, with Ajie Sudarmaji Muksin, 1975), *Mati Mati Mati* (Death, Death, Death, 1975), *Bayi Mati* (The Dead Baby, 1978), and *Catatan-catatan Mira Sato* (Notes by Mira Sato, 1978). His collections of short stories include *Manusia Kamar* (The People in the Room, 1988), *Negeri Kabut* (Land of Mist, 1996), *Iblis Tidak Pernah Mati* (The Devil Never Died, 1999), and *Mengapa kau culik anak kami?* (Why Did You Kidnap Our Children? 2001).

[41] For the English translation of the title story, "Saksi Mata" (Eyewitness), see Lingard et al. 1995, 41–48.

[42] On East Timor, see Fox and Soares 2000; and Schwarz 1994.

[43] Ajidarma's description of the background to writing the stories was first published as the introduction to the English translation in 1995 and then incorporated into a collection of essays entitled *Ketika Jurnalisme Dibungkam, Sastra Harus Bicara* (When Journalism Is Gagged, Literature Must Speak, 1997). He also incorporated direct descriptions of events in Dili into his book *Jazz, Parfum, dan Insiden* (Jazz, Perfume, and the Incident 1996), English translation in Harris 2002. Other translations of Ajidarma's work can be found in Bodden 2002. For further information see Bodden 1999, 153–56.

[44] Oka Rusmini, a novelist and short story writer, was born in Jakarta on 11 July 1967; see her short story collection *Sagra* (2001) and novel *Tarian Bumi* (2000).

[45] This classical story is told in the *Para Raton*; see the English translation by Phalgunadi (1996).

Bibliography

Ajidarma, Seno Gumira. 1994. *Saksi Mata* [Eyewitness]. English translation listed under Jan Lingard. Yogyakarta: Bentang.

―――. 1996. *Jazz, Parfum, dan Insiden* [Jazz, Perfume, and the Incident], English translation listed under Gregory Harris. Yogyakarta: Yayasan Bentang Budaya.

―――. 1997. *Ketika Jurnalisme Dibungkam Sastra Harus Bicara*. [When Journalism is Gagged, Literature Must Speak]. Yogyakarta: Yayasan Bentang Budaya.

Allen, Pamela, ed. 1995. *Women's Voices: An Anthology of Short Stories by Indonesian Women Writers*. Melbourne: Longman.

Anonim. [1926] 2000. "Batoe jang Berhikajat" [The Stone with a Story]. In *Antologi Cerpen Periode Awal* [An Anthology of Short Stories: The Early Period], edited by Erlis Nur Mujingsih et al., 12–18. Jakarta: Pusat Bahasa, Departemen Pendidikan Nasional.

Aveling, Harry. 2001. *Secrets Need Words: Indonesian Poetry, 1966–1998*. Athens: Center for International Studies, Ohio University.

Aveling, Harry, ed. and trans. 1975. *A Heap of Ashes* by Pramoedya Ananta Toer. St. Lucia, Queensland: University of Queensland Press.

―――. [1978] 2001. *Secrets Need Words*. Abracadabra. Jakarta: Metafor.

―――. 1976. *From Surabaya to Armageddon: Indonesian Short Stories*. Singapore: Heinemann Educational Books.

Bodden, Michael H. 1999. "Seno Gumira Ajidarma and Fictional Resistance to an Authoritarian State in 1990s Indonesia." *Indonesia* 68 (October): 153–56.

―――. trans 2002. *Jakarta at a Certain Point in Time: Fiction, Essays, and a Play from the Post-Suharto Era in Indonesia,* by Seno Gumira Ajidarma. Victoria, BC: Centre for Asia-Pacific Initiatives, University of Victoria.

Bruine Boonen. [1929] 2000. "Papa, Mama Kemana" [Daddy, Where Is Mummy?]. In *Antologi Cerpen Periode Awal,* edited by Erlis Nur Mujiningsih et al., 57–62 . Jakarta: Pusat Bahasa, Departemen Pendidikan Nasional.

Davidson, Jeremy. 1982. "The Modern Short Story in South East Asia: An Introduction." In *The Short Story in South East Asia: Aspects of a Genre,* edited by J. Davidson and H. Cordell, 1–27. London: School of Oriental and African Studies, University of London.

Danarto. 1974. *Godlob: 9 Cerita Pendek* [Godlob: Nine Short Stories]. N.p.: Rombongan Dongeng dari Dirah. Translated by Harry Aveling as *Abracadabra* in 1978.

———. 1987. *Godlob: Kumpulan Cerita Pendek*. Jakarta: Grafitipers.

Djati, Widodo, ed. 1995. *Antologi Cerita Pendek Indonesia Modern pada Zaman Jepang dalam Majalah Panji Pustaka*. Jakarta: Departemen Pendidikan dan Kebudayaan.

Djati, Widodo, and Suryati Syam, eds. 1994. *Tiga Puluh Cerita Pendek Indonesia Modern: Tahun 1920–1940*. Jakarta: Pusat Pembinaan dan Pengembangan Bahasa.

Erlich, Victor. 1965. *Russian Formalism: History, Doctrine*. The Hague: Mouton.

Feith, Herb. 1963. "The Dynamics of Guided Democracy." In *Indonesia*, edited by Ruth T. McVey, 309–409. New Haven: HRAF Press.

Foulcher, Keith. 1969. "The Events Surrounding 'Manikebu.'" *Bijdragen tot de Taal-, Land- en Volkenkunde* 125.4: 429–65.

———. 1986. *Social Commitment in Literature and the Arts: The Indonesian "Institute of People's Culture," 1950–1965*. Clayton, Vic.: Centre of Southeast Asian Studies, Monash University.

———. 1993a. "The Early Fiction of Pramoedya Ananta Toer, 1946–49." In *Text/Politics in Island Southeast Asia: Essays in Interpretation,* edited by D. M. Roskies, 191–220. Athens: Center for International Studies, Ohio University.

———. 1993b. "Literature, Cultural Politics, and the Indonesian Revolution." 221–256 in *Text/Politics in Island Southeast Asia: Essays in Interpretation*. Edited by D. M. Roskies. Athens, Ohio: Ohio University Center for International Studies.

Fox, James J., and Dionisio Babo Soares. 2000. *Out of the Ashes: The Destruction and Reconstruction of East Timor*. Adelaide: Crawford House.

Geertz, Clifford. 1960. *The Religion of Java*. Glencoe, IL: Free Press.

Geertz, Hildred. 1963. "Indonesian Cultures and Communities," In *Indonesia,* edited by Ruth McVey, 24–96. New Haven: Council on Southeast Asian Studies, Yale University.

Goenawan Mohamad. 1969. "Njanji Sunji jang Kedua." *Horison* (February): 41–45.

Harris, Gregory, trans. 2002. *Jazz, Perfume, and the Incident*, by Seno Gumira Ajidarma. Jakarta: Lontar Foundation.

Harvey, J. 1965. *Character and the Novel*. Ithaca: Cornell University Press.

Hill, David, ed. 1998. *Beyond the Horizon: Short Stories from Contemporary Indonesia*. Clayton Vic.: Asia Institute, Monash University.

Idrus. [1948] 1990. *Dari Ave Maria ke Jalan Lain ke Roma*. Jakarta. Balai Pustaka.

Jedamski, Doris. 1992. "Balai Pustaka: A Colonial Wolf in Sheep's Clothing." *Archipel* 44:23–46.

Johns, Anthony Hearley. 1963. "Genesis of a Modern Literature." In *Indonesia*, edited by Ruth McVey, 410–437. New Haven: Council on Southeast Asian Studies, Yale University, by arrangement with HRAF Press.

———. ed. 1979. *Cultural Options and the Role of Tradition: A Collection of Essays on Modern Indonesian and Malaysian Literature*. Canberra: Faculty of Asian Studies in association with the Australian National University Press.

———. [1963] 1979. "Pramudya Ananta Tur, the Writer as Outsider: An Indonesian Example." In *Cultural Options and the Role of Tradition*, edited by Anthony Johns, 96–108. First published in *Meanjin*.

Kayam, Umar. 1976. "Bawuk." Translated by Harry Aveling. In *From Surabaya to Armageddon: Indonesian Short Stories*, edited by Harry Aveling, 135–162. Singapore: Heinemann Educational Books.

Klein, Leonard S., ed. 1988. *Far Eastern Literatures in the Twentieth Century*. Harpenden, U.K.: Oldcastle Books.

Koentjaraningrat, R. M. 1975. *Introduction to the Peoples and Cultures of Indonesia and Malaysia*. Menlo Park, CA: Cummings.

Kommer, H. 1982. "Tjerita Nji Paina" [The Story of Nji Paina]. In *Tempo Doeloe*, edited by Pramoedya Ananta Toer, 315–29. Jakarta: Hasta Mitra.

Kratz, E. U. 1982. "The Indonesian Short Story After 1945." In *The Short Story in South East Asia: Aspects of a Genre*, edited by Jeremy Davidson and H. Cordell, 139–66. London: School of Oriental and African Studies, University of London.

Lane, Max, trans. 1979. *The Struggle of the Naga Tribe: A Play by Rendra*. St. Lucia, Queensland: University of Queensland Press.

Lingard, Jeanette, ed. 1995. *Diverse Lives: Contemporary Stories from Indonesia.* Kuala Lumpur: Oxford University Press.

Lingard, Jeanette, Bibi Langker, and Suzan Piper, trans. 1995. *Eyewitness* by Seno Gumira Ajidarma. Sydney: ETT Imprints.

Madjoindo, A. Dt. 1994. "Kalau Ibu Meninggal . . ." (If Mother Dies . .). In *Tiga Puluh Cerita Pendek Indonesia Modern: Tahun 1920–1940*, edited by Widodo Djati and Suryati Syam, 87–91. Jakarta: Pusat Pembinaan dan Pengembangan Bahasa.

Maier, Hendrik, M. J. 1999. "Flying a Kite: The Crimes of Pramoedya Ananta Toer." In *Figures of Criminality in Indonesia, the Philippines, and Colonial Vietnam*, edited by Rudolf Mrazek and Vicent L. Rafael, 231–258. Ithaca: Southeast Asia Program, Cornell University.

Mandank, Or. 1994. "Surat dari Ibu" [A Letter from Mother]. In *Tiga Puluh Cerita Pendek Indonesia Modern: Tahun 1920-1940,* edited by Widodo Djati and Suryati Syam, 63–67. Jakarta: Pusat Pembinaan dan Pengembangan Bahasa.

McVey, Ruth, ed. 1963. *Indonesia.* Survey of World Cultures, no. 12. New Haven: Council on Southeast Asian Studies, Yale University, by arrangement with HRAF Press.

Mona, Matu. [1942]1995. "Gegap Gempita di Medan Perang Timur" [Thunder on an Asian Battlefield]. In *Antologi Cerita Pendek Indonesia Modern pada Zaman Jepang dalam Majalah Panji Pustaka*, edited by the Widodo Djati, 12–19. Jakarta: Departemen Pendidikan dan Kebudayaan.

Mujiningsih, Erlis Nur, Sri Sayekti, and Atisah, eds. 2000. *Antologi Cerpen Periode Awal.* Jakarta: Pusat Bahasa, Departemen Pendidikan Nasional.

N. Asia. [1945] 1995. "Menuntut Bela" [Defense]. In *Antologi Cerita Pendek Indonesia Modern pada Zaman Jepang dalam Majalah Panji Pustaka,* edited by Widodo Djati, 148–51. Jakarta: Departemen Pendidikan dan Kebudayaan.

Nio, Joe Lan. 1962. *Sastera Indonesia-Tionghoa.* Jakarta: Gunung Agung.

Pamasuk Eneste. 2001. *Bibliografi sastra Indonesia: Cerpen, Drama, Novel, Puisi, Antologi, Umum.* Magelang: IndonesiaTera.

Phalgunadi, I Gusti Putu, trans. 1996. *The Pararaton: A Study of the Southeast Asian Chronicle.* New Delhi: Sundeep Prakashan.

Prihatmi, Th. Sri Rahayu. 1989. *Fantasi dalam Kedua Kumpulan Cerpen Danarto: Dialog antara Dunia Nyata dan Tidak Nyata.* Jakarta: Balai Pustaka.

Quinn, George. 1988. "Indonesian Literature." In *Far Eastern Literatures in the Twentieth Century,* edited by Leonard S. Klein, 54–72. Harpenden, U.K.: Oldcastle Books.

Robson, Stuart Owen. 2002. *From Malay to Indonesian: The Genesis of a National Language.* Working Papers no. 118. Clayton, Vic.: Centre of Southeast Asian Studies, Monash University.

Rosidi, Ajip. 1959. *Tjerita pendek Indonesia.* Jakarta: Djambatan.

Rosidi, Ajip. ed. 2002. *Menuju Kamar Durhaka: Kumpulan Cerpen* by Utuy Tatang Sontani. Jakarta: Pustaka Jaya.

Roskies, David, trans. and ed. 1997. *Black Clouds over the Isle of God, and Other Modern Indonesian Short Stories.* Armonk NY: M. E. Sharpe.

Rusmini, Oka. 2000. *Tarian Bumi: Sebuah Novel.* Magelang: IndonesiaTera.

———. 2001. *Sagra.* Magelang: IndonesiaTera.

Salmon, Claudine. 1981. *Literature in Malay by the Chinese of Indonesia: A Provisional Annotated Bibliography.* Paris: Éditions de la Maison des Sciences de l'Homme.

Salmon, Claudine, ed. 1987. *Literary Migrations: Traditional Chinese Fiction in Asia, Seventeenth-Twentieth Centuries.* Beijing: International Culture Pub.

———. 1992. "Introduction." In *Le Moment "Sino-Malais" de la Litterature Indonesienne,* edited by Claudine Salmon. Paris: Cahier d'Archipel.

Satyagraha Hoerip [Soeprobo]. 1979. *Cerita Pendek Indonesia,* vol.1. Jakarta: Department of Education and Culture. vol. 1.

———. 1984. *Cerita Pendek Indonesia.* Vols. 2–4. Jakarta: Department of Education and Culture.

———. 1991. *New York after Midnight: Eleven Indonesian Short Stories.* Jakarta: Executive Committee, Festival of Indonesia.

Schwarz, Adam. 1994. *A Nation in Waiting: Indonesia's Search for Stability.* London: Allen and Unwin.

Sen, Krishna, and David T. Hill. 2000. *Media, Culture, and Politics in Indonesia.* Oxford: Oxford University Press.

Situmorang, Sitor. 1956. *Pertempuran dan Salju di Paris.* Jakarta: Dian Rakjat.

———. 1963. *Pangeran*. Bandung: Kiwari.

Sontani, Utuy Tatang. 1951. *Orang-orang Sial Sekumpulan Tjerita Tahum 1948–1950*. Jakarta: Balai Pustaka.

———. 2002. *Menuju kamar Durhaka: Kumpulan Cerpen*. Jakarta: Dunia Pustaka Jaya.

Surjomihardjo, Abdurrachman, ed. 2002. *Beberapa Segi Perkembangan Sejarah pers di Indonesia*. Jakarta: Penerbit Buku Kompas.

Suryadinata, Leo. 1996. *Sastra Peranakan Tionghoa Indonesia*. Jakarta: Grasindo.

Sykorsky, W. V. 1980. "Some Additional Remarks on the Antecedents of Modern Indonesian Literature." *Bijdragen tot de Taal-, Land- en Volkenkunde van Nederlandsch-Indie* (BKI), 136.4: 498–516.

Teeuw, A. 1967. *Modern Indonesian Literature*. Vol. 1. The Hague: Nijhoff. Vol. 1.

Toer, Pramoedya Ananta, ed. [1982] 2003. *Tempo Doeloe: Antologi Sastra Pra-Indonesia*. Jakarta and New York: Lentera Dipantara and Hyperion East. New York: Hyperion East.

Toer, Pramoedya Ananta. 1996. *Child of All Nations*. Translated by Max Lane. New York: Penguin.

———. 2004. *Cerita dari Blora* [All That Is Gone]. Translated by Willem Samuels, 1–30. New York: Hyperion East.

Watson, C. W. 1971. "The Antecedents of Modern Indonesian Literature." *Bijdragen tot de Taal-, Land- en Volkenkunde van Nederlandsch-Indie* (BKI), 124.4: 417–433.

Zaini-Lajoubert, Monique. 1988. "Syair Cerita Siti Akbari Karya Lie Kim Hok (1884), Penjelmaan Syair Abdul Muluk (1846)." In *Far Eastern Literatures in the Twentieth Century*, edited by S. Klein, 277–321. Harpenden, U.K.: Oldcastle Books.

9

The Modern Vietnamese Short Story
Peter Zinoman

The origins and early development of the modern Vietnamese short story must be understood within the context of changes generated by French colonialism in the late nineteenth and early twentieth centuries: the transition from an ideographic to a romanized writing system; the expansion of literacy through the growth of a Franco-Vietnamese school system; the development of capitalist economic relations; the emergence of new urban classes and the rise of a powerful, radical, nationalist movement. Subsequently, the fortunes of the literary genre were conditioned by the major historical developments of the postcolonial era; military conflict between colonial and anticolonial forces, territorial division, a civil war fueled by the cold war, the communist victory; and the eventual growth of a market economy under the continued political leadership of the Communist Party.

While these changes shaped the evolution of modern prose literature in general, additional factors conditioned the specific development of the short story. It is instructive that the genre has flourished during two of the four discrete periods conventionally employed to categorize the history of modern Vietnamese literature: the "late colonial period," between 1930 and 1945; and the recent period identified with the introduction of market socialism in 1986. Both eras witnessed explosive growth in the publication of newspapers and periodicals and hence a dramatic increase in the number of arenas for the production and consumption of short stories. Both eras have been characterized by unusual degrees of intellectual freedom and political competition, creating space for writers to pursue a variety of personal visions. Moreover, writers from both eras saw themselves as leaders of a cultural restoration following an immediate past characterized by artistic and intellectual stagnation. In such highly charged contexts, the brevity and accessibility of the short story form made it an ideal literary instrument for writers to contribute to the central political and cultural projects of their day.

The Precolonial Background

The forcible incorporation of the Vietnamese population of the Red River Delta into the Chinese empire between 111 BCE and 939 CE prevented the early development of a Vietnamese writing system and stunted the growth of a vernacular literature (Taylor 1983). Indeed, virtually all Vietnamese-authored texts produced during the first millennium were written in Chinese and hence remained inaccessible to all but a tiny, sinophilic, Vietnamese elite. Although Vietnamese scholars eventually developed an ideographic system to render their own language using modified Chinese characters (*nom*), the fact that mastery of the new system was predicated on a prior knowledge of Chinese prevented it from providing the basis for a popular literature (DeFrancis 1977, 20–35). Despite several remarkable literary achievements, particularly in *nom* poetry, the role of written literature in the cultural life of the vast majority of the population remained extremely limited.[1]

The Early Colonial Period: 1862-1930

The history of modern literature in Vietnam begins with the abrupt abandonment of both Chinese and *nom* in the late nineteenth century and their replacement by *quoc ngu,* a romanized writing system devised by French missionaries in the seventeenth century (DeFrancis 1977, 48–69). This extraordinary transition, arguably the most significant development in modern Vietnamese cultural history, was facilitated by a remarkable convergence of interests among colonial and anticolonial forces. The colonial state hoped that the suppression of Chinese writing and the promotion of *quoc ngu* would sever the Vietnamese elite from the pernicious influence of anti-imperialist, anti-Western, and social revolutionary texts, which radiated threateningly from China and Japan. Concurrently, patriotic scholars, led by Phan Boi Chau and Phan Chau Trinh, supported the adoption of the easy to learn romanized script as a vehicle for the mass dissemination of anticolonial and nationalist ideas. In addition, *quoc ngu* had long enjoyed a limited currency among the largest and most reliable community of local collaborators: the Catholic minority (Osborne 1969, 89–109).

Driven by this unlikely consensus and the rapid development of the colonial school system after 1917, the movement to replace characters with *quoc ngu* induced a dramatic reorientation in Vietnamese cultural and intellectual life.[2] It was experienced initially by the generation that attended colonial schools in the 1910s and 1920s and entered the colony's tumultuous cultural and political arenas during the 1930s and 1940s.[3] While scholars tend to emphasize what members of this new colonial-educated elite gained in terms of their knowledge of Western civilization, what they lost is equally significant. By the third decade of the twentieth century, the educated youths of Vietnam (now largely ignorant of written Chinese, *nom* and Sino-Vietnamese) had lost the linguistic capacity to explore their own literary and intellectual heritage. As this profound cultural rupture became increasingly apparent, members of the young elite attempted to assemble a new tradition almost literally from scratch. Given the urgency of their predicament, writers turned to poetry and the short story as the forms most easily mastered and mobilized as building blocks for the creation of a new literary tradition.

The relationship between the development of the short story and the cultural project of the first generation of educated Vietnamese to effectively cut themselves off from the Sino-Vietnamese ideographic tradition can be seen in the relative neglect of the short story until the emergence of this elite in the late 1920s and 1930s. Other than Huynh Tinh Cua's *Stories for Fun* (*Truyen Giai Buon*, 1980), Nguyen Trong Quan's *The Tale of Lazaro Phien* (*Truyen Thay Lazaro Phien*, 1887) and a handful of stories in Nguyen Van Vinh's *Dong Duong Tap Chi* (*Indochina Review*, 1913–17), few early writers experimented with the short story form.[4] Nor did the genre's fortunes improve significantly with the foundation of *Nam Phong*, Pham Quynh's influential and long-running *quoc ngu* literary monthly, established in Hanoi in 1917.[5] In the 210 issues published during *Nam Phong's* seventeen-year existence, only thirty-four short stories were published, roughly two per year (Lai Van Hung 1989, 258–59). The journal's relative neglect of the genre reflected Pham Quynh's conviction, clearly expressed in an essay he penned in 1921, that the novel represented the highest achievement of modern literature (Pham Quynh 1996). Pham Quynh's novelistic bias was probably buttressed by the popular success of Ho Bieu Chanh, the prolific southerner who produced over a dozen widely read novels during the 1910s and 1920s, and by the sensational public impact of two novels published in the mid 1920s: Nguyen Trong Thuat's *The Watermelon* and Hoang Ngoc Phach's *Pure Heart*.[6]

The Late Colonial Period: 1930-45

While the first sixty years of French rule (1862–1918) witnessed the publication of only thirty *quoc ngu* periodicals, the emergence of the new elite in the late 1920s coincided with a dramatic proliferation of newspapers and magazines in romanized script. Indeed, the French sociologist André Dumarest pointed to a taste for newspapers as one of the defining cultural features of this new class (McHale 1995, 177). To meet the surging demand, enterprising editors founded over forty new *quoc ngu* dailies, weeklies, and monthlies between

1926 and 1930 (DeFrancis 1977, 213). Another four hundred appeared during the 1930s (217). These included explicitly literary journals, as well as newspapers and general interest publications, that regularly set aside space for short fiction or serialized novels. The relaxation of colonial censorship during the Popular Front era in France (1935–39) accelerated further the growth of *quoc ngu* publications in Indochina and broadened the kind of subject matter allowed in print.

A consequence of the ensuing demand for material created by the unprecedented growth in colonial publishing during the 1930s was to transform fiction writing into a profession. During this period, editors paid as much as five piasters per short story, enough for productive and popular writers to earn a modest living (Nguyen Danh Manh 1996). As important as the financial incentives, members of the new elite were drawn to writing by the seductive prospect of a literary lifestyle (*song nghe si*) and the attractions of fame and social prestige. Forming literary circles, frequenting opium dens, patronizing brothels, and gathering at cafés, where they contemplated philosophy, politics, and the latest trends in metropolitan art and literature, writers cut a romantic figure in late colonial society.

The cultural milieu of colonial era writers has been vividly captured in the work of Nam Cao, one of the era's most brilliant practitioners of the short-story form. In his story, "Doi Thua" (A Useless Life), a young writer who dreams of "someday winning the Nobel Prize," struggles to balance domestic responsibilities with his desire to lead the restless, carefree life expected of a serious author (Nam Cao 1977b, 67–78). In "Doi Mat" (A Pair of Eyes), Nam Cao employs a conversation between an accomplished but ultimately conservative author and an idealistic literary neophyte to explore the political and aesthetic dilemmas writers faced as the radical anti-colonial movement rose to challenge the power of the colonial state (Nam Cao 1977b, 414–28).

The abundance and diversity of *quoc ngu* fiction produced during the late colonial period make it difficult to identify dominant stylistic or topical trends. Vietnamese scholars writing inside the country have typically employed an ideologically driven division between realists (*hien thuc*) and romantics (*lang man*) to categorize the voluminous prose fiction of the era.[7] According to this scheme, writers associated with the allegedly romantic movement known as Tu Luc Van Doan (Self-Strength Literary Group), such as Nhat Linh and Khai Hung, are characterized by their tendency to focus on the psychological anxieties of the urban bourgeoisie and to lament the injustices of the Confucian family system.[8] On the other hand, the realists, represented by Nguyen Cong Hoan, Nguyen Hong, Ngo Tat To, To Hoai, and Nam Cao, strove to reveal the lives of the underclass and the destructive social consequences of colonial capitalism.

This realist tendency is illustrated in Nguyen Cong Hoan's short story, "Kep Tu Ben" (Tu Ben the Actor) from the collection of that name. It opens with a brief preface that explains the plight of the protagonist, Tu Ben.

> However, for over a month now, he has not performed. For over a month now, his father has been sick. For over a month now, in a dark loft in the small house at the end of Sam Cong Lane, Tu Ben has listened to his father's moans mingling with the sad whistle of the medicine kettle. The sound depresses Tu Ben and he cannot think about work. As his father's condition worsens, Tu Ben exhausts his savings to buy medicine. Finally, with no other options, he beings to borrow money from several wealthy theater owners. (Yamada 2002, 273, trans. by Peter Zinoman and Nguyen Nguyet Cam)

Caught in the double bind of ministering to his critically ill father or acting in the play *The Obsequious Mandarin* in order to buy the medicine his father desires, Tu Ben decides to take the "comic" role in the play. While feigning humor he does not feel, he finds out after the play that he has just missed his father's death. The high-profile debates about art for art's sake and Nguyen Cong Hoan's (putatively realist) short story collection *Kep Tu Ben,* which erupted during the 1930s, are often seen to embody the conflict between the realist and romantic orientations in late colonial literature.[9]

While not without value, such an analysis fails to account for the extraordinary richness and complexity of the late colonial literary scene.[10] In the late 1930s, for example, Thach Lam, a major figure within the reputedly romantic Tu Luc Van Doan group (he was Nhat Linh's brother) published three powerful collections of short stories that explored the lives of the urban, petite-bourgeoisie, the rural peasantry, and the suburban poor.[11] Moreover, two of the most prolific and brilliant prose stylists of the 1930s, Vu Trong Phung and Nguyen Tuan, wrote a huge body of morally and politically ambiguous fiction that continues to stubbornly resist one-dimensional systems of classification.[12]

The quantity and diversity of Vietnamese prose fiction produced during the late colonial era is better reflected in the colorful system devised by the literary critic Vu Ngoc Phan in 1942 to impose some order on the youthful history of *quoc ngu* writing. In his encyclopedic opus *Nha Van Hien Dai* (Modern Writers), Phan assessed the work of almost three dozen interwar fiction writers, virtually all of whom employed the short story form (some more than others). Instead of trying to streamline and pigeonhole their efforts, he divided their work into wide-ranging categories: topical fiction, moral fiction, fantastic fiction, journalistic fiction, comic fiction, realist fiction, social fiction, detective fiction, and fiction of cultural mores (Vu Ngoc Phan, 1994). What Phan's system forfeited in terms of classificatory elegance it more than made up for in its ability to convey a sense of the tremendous urgency, energy, and variety that characterized Vietnamese efforts, in the 1930s, to create a modern literary tradition almost literally from scratch.

Civil War and Revolutionary Transformation: 1945-75

The most important development in Vietnamese literature after World War II was its dramatic bifurcation between 1946 and 1975 along an axis that was both geographical and political. In short, Vietnamese literature produced in communist-ruled territories underwent a radical transformation while literary culture in noncommunist areas was marked by significant continuities with historical patterns emergent from the late colonial era. Several factors, however, complicate this fragmented portrait of continuity in the noncommunist South and change in the communist North. These include the rise to prominence of new themes (military conflict and civil war) and foreign influences (American) in southern literature, the continuation of regionally specific northern literary trends within the South as a consequence of mass migrations of writers and readers across the seventeenth parallel following the Geneva Accords, and the enhanced contribution and significance of women writers in both the North and the South after 1954.

Starting in the mid-1940s, the Communist Party devised detailed guidelines on the form and content of acceptable literature (Truong Chinh 1977, 217–301). Following models developed by Chinese and Soviet cultural officials during the Maoist and Soviet eras, Vietnamese writers under communist rule were urged to glorify the party, serve its war efforts, and persuade the population of the merits of its economic and social policies. All literature was to be assessed based on the presence or absence of three requisite "orientations": a national orientation (*tinh dan toc*), a scientific orientation (*tinh khoa hoc*), and a mass orientation (*tinh dai chung*). Literary mavericks did not last long in this climate, especially if they refused to adopt prescribed models of socialist realism or celebrate cardboard paragons of "revolutionary heroism" (*anh hung cach mang*). While a fleeting relaxation of censorship and cultural policing in the late 1950s gave rise to the irreverent, politically incorrect Literary Humanism Movement (Nhan Van Giai Pham), its leaders were quickly suppressed and literature returned, for the following twenty-five years, to the sterile course on which it had previously been set.[13]

In the South, the power of the government to monitor and control cultural production and the press was partially mitigated by the endurance of a republican tradition sanctioning freedom of expression that had underwritten the colonial state's relatively tolerant attitude toward Vietnamese artistic, intellectual and political discourse—in Saigon especially—during the late 1930s. Emblematic of this tradition was a law passed by Ngo Dinh Diem's government in February 1956 that freed the Vietnamese-language press from official censorship. While southern governments employed a host of other means—both arbitrary and institutional—to harass, intimidate, and silence writers and journalists, the intellectual and literary cultures of the Republic of Vietnam remained dynamic and freewheeling, especially compared to their tightly controlled counterparts north of the seventeenth parallel. In early 1975, Saigon boasted roughly 1,000 printing shops, 150 privately owned publishing houses, and scores of independent newspapers and journals managed by a wide range of individuals, parties, and associations. The large number of periodicals, in turn, ensured the existence of many arenas for the publication of short stories and encouraged a proliferation of schools and styles that recalled the exciting and diverse literary atmosphere of the late colonial era (Vo Phien 1986).

The development of short fiction in southern Vietnam was energized further by the southward migration of roughly a million people in 1954, including a handful of prominent northern writers. These included Nhat Linh, Vu Bang, Nguyen Vy, Vu Hoang Chuong, Doan Quoc Si, Mai Thao, Duong Nghiem Mau, Thanh Tam Tuyen, Vien Linh, and Duyen Anh among others. When combined with the efforts of important southern authors such as Son Nam, Binh Nguyen Loc, Vo Phien, Cung Tich Bien, and Nguyen Xuan Hoang, this influx of northern literary talent allowed Saigon, for the first time in its history, to rival Hanoi as the center of Vietnamese literary life.

The dynamism of literature in southern Vietnam was further enhanced by new foreign influences such as existentialism, the *nouveau roman*, and contemporary American literature, none of which was permitted to make significant inroads in the North. Some of these influences are illustrated in Vo Phien's story "Unsettled." In it the life of the protagonist, Hieu, unfolds through a psychological landscape of loss covering the war years in Vietnam through the 1950s.

> Hieu thought about the myth of Orpheus going to the underworld to ask for his wife's return to earth. His request was granted, but he was only allowed to bring Eurydice back on the condition that he not gaze upon her before their return. Orpheus was elated. But on the way back, his curiosity got the better of him. He took one look at his wife, causing her to vanish. Hieu suspected that if he were still caught up in events, still being pushed forward, perhaps he could be blind and have faith in what lay at the end

of the road. But he had given up halfway, paused and looked directly at life. His scrutinizing gaze made life lose all its color, becoming pale and distorted, like Eurydice! What could he do now? (Yamada 2002, 296, trans. by Bac Hoai Tran and Courtney Norris)

Finally, the greater freedom that southern writers enjoyed allowed them to explore through their writing the themes of war and civil conflict in a much more profound way than could their counterparts in the North. The innovative quality of southern Vietnamese war writing may be seen in the short stories of Nguyen Vu and Y Uyen and in the nonfiction reportage of Phan Nhat Nam.

The manpower requirements that the military conflict imposed on both northern and southern Vietnamese society resulted in one of the few agreeable literary developments of the war years: the growth of the first substantial body of literature produced by Vietnamese women. During the late 1960s, a number of talented female writers—Nguyen Thi Hoang, Nha Ca, Tuy Hong, Trung Duong, Nguyen Thi Thuy Vu, and Tran Thi Ngh—appeared in rapid succession on the southern literary scene (Cong-Huyen Ton-Nu Nha-Trang 1987). In the North, party efforts to facilitate female inroads into what had previously been male occupational preserves contributed to the emergence of a number of professional women writers: Nguyen Thi Ngoc Tu, Vu Thi Thuong, Le Minh Khue, and Duong Thi Xuan Qui.

Among them, Le Minh Khue, who joined the People's Army in 1965 at age sixteen, writes of both the tragedy and the hope that marked her generation, including the loss of love and idealism. One of her most accomplished stories, "A Small Tragedy," spans singular events of great consequence in modern Vietnamese history: the land reform period and its impact on the wealthy, and the U.S.-Vietnam war and its aftermath. These events are explored through the personal observations of Thao, a young female journalist. In the course of an investigation she finds that murders of the past still haunt certain members of her own family in the present.

> In fact, nothing was really so terrible in a country that had seen nothing but uprootedness, war, and sorrow. I used to think that in old times, people just made up the story of "The Stone Woman Waiting for her Husband's Return." I thought they were wrong to believe that human struggle was futile within the grip of fate and wrong to lament over the heart-breaking predicaments of the world. But who could have guessed that such a misfortune could happen to Uncle Tuyen's family? However, each era reaps its own tragedies. (Le Minh Khue 1997, 206)[14]

While institutionalized political pressure sapped the creative vitality of the work of women writers as profoundly as the fiction produced by men, the development of a solid core of northern women writers during the war prefigured the leading role women would assume in the dominant literary movement of the postwar era.

Doi Moi: 1986-Present

While Vietnamese literature during the first decade of the postunification era (1975–86) was hampered by the same political and institutional constraints that debilitated northern literature during the war years, the Renovation Policy (Doi Moi) introduced in 1986 ushered in a period of literary dynamism reminiscent of the late colonial era.[15]

By the late 1970s, careful observers could detect a growing desire among Vietnamese intellectuals for cultural renewal after the malaise of the war years. Disenchantment with the party grew not only due to its poor handling of the economy but because increasing numbers of people were becoming alienated by the narrowness of its cultural and media institutions (Phuong Kien Khanh 1990). Samizdat literature and critical essays began circulating widely in the early 1980s. And, in an influential series of articles, the literary critic Hoang Ngoc Hien attacked the hegemony of socialist realism and coined the pejorative phrase "dutiful literature" (*van chuong phai dao*) to characterize the insipid quality of fiction-writing over the past thirty years.[16]

This simmering discontent was given focus and direction by the party's general secretary, Nguyen Van Linh, and the Doi Moi policy he introduced at the Sixth Party Congress. While much attention has been paid to the market reforms introduced by Doi Moi, changes in intellectual life have been equally dramatic. Most importantly, Doi Moi inaugurated the relaxation of press controls, which led to a rapid increase in the number of newspapers and journals and an expansion of the kinds of things they could print. Moreover, anticipating that economic liberalization would lead to an increase in corruption, Linh appealed directly to writers to use their talents to expose graft, inefficiencies, and injustices within the system.[17]

As during the 1930s, the simultaneous growth of print capitalism and an officially sanctioned expansion of freedom of expression generated rich literary dividends. And again, short stories proved to be the medium of choice. In 1986, several journals began publishing an extraordinary body of short fiction by a previously unknown writer named Nguyen Huy Thiep.[18] Politically daring and stylistically innovative, Thiep's stories sent shock waves through the literary world. Perhaps no story generated as much critical attention as

"Tuong Ve Huu" (The General Retires), Thiep's uncompromising exploration of the aimlessness and moral bankruptcy of life in postwar Hanoi. According to the historian Greg Lockhart, close to one hundred critical reviews of Thiep's work appeared in the year following the publication of the story (1991, 3). Over the next five years, literary magazines published three dozen more stories by Thiep, including a brilliant trilogy of pseudo-historical tales read by many as an unprecedented critique of contemporary Vietnamese politics and society (Zinoman 1992).

One of these tales, "Fired Gold," ends with three possible conclusions so the reader can select the one he or she feels is most suitable, an oblique criticism of the metanarrative of historical veracity.

Courtesy of Oxford University Press (China) Ltd

> The memoir of the anonymous Portuguese ends here. I, the writer of this short story, have already endeavored to search the content of ancient texts and memories of aged men, yet I have uncovered neither documents nor individuals with information on The Valley of the Ravens and the Europeans who entered it during Gia Long's reign. Over many years, all my attempts have been in vain. I therefore offer three conclusions to the story, so that each reader can select the one which he or she feels is most suitable. (Nguyen Huy Thiep 1994, 24)

It is arguable that the raw power and deft elegance of Thiep's writing has single-handedly elevated *quoc ngu* prose fiction to a higher level.

While other Doi Moi writers continue to look to village life and wartime experiences for much of their material, they have devised new and exciting ways to approach these familiar topics. Writers such as Bao Ninh, Nguyen Quang Lap, and Le Luu have virtually redefined the war story by replacing the old, exclusive focus on military heroism and patriotic sacrifice with forthright explorations of the physical and emotional costs of war.[19] Others, such as Ta Duy Anh and Duong Thu Huong, have employed fiction to critically reassess the party's early efforts at socialist transformation.[20]

Duong Thu Huong's novels and short stories often reflect more than a critique of socialist transformation. She also pragmatically and honestly explores the consequences of gender, the disparity caused by social privilege, and the failed expectations of marriage. The latter is a poignant theme in "The Story of an Actress" (1985), a coming of age tale that explores the existential issue of free will through the contrasting lives of two young women, Thom and Be. One's success and the other's failure, due to their own decisions, are framed through a mutual sense of loss over their innocence as childhood friends, catching fish and crabs surrounded by the verdant, natural beauty of rural Vietnam. A melancholic but insistent desire to recapture the joyful innocence of a childhood friendship is expressed in the following passage.

> "In those days, we lived to happily and joyfully."
> "In those days, we really lived."
> In her eyes I found a shadow of the childhood rains. The rains that weren't rains, but an overflowing, endless celebration. In our hearts they created melodious sounds and sparkling magical colors, remaining like a fresh breeze for our souls. And thanks to those memories, we'll again find the blue smoke, the taste of delicious baked fish, and the clear autumn horizon . . .
> (Yamada 2002, 320, trans. by Bac Hoai Tran and Courtney Norris)[21]

The exploration of loss, whether through war or failed relationships, poignantly haunts Duong Thu Huong's fiction.

Another remarkable aspect of the Doi Moi era has been the leading role assumed by women in the field of literature. In addition to Duong Thu Huong, whose extraordinary international stature dwarfs virtually all of her contemporaries,—women such as Pham Thi Hoai[22] and Le Minh Khue—can be counted among the country's most skilled and influential writers.[23] That the leadership of an even more recent literary generation (post–Doi Moi?) is dominated by women writers such as Phan Thi Vang Anh confirms the durability of gains made by women during the Doi Moi era.[24]

Editor's Note

Contemporary Vietnamese literature has become a global enterprise of multiple languages and locations. The development of the contemporary Vietnamese short story, especially after the fall of Saigon in 1975, must also be traced beyond the borders of Vietnam along the various pathways of exile writers, members of the Vietnamese diaspora.[25] Their literary activity stretches from Australia, France, and Germany to the United States and elsewhere. The Internet has become an important transnational source linking them across the diaspora.[26]

Among those writing from America, Linh Dinh has done much to promote the modern Vietnamese short story, first through the anthology *Night, Again: Contemporary Fiction from Vietnam* (Dinh 1996). This collection was preceded by Greg Lockhart's well-received translation of Nguyen Huy Thiep's short stories under the title *The General Retires and Other Stories* (Nguyen Huy Thiep 1992). This was followed by Wayne Karlin's efforts at Curbstone Press with the publication of *The Other Side of Heaven: Post-war Fiction by Vietnamese and American Writers* (Karlin et al. 1995), *The Stars, the Earth, the River: Short Fiction by Le Minh Khue* (Karlin 1997), and *Behind the Red Mist: Fiction by Ho Anh Thai* (Ho Anh Thai 1998). Among the short-story anthologies, John Balaban and Nguyen Qui Duc's *Vietnam: A Traveler's Literary Companion* (1996) added to the translation momentum of Vietnamese modern literature during the 1990s in the United States, making it the most translated literary tradition of any country in Southeast Asia. One early source of this enterprise was Yale University's Council on Southeast Asian Studies, which beginning in 1981 promoted the publication of two journals—*Viet Nam Forum* and *Lac Viet* — under the editorial direction of Huynh Sanh Thong. Dan Duffy took over the editorial responsibilities from 1994 until the series ended in 1997. Many translations of short stories and essays on Vietnamese literature were included in these journals. An anthology of Vietnamese American writers was published in 1998, *Watermark: Vietnamese American Poetry and Prose* (Tran, Truong, and Luu 1998). It also contains a short story by the bilingual writer Linh Dinh.

Writing in both English and Vietnamese, Dinh represents a distinctive form of intellectual globalism found among a certain set of Southeast Asian writers and filmmakers who are multilingual and travel throughout the world promoting a new, more experimental literature and cinema with cultural traces from multiple locations.[27] His stories in *Fake House Stories*

Courtesy of Curbstone Press

(2000) reflect this multiplicity of localities and identities as he depicts an array of American, Korean, Vietnamese, and Taiwanese characters in various geographical settings.[28] There is no one site that indicates a cultural location signifying "home." His latest short story collection, *Blood and Soap* (2004), a set of "modern fables," continues his impressionistic, postmodern exploration of language and locality. Linh Dinh's nomadic lifestyle clearly signifies the dissolution of national boundaries as a container for a unique literary culture, as the experience of Vietnamese identity and its literary representations have become a globalized phenomena.

Notes

[1] For a remarkable introduction to the tradition of *nom* poetry in English translation, see Huynh Sanh Thong 1979.

[2] For the development of the Franco-Vietnamese school system, see Kelly 1975.

[3] The development of this new elite is treated in Marr 1981. He refers to it as the "intelligentsia" to distinguish it from previous elites, which were rooted in the scholar-gentry class.

[4] Two innovators of the Vietnamese short story, Pham Duy Ton and Nguyen Ba Hoc, published early influential examples of the genre in *Dong Duong Tap Chi*. For an excellent treatment of Pham Duy Ton and his work, see Schaffer 1994. The career of Nguyen Ba Hoc is treated by Hoang Ngoc Thanh 1973, 226–29.

[5] For background on Pham Quynh, see O'Harrow 1973.

[6] For the emergence of the novel in Vietnam, see Schafer and The 1993; and Cao Thi Nhu Quynh and Schafer 1988. For additional information on Hoang Ngoc Phach, see Nguyen Hue Chi 1996.

[7] For example, see Tran Van Giap et. al. 1971–72, 48.

[8] Khai Hung published four short story collections: *Doc Duong Gio Bui* (1936), *Tieng Suoi Reo* (1937), *Doi Cho* (1939), *Doi Mu Lech* (1939). Nhat Linh published two: *Toi Tam* (1936), and *Hai Buoi Chieu* (1937). And they jointly authored one: *Anh Phai Song* (1937). For a brief treatment of their careers, see Huynh Sanh Thong 1984, 99–195.

[9] For a treatment of these debates, see Hue Tam Ho Tai 1987, 63–83.

[10] This argument is made by Nguyen Hoanh Khung (1994) in his introduction.

[11] These collections were *Gio Dau Mua*, *Nang Trong Vuon*, and *Soi Toc*.

[12] For their collected works, see Nguyen Dang Manh 1993; and Ly Huy Nguyen 1994, 1996, 2000. For a translation of a novel by Vu Trong Phung, see Zinoman 2004.

[13] For a discussion of Nhan Van Giai Pham, see Boudarel 1991. For information on Vietnamese perspectives of the war in Vietnam see Schaffer 1997.

[14] A redacted version of this story appears in Balaban and Nguyen 1996, 53–89.

[15] For further information on post Doi Moi writers, see Healy 2000 and Nguyen Ngoc 2008.

[16] See, for example, Hoang Ngoc Hien 1979.

[17] See Nguyen Van Linh 1991.

[18] For an extensive treatment of Nguyen Huy Thiep and his work, see Zinoman 1994.

[19] English translations of work by these three can be found in Karlin et al. 1995.

[20] For English translations see Duong Thu Huong 1993, 1995. For a translation of a short story by Ta Duy Anh, see Lowe 1995.

[21] Only one other short story has been translated to date: "The Shelter" in Balaban and Nguyen. 1996, 14–27. Many of her novels have been translated; see Duong Thu Huong 1993, 1995, 2000, 2002.

[22] Pham Thi Hoai now spends time between Hanoi and Berlin as a Vietnamese transnational. Her insightful commentary on Doi Moi and contemporary Vietnamese literature is published through the International Institute at the University of California (2004).

[23] English translations of short fiction by Le Minh Khue and Pham Thi Hoai can be found in Linh Dinh 1996.

[24] For an English translation of Phan Thi Vang Anh's "Pantomime," see Nguyen Nguyet Cam 1995.

[25] On this issue, limited to the United States, see Linda Vo 2000. Dao Strom (2003) explores the Vietnamese American experience. One of the first explorations of the "exile experience in America," a genre so popular in the United States, was by Jade Ngoc Quang Huynh (1994); one of the most successful is Andrew Pham's *Catfish and Mandala* (1999). Aimee Phan (2004) fictionalizes this experience in a set of linked stories. Linda Le writes in French from France about being Vietnamese there. A number of her novels have been translated (Allen 1996). Monique Truong, situated in the United States, writes of being Vietnamese in France (2003).

[26] For example, see the online literary magazine *Da Mau* http://damau.org, edited by Thuy Dinh and published bimonthly in Vietnamese and English.

[27] The Thai American writer Rattawut Lapcharoensap (2005) also exemplifies this trend, along with the Thai filmmaker Pen-Ek Ratanaruang. See Susan F. Kepner's "Thai Short Fiction of the Modern Era," Chapter 1 in this collection.

[28] Although Linh Dinh is bilingual, many of these English-language short stories were translated into Vietnamese by Phan Nhien Hao and published in *Hop Luu* (Dinh 2000, iv).

References

Allen, Esther, trans. 1996, *Slander,* by Linda Le. Lincoln: University of Nebraska Press.

Bac Hoai Tran and Courtney Norris, trans. 2002. "The Story of an Actress" by Duong Thu Huong. In *Virtual Lotus: Modern Fiction of Southeast Asia*, edited by Teri Shaffer Yamada, 298–320. Ann Arbor: University of Michigan Press.

Balaban, John, and Nguyen Qui Duc, eds. 1996. *Vietnam: A Traveler's Literary Companion.* San Francisco: Whereabouts Press.

Boudarel, Georges. 1991. *Cent Fleurs Écloses dans la Nuit du Vietnam: Communisme et Dissidence, 1954–1956.* Paris: Jacques Bertoin.

Cao Thi Nhu-Quynh and John C. Schafer. 1988. "From Verse Narrative to Novel: The Development of Prose Fiction in Vietnam." *Journal of Asian Studies* 47.4 (November): 756–77.

Cong-Huyen-Ton-Nu Nha-Trang. 1987. "Women Writers of South Vietnam (1954–1975)." *The Viet Nam Forum* 9 (winter–spring): 149–221.

DeFrancis, John. 1977. *Colonialism and Language Policy in Viet Nam.* The Hague: Mouton.

Dinh, Linh, ed. 1996. *Night, Again*: *Contemporary Fiction from Vietnam.* New York: Seven Stories Press.

———. 2000. *Fake House: Stories.* New York: Seven Stories Press.

———. 2004. *Blood and Soap: Stories.* New York: Seven Stories Press.

Duong Thu Huong.1993. *Paradise of the Blind.* Translated by Nina McPherson and Phan Huy Duong. New York: Morrow.

———. 1995. *Novel without a Name.* Translated by Nina McPherson and Phan Huy Duong, New York: Morrow.

———. 1996. "The Shelter." Translated by Phan Huy Duong and Nina McPherson. In *Vietnam: A Traveler's Literary Companion*, edited by John Balaban and Nguyen Qui Duc, 14–27. San Francisco: Whereabouts Press.

———. 2000. *Memories of a Pure Spring.* Translated by Nina McPherson and Phan Huy Duong. New York: Hyperion East.

———. 2002. *Beyond Illusions.* Translated by Nina McPherson and Phan Huy Duong. New York: Hyperion East.

Duffy, Dan, ed. 1997. "North Viet Nam Now: Fiction and Essays from Ha Noi." *The Viet Nam Forum* no. 15. New Haven: Council on Southeast Asian Studies, Yale University.

Healy, Dana. 2000. "Literature in transition: an overview of Vietnamese writing of the Renovation Period." In *The Canon in Southeast Asian Literatures: Literatures of Burma, Cambodia, Indonesia, Laos, Malaysia, the Philippines, Thailand and Vietnam*, edited by David Smyth, 41–50. Richmond, Surrey: Curzon.

Ho Anh Thai. 1998. *Behind the Red Mist: Fiction by Ho Anh Thai*. Edited by Wayne Karlin. Willimantic: Curbstone Press.

Hoang Ngoc Hien. 1979. "Ve Mot Dac Diem Chua Van Hoc Va Nghe Thuat O Ta Trong Giai Doan Vua Qua" [On a Main Point of Our Literature and Art in the Period Just Passed]. *Van Nghe* 23 (June).

Hoang Ngoc Thanh. 1973. "Quoc Ngu and the Development of Modern Vietnamese Literature." In *Aspects of Vietnamese History*, edited by Walter Vella, 191–236. Honolulu: University of Hawai'i Press.

Hue Tam Ho Tai. 1987. "Literature for the People: From Soviet Policies to Vietnamese Polemics." In *Borrowings and Adaptations in Vietnamese Culture*, edited by Truong Buu Lam, 63–83. Southeast Asia Papers no. 25. Honolulu: Center for Asian and Pacific Studies, University of Hawai'i at Manoa.

Huynh, Jade Ngoc Quang. 1994. *South Wind Changing*. Saint Paul, Mn.: Graywolf Press.

Huynh Sanh Thong. 1979. *The Heritage of Vietnamese Poetry*. New Haven: Yale University Press.

———. 1984. "Main Trends of Vietnamese Literature between the Two World Wars." *The Viet Nam Forum* 3 (winter-spring): 99–125.

Karlin, Wayne, ed. 1997. *The Stars, the Earth, the River: Short Fiction by Le Minh Khue*. Willimantic, CT: Curbstone Press.

Karlin, Wayne, Le Minh Khue, and Truong Vu, eds. 1995. *The Other Side of Heaven: Post-war Fiction by Vietnamese and American Writers*. Willimantic, CT: Curbstone Press.

Kelly, Gail Paradise. 1975. "Franco-Vietnamese Schools, 1918–1938." PhD Diss., University of Wisconsin.

Lai Van Hung, ed. 1989. *Truyen Ngan Nam Phong* [The Stories of Nam Phong]. Hanoi: Khoa Hoc Xa Hoi.

Lapcharoensap, Rattawut. 2005. *Sightseeing: Stories*. New York: Grove.

Le Minh Khue. 1997. "A Small Tragedy." Translated by Bac Hoai Tran. In *The Stars, the Earth, the River: Short Fiction by Le Minh Khue*, edited by Wayne Karlin, 178–217. Willimantic, CT: Curbstone Press.

Lockhart, Greg. 1991. "Nguyen Huy Thiep and the Faces of Vietnamese Literature." In *The General Retires and Other Stories*, by Nguyen Huy Thiep, 1–38. Singapore: Oxford University Press.

Lowe, Viviane, trans. 1995. "The Broken Curse," by Ta Duy Anh. *Manoa: A Pacific Journal of International Writing* 7.2 (winter): 142–156.

Lu Huy Nguyen, ed. 1994, 1996, 12000. *Tuyen Tap Nguyen Tuan, I, II, and III* [Collected Works of Nguyen Tuan, Vols 1, 2, and 3). Hanoi: Van Hoc.

Marr, David G. 1981. *Vietnamese Tradition on Trial, 1920–1945*. Berkeley: University of California Press.

McHale, Shawn. 1995. "Printing and Power: Vietnamese Debates over Women's Place in Society, 1918–1934." 173–194 in *Essays into Vietnamese Pasts*, edited by Keith Taylor and John K. Whitmore, 1–38. Studies on Southeast Asia, no. 19. Ithaca: Southeast Asia Program, Cornell University.

Nam Cao. 1977. "Doi Thua" [A Useless Life]. 67–78 in *Nam Cao: Tac Pham Tap II* [Collected Works of Nam Cao. Vol. II]. Hanoi: Van Hoc.

———. 1977a. "Doi Mat" [A Pair of Eyes]. Pp. 414-428 in *Nam Cao: Tac Pham Tap II* [Collected Works of Nam Cao, Vol. 2]. Hanoi: Van Hoc.

Nguyen Cong Hoan. "Tu Ben The Actor." Translated by Peter Zinoman and Nguyen Nguyet Cam. In *Virtual Lotus: Modern Fiction of Southeast Asia*, edited by Teri Shaffer Yamada, 272–78. Ann Arbor: University of Michigan Press.

Nguyen Dang Liem, comp. 1973. *Aspects of Vernacular Languages in Asian and Pacific Societies*. Honolulu: Southeast Asian Studies Program, University of Hawai'i.

Nguyen Dang Manh, ed. 1993. *Tuyen Tap Vu Trong Phung, I and II* [Collected Works of Vu Trong Phung, Vols. 1 and 2]. Hanoi: Van Hoc.

———. 1996. Interview with the author, 21 December, Hanoi.

Nguyen Hoanh Khung. 1994. Introduction to *Van Xuoi Lang Man Vietnam (1930–1945), Tap I* [Vietnamese Romantic Literature (1930–1945), Vol. 1]. Hanoi: Khoa Hoc Xa Hoi.

Nguyen Hue Chi, ed. 1996. *Hoang Ngoc Phach: Duong Doi Va Duong Van* [Hoang Ngoc Phach: Life and Literature]. Hanoi: Van Hoc.

Nguyen Huy Thiep. 1992. *The General Retires and Other Stories*. Translated by Greg Lockart. Singapore, New York: Oxford University Press.

———. 1994. "Fired Gold." Translated by Peter Zinoman. *Viet Nam Forum* 14:18–25.

Nguyen Nguyet Cam, trans. 1995. "Pantomime," by Phan Thi Vang Anh. *Manoa: A Pacific Journal of International Writing* 7.2 (winter): 101–12.

Nguyen Ngoc. 2008. "An Exciting Period for Vietnamese Prose." *Journal of Vietnamese Studies* 3.1 (Winter): 193–219.

Nguyen Van Linh. 1991. "Let Writers and Artists Actively Contribute to Renovation." *Vietnamese Studies*, new ser., no. 21: 117–125. Hanoi: Foreign Language Publishing House.

O'Harrow, Stephen. 1973. "French Colonial Policy towards Vernacular Language Development and the Case of Pham Quynh in Viet-Nam." In *Aspects of Vernacular Languages in Asian and Pacific Societies,* compiled by Nguyen Dang Liem, 113–135. Honolulu: Southeast Asian Studies Program, University of Hawai'i.

Osborne, Milton E. 1969. *The French Presence in Cochinchina and Cambodia: Rule and Response (1859–1905)*. Ithaca: Cornell University Press.

Pham, Andrew X. 1999. *Catfish and Mandala: A Two-Wheeled Voyage through the Landscape and Memory of Vietnam*. New York: Picador.

Phan, Aimee. 2004. *We Should Never Meet: Stories*. New York: St. Martin's Press.

Pham Quynh. 1996. "Khao Ve Tieu Thuyet" [Research on the Novel]. In *Khao Ve Tieu Thuyet: Nhung Y Kien, Nhung Quan Niem, Cua Cac Nha Van, Nha Nghien Cuu O Viet Nam Tu Dao The Ky XX Cho Den 1945* [Research on the Novel: Ideas and Conceptions of Vietnamese Writers and Researchers from the Start of the Twentieth Century to 1945], edited by Vuong Tri Nhan. 115–57. Hanoi: Nha Van.

Pham Thi Hoai. 1997. *The Crystal Messenger*, translated by Ton-That Quynh Du. South Melbourne, Australia: Hyland House Printing.

———. 2004. "The Machinery of Vietnamese Art and Literature in the Post-Revolution, Post-Community, and Post-Modern Period." Center for Southeast Asian Studies Occasional Papers. Los Angeles: International Institute, eScholarship Repository, University of California.

Phan Thi Vang Anh. 1995. "Pantomime." Translated by Nguyen Nguyet Cam. *Manoa: A Pacific Journal of International Writing* 7.2: 101–12.

Phuong Kien Khanh, 1990. *Glasnost in Vietnam: Limits to Openness.* Indochina Reports, no. 25. Singapore: Information and Resource Center.

Schafer, John C. and The Uyen. 1993. "The Novel Emerges in Cochinchina." *Journal of Asian Studies* 52.4 (November): 854–84.

Schafer, John C. 1994. "Pham Duy Ton: Journalist, Short Story Writer, Collector of Humorous Stories." *Viet Nam Forum* 14:103–24.

———. 1997. "Vietnamese Perspectives on the War in Vietnam: Annotated Bibliography of Works in English." http://yale.edu/seas/bibliography (November 24, 2008). *Lac-Viet* no.17.

Strom, Dao. 2003. *Grass Roof, Tin Roof.* Boston: Houghton Mifflin.

Taylor, Keith Weller. 1983. *The Birth of Vietnam.* Berkeley: University of California Press.

Taylor, Keith Weller and John K. Whitmore, eds. 1995. *Essays into Vietnamese Pasts*. Studies on Southeast Asia, no. 19. Ithaca: Southeast Asia Program, Cornell University.

Tran, Barbara, Monique T. D. Truong, and Truong Khoi Luu, eds. 1998. *Watermark: Vietnamese American Poetry and Prose.* New York: Asian American Writers' Workshop.

Tran Van Giap, Nguyen Tuong Phuong, Nguyen Van Phu, and Ta Phong Chau. 1971–72. *Luoc Truyen Tac Gia Vietnam Tap II* [Almanac of Vietnamese Writers, Vol. 2]. Hanoi: Khoa Hoc Xa Hoi.

Truong Chinh. 1977. "Marxism and Vietnamese Culture." In *Truong Chinh: Selected Writings*, 217–301. Hanoi: Foreign Languages Publishing House.

Truong, Monique T. D. 2003. *The Book of Salt.* Boston: Houghton Mifflin.

Wu, Jean Yu-wen Shen, and Min Song, eds. 2000. *Asian American Studies: A Reader*. New Brunswick, NJ: Rutgers University Press.

Vella, Walter F., ed. 1973. *Aspects of Vietnamese History*. Asian Studies at Hawai'i, no. 8. Honolulu: University of Hawai'i Press.

Vo, Linda Trinh. 2000. "The Vietnamese American Experience: From Dispersion to the Development of Post-refugee Communities." In *Asian American Studies: A Reader*, edited by Jean Yu-wen Shen Wu and Min Song, 290–305. New Brunswick, NJ: Rutgers University Press.

Vo Phien. 1986. "Writers in South Vietnam, 1954–1975." *Viet Nam Forum* 7: 176–99.

———. 2002. "Unsettled." Translated by Bac Hoai and Courtney Norris. In *Virtual Lotus: Modern Fiction of Southeast Asia*, edited by Teri Shaffer Yamada, 284–98. Ann Arbor: University of Michigan Press.

Vu Ngoc Phan. 1994. *Nha Van Hien Dai: Phe Binh Van Hoc* [Modern Writers: Literary Criticism]. TP Ho Chi Minh City: Van Hoc.

Yamada, Teri Shaffer, ed. 2002. *Virtual Lotus: Modern Fiction of Southeast Asia.* Ann Arbor: University of Michigan Press.

Zinoman, Peter. 1992. "Nguyen Huy Thiep's Vang Lua and the Nature of Intellectual Dissent in Contemporary Vietnam." *Viet Nam Generation Journal and Newsletter* 3.4 (January) online.

———. 1994. "Declassifying Nguyen Huy Thiep." *positions: east asia cultures critique* 2.2 (fall): 294–318.

Zinoman, Peter ed. 2004. *Dumb Luck: A Novel by Vu Trong Phung.* Translated by Peter Zinoman and Nguyen Nguyet Cam. Ann Arbor: University of Michigan Press.

10

The Story of the Philippine Short Story in English
Cristina Pantoja Hidalgo

The history of Philippine literature is inextricable linked to the history of the country, which is a history of repeated colonization. This relationship is most obvious in the case of the novel in English, where the country's history is itself the subject of many works. But it is also apparent in the case of the short story, as this essay hopes to show.

The story of the development of the Philippine short story in English must start with the fact that it is *in English*. And from the beginning the writers in English themselves have been sharply aware of this. Francisco Arcellana, a National Artist for Literature, called it "a historical mistake," the "not enviable situation" of the short story writer in English of the 1930s, "drawing substance" from a life "lived in a language different from the language he uses" (1967, 607).

N. V. M. Gonzalez, Arcellana's contemporary and another National Artist for Literature, describing his own early work, echoed Arcellana.

> The life I described quite literally spoke a different language—and became a different life. Rendered in an alien tongue, that life attained the distinction of a translation even before it had been made into a representation of reality, and then even before becoming a reality of its own. (1995, 62)

It was clearly a formidable struggle for Gonzalez. He was a country boy without the privileges of a college education from the city or early knowledge of the language, which had become the language of power, and certainly with no understanding of the full import of the nation's colonial past and neo-colonial future. The legendary A. V. H. Hartendorp, publisher and editor of the prewar *Philippine Magazine*, accepted two of his early stories. Not having had the advantage of being taught by American professors at the University of the Philippines (UP), Gonzalez felt that it was "the novelty of the *kaingin* as a setting for a fictional work that "opened the pages" of the *Philippine Magazine* to him (65).[1]

So began Gonzalez's journey from a small town in Romblon to the capital city to become a journalist and then a teacher at the UP, to the United States where he eventually would become a professor and director of a creative writing program, and back to the Philippines to receive an honorary doctorate and the country's highest award, National Artist for Literature, before his death in 1999.

Another contemporary, Jose Garcia Villa, was born in Manila, studied at the UP and became the center of its literary life, moved to New York City (in 1929 or 1930), became part of a literary coterie, and published poems that received the praise of Dame Edith Sitwell.

Yet another contemporary, Carlos Bulosan, stowed away on a ship bound for the United States. But a different fate awaited him. Poverty and alcoholism led to illness and death. Nonetheless, *The Laughter of My Father*, a collection of his short stories, was well received when it was published in 1944. (This "triumph" was to be followed by three novels: Celso Carunungan's *Like a Big Brave Man* ([1944] 1960), Stevan Javellana's *Without Seeing the Dawn* [1947], and Edilberto Tiempo's *Watch in the Night* [1953], all about the Japanese war in the Philippines.)

Filipinos were "making it." But there was a price attached: isolation from other Filipinos. Filipino writers in English were writing for American teachers, editors, and critics. For a long time, this was to remain the gauge of a story's worth—acceptance in America.

Gonzalez tried writing in Tagalog.[2] But his friends, who were editors of Tagalog magazines, advised him against this move.

> The accepted idea of writing was that one composed for the masses [the *pambakya* then being produced] or for the elite [the *pampanitikan* – pieces that might be considered for a literary prize]. These notions appeared to have gotten a firm hold not only among editors but throughout the publishing industry. (86)[3]

So Gonzalez returned to English.

From the start, however, Filipino fictionists in English were determined to sound different from their American and British models. Among the earlier writers, Manuel Arguilla is often cited for having most effectively used English to express a thoroughly Filipino experience and sensibility. The eminent scholar and professor, Leopoldo Yabes, recorded Hartendorp's comments on Arguilla's use of English "as if it were a Philippine dialect—so adequately does he find it for his purpose." Yabes himself said of Arguilla that his was "perhaps. . . the only really authentic voice. . . unashamedly Filipino" (1975a, xxxi-xxxiv).

And Arcellana wrote, "I don't believe that more beautiful writing has ever been achieved by any other Filipino. It is writing so lucid and luminous, that is, so clear and so radiant. His language is English and yet it is Filipino" (1967, 614). In fact, there are writers who believe that all of Philippine literature in English is characterized by this effort to "colonize" English, the best-known articulation of which is probably Gémino H. Abad's distinction between writing *in* English and writing *from* English.[4]

The Hispanic Period (1565-1897)

Spain established its first permanent settlement in the Philippines in 1565. A native syllabary was in existence, but scholars now know that it was not used for either recording or producing songs and other types of works that might be considered "literary."

As Resil Mojares has shown in his groundbreaking study of the development of the Filipino novel, fiction in the Philippines is rooted in a tradition of local oral narratives—oral epics, ballads, tales, and other folk narratives. Later the Spaniards introduced other narrative types, lives of saints, parables, fables, and metrical romances, local versions of which came to be known as the *awit* and the *corrido*. (1983, 73–80) The popularity of these narratives extended to the first quarter of the twentieth century. Printing was the monopoly of the Catholic religious orders, which meant that early written literature was entirely religious in nature. The first prose works in the country, chiefly lives of saints and manuals of conduct, date only from the nineteenth century (Lumbera and Lumbera 1982, 42).

Philippine literature during this period reached its apex with the Propaganda Movement (ca.1862–96), which consisted of the Filipino expatriates in Spain who were later to become the heroes of the Philippine Revolution and who, ironically, wrote primarily in Spanish. They were mainly essayists, and their vehicle was the newspaper *La Solidaridad* (1889–95).

Influenced by the European Enlightenment and the spirit of scientific inquiry, José Rizal's novels, *Noli Me Tangere* (1887) and *El Filibusterismo* (1891), are early examples of Filipino realist fiction but are obviously influenced by both the native traditional literature and European literatures in several languages.[5]

The Europe-based reformist movement was unsuccessful, and by the end of the nineteenth century Filipino intellectuals were being drawn to the radical revolutionary movement called the Katipunan. General Emilio Aguinaldo led the victorious forces and proclaimed the country's independence in Cavite.[6] But, rather than surrender to the Filipinos, Spain chose to cede the Philippines to the United States in the Treaty of Paris in 1898. Pretending to be the allies of the Filipino revolutionaries, the Americans prevented Aguinaldo from entering Manila and soon established a new colonial government. Filipinos found themselves fighting a new war, the terribly uneven Philippine-American War of 1900-1904.

The American Period (1898-1945)

The Americans established a public school system with English as the medium of instruction, and in 1908 they founded the UP as an alternative to the Catholic University of Santo Tomas and the other colleges run by the Spanish religious orders. It was to serve as a training ground for the young Filipinos who were to become the new English-speaking elite.

> Unlike the ilustrados of the late nineteenth century who belonged to the socio-economic elite, the new elite came from a broader sector of the populace.
> ... It was within the ranks of these intellectuals... that Philippine writing in English had its beginnings. (Lumbera and Lumbera 1982, 96–97)[7]

The last part of the nineteenth century had been a rich period for the novel in Tagalog and the other Philippine languages. Spanish was declining, and proficiency in English still left much to be desired. But the authors of these novels—mainly serialized in the popular press—had no access to the education received by Rizal, nor did they have his cosmopolitan background. The result was a widening split between "highbrow" and "lowbrow" literature and the emergence of the concept of the *bakya* crowd. The gap grew wider as members of the intelligentsia became more proficient in English and more Americanized in their tastes.

Most literary critics agree that it was in the field of the short story that Filipino writers in English quickly began to excel. Leopoldo Yabes referred to its "remarkable, almost phenomenal growth..." (1975a, xix) and Pura Santillan-Castrence noted, "The remarkable feat of some of the contributors is the quickness with which they produced works in a language entirely foreign to them..." (1967, 548).

By the 1920s, English was entrenched. Magazines such as *Philippine Magazine* (1904–41) and the *Philippines Free Press* (1908–72) had been established, and young writers were flocking to organizations like the UP Writers' Club (founded in 1927), the Philippine Book Guild (1936–40), and the Philippine Writers' League (1939–41). But this privileging of English slowed down the development of literature in the Philippine languages, including Tagalog, and alienated writers in English from the popular culture (Mojares 1983, 349).

In 1933, Jose Garcia Villa published his collection of short stories, *Footnote to Youth,* which earned warm praise from the American critic Edmond O'Brien. He also began his annual project of compiling what he regarded as the best Filipino short stories in English, a project he sustained until 1940, which, in Arcellana's view, was instrumental in "defining" and giving "direction" to the short story in English (1967, 609).

The Philippine Commonwealth was established in 1935 with a new constitution that provided for the granting of independence after a trial period of ten years. This period of peace, prosperity, and relative stability was good for literature.

In 1940, Leopoldo Yabes tried to put together what he intended to be a representative collection of the Philippine short stories that had been published since 1925. The first volume (covering 1925–40), which contained sixty-six stories by about thirty-one writers, was not published until 1975. Of these writers, eight eventually published story collections of their own: Jose Garcia Villa (1906–97), Arturo Rotor (1907–88), Bienvenido Santos (1911–95), Manuel Arguilla (1910–44), N. V. M. Gonzalez (1915–99), Estrella Alfon (1917–83), Nick Joaquin (1917–2004) and Francisco Arcellana (1916–2002). Santos, Gonzalez, and Joaquin also became novelists, and Villa, Gonzalez, Joaquin, and Arcellana were eventually to be named National Artists.[8]

It is worth noting that this anthology included several women: Paz Marquez Benitez (1894–1983) and Paz Latorena (1927–43) (who were also regarded as excellent English teachers), Loreto Paras Sulit (1908–?), Estrella Alfon, Lydia C. Villanueva (who married Manuel Arguilla) (1913–69), and Ligaya Victorio-Reyes (dates unknown).

Describing what was regarded as a good short story, Yabes wrote:

> Most important of all it must have a sense of completeness. . . a completeness of mood, character, or event. . . . [It] should have a sense of direction, know where it is going. . . . Being a dramatic art [it] demands an organic completeness, demands finality. (1975a, xxxi)

The approved technical strategies included a style marked by restraint, indirection, subtlety, and a deliberate effort toward universality of theme (xxxi–xxxii). That these qualities were derived from the writers' readings of Western models is undeniable. Yabes himself has mentioned the writers who influenced the prewar generation of Filipino writers in English: Guy de Maupassant, O. Henry, Edgar Allan Poe, Sherwood Anderson, Ernest Hemingway, Wilbur Daniel Steele, Dorothy Parker, and William Saroyan.

For Bienvenido and Cynthia Lumbera, Manuel Arguilla and Arturo Rotor were "the finest short story writers of their time. . . . Between the two of them, they covered a broad range of subject matter and themes drawn from the experience of Filipinos in the 1930s" (Lumbera and Lumbera 1982, 97). Arguilla is best known for his stories set in an idyllic countryside (e.g., "Midsummer"). However, his later fiction takes place in the dark alleys and cramped tenement houses of Manila (e.g., "Caps and Lower Case"). Both story types are to be found in the collection *How My Brother Leon Brought Home a Wife, and Other Stories* (Arguilla 1940). Rotor, for his part, always wrote of the inner city, usually from the point of view of a doctor who encountered all manner of suffering through his patients. His first collection is *The Wound and the Scar* (1937). Today both writers continue to be highly regarded, although Arguilla's city fiction fares better than the stories set in the countryside.

Just before World War II the Philippines went through a period of agrarian unrest. Jose Garcia Villa, who was regarded as a kind of "literary dictator" at the UP and was widely known for his aestheticism, found himself being challenged by younger writers, who had discovered an alternative critical framework (in his very own backyard, as it were) in socially committed literature, as elaborated by Salvador P. Lopez in "Literature and Society" ([1940] 1998). This movement was at least partly influenced by literary developments in the United States, specifically by American "proletarian literature." As Manuel Viray put it, "When John Steinbeck wrote *In Dubious Battle*, John Dos Passos, *U.S.A.*, James T. Farrell *Studs Lonigan*. . . there was an embarrassment of proletarian stories in the Philippines" (1953, 331).[9]

Soledad Reyes regards "Literature and Society" as the first example of literary theory in Philippine literary scholarship.[10] The attempt to enlist literature in the struggle to transform society, rather than just recording it, became the defining characteristic of one important type of fiction in English: "Of all the ends to which he may dedicate his talents, none is more worthy than the improvement of the condition of man and the defense of his freedom" (Lopez [1940] 1998, 379). This school of fiction was to become dominant during the period immediately preceding the declaration of martial law by Ferdinand Marcos in 1972.

In the same year, the Commonwealth Literary Awards were established. One of the Awards' aims was "to encourage creative works that record or interpret the contemporary scene, or that deal with the social and economic problems of the individual and of society over and above those that are merely concerned with fantasy or mysticism or vain speculation" (Dalisay 2002, 139). This reinforced the Lopez position.

However, for Arcellana, N. V. M. Gonzalez was "the genius of the 1930s," in particular because of the "astonishing suggestiveness" and "epic simplicity" of the stories in his first collection, *Seven Hills Away and Other Stories* (1947). It seems to me, though, that Gonzalez's most significant achievement in this and his other story collections, such as *Children of the Ash-Covered Loam* (1977), is his attempt to bring to life (in English) the quality, rhythms, and nuances of the days and nights lived by the *kaingin* farmers of Mindoro, thus creating an enduring myth of the Filipino peasant for the national imagination. This sensibility, described by Arcellana as Gonzalez's ability to present a "postage stamp of native soil," is captured in one of his most popular stories in that collection: "Lupo and the River" (Arcellana 1967, 616–17).

> Below, in the broken shade that the roof frame made on the ground, Tio Longinos was busy with his mallet and chisel. Pisco climbed the post, and, with his upturned foot, received one end of the heavy beam that Lupo lowered to him. With his own loop of rattan, and bending over, Pisco caught the beam and pulled. Lupo taught him to work the rattan this way and that, never sacrificing pattern for strength, never losing purpose, and yet taking care to make out of something ordinary a beautiful thing. Pisco could not help feeling that it was from Lupo that all this wisdom of the rattan had come, and he thought he saw Tio Longinos smiling quietly to himself there below. (Gonzalez 1977, 46–47)

This was an important development in the short story in English: the deliberate effort of writers to locate themselves, to find that bit of earth they could claim through their fiction.[11]

In 1940, Nick Joaquin's publication of "Three Generations" in *Graphic* created a stir. If Gonzalez's territory was the farms of the Mindoro peasants, Joaquin's was the homes of the middle-class Manileños, whose forbears were the Intramuros[12] *ilustrados*. But Joaquin's more important contribution at this point was his brilliant use of the English language and his mastery of the techniques of fiction. "May Day Eve" provides an example of this mastery.

> "And what did you see, Mama? Oh, what was it?" But Doña Agueda had forgotten the little girl on her lap: she was staring past the curly head nestling at her breast and seeing herself in the big mirror hanging in the room. It was the same room and the same mirror but the face she now saw in it was an old face—a hard, bitter, vengeful face, framed in graying hair, and so sadly altered, so sadly different from that other face like a white mask, that fresh young face like a pure mask that she had brought before this mirror one wild May Day midnight years and years ago." (1962, 28)

A tale of love and betrayal in three generations of one family set against a lavishly romantic backdrop of horse-drawn carriages and candlelit rooms, "May Day Eve" is written in a lush, lyrical, cadenced language using sophisticated narrative strategies, including multiple points of view, time shifts, stream of consciousness, and other modernist techniques.

The Postwar Period (1946-60)

The Pacific War brought the Japanese to the Philippines as another army of occupation. Japanese language became compulsory in Philippine schools, and Tagalog was pushed as the national language. Only the Tagalog magazine *Liwayway* was allowed to continue publishing. No writing in English was allowed.

The Philippines remained under Japanese rule from 1942 to 1945. Then, after "liberation" in 1946, the devastated country was suddenly "granted" its much longed for and long-delayed independence. However, American influence on Philippine life and culture, including literature, remained strong, not only because several treaties ensured economic dependence on the former colonial masters, but because of the Fulbright program, which granted scholarships, fellowships, and so on to almost all important Filipino artists and scholars, thus guaranteeing their firsthand exposure to American culture.[13]

In the critical introduction to the sequel to his first anthology (covering the years 1941–55), Yabes made three observations about the 154 collected stories: (1) no "remarkable" stories were published about the battles of Bataan and Corregidor, although there were some fine stories about the Death March,[14] the concentration camps, the guerrilla activities, and the harrowing Battle of Manila; (2) sex as a subject was beginning to be handled with more frankness; (3) the stories covered the whole of the country, including its ethnic and cultural minorities;[15] and (4) there was an increase in the number of stories set in foreign lands (1981, xviv).

More war narratives were to be written later, notably by women, such as Edith Tiempo, Lina Espina-Moore, Aida Rivera-Ford, Linda Ty-Casper, Gilda Cordero-Fernando, and Cecilia Manguerra Brainard. Greater candor in the handling of sex as a subject would characterize modern fiction by both men and women. The tendency to range far and wide where subject matter is concerned is another important quality of the short story in English and one that became more pronounced in contemporary literature. And stories "set in foreign lands," which began with Bienvenido Santos ("The Scent of Apples"), increased in number when the "Fil-ams," the third generation of expatriate or immigrant Filipinos, came of age.

Another development, which Yabes failed to mention was that some of the stories deviated from the conventional realist mode, for example, Francisco Arcellana's "The Wing of Madness."[16] And Nick Joaquin's tales, "The Legend of a Dying Wanton," seem to anticipate magical realism. Here is yet another important characteristic of the Filipino short story in English —the value placed on originality where technical strategies are concerned.

Among the new writers included in the second Yabes anthology were some who would become leading literary figures later: the spouses Tiempo (Edilberto and Edith), who would be named National Artists for Literature in 2000; F. Sionil José, who would be named National Artist for Literature in 2001; and Kerima Polotan, regarded by some as the country's most important woman writer in English.

Polotan's fiction has not received the attention it deserves, perhaps because it was overshadowed by the fiction of her male contemporaries, Gonzalez, Arcellana, Joaquin, and Bienvenido Santos. Her short fiction—collected in *Stories* (1968a)—are among the most emotionally powerful and technically accomplished to have been written by Filipinos in any period.[17]

Edith Tiempo's essay "The Short Stories" (1953) in *Philippine Writing*, an anthology of Philippine literature, edited by T. D. Agcaoili, is a good summary of the fictional qualities considered important by someone who was to exercise tremendous influence on literary production. Tiempo's essay described what she called a "successful story" in terms espoused by New Criticism, which she and her husband, Edilberto Tiempo (both of them newly returned from the University of Iowa), were introducing into Silliman University in Dumaguete:[18] "In the short story when we define structure we really set down the rules for writing a successful story" (xi).

Tiempo's "rules" were a refinement of the same qualities admired by the fictionists of the prewar period—technical strategies contributing toward organic unity and a striving toward universality of theme. And it was the Polotan story "The Virgin" that Tiempo used as an example of a "successful story" (1953, xix). This is the story of a lonely spinster's struggle against the attraction she feels for a much younger man from the lower classes. Its language is both limpid and lyrical, and the frankness with which it deals with both the class divide and woman's sexuality is unusual for its time.

> And yet Miss Mijares did think of love. Secret, short-lived thoughts flitted through her mind—in the jeepneys she took to work when a man pressed down beside her and through her dress she felt the curve of his thigh. . . . And in the movies, ah the movies, to sink into a seat as into an embrace, in the darkness with a hundred shadowy figures about her and high on

the screen, a man kissing a woman's mouth while her own figures stole unconsciously to her unbruised lips. (Polotan 1968b, 24)

Other good examples would be Tiempo's own stories, including "The Black Monkey," which tells of a woman lying helpless in a tree house, where she might be safe from the Japanese soldiers but not from either the monster without or the monster within.

In the same Agcaoili anthology, N. V. M. Gonzalez was worrying over the conflicting demands between earning a decent living and producing literature that would satisfy standards learned from the West (Gonzalez, 1953, 227–28). This suggests that the tastes of readers (who, if they bought literary works, would have enabled writers to earn a decent living from their books) did not conform with the standards the writers had set for themselves, a gap that continues to plague Philippine fiction in English today.

The appearance of Gilda Cordero-Fernando and Gregorio C. Brillantes marks the entrance into the scene of writers who are products of the so-called exclusive Catholic schools.[19] But there is nothing parochial about their work. In fact, Cordero-Fernando's stories (collected in *Butcher, Baker, Candlestick Maker* [1962]) and Brillantes's stories (collected in *The Distance to Andromeda and Other Stories* [1960]) are a high point in the development of the Philippine short story in English. Mastery of the medium has reached the point of apparent effortlessness. Gone are all traces of stiltedness, of awkwardness.

Cordero-Fernando's "High Fashion," with its androgynous fashion designer protagonist, is a satirical fairy tale about the foibles of Manila's socialites. Brillantes's "The Distance to Andromeda" is a tale of an adolescent boy's attempts to grapple with the mysteries and meaning of the vast universe and his own existence in it while around him life in all its mundane detail goes placidly on. This writing is characterized by ease and elegance. Its perspective is both urbane and ironic. These qualities—a highly sophisticated fictional technique and an ironic point of view—were to characterize much of the fiction in English of the next decades.

An important development in the literary scene in the late 1940s and early 1950s was the establishment of the Short Story Writing Contest by the Philippines Free Press in 1949 and of the Carlos Palanca Memorial Literary Awards in 1950. These awards—which are ongoing—have undoubtedly been a major source of both encouragement and inspiration for writers, and have done their share in contributing to the shaping of what we might call the "poetics" of the Philippine short story in English.

The Contemporary Period (1960-2000)

The *Philippine P. E. N. Anthology of Short Stories,* edited by Francisco Arcellana (1962), and *Equinox 1: An Anthology of New Writing from the Philippines,* edited by F. Sionil José (1965), provide a useful overview of the scene a decade after publication of the Agcaoili anthology. Stories by older writers such as F. Sionil José and Gilda Cordero-Fernando are part of the *P. E. N. Anthology,* but also included are some new names, including Erwin Castillo, César Aquino, and Wilfredo Sanchez.

Today the stories by the younger writers may strike the reader as rather dense, highly impressionistic, and perhaps even self-indulgent. A change had taken place. Writers were no longer preoccupied with language in the sense of its being a foreign language. They were more interested in testing its possibilities and experimenting with different techniques. In his introduction to *Equinox,* Andres Cristobal Cruz points out that the writers—José V. Ayala, G. Burce Bunao, Lilia Pablo Amansec, Norma Miraflor—are "pervasively subjective," perhaps because they are writing in a borrowed language (surely a *non siquitur*): "Involved in language, the human event is explored partially. Commitment seems to be to art first, and to life, second..." (1965, 7).

Courtesy of Random House, Inc.

This, then, is the defining quality of another type of Filipino short story in English that is as strong in its way as socially committed writing: writing that might be said to be enamored of language, writing that tends to be subjective, impressionistic, more interested in reflection than action. The debate between Villa and Lopez had obviously not been settled and would continue to rage.[20]

The American critic Leonard Casper's observation reflected the same note sounded earlier by N. V. M. Gonzalez: the problem of a lack of audience for Philippine writing in English. In the preface to his *Modern Philippine Short Stories* (Casper, 1962), he commented that "to write honestly *about* his people" the Filipino writer in English apparently "must risk not writing *for* them" (xvii). And yet it was undeniable that Filipino writing in English was gaining some international recognition.[21]

The 1960s were a kind of golden age for magazine publishing, with the *Philippines Free Press*, *Graphic,* and the *Asia Philippines Leader* publishing stories of unusually high quality. The writers on the staff of these magazines included some of the most important writers in English: Nick Joaquin, Kerima Polotan, Gregorio C. Brillantes, Wilfredo Nolledo, Jose Lacaba Jr., Luis Teodoro, and Ninotchka Rosca. This was also a period of maturity for Nick Joaquin, Kerima Polotan, Bienvenido Santos, F. Sionil José, and Linda Ty-Casper, who were now producing novels. By this time, Philippine universities were beginning to offer graduate courses in Philippine literature, and writers were beginning to change their minds about publication abroad being the only path to literary achievement (Gonzalez 1967, 540).

On the eve of the political upheaval that would have a major impact on the literati, Philippine literature in English found a defender in Bienvenido Lumbera, a prominent nationalist scholar and later a staunch advocate of the national language as a literary language. Lumbera claimed that literature in English was superior to literature in Filipino. He attributed this superiority (i.e., its greater complexity and sophistication) to the ironic vision of the writers, a vision that he traced to the Western tradition behind this branch of literature and to extraliterary factors such as the peculiar position of the writer in English in society, a position similar to that of the *ilustrado* in the previous century (1967, 14–15).

The opposite view was to be expressed a couple of years later by, among others, Luis Teodoro.

> Those who write in English—whatever their degree of political consciousness—of necessity address themselves to an audience forming a minor segment of our population and concentrated on the intelligentsia. We can expect that audience to further dwindle as the nationalist struggle gains momentum. (1968–69, 5)

The Villa-Lopez debate had taken on a new dimension, with English being somehow associated with the art for art's sake position and Filipino with the art for society position, an obvious case of oversimplification.

The late 1960s and early 1970s were a troubled time for the country. Student power movements were sweeping campuses all over the world in the wake of the massive protest actions against the Vietnam War. In the Philippines, the movement took a radical nationalist turn, a vehement attack on imperialism, feudalism, and bureaucrat capitalism. Ferdinand Marcos was seen as the very embodiment of these evils.

The unrest had the effect of politicizing writers. The chief influences were Mao Zedong's "Talks at the Yenan Forum," Jean-Paul Sartre's concept of the writer as *engagé*, and the rewriting of Philippine history in the essays of Renato Constantino.[22] Mao Zedong had drawn a sharp distinction between artistic and political criteria in the evaluation of a literary work. The subjective, precious, mannered style of the earlier decade, and the predilection for purely personal concerns—such as the search for identity, romantic love, or the absurdity of life —were now regarded as reactionary, a manifestation of "decadent bourgeois tendencies." Teodoro's "The Trial of Professor Luis Riesgo" is probably one of the best examples of this type of story. Written in the social realist mode, it focuses on an actual case during the witch hunt of the 1950s on the UP campus.

This turbulent period, now known as the First Quarter Storm, was to culminate in the declaration of martial law in September 1972. The Marcos dictatorship, which lasted from 1972 to 1986, was a not a good time for literature. Government controls were imposed on media. Literary publishing houses, still in their infancy, almost came to a standstill. But the Carlos Palanca Memorial Awards for Literature were still awarded each year. (Among the new writers to receive prizes for their short stories during this period were Elsa Martinez-Coscolluela, Cristina Pantoja Hidalgo,[23] Renato Madrid, Jaime An Lim, Leoncio Deriada, and Rowena Tiempo-Torrevillas.) And new periodicals were established to replace the ones that had been shut down.

The magazine *Focus Philippines,* founded in 1972, immediately began to publish fiction and offer literary awards. However, a cursory glance at the list of winners in its early years will reveal the marked absence of familiar names.[24] Many writers refused to be reconciled to the Marcos regime. As Richard Croghan observed, "This magazine has become one of the main outlets for new writers. But so far, the results have not been impressive. . . . In general, the writers seem afraid to truly express themselves" (1975, 250).

Croghan also noted the consensus (arrived at during a National Seminar on Bilingual Education held at Ateneo de Manila University in 1974) that Filipino would increasingly become the medium of instruction in Philippine schools. This meant, Croghan said, that the quality of English would change, would perhaps even become a kind of pidgin (although he did not use the term, preferring to speculate on "Englipino" or "Pilipinish"). It appeared that the future of Philippine literature in English was uncertain. But, Croghan added, "Whatever the future may bring. . . in this Modern Period of Philippine

Literature in English, the literary style and content have become more Filipino than ever before" (1975, 250–51).

In the meantime, Marcos's hard-line policies were causing Filipino writers to take stock and seriously consider the role of the writers in the so-called New Society. Martial law may have been the catalyst that eventually turned many writers to historical fiction.

In 1973, the Marcos government issued Proclamation no. 1144, providing special awards to individual artists in recognition of "artistic and literary accomplishment at its highest level, and. . . to elevate creative expression in all its forms to its rightful status as the vanguard of the country's spiritual development." Significantly, the first writer to be honored as a National Artist for Literature was Jose Garcia Villa.

Martial law finally came to an end after a popular peaceful uprising—known as People Power or the EDSA Revolution—toppled the dictator, restored democracy, and made Corazon Aquino (the widow of the slain opposition leader Benigno Aquino, Jr.) president. Literature flourished, as did the publishing industry and other media.

The Present Scene and Prospects for the Future

The predictions, Croghan's included, appear to have been wrong. For all that, the audiences for literature (in English or Filipino) remain miniscule (the average print run for a collection of short fiction or a novel is one thousand copies). Despite the fact that no writer can survive solely on writing fiction or poetry, and despite the deterioration in English-language proficiency in the country as a whole, there are more writers in English than ever before.[25] In his introduction to a special literary issue of *Philippine Studies* in 1995, Emmanuel Torres had this to say about the language issue.

> The language question—to write in English or Filipino?—which so preoccupied nationalists in the sixties/seventies, has been superseded by a pragmatic attitude. . . . The key to literary survival and development appears to be proficiency in both Filipino and English, something taken for granted these days. . . . [The writers] write in whichever language serves the given literary material better with the confidence of those familiar with more than one language and one culture. Bilingual proficiency among today's better-known young writers is commonly seen as an advantage. (1995, 286)

And Jose Y. Dalisay, Jr. noted :

> Our young writers today use English unapologetically, refusing to be burdened by colonial guilt; quite a number of them write bilingually. Indeed, we are witnessing the continuing de-Americanization of English, its appropriation by Filipino writers for Filipino subjects and purposes. (2002, 145)

In the field of fiction, many of the older writers, such as Edith Tiempo and F. Sionil José, are still writing. And the writers of the next generation are at the peak of their powers. Alfred A. Yuson, a member of the Carlos Palanca Hall of Fame,[26] reflects the best of this generation. His short story "The Music Child" (1991) winner of the 1992 S. E. A. Write Award, reflects an interest in socially critical realism. While in the jungle investigating a human interest story about indigenous music, the journalist protagonist finds himself embroiled in violence against a tribal group that is trying to protect its environment from illegal deforestation while he is interviewing one of its supporters.

> Five years ago they began to have problems with big logging companies. But they had stood their ground and the encroachment stopped. Now it appeared that the new group was determined to have its way. He himself was quite resigned to the thought that their mountains would soon be stripped naked and dry. . . . Violence had already claimed the lives of his friends who had tried to block the road with rocks and dead trees. (Yamada 2002, 247)

Yuson writes in different genres and is equally at home with realism, fantasy, broad farce, sophisticated comedy, postmodernism, and magical realism.[27] His two prize-winning novels—*Great Philippine Jungle Energy Café* (1988) and *Voyeurs and Savages* (1998)—combine all of these modes.

Jose Y. Dalisay, Jr., also a member of the Carlos Palanca Hall of Fame, writes stories that combine a starkly simple realism with poignant lyricism.[28] Among the most moving is "Amnesty," which records the encounter of a man and a woman, former comrades in the resistance movement, who find themselves side by side on a bus. The man turned his back on political activism and has survived under the Marcos government. The woman's husband was killed by the military, and she suffered long years of imprisonment. With the victory of People Power, the protagonist finds himself jobless, and the woman is suddenly free, so the meeting is fraught with irony. Dalisay has also published an award-winning novel, *Killing Time in a Warm Place* (1992).

Charlson Ong is the first major writer to focus on the Chinese Filipino experience (in three story collections).[29] He is also one of the few major writers with the ability to turn grim reality into fine comedy. In "Mismanagement of Grief," for instance, a young man insists on confronting his father with all the family skeletons during the wake of a young relative who had been kidnapped and then killed during a botched rescue attempt. Ong's first novel, *An Embarrassment of Riches* (2000), is a political satire that won the second prize for the novel in the prestigious, government-sponsored Centennial Literary Awards.

After two decades of writing in Filipino, Rosario Lucero has returned to English with *Feast and Famine: Stories of Negros* (2003), an award-winning collection that reconstructs the author's mad, magical, rollicking, ribald, and endlessly fascinating Negros.[30] The funniest story in the book is probably "The Death of Fray Salvador Montano, Conquistador of Negros," which is an account of the ludicrous misadventures of a well-meaning friar in his efforts to turn the natives into good Christians.

And then there is a whole slew of even younger writers, who already have individual short story collections to their names and national prizes under their belts: Vicente Groyon, Katrina Tuvera, Menchu Sarmiento, Romina Gonzalez, Lakambini Sitoy, Clinton Palanca, Luis Katigbak, Angelo Lacuesta, F. H. Batacan, and Tara FT Sering.

The literary production of these young writers is amazingly diverse, in both content and style. They write with aplomb about many subjects that a previous generation of writers considered taboo. Issues of gender, ethnicity, and the environment figure prominently. But so do other themes, including the traditional ones of love, death, loss, betrayal, power, guilt, and so on. Most of the stories are very sophisticated, very self-conscious, urban tales. The high degree of stylistic skill is probably the result of the fact that many of them have not only attended creative writing workshops but are graduates of new university creative-writing programs. Most are familiar with the work of Jorge Luis Borges, Italo Calvino, Salman Rushdie, Jamaica Kincaid, Arundhati Roy, Milan Kundera, Ben Okri, Tewfik Saleh, J. M. Coetzee, A. S. Byatt, Jeanette Winterson, and John Barth. Their narrative strategies are obviously influenced by postmodernism, magical realism, the other arts, the media, the Internet, and popular culture (comic books, MTV, anime, etc.).

Obviously these texts are the products of the age of technology, cyberspace, and globalization, as well as of their own country's troubled history and unrelenting socioeconomic and political problems. It would be absurd to ask whether these stories are "Filipino." Even the most experimental among them are undeniable Pinoy,[31] and not just because of a new awareness of the significance of local mythology and an interest in the retrieval of forgotten aspects of Philippine culture.

Katigbak writes slick, minimalist urban tales, some of them self-consciously metafictional, such as "Birthday," whose protagonist one day simply forgets who he is. Romina Gonzalez uses both realist and nonrealist techniques to tell particularly dark tales about such subjects as voyeurism, racism, and incest, through which runs a deeply ironic sense of humor. For instance, in "Rock," the young female protagonist has nocturnal adventures with a rocking horse that might actually be her brother. A heavy-handed sort of feminism characterized Lakambini Sitoy's early stories. But her more recent stories are more subtle, sensitive narratives about very young protagonists—such as the terrified victim of an urban vampire, a pedophiliac ("Vampire"), and the small daughter of a security guard who seeks safety from her unstable world in a TV show about wild animals in their natural habitat ("Jungle Planet"). Groyon explores sinister truths lurking just beneath apparently placid, even genteel, surfaces, such as possible sexual abuse implicitly condoned by school authorities ("What I Love Or Will Remember Most About High School?").

What might be the reason for such a flowering?

Publishers—including small new ones such as Milflores Publishing—have done their share to make literature an attractive occupation. Even the university presses now carry literary titles as a matter of course, which was not true even as late as the 1970s. Journalists who come from the same universities that produce the creative writers, and who themselves may be creative writers in secret, give literary events and awards good media coverage.

Another important factor must be the recognition given by academe to creative writing as a distinct discipline. As we have seen, academe has been involved in literature since the establishment of the UP early in the twentieth century. But the formalization of this connection through creative-writing programs, workshops, centers, and so on has increased creative writing's prestige, with major universities competing to get prominent writers onto their faculties.

Finally, there is the impact of the breakthrough being enjoyed by Filipino writers living abroad. We refer to them as "Fil-ams" because most of them are based in the United States. Unlike the second generation of expatriate writers (Villa, Bulosan, Santos),[32] many among them have made their names abroad by writing not about the immigrant experience but about the mother country.[33] Ninotchka Rosca, Jessica Hagedorn, Cecilia Manguerra Brainard, Rowena Tiempo-Torrevillas, Bino Realuyo, Marianne Villanueva, Michele Skinner, M. Evelina Galang, Eric Gamalinda, R. Zamora Linmark, Mar Puatu, Peter Bacho, Brian Ascalon Roley, Paulino Lim Jr., and ER Escober write from the United States; Arlene J. Chai, Merlinda Bobis, and Cesar Leyco Aguila live in Australia; Norma Miraflor, F. H. Batacan, Tara FT Sering, Noelle Q. de Jesus (Noelle Chua), and Nadine Sarreal live in Singapore; and Reine Arcache Melvin lives in Paris. Some of them continue to publish in the Philippines. Many visit the country regularly. Although these writers reside outside of the Philippines, their fiction is often set within the country.

Marianne Villanueva's short story "The Mayor of the Roses" provides an example of this. A socially reflective recounting of an actual rape-homocide reported in the Manila newspapers, it graphically reconstructs the tragic and violent death of a former beauty queen along with the callousness of the mayor who allowed it. Politically protected, he escapes much punishment.

Courtesy of Marianne Villanueva

> Much, much later, when I was myself again, I opened a newspaper and there was his picture. I couldn't mistake that shock of hair that looked like a rug, those pig eyes. He was sitting in a bathtub, and, from what I could see of him, was apparently naked. The caption said that the picture had been taken in jail. But the Mayor was smiling. The article said the Mayor's bathwater was sprinkled with rose petals provided by his loving wife, Bai, the new Mayor of Calauan. (Yamada 2002, 262)[34]

Through the Internet, these writers maintain close contacts with Filipino writers based in the Philippines and contribute to books published locally and locally hosted Web sites. In turn, they invite Filipino writers to contribute to books published abroad and arrange for readings, lectures, and so on when the latter visit. This is simply another aspect of globalization.

Although these writers reside outside of the Philippines, their fiction is often set within the country. However, the effects of this diaspora on writing in English in the Philippines have not yet been measured. One possible negative effect is that it could alienate Philippine writing in English even more from

Philippine writing in Filipino and the other Philippine languages, as English is the primary language of cyberspace.

In what language will the fiction of the future be written? I believe it is likely that many writers will continue to write in English, and Philippine literature in English will continue to enjoy the prestige it does today, as long as America remains a superpower if not *the* superpower. The desire on the part of the writers to enter into world literature antedated economic policies of globalization. It is not likely to go away now.

On the other hand, bilingualism will increase. And, given encouragement of the retrieval of regional cultures,[35] multilingualism may increase as well. It is also possible that the fiction of the future will not be written in what we call "standard English." It might go the way of Jamaica Kincaid or Arundhati Roy. It might be written in "Filipino English" or "Taglish." The Fil-am writer R. Zamora Linmark has already taken fiction in that direction with the novel *Rolling the R's* (1995), which uses the pidgin of the Filipino plantation workers of Hawaii. The dialogue in Tara FT Sering's novella *Getting Better* (2003) is in yuppie Taglish. Antonio A. Hidalgo has written a story ("D Many Txts of Luv") entirely in the language of texting, which is neither English nor Filipino nor even Taglish but a kind of code.

I also believe that the issue of audiences and markets will become increasingly more important. Popular culture—comic books, malls, high fashion, and beauty contests—is now a legitimate area of study in universities. The late Levi Celerio, composer of numerous popular songs, was recently named a National Artist, as were the film directors Lino Brocka and Ishmael Bernal. They have worthy successors in Mark Meily and Jeffrey Jaturian, among others, who are mixing comedy and postmodern techniques with surprising effects. The Manila Critics' Circle now includes comic books among the categories of its annual National Book Awards, and academics mount comic book exhibits in the Cultural Center of the Philippines and participate in international comic book conferences and fairs.

Obviously popular literature can be written in English as well as Filipino. And the most serious themes can be presented in a light manner so that they will appeal to larger audiences. The binary of *bakya* crowd versus literati no longer holds. The University of the Philippines Press recently published a crime novel and a novella that belongs to the popular genre known as "chick lit" as part of its Jubilee Student Edition. The crime novel *Smaller and Smaller Circles*, by F. H. Batacan (2002), won three prestigious national awards and has gone into four printings. Sering's second chick lit novella, *Almost Married* (2003), won a National Book Award and has sold ten thousand copies so far.

Many young writers are experimenting with creative nonfiction. Others are going multimedia. There is a proliferation of e-zines and blogs and Web sites carrying fiction and other literary works. Bars and cafés feature the "spoken word" along with jazz bands and solo singers. The UP's Institute of Creative Writing recently sponsored a poetry-writing contest that required participants to text in their entries. Which of these directions will prove enduring is anyone's guess. But one thing seems clear: the scene is an immensely exciting one. The unstable political and economic conditions prevailing in the country for the past decades have not proven a deterrent to literary production. On the contrary, they seem to have had the effect of stimulating and challenging writers. As the country lurches fitfully through the first decade of the twenty-first century, the scene may well become even wilder.

Notes

[1] *Kaingin* (slash and burn) is a method of cultivation or preparation of land for planting by burning all the trees and weeds.

[2] Tagalog, the language of Manila and surrounding regions (now called the National Capital Region) is the basis of Filipino, the official national language of the Philippines.

[3] *Bakya* refers to wooden clogs, associated in the popular imagination with the lower classes, which were not in the habit of wearing shoes. Hence, *pambakya* would be, literally, "for the lower classes." *panitikan* is "literature." Hence, *pampanitikan* means "for the literati."

[4] On this distinction, see Abad (2002), who wrote, "Our concern now is what we have made of English: at first indeed we wrote *in* English, and freely borrowed and adopted, and then, we wrought *from* English, and forged (in its double sense) ourselves and our own scene where we worked out our own destiny" (18). See also, Dalisay, (2002): "Indeed we are witnessing the continuing de-Americanization of English, its appropriation by Filipino writers for Filipino subjects and purposes" (145). For an overview of the Philippine short story in English see Hidalgo 2004.

[5] José Rizal, the country's national hero, was accused of treason and executed by the Spanish colonial government.

[6] Cavite is a province located on the southern shores of Manila Bay in the Calabarzon region in Luzon.

[7] The term *ilustrado* refers to the members of native elite, many of them mestizo Spanish or mestizo Chinese.

[8] Jose Garcia Villa received the award in 1973, Nick Joaquin in 1976, Francisco Arcellana in 1990, and N. V. M. Gonzalez in 1997.

[9] The Marxist critic Petronilo Bn. Daroy also attributed the critical formulations for the literature of "social consciousness," as articulated by Salvador P. Lopez, to the canons of social protest in the United States (1969, 260–61).

[10] "Whether celebrating literature's didactic functions or stressing the aesthetic components of literature, the majority of critics in the past did not see the need to abstract from the data and theorize on any issue related to the practice of literature. An exception was Salvador Lopez who ". . . argued the need for committed literature" (Reyes 1987, 79).

[11] Estrella Alfon was thus to claim Cebu; Antonio Enriquez, Cagayan de Oro; Gregorio C. Brillantes, Tarlac; Erwin Castillo, Caite; and so on.

[12] Intramuros (literally, "between walls") was the old walled city inside Manila, where the Spaniards and the native elite resided during the Spanish colonial period.

[13] Americans have themselves commented on this ironic "dependent independence." For instance, "Just as they had pressed Roxas into a favorable bases agreement, so the Americans exerted leverage on the Filipinos to obtain economic preferences. Americans paradoxically acquired greater privileges in the Philippines during the postcolonial years than they had during the colonial period" (Karnow 1989, 323).

[14] After the attack on Pearl Harbor, General Douglas MacArthur declared Manila an open city and moved his headquarters to Bataan. However, he evacuated soon after, and his Filipino allies were left to hold the fort at Bataan and Corregidor, which they did for four agonizing months. After the fall of Corregidor came the forced march of war prisoners to Capas, which has come to be known as the Death March because of the number of men who did not survive it.

[15] This led Yabes to observe that "the Filipino short story in English is more truly national than the Filipino short story in the native Philippine languages and in Spanish. In other words it presents a more truly comprehensive picture of the life and culture of the Filipino people in its varied aspects" (1981, xiv).

[16] In fact, Arcellana was a bold experimenter from the start. Consider "Trilogy of the Turtles" (1990, 26–32). This may be why Yabes was skeptical about his worth as a writer. "I have not yet been able to determine to which group Arcellana belongs," Yabes wrote. "He may really be a genius, as Villa has pronounced; but he may also be a mediocrity or merely a skilled craftsman" (1981, xxxiii).

[17] It was only in the late nineties that all of Polotan's books, including her award-winning novel, *The Hand of the Enemy* (1962), were retrieved and reprinted by the University of the Philippines Press.

[18] Dumaguete is a city in Negros Oriental, south of Manila in the Central Visayas region.

[19] Gilda Cordero-Fernando was educated at Saint Theresa's College, a Catholic college exclusively for women, and Gregorio C. Brillantes at Ateneo de Manila

University, a Jesuit college exclusively for men. These "exclusive" Catholic schools continue to be preferred by the Filipino upper and middle classes today chiefly because of the high quality of education they provide.

[20] The debate referred to is the art for art's sake view of Jose Garcia Villa versus the art for society view represented by Salvador P. Lopez (see Lumbera and Lumbera above.)

[21] For instance, there was Donald Keene's response to Leonard Casper's second anthology, *New Writing from the Philippines* (1966): "Whatever course Philippine literature may take, we are certainly fortunate that there are now Filipinos who can speak to us beautifully in our own language, without risking the terrible hazards of translation. . . . The collection as a whole is of even more importance than the individual excellences. It is an admirable testimony to the emergence of another important branch of English literature" (cited in Gonzalez 1995, 27).

[22] Constantino's books include his own and those he co-authored: *The Making of a Filipino* (1969), *The Philippines: A Past Revisited* (1975), and *The Philippines: The Continuing Past* (1978).

[23] My story "The Painting," written in 1992, reflects the continuing development of writers who endured the 1970s. A lyrical narrative with elements of magical realism, it contains a complex plot with the past mirrored in the present, reflecting the failure of the *ilustrados*, including José Rizal, to bring about enduring change in the Philippines. It is reprinted in Yamada 2002, 221–35.

[24] Juan Tuvera and Kerima Polotan Tuvera, who were known to be closely connected with the Marcos family, published *Focus Philippines* (*Focus Magazine*).

[25] The *Philippines Free Press* and *Philippine Graphic* pay between 800 to 1,000 pesos for a short story (less than 20 dollars). The glossies (*Metro, Mega, Preview,* etc.) pay slightly more—1,500 to 2,000 pesos (30 to 40 dollars)—but they carry feature articles and essays, not short stories. Most writers—of whatever language—have regular jobs in academe, in the media, in advertising, or on the staffs of politicians, and write fiction and poetry "on the side." This includes even the highest-paid writers today, namely, film scriptwriters.

[26] Writers who win a Carlos Palanca first prize five times (in any or all genres) become part of the Carlos Palanca Hall of Fame.

[27] Yuson's stories are collected in *The Music Child and Other Stories* (1991) and *Eight Stories* (2002).

[28] Thus far, Dalisay has published three short story collections: *Oldtimer and Other Stories* (1984), *Sarcophagus and Other Stories* (1992), and *Penmanship and Other Stories* (1995).

[29] Ong's books are *Men of the East and Other Stories* (1999), *Woman of Am-Kaw and Other Stories* (1992), and *Conversion and Other Fictions* (1996).

[30] Negros Oriental and Negros Occidental are neighboring provinces in the Philippine south.

[31] *Pinoy* is an affectionate abbreviation for "Filipino." It does not have the derogatory connotations attached to "flip," a word originally coined by American soldiers during the Philippine-American War.

[32] The first generation would be the Propaganda Movement, the expatriate Filipinos who wrote from Spain.

[33] The Filipino-American critic, Oscar Campomanes, has suggested that this is a "strategy for making themselves 'visible' in a country which has in effect 'erased' them from its history, a means of coping with their exile which is different from that taken by the first generation of expatriate." He refers to the systematic erasure from official history of the U.S. of the colonial project in the Philippines (1995, 159-192).

[34] This story was subsequently republished in Villanueva's *Mayor of the Roses: Stories* (2005).

[35] Such encouragement is provided, for example, by the National Commission for Culture and the Arts, for example, which regularly gives grants to research of this sort; and by graduate programs, like the Comparative Literature Program in the UP, where students are urged to do primary research in the languages and literatures of their own regions.

References

Abad, Gémino H. 2002. "Mapping our Poetic Terrain: Filipino Poetry in English from 1905 to the Present." in *The Likhaan Anthology of Philippine Literature in English, from 1900 to the Present*, edited by Gémino H. Abad, 3–23. Quezon City: University of the Philippines Press.

Alfon, Estrella. 2000. "English." In *The Estrella D. Alfon Anthology: A Critical Edition*, 62–69. Manila: De La Salle University Press.

Arcellana, Francisco, ed. 1962. *Philippine P.E.N. Anthology of Short Stories*. Manila: Philippine Chapter, International P.E.N.

Arcellana, Francisco. 1967. "Period of Emergence in the Short Story." In *Brown Heritage*, edited by Antonio Manuud, 603–617. Quezon City: Ateneo de Manila University Press.

Agcaoili, T. D. 1953. Foreword. In *Philippine Writing: An Anthology*, edited by T. D. Agcaoili, vii-ix. Manila: Archipelago Publishing House.

Arguilla, Manuel. 1940. *How My Brother Leon Brought Home a Wife, and Other Stories*. Manila: Philippine Book Guild.

Bernad, Miguel A. and Alfred Stirling. 1961. *Bamboo and the Greenwood Tree: Essays on Filipino Literature in English*. Manila. Bookmark.

Campomanes, Oscar. 1995. "Filipinos in the United States and Their Literature of Exile." In *Discrepant Histories: Translocal Essays on Filipino Cultures*, edited by Vicente L. Rafael, 159–92. Philadelphia: Temple University Press.

Casper, Leonard, ed. 1962. *Modern Philippine Short Stories*. Albuquerque: University of New Mexico Press.

Casper, Leonard. 1966. *New Writing from the Philippines: A Critique and Anthology*. Syracuse, NY: Syracuse University Press.

Constantino, Renato. 1969. *The Making of a Filipino (A Story of Philippine Colonial Politics)*. Quezon City: Malaya Books.

———. 1970. *Dissent and Counter-consciousness*. Quezon City: Malaya Books.

Constantino, Renato, and Letizia R. Constantino. 1978 (1982). *The Philippines, the Continuing Past*. Quezon City: Foundation for Nationalist Studies.

Croghan, Richard. 1975. "The Modern Period: 1960 to 1974." In *The Development of Philippine Literature in English (since 1900)*, 249–53. Quezon City: Alemar-Phoenix Publishing House.

Cruz, Andres Cristobal. 1965. "Philippine Writing in English: A Need for Affirmation and Renewal." In *Equinox 1: An Anthology of New Writing from the Philippines*, edited by F. Sionil José, 1–7. Manila: Solidaridad.

Dalisay, Jose Y., Jr., 1984. *Oldtimer and Other Stories*. Manila: Asphodel.

———. 1992. *Sarcophagus and Other Stories*. Quezon City: University of the Philippines Press.

———. 1995. *Penmanship and Other Stories*. Metro Manila: Cacho Publishing House.

———. 2002. "The Filipino Short Story in English: An Update for the '90s." In *Likhaan Anthology of Philippine Literature in English,* edited by Gémino H. Abad, 139–46. Quezon City: University of the Philippines Press.

Daroy, Petronilo Bn. 1969. "Aspects of Philippine Writing in English." In *The "Urian Lectures" on Philippine Literature, Philippines Studies Quarterly* 17.2 (April) 249–65. Quezon City: Ateneo de Manila University Press.

Galdon, Joseph, ed. 1972. "Introduction." In *Philippine Fiction, Essays from Philippine Studies, 1953–1972,* xi–xvii. Quezon City: Ateneo de Manila University Press.

Gonzalez, N. V. M. 1953 "Imaginative Writing in the Philippines." In *Philippine Writing: An Anthology*, edited by T. D. Agcaoili et al., 321–28. Manila. Archipelago.

———. 1967. "The Difficulties with Filipiana." In *Brown Heritage*, edited by Antonio G. Manuud, 539–45. Quezon City: Ateneo de Manila, University Press.

———. 1977. "Lupo and the River." In *Children of the Ash-Covered Loam and Other Stories*, 23–75. Metro Manila: Bookmark.

———. 1995. "Kalutang: A Filipino in the World." In *Work on the Mountain*, 35–94. Quezon City: University of the Philippines Press.

Hidalgo, Cristina Pantoja. 2004. "The Philippine Short Story in English: An Overview" *World Englishes* 23.1: 155–168.

Joaquin, Nick. 1961. *The Woman Who Had Two Navels: A Filipino Novel*. Manila: Regal.

———. 1962. "May Day Eve." In *Nick Joaquin's Selected Stories,* 24–36. Manila: A. S. Florentino.

José, F. Sionil. 1962. *The Pretenders*. Manila: La Solidaridad.

José, F. Sionil. ed. 1965. *Equinox 1: An Anthology of New Writing from the Philippines.* Manila: La Solidaridad.

Karnow, Stanley. 1989. *In Our Image: America's Empire in the Philippines.* New York: Random House.

Lopez, Salvador. P. [1940] 1998. "Literature and Society." In *The Likhaan Anthology of Philippine Literature in English, from 1900 to the Present*, edited by Gémino H. Abad, 400–407. Quezon City: University of the Philippines Press.

Lumbera, Bienvenido. 1967. "Philippine Literature and the Filipino Personality." In *Brown Heritage: Essays on Philippine Cultural Tradition and Literature,* edited by Antonio G. Manuud, 1–15. Quezon City: Ateneo de Manila University Press.

Lumbera, Bienvenido and Cynthia N. Lumbera, eds. 1982. *Philippine Literature: A History and Anthology.* Manila: National Book Store, Inc.

Mojares, Resil B. 1983. *Origins and Rise of the Filipino Novel: A Generic Study of the Novel until 1940.* Quezon City. University of the Philippines Press.

Ong, Charlson. 1992. *Woman of Am-Kaw and Other Stories.* Pasig: Anvil Publishing.

———. 1996. *Conversion and Other Fictions.* Pasig: Anvil Publishing.

———. 1999. *Men of the East and Other Stories.* Diliman, Quezon City: University of the Philippines Press.

Polotan, Kerima. 1962. *The Hand of the Enemy.* Manila: Regal.

———. 1968a. *Stories.* Manila: Bookmark.

———. 1968b. "The Virgin." In *Stories,* 22–32. Manila: Bookmark.

Reyes, Soledad. 1987. "Philippine Literary Studies, 1970–85: Some Preliminary Notes." *Philippine Studies* 35.1: 71–92.

Rotor, Arturo B. 1937. *The Wound and the Scar: Selected Stories.* Manila: Philippine Book Guild

Santillan-Castrence, Pura. 1967. "The Period of Apprenticeship." In *Brown Heritage,* edited by Antonio G. Manuud. Quezon City: Ateneo de Manila University Press, 546–74.

Santos, Bienvenido N. 1965a. *Villa Magdalena: A Novel.* Quezon City: New Day.

———. 1965b. *The Volcano.* Quezon City: Phoenix.

Teodoro, Luis V. 1968–69. "Literature and Social Reality." In *Philippine Collegian*. First Semester.

Tiempo, Edith. 1953. "The Short Stories." In *Philippine Writing: An Anthology*, edited by T. D. Agcaoili, xi–xx. Manila: Archipelago.

Torres, Emmanuel. 1995. "Introduction: Pinoy Writing at the Turn of the Asia-Pacific Century." *Philippine Studies: New Writing from the Philippines*, 43:285–94.

Ty-Casper, Linda. 1964. *The Peninsulars: A Novel*. Manila: Bookmark.

Villanueva, Marianne. 2005. *Mayor of the Roses: Stories*. Oxford, OH: Miami University Press.

Viray, Manuel. 1953. "Certain Influences in Filipino Writing." In *Philippine Writing: An Anthology*, edited by T. D. Agcaoili, vii–ix. Manila: Archipelago.

Yabes, Leopoldo Y. 1975a. "Prefatory Note." In *Philippine Short Stories, 1925-1940*, edited by Leopoldo Y. Yabes, vii-x. Quezon City: University of the Philippines Press.

———. 1975b. "Postscript: Thirty-five Years Later." In *Philippine Short Stories, 1925-1940*, edited by Leopoldo Y. Yabes, xviv–xlvi. Quezon City: University of the Philippines Press.

———. 1981. "Preface." In *Philippine Short Stories, 1941–1955: Part I (1941–1949)*, edited by Leopoldo Y. Yabes, vii-x. Quezon City: University of the Philippines Press.

Yamada, Teri Shaffer, ed. 2002. *Virtual Lotus: Modern Fiction of Southeast Asia*. Ann Arbor: University of Michigan Press.

Yuson, Alfred. 1991. *The Music Child and Other Stories*. Manila: Anvil.

———. 2002. *Eight Stories*. Diliman, Quezon City: University of the Philippines Press.

The Contemporary Short Story in Filipino
Rosario Torres-Yu

Prior to colonization, Filipinos had a strong oral literary tradition consisting of epics, songs, short poems, folklore, mimetic dances, and rituals. Oral literature was produced in communal societies found in most parts of the territory and in sultanate societies in the south. In particular, prose narratives, consisting of origin myths, legends, hero tales, and fables, were told from generation to generation to explain natural phenomena, past events, and existing beliefs with no reference to author(s) because the concept of an individual author, as introduced in colonial times, did not yet exist. These narratives, which exemplified the indigenous sense of humor and wit, were shared communally.

The literary historian and critic Bienvenido Lumbera reads against the colonial perspective imposed on the literary traditions of the early Filipinos. He finds that it is the Asian way of seeing that animates these native traditions and allows us to recognize their value. The early Filipinos used these traditions to filter the Western culture that colonizers brought from Europe (Lumbera and Lumbera 1997, 5). The colonial experience of more than three hundred years under Spain and forty-five years under the Americans, however, eroded this Asian perspective in a long process of accommodation and resistance. What emerged from this experience was and still is the national goal of defining Filipino culture and authentic identity. Writers have been in the forefront of this quest for self-definition.

In this essay I will discuss the significant historical, political, and literary conditions that influenced the development of the contemporary short story in Filipino. What I hope to foreground is the resolute effort of Filipino writers to master and transmute the short story as a genre used to narrate a people's struggle against colonialism. In recent times, the short story writers in Filipino and the regional languages have responded to changing conditions and new ways of seeing. They have continued to produce stories informed by the various factors affecting a Filipino's sense of self and nation.

Conditions That Nurtured Traditions

The printing and publishing enterprises that used to be under church control and censorship were liberated from this restraint with the demise of Spanish colonial rule in 1898. Individual publishers ventured into commercial publishing of newspapers and magazines that carried short stories, serialized novels, and poems. Some of these publications that later became institutions of popular literature in the vernacular were *Liwayway* (1922),[1] *Bisaya* (1930), *Hiligaynon* (1934), *Bannawag* (1934), and *Kalendariong Bikol* (1929).[2] As these publications gained popularity with readers of vernacular literature, writers emerged to provide them with stories.

There has been a renewed interest in vernacular expression as part of a national literature. Recent studies on writing in Philippine languages are now useful in understanding the larger picture of fiction as it developed in a country previously dominated by studies on English and Tagalog fiction. In order to appreciate how important this is, I need to emphasize that the Philippines, an archipelago of 7,107 islands, is multilingual and multicultural. There are over seventy languages and dialects, all closely related to the Austronesian (Malayo-Polynesian) family of languages. They include eight major linguistic groups: Tagalog, Cebuano, Ilocano, Hiligaynon, Bicol, Waray-Waray, Pampango, and Pangasinan. Filipino, based on Tagalog, is now the national language of the Philippines and the most widely spoken linguistic group (*Encyclopedia Britannica* 2007).

Under colonial rule, the natives were not aware of the concept of "nation" or "Pilipino nationality." National awareness was the product of a long struggle for independence. As in Indonesia, the issue of developing a national language became inexorably linked to this struggle. It was during American rule that the twin issues of independence and national language began to create a deep cultural divide. The use of English in government, commerce, and education bestowed privilege on those who spoke it and a position of power among the natives.[3] The rest, who barely learned English in the public school system or never went to school at all, and those living far from the cities and urban centers or in upland tribal communities, used their own languages and preserved their indigenous ways of life.

A passionate controversy among writers has existed over the literary use of English as opposed to Tagalog, also referred to as Filipino. In 1939, the first president of the Philippine Commonwealth, Manuel Luis Quezon, declared Filipino the national language; subsequently it was mandated as the lingua franca in the 1987 Philippine Constitution. As the controversy unfolded, literature written in English and Tagalog—representing the protagonists in the language conflict—became more prominent. The effect of this development on the short story will be discussed in the succeeding sections.

The Tradition of Popular Fiction

The earliest short stories in the vernacular appeared in Tagalog in the form of the *dagli* (vignette), *asoy* (story) of Hiligaynon, and *kuwentong bayan* (folklore) of Bikol.[4] These were published in commercial magazines such as *Liwayway,*[5] *Hiligaynon,* and *Kalendariong Bikol* in the first decade of the 1900s.[6]

In Tagalog, the *dagli* was written in the tradition of the nationalist propaganda literature of the Spanish period. It tackled the themes of anti-Americanism, the colonial mentality among Filipinos, the condition of workers, agrarian problems and usury. The pioneering writers of this early form of fiction were Antonio Abad, Iñigo Ed. Regalado, Juan Arciwals, and Antero Gempesaw.[7]

In Hiligaynon, the short story began with precolonial folklore. These early short stories formed part of the tradition of religious and moralistic literature of the Spanish period. These were reshaped in the mold of O. Henry's or Edgar Allan Poe's short stories, which were introduced through high school textbooks on American literature (Deriada 2000).

The first short stories in Bikol, just like those in Hiligaynon, were derived from folklore. Two of the three short stories published in *Sanghiram* (1927) were about Juan Osong, a popular character in trickster tales; another was about a man who lost his wits trying to learn how to cook a crab for his fiancée. According to Realubit (2001), the short story as a genre began in 1929 with the publication of Nicolasa Ponte de Perfecto's short stories. Four of her stories, which appeared in *Kalendariong Bikol,* had already veered away from the folktale form by employing good characterization, direct narration, and devices such as the elements of surprise and suspense (2001, 51). After these beginnings, the short stories that dominated commercial publications had either popular themes, including love, romance, and domestic relationships, or moralistic stories, which almost always projected the idea that good is rewarded while evil is punished.

According to Melendrez-Cruz, the abandonment of the nationalist themes in Tagalog short stories, after the first decade of the 1900s, was the result of the colonial education fostered in the public school system (Samson et al. 1994, 174–79). Writers were immersed in American culture and tried to master English and the form of the Western short story. In schools and universities, it was forbidden to speak the native language; to enforce this, those who broke the injunction were fined. When Liwayway Arceo, an established fiction writer in Tagalog, was interviewed in 1998, she recalled that it was this experience that nurtured her desire to become a writer in her native language.[8]

These developments also signaled another kind of categorization of writers: the binary of English or the vernacular. This oppositional process—popular versus serious literature, English versus vernacular—created traditions that were opposed to each other in form and content along with tension between the old and the new.

Popular versus Academe

The older writers took full control of the popular outlets for literary works and were opposed to any kind of deviation from the conventions of commercial publishing. Most of them had been working in the publishing industry so they had learned to write through the example of commercial publications. Some had also been exposed to Anglo-American literature in the school system.

Sentimentalism was fashionable among the Tagalog-language short story writers until the eve of World War II. It was inherited from Anglo-American romanticism but not the kind of romanticism that emphasized individualism through a rebel protagonist. As a consequence, the moralistic, Christian worldview of predestination dominated the stories. Readers were also entertained by romance, especially love stories about successful liaisons between the rich and the poor. Many of these stories are included in Abadilla and del Mundo's *Mga Kuwentong Ginto, 1925–1935* (Best Stories, 1925–1935 [1936]) and Pedrito Reyes's *50 Kuwentong Ginto ng 50 Batikang Kuwentista* (Fifty Best Stories of the Fifty Best Fiction Writers [1998]).

From the 1930s to the 1950s, the popular Bicol short stories that appeared in *Bicolana* and *Bicolandia* explored the theme of love. Only a few of these stories were good in terms of characterization and plot. The characters were either paragons of virtue, simpletons, clowns, or negative representations of the ideal. Devices used to develop the plot were letters, barrio meetings, and rumors. Maria Lilia F. Realubit identifies Ana T. Calixto as the most popular fictionist during this period (1999).[9]

By the second decade of American rule, Filipinos had learned English and were writing in that language. Writers came from the ranks of teachers and critics of literature in the universities, who used Western literary canons as models of good writing. According to Bienvenido L. Lumbera, the finest short story writers of their time were Arturo B. Rotor (1907–88) and Manuel E. Arguilla (1910–44). They covered a broad range of subject matter and themes drawn from the experiences of Filipinos in the 1930s. Comparing the two, Lumbera considers Rotor the "sensitive chronicler of the inner life of the Filipino in the city" whereas Arguilla was the "meticulous painter of the country scenes in his best loved stories where he captured the gentler aspects of Philippine rural life" (Lumbera and Lumbera 1997, 97).

Lucila Hosillos' own investigation of the experience of Filipino writers in English leads her to observe that writing in English went through the stages of emulation, stimulation, experimentation, and creativity (1984, 110). She asserts that the Filipino writers' response to colonial experience should not be lost on the present crop of writers.

> The Filipinization of the Western short story is a collective effort of Filipino writers, especially of those who took up the challenge to experiment with its forms during its formative stage. Thus although foreign influences were seminal and overpowering, the Filipino writer has still been able to transmute them into entities with his originality that he may call his artistic creations his own and that of his people. (120)

Writers in the regional languages were likewise influenced by Western literary standards. Tagalog writers, who were educated in English and aspired to write in the tradition of the Western short story, succeeded just like their counterparts in English. Deogracias Rosario (1894–1936) was one such writer. He was considered "The Father of Tagalog Fiction" in recognition of his skill and craft, much like the English writers. Writing in the realistic mode, his stories depicted the ongoing Americanization of Philippine society at that time. Supporting this trend was the organization of writers in Panitikan led by Alejandro G. Abadilla and Clodualdo del Mundo, Jr., who both used literary criticism in their aim to modernize the short story.

In the domain of the Cebuano short story, Marcel M. Navarra (1914–84), who was recognized as the "Father of Cebuano Literature," also wrote stories in the Western mode. His exposure to the ideas of the avant-garde Filipino writer Jose Garcia Villa and foreign writers (including O. Henry, Guy de Maupassant, Theodore Dreiser, and Ernest Hemingway) enabled him to be more critical of the works he chose for publication in *Bisaya,* which he edited. As a result, many of the stories published before the outbreak of the war were no longer as didactic and romantic as those published in the previous years (Maceda 1986).

To summarize these developments, two kinds of traditions had emerged on the literary landscape before the outbreak of World War II. One was the tradition of popular fiction, supported by a large number of vernacular-language authors who were influenced by popular conventions. The other was the modernist tradition, supported by authors influenced by Western literary traditions who published in campus literary journals and anthologies.

These two traditions of literary production continued even after the war with the introduction of New Criticism from the United States. The influence of this literary theory became more intense among writers and critics in the Philippines during the 1950s and greatly influenced the concept of "good" fiction. New Criticism, which emphasized aestheticism and avoided politics, coincided with the onset of the cold war and with it the spirit of anticommunism that pervaded the political climate. This antipolitical orientation informed the judges of important literary contests such as the competitions sponsored by the *Philippines Free Press* and the Don Carlos Palanca Memorial Awards for Literature, the country's most prestigious national literary contest, established in 1950. It should be emphasized, however, that initially the effect of modernism on the writing of the short story as a genre was progressive. The writers tried to "transmute," as Hosillos puts it, the Western short story form so that it could reveal the true condition of Filipinos under colonialism. Filipino writers indigenized the form during this process (Hosillos 1984, 92–120). Too much preoccupation with the craft and technique of writing in the 1950s, however, sanitized fiction and other genres of any political subject matter and themes. It moved writing farther away from the earlier mainstream tradition of nationalist commitment.

Social Commitment versus Art for Art's Sake

It is important to note that, beyond the language issue, ideological tension did exist between the two basic groups of writers. There were writers who wrote about social realities, especially in the 1930s. During this time, the country was experiencing revolutionary conditions that developed into peasant uprisings led by the Communist and Socialist parties of the Philippines under the leadership of Crisanto Evangelista and Pedro Abad Santos. In this context, Salvador Lopez (1911–93), a writer in English, would strongly criticize Filipino English-language writers, who he felt were too preoccupied with art for art's sake. He challenged them to abandon Villa's aestheticism and confront what was happening in society. Some writers formed the Philippine Writer's League to give organizational expression to Lopez's call. Among the first to respond was Arguilla, who veered away from his idyllic stories of life in the countryside and wrote about radical workers and peasants in stories such as "Caps and Lower Case" and " Epilogue to Revolt." The same change of perspective happened to the Tagalog fictionist Brigido Batungbakal, who turned his back on a form of avant-gardism exemplified in his "Ngayong Gabi" (Tonight) and wrote about the class struggle, labor, and capital in "Aklasan" (Strike) (Lumbera and Lumbera 1997, 102).

There was another kind of rebellion staged by Tagalog writers of fiction, which derived its impulse from Western literary influence. In the first half of the 1960s, young writers from the university would muster the courage to challenge the dominance of the older generation of writers who continued to control the popular publications. The fiction of these new writers was published in the conservative magazine *Liwayway* when the literary editor, Liwayway Arceo, introduced a section for younger writers. But the young ones were not satisfied with this gesture. Bemoaning the lack of realism in popular fiction, they wrote stories to influence the development of Tagalog fiction. *Mga Agos sa Disyerto* (Streams in the Desert) is considered to be a collection of the best fiction by these young writers (Abueg 2000, 3). These stories presented liberal individualism in direct opposition to the prevalent Christian worldview. Armed with naturalism as their literary mode, these writers explored a broad range of subjects: social conflict, poverty and violence in the city, triumph over hardship, domestic relations, filial love, and education as a means to the development of the individual. Their stories reveal the antagonistic character of social relations in Filipino society. Rogelio Sikat's story "Tata Selo" (Old Selo) tackles the social injustice of the landlord-tenant conflict, which dates to the time of Spanish colonial rule (Abueg et al. 1993, 212–18 [1964]).[10] This theme is represented through the personal tragedy of Tata Selo, whose landlord divests him not only of his farm but, even worse, of his honor.

The landlord, after sending Tata Selo several notices demanding that he leave his land, starts to beat him and is killed by Tata Selo in self-defense. From the point of view of the landlord, Tata Selo had lost his right to cultivate the land the moment he lacked the strength to work. It is the landlord, not the tenant, who has the power over the land, as well as the power over the very person of the tenant, including all the members of his household. Thus, Tata Selo's daughter suffers, too, when she is raped while trying to see her father in the stockade. The story is much praised for its use of subtlety and control as the following scene exemplifies.

> It is around four in the afternoon. It is still hot although the sun's rays are about to disappear. There is a little shade near the wall in the stockade, but Tata Selo is not there. He is in the sunlight, holding the steel bars in front of the stockade, looking out. The red rays of the sun reflect in his eyes making it difficult to see. . . . Now, he is no longer muttering about the land.
>
> "Everything is lost, everything, ay! Everything is taken away from us," he mutters, clutching the bars. (Abueg et al. 1993, 218 [1964], translation by Rosario Torres-Yu)

Although it was short-lived, there were young, university-bred Cebuano writers, such as Godofredo Roperos and Tiburcio Bagiuo, who attempted a similar literary rebellion. Modern stories that were introspective and thematic began to appear in *Bisaya*. As a consequence, however, the circulation of the magazine suffered. When the management noticed the decline in readership, it stopped publishing this kind of story.

The Question of Alignment and Commitment

From the mid-1960s until the imposition of martial law in 1972, there was a resurgence of nationalism and youth activism. The national democratic movement, led by the reestablished Communist Party of the Philippines (CPP-NPA), used the universities to launch the so-called Second Propaganda Movement.[11] This cultural movement was directed against the imperialist and feudal domination of the elite whose power held sway over the lives of the greater mass of poor and powerless people. It was a period of heightened awareness of class conflict. Student activists rallied and protested against many issues: the Vietnam War; the oil price hike; U.S. neocolonial control of the economy, politics, and culture; the colonial system of education; and almost anything else that represented power.

In this political climate, writers and intellectuals were confronted with the difficult questions of alignment and commitment. For whom does one write? This was the question problematized by a radical organization of writers, the Pambansang Samahan ng Manunulat para sa Sambayanan (National Organization of Writers for the People, or PAKSA). The domain of literature was also influenced by the militant nationalist movement, demanding radical changes in almost all aspects of life, including education and the university's role in social emancipation. In fact, literary criticism, particularly New Criticism, came under severe attack from the proponents of Marxist criticism. The debate on form and content was resolved in favor of writing for the great mass of people who needed to be awakened and mobilized for social change. Thus, the issue of language for writers was likewise resolved in favor of Filipino, known then as Tagalog.

The publication of the anthology *Sigwa* (Storm, 1972) manifested a radical shift in the development of the Filipino short story. Using the metaphor of a storm to signify the impending revolutionary change—sweeping, violent, irrepressible, and critical of the status quo—the stories pushed the radicalism of the 1960s social realists one notch higher. Instead of a defeatist view, the stories portrayed characters who were no longer fighting alone and being overcome by powerful social forces. Characters were imbued with a correct understanding of individual problems rooted in class conflict; they recognized the need to unite with the other oppressed classes in a movement for change. These stories hoped to accomplish the task that PAKSA had laid out for committed writers: to educate the public on the need for revolutionary action.

In Ricardo Lee's short story "Si Tatang, si Freddie, si Tandang Senyong at iba Pang Tauhan ng Aking Kuwento" (Tatang, Freddie, Old Senyong, and Other Characters of My Story), personal and historical events frame the story of a writer's political awakening and his transformation into a socially committed individual. In this story, the turning point in the life of the self-absorbed character who is a writer occurs when he witnesses the massacre of the Lapiang Malaya.[12] He becomes interested in Tatang de los Santos as the subject for a story. He starts visiting this old man in a mental hospital. As the writer-protagonist becomes more intimate with him, the reasons why people like Tatang are driven to organize themselves in pursuit of messianic goals become clear. The peasant's long history of social injustice is clearly shown to be deeply rooted in a class-based social structure in which the big landlords exploit the peasants who till the land. In the end, the writer realizes that he has his own struggle to wage as an employee of the publishing house where he writes, and so he joins the union of journalists.

Fanny Garcia's story "Alamat ng Sapang Bato" (The Legend of Sapang Bato, 1978) has a middle-class character, Minda, who works as a secretary in a home for elders. Minda, having long nurtured the desire to become a writer, meets Lola Victoria, who, unlike the rest, is unhappy to be a resident. Lola Victoria incessantly talks of Sapang Bato, where she comes from. Again, as in Lee's story, the writer-character's subject, here Lola Victoria, enlightens her to larger social realities. In the end, she will not only sympathize with Lola Victoria but will write about Sapang Bato. She begins her story with a sentence that Lola Victoria often mutters: "Ineng, nandoon ang pag-asa" (Girl, hope lies there) while pointing to the mountains. Given the revolutionary context, the mountains clearly allude to that subversive option for the oppressed.

One writer of Bikol popular literature, Rogelio Basilio, stands out for his subject matter, which ranges from land-grabbing and local politics to the plight of *provincianos* in the cities. In one of his stories, "Kaipohan an Pagbabago sa Politika" (Change Is Necessary in Politics), a socially critical theme is developed through Sabas, an ordinary peasant who runs for mayor and defeats the traditional politicians who come from the rich families in town. With the support of the townspeople, electoral politics is no longer dominated by the rich and powerful. Change is possible, something that was generally considered impossible in earlier times (Realubit 2001).

Hiligaynon writers also responded to the call for relevance. Hosillos refers to the late 1960s, when a group of socially conscious writers embarked on a self-help project, resulting in a collection of short stories, *Bahandi* (Gem), published in 1970. Although originally intending to focus only on stories with social relevance, the editor Juanito Harcella finally had to include other kinds of stories to complete the collection. The forty-six writers whose stories were reprinted from *Hiligaynon* contributed to the printing cost. Social realism was also expressed in some novels, such as Lino V. Moles's *Kalayo sa Sidlangan* (Fire in the East), serialized in *Hiligaynon* in 1971, and some novellas (Hosillos 1992, 279).

From the imposition of martial law on 21 September 1972, until Ferdinand Marcos was deposed in February 1986, the country's political and social conditions heightened the need for people—writers included—to confront the question of alignment and commitment in a highly polarized society. Publications were controlled through censorship. Freedom of the press, together with other basic human rights, was suspended. A curfew was imposed. Both urban and rural areas became sites of ideological and armed conflict between those who supported a dictatorial regime and those who opposed it. The state declared that writing against the official slogan, "revolution from the center," was a crime against national security. Nevertheless, repression, censorship, military abuse, violations of human rights, and worsened economic conditions further fueled the underground revolutionary movement. By the close of the 1970s, the martial law regime and its allies had become isolated from the people and the middle class had aligned itself with the rapidly growing antidictatorship movement.

The growth and spread of the revolutionary movement breathed new life into regional languages. Using traditional literary forms that were indigenous to their area, writers in the movement wrote in native languages and infused their work with revolutionary content. Writers associated with various social sectors—the universities, the parishes, the labor unions, and to a limited extent the mass media—supported the antidictatorship movement in their own way.

The Growth of People's Literature

From the 1970s onward, the revolutionary conditions of Philippine society nurtured the rich soil on which a people's literature thrived. People's literature, including both official and underground publications, portrayed the Marcos dictatorship as a common enemy. This literature for the masses could be socially relevant, nationalist, or revolutionary. One literary pattern that emerged as it developed included (1) a critical analysis of the basic problems of society and the social forces creating them; (2) an exposition of false consciousness in order to reveal the truth; and (3) a statement, direct or indirect, on the need to oppose oppression by joining the national democratic movement.

Within the realm of revolutionary literature, a new development occurred regarding authorship. Traditionally, writers came from the ranks of the upper- and middle-class intellectuals who possessed the inclination to pursue a career in writing. This time, writers emerged from the ranks of workers, peasants, and communist fighters (Guillermo 1996, 367–70).

In Guillermo's analysis of the stories produced in the underground press, he observes that popular characters come from the working class, the peasants, or the petite bourgeoisie. The plot typically follows a similar pattern: the character experiences social inequity but in the process of overcoming this experience gains a broad understanding of society and how change can be effected by joining the mass movement. In the end, the protagonist resolves to work full time for the revolutionary movement. The first short story published in the underground press during martial law, "Kasama" (Comrade), is a story of a street hooligan who becomes a squad leader of the New People's Army (NPA). As the story evolves, the plot reveals different aspects of revolutionary work in the countryside and the different traits of a revolutionary: patience, trust, love for the masses in the face of death, and commitment to the revolution. Guillermo likewise notes the choice of children as main characters (1996, 369). In stories such as "Ang Batang NPA" (The Young NPA) and "Ka Dadong" (Comrade Dadong), the main characters are ordinary children who live in the guerrilla zones and perform tasks appropriate to their age. In another story, "Dalawang Bata at ang Baril" (Two Children and a Gun), two children outwit some soldiers and take a gun without being noticed. Guillermo observes that such stories about and for children assure the revolution of experienced and tempered fighters in the years ahead since children have listened to such stories since infancy (370). Some of the stories produced by the underground press became available to the public in *Kamao* (Fist), an anthology published by the cultural division of the government (Salanga 1987).

Another significant development of this period concerns language. In the 1960s, young writers had already attempted to bring the language of fiction closer to daily speech, the language of the street. Following this initiative, Jun Cruz Reyes in 1981 extended the limits by using colloquial Filipino in his *Utos ng Hari at Iba Pang Kuwento* (The King's Command and Other Stories). The story "Utos ng Hari" (74–85) revolves around the protagonist, Jojo, a high school student who does not seem to fit in a special school for science, ironically because he has an independent mind.[13] Skepticism has no place in this school; thus, Jojo suffers the intolerance and prejudice of his teachers, who are content with traditional and sometimes stale knowledge. Although he chooses to be quiet in class, he carries on an interior monologue while humoring authority.

> Ay, sense of propriety, at de-quo-rum, talagang nakatataranta. Clean cut (pagsuklayin mo si Einstein). White polo shirt at black pants (pagdisentihin mo si Kristo). Naiisip ko tuloy kung propriety din 'yung tawag sa mga teacher kung nakadamit civilian sila kapag Miyerkules. 'Yun bang parang a-attend sila ng party. 'Yun bang ang tipo ng tela ay mapapansin agad at mapapagsabihang "Ay, ang ganda, saan mo nabili? Siguro ang mahal ano?. . . At para talaga mapansin, kailangang humahalimuyak din sila sa bango. . . sa kanilang "ganda" at "ningning," para kang nakakita ng X'mas tree sa isang mahal na araw. 'Yun ang proper sa kanila. (Reyes 1981, 83)

> Oh, sense of propriety, of de-quo-rum, it's really confusing. Clean cut (let Einstein comb his hair). White polo shirt and black pants (make Christ look decent). I am thinking, is it propriety that teachers wear civilian clothes on Wednesdays as if they are going to a party. The type of clothing material, which calls attention and elicits remarks such as, "Oh, how pretty, where did you buy that? That must be pretty expensive. . ." And to be really noticed, it is necessary to radiate with fragrance. . . . In their "beauty" and "charm," it seems like you are looking at a Xmas tree during the season of Lent. That, to them, is proper. (Reyes, 1981, 83, translation by Rosario Torres-Yu)

The use of regional languages by the underground revolutionary movement contributed to the awareness of the importance of regional literature. Literature in regional languages was produced in order to reach the masses in the region or province where NPA bases had been established. Guillermo mentions the poem "Ortelano: Ing Bayaning Era Balu" (The Peasant, Unknown Hero), written in Kapampangan by a peasant activist. It became one of the most popular poems among peasant audiences, especially after it was translated into Filipino (1996, 361).

Liberal Democracy and Literary Bloom

The overthrow of the Marcos dictatorship in February 1986 gave the Pilipinos a feeling of empowerment experienced through the "People Power Revolution." Corazon Aquino, the widow of slain opposition leader Senator Benigno Aquino, was catapulted to the presidency. Her leadership did not provide immediate stability because of as series of attempted coups d'état. The economy that Marcos left behind was in bad shape. Natural calamities, such as the eruption of Mount Pinatubo and the earthquake in 1991, worsened the country's fiscal situation. Nevertheless, the people remained patient and optimistic. They welcomed the lifting of the curfew and the restoration of basic freedoms, including a free press, although many of the laws decreed during martial law remained in force. For the radical Left, the release from prison of political detainees, led by Jose Ma. Sison and Bernabe Buscayno, temporarily projected a climate of peace for the country. It was temporary because the mass movement led by the political Left soon came to perceive the Aquino government as the restoration of the pre-martial-law dominance of the elite along with their inability to institute fundamental changes in property relations and governance. In the countryside, the people's war continued with government troops facing two enemies: the revolutionary movement led by the CPP-NPA and the secessionist Moro National Liberation Front.

It was in this context that writers would resume writing. Perhaps on account of the new climate of freedom, many new names, especially those of young women and gay writers, emerged in the 1990s. This development continues to the present.

Other factors sparked new interests and trends that affected writing in general and the writing of the short story in particular.

1. The spread of the feminist movement
2. The establishment of creative writing centers in the cities and universities
3. The spread of writers' organizations
4. The reorientation of the government's cultural agency, the Cultural Center of the Philippines (CCP)
5. The establishment of another agency, the National Commission on Culture and the Arts (NCCA)
6. The formation of nongovernmental organizations (NGOs) working with special interests
7. The proliferation of publication venues (campus organizations, commercial presses, university presses, and organizations of writers)
8. The establishment of more literary competitions and awards
9. Renewed importance given to regional literature
10. The influence of theories and perspectives on literary studies from the West, including postcolonial, postmodernist, and reader-response theories

From a different perspective, many of these factors may appear to foster cultural apparatuses that work in concert to elicit a consensus in civil society. To be sure, there will be interventions and subversions by the social movement and the writers themselves. The dynamic these dialectical processes produce can help us to understand some of the changes discussed in the following section.

Gender Awareness

Women were one of the sectors of society that became organized in the anti-dictatorship struggle immediately after the 1983 assassination of Benigno Aquino. Women from all classes and varied concerns became involved in political actions. Various groups would later become federated with GABRIELA, a national umbrella organization of women's groups with a nationalist, democratic, and feminist orientation. This movement of women brought some reforms, notably in the adoption of a new Family Code, the formation of the National Commission on the Role of Women, the formation of a number of Women's Studies Centers in leading universities in Metropolitan Manila, and the offering of academic programs in women's studies. All of these had an impact on writers, especially women.

During this period, a number of canonized short story writers and feminist critics recognized and gave their works new perspectives. These writers include Liwayway Arceo (1920–99), a multitalented writer, who was awarded the Carlos Palanca Literary Prize for Short Story in Filipino in 1962. Her "Lumapit, Lumayo ang Umaga" was produced as an award-winning film in 1975. Genoveva Edroza-Matute received recognition by the Cultural Center of the Philippines in 1992 for promoting the quality of the Tagalog short story. She translated a collection of her short stories and essays into English (1998). Lualhati Bautista, also a prominent screenwriter

Virginitarian and Other Stories, by Mayette Bayuga. Courtesy of the University of the Philippines Press.

and novelist, received first prize in the Carlos Palanca Memorial Awards for Literature in 1982 for her short story "Tatlong Kuwento ng Buhay ni Juan Candelabra" (Three Stories in the Life of Juan Candelabra). Other remarkable women writers include Fanny Garcia, and Lilia Quindoza Santiago. Joining this group is a younger generation of women writers, including the poet and fictionist Joi Barrios, Mayette Bayuga, and artist-writer Chit Balmaceda Gutierrez.

Feminist critics and teachers of literature in the universities have published anthologies of women writers.[14] Graduate students in the universities, particularly at the University of the Philippines, Ateneo de Manila University, and De La Salle University, are engaged in feminist literary criticism and gender studies.

The New Orientation and Direction of Literary Apparatuses

Universities, organizations of writers, and certain cultural agencies of the government have assumed an active role as centers of literary production. The University of the Philippines Creative Writing Center (UP-CWC) and Silliman University regularly conduct national workshops for writers. In recent years, the University of Santo Tomas, a sectarian university, also established a Creative Writing Center. The UP-CWC, established in 1978 and renamed the Institute of Creative Writing in 2002, regularly publishes anthologies of works considered by editors to be the best of the year. These anthologies, published since 1995, have introduced the best writers to the general public.[15] The Institute of Creative Writing also sponsors a monthly online journal, *Likhaan Online*, with archives dating back to 1999, which publishes short stories by emerging writers.

Writers groups such as Unyon ng mga Manunulat sa Pilipinas (Writers' Union of the Philippines), Pambansang Unyon ng Manunulat (National Union of Writers), and KATHA (Fiction) have also attracted more writers. Of these groups, KATHA has paid particular attention to the short story and tried to popularize it through a radio program apart from its publications. In response to the observation that short story writing in the country had reached a dead end, young writers joined together to revive writing in this genre. The result was the publication of five anthologies since 1989, the year the organization was formed. The following collections included contributions from KATHA's members: *Engkuwentro* [Encounter, 1990], *Habilin* (Entrust, 1992) *Impetu* (Impetus, 1991), *Alagwa* (de Guzman and V. C. Nadera, eds. [Falling Kite, 1997]), and *Relasyon* (Liaison 1999 [Tolentino and Sicat 2000]).

These anthologies are organized according to themes. *Relasyon*, a collection of twenty-nine stories, treats the subject of personal relations in connection with the issues of reproduction and sexuality. There are both happy and unhappy stories about marriage. Many of the stories invite readers to take a serious look at interpersonal relations. Others are disturbing, making one think twice before considering a relationship. There are also stories that effectively interrogate long-held views on gender roles and sexual orientation.

A number of these stories feature narrative experimentation. Joi Barrios goes back to the early form of the Tagalog short story, *dagli,* in her "Ang Babae sa Tabindagat (Isang Kuwentong Di Naging Nobelang Romantiko)" (A Story That Did Not Evolve into a Romantic Novel) (Tolentino and Sicat 1999, 279–80). Eli Guieb, in "Horoscope," appropriates the format of a horoscope to structure several vignettes. The vignettes run parallel, akin to the horoscope's format, revealing an array of events occurring simultaneously (203–16). In "Palabas" (Show), Rolando B. Tolentino presents the melodramatic unfolding of a breakup through dialogue heard while a television set blares on and on (59–66). Vim Nadera, in "Beinte-beinteng Bisyon sa Loob ng Toyotang Wala sa Japan" (20/20 Vision Inside a Toyota Not in Japan) uses the format of an open letter or memorandum (101–104). Rommel Rodriguez's "Long Distance" renders the story in the form of a phone conversation (77–84). In all these experimentations, we see the writers deconstructing the conventional plot to explore new ways of unfolding the action (Torres-Yu 1999a, ix).

The reorientation of the Cultural Center of the Philippines after the 1986 EDSA Revolution favored the production of national literature and art in general. During martial law, the center was used by the dictatorship to showcase foreign culture at the expense of national culture. Under the leadership of Artistic Director Nicanor Tiongson, a professor at the University of the Philippines, the center embarked on the development of a national culture that included public participation. A Coordinating Center for Literature set up within the CCP existed until 1995, dispensing writing grants to qualified writers in Filipino, Iloko, Cebuano, Hiligaynon, Bikol, Kinaray-a, Aklanon, Tagalog, and English. According to Beltran, a total of seventy-seven individual writers and eighteen groups of writers and institutions received grants (1999). The CCP also published the works produced through the grants in twenty-nine issues of *Ani* (Harvest). These issues include special collections of works in regional languages. Unfortunately, according to Herminio Beltran, this healthy support given to writers and performers stopped in 1995 when the center experienced financial problems.

Voices from the Outside

Literary studies in the universities—dominated in the 1960s by the formalists of New Criticism and in the 1970s by the Marxist critics—were challenged by the entry of relatively new theories and perspectives from the West. Poststructuralism, reader-response theory, postcolonial theory, neo-Marxism, and postmodernism contributed to the new discourse on literature and literary production. This development, in particular, provided the basis for rethinking old and prevailing attitudes toward formerly discredited kinds of writing—literatures from the regions, writings by women, gays, youth, workers, and peasants, and popular literatures—which for a long time had been considered insignificant if not escapist and trashy.

Regional literature in particular assumed greater importance in connection with the national agenda of developing a national literature. To be sure, there were different and sometimes opposing views on how national literature should be developed, but there was at least an agreement on the need to develop one. As a result, many authors were encouraged to write in two or three languages. The Palanca Awards, the country's most prestigious awards in literature, threw in its support by introducing new categories in the short story in Hiligaynon, Iluko, and Cebuano. The Hiligaynon magazine *Quin Baterna* established a competition in the Hiligaynon short story that lasted until 1997. It was during this time, according to Leoncio Deriada, that Alicia Tan Gonzales, an important fiction writer in Hiligaynon, was discovered (2000). Another proof that regional writers had found their voice is a collection of works in fiction and poetry edited by Merlie Alunan, *Fern Garden: An Anthology of Women Writing in the South* (1998), published through the support of the NCCA Committee on Literature. On writing from the south, Alunan explains:

> For the southern writer, the concept of the north includes a colonizing national language that reduces the regional languages to secondary status. Away from the center, southern lifeways thrive on their own. These lifeways yield their own stories and breed their own unique modes of thinking and seeing. . . . The diversity of language also implies a diversity of attitudes and habits of thinking and feeling. Most, if not all of the women represented in this volume write in English. Those who write in their native tongue are aware of the politics of their choice, realizing it as an effort to restore or regain lost ground and to reassert them as medium for the works of the imagination. (3)

Deriada sees a problem in contemporary writing in the Hiligaynon short story genre, which is the polarization of two groups of writers: popular and academic. The second group, according to him, is composed of individuals who are conversant in world literature and are bilingual or multilingual. It also consists of English majors whose works are published in journals and national publications and who receive writing grants and awards. This group of writers is more daring in its themes. For instance, Alicia Tan Gonzales' story "Isa Ka Pungpong ng Rosas" (A Bunch of Roses), which won third place in the short story category of the Palanca Memorial Awards for Literature in 1997, is about a man-tired woman who happily contemplates having a lesbian relationship. Peter Nery's "Lirio", which won first prize in the same contest, is about a mute girl named Lirio who is gang-raped by policemen. While struggling against them, butterflies fly out of the little girl's mouth. There is also a story by Alex C. Santos, "Sastre" (Tailor), about a homosexual who runs away to avoid constant beating by his father. He returns only after his father's death, shocking the whole town by coming home in a woman's red dress (Deriada 2000).

Another related development is that many of the authors are writing in multiple languages. Rosario Lucero, for instance, wrote short stories in English before she wrote in Filipino. Encouraged by the Tagalog fiction writer Rogelio Sikat, Lucero sets her story "Demonyo" (Devil) in Negros, the southern province where she grew up (Chua 1999, 103–32). The story won an award in the 1990 Cultural Center of the Philippines literary contest.

Told from a child's perspective, "Demonyo" succeeds in depicting the delicate subject of rape and insurgency without being dominated by the usual partisan point of view. Two children, Nena and Jose, grow up together in a hacienda. The girl is the daughter of a fishpond owner while the boy is the son of one of the workers employed there. Unaware of their class differences, the two become childhood friends. In fact, Nena seems to have developed a special fondness for the boy. The military strafes the hut of Jose's family. He pretends to be dead while his mother and sister are raped. He does not escape torture and sexual violence but is not killed. In a surprising reversal of the protagonist-antagonist position, the boy turns against Nena while the two are in the wooded section near the fishpond looking for Jose's other sister, Mimay. Overcome by rage, he unleashes his wrath on Nena and rapes her. The girl, unable to understand what has possessed Jose, protects the boy nevertheless by not telling her family about the incident. The reader is disturbed at the end of the story by feelings about the children and the ramifications of the ongoing war. The story succeeds, too, in weaving together the politics of class conflict and sexual politics with great subtlety.

New Perspectives in Literary Studies

The developments of the 1980s have continued to influence writers during the1990s and up to the present. In addition, new perspectives and theories on literary studies from the West have reached writers, faculty, and students of literature in the academy via books and the Internet and through academics financed by scholarships for study abroad. Fairly recent developments in the short story reveal the effects of innovative ways of reading and writing informed by these new theories. Writers are vigorously tackling the many facets of identity formation and ideology by probing such categories as class, gender, ethnicity, and race. Related to this is the young writers' self-conscious drive to break with tradition, in both content and form, and to push boundaries between genres to create new forms of literary expression.

Many works being published and read in campus publications and anthologies are by some of these writers, Joi Barrios and Luna Sicat-Cleto, to name a few.[16] Among the stories about sexuality and gender, there is a continuing interrogation of patriarchy as well as a celebration of the affirmation of feminist assertion. Mayette Bayuga's story "Baliw" (Insane), which appears in the anthology *Ang Aklat Likhaan ng Tula at Maikling Kuwento, 1996,* edited by Joi Barrios and Jun Cruz Reyes (71–78), interweaves the experiences of Soreen and Be, two married women. Both have abusive and adulterous husbands. Both stay married until they can no longer bear the psychological pain and become insane. Soreen's subplot continues to unfold after Be's hospitalization. She has been working as a domestic laborer in Hong Kong to help her family. When she finally returns home for good, Soreen discovers that her husband has squandered all the money she sent him. She also learns that he has been having an affair with their best friend. No longer able to endure his violence and betrayal, she becomes violent herself and is taken to a mental hospital.

The Likhaan Book of Poetry and Short Fiction, edited by Domingo G. Landicho and Lilia Qunidoza Santiago. Courtesy of the University of Philippines Press.

Reading the story of these two women reminds one of Sisa, a character in José Rizal's canonical novel *Noli Me Tangere* (1887), who is an archetype of the suffering wife and mother and ultimately goes insane. Bayuga's story reminds readers that there are still many Sisas in their midst and urges them to keep on questioning much of the traditional thinking that social institutions perpetuate in order to control women. Religion is one institution that the story implicates. One clever detail is a scene in which Be is waiting for her husband while the television is on. While waiting, Be watches a late show in which the charismatic Christian group El Shaddai is holding a worship service. The preacher exhorts women to heed the biblical passage "Women, put yourselves under the dominion of your husbands." Irony, and even sarcasm, directed against religion is consequently achieved when the reader perceives the contrast between the two women's experiences and the biblical teaching. The theme assumes greater importance in the context of a predominantly Catholic country.

In another story, Glecy Atienza's "Noong Unang Panahon, sa May Di Kalayuan" (In the Early Days, in a Not So Faraway Place), two narratives run parallel to each other like two monologues in a play being recited simultaneously. The first narrative is that of a young son speaking of Wonder Woman as a metaphor for his mother. The second is that of the mother talking to her son, recalling the past and explaining why he grew up without a father. The story ends on a happy note dominated by the son's point of view. The son accepts the difference in the lifestyle he and his mother lead and sees the way he was raised as being almost magical, a feat only a Wonder Woman could achieve. Empowered, he looks to the future with much optimism.

> Wonder Woman has many more stories. What I always have in mind, though, is that I will pursue my plan to go into the outer space. Of course, she will be with me. I will become a scientist, and then we will ride a space ship.
>
> By the way, I will also become a father when I grow up. And I will give my children all the powers that Wonder Woman gave me. (Barrios and Reyes 1998, 58; translation by Rosario Torres-Yu).

Honorio Bartolome de Dios, Eugene Evasco, and Rommel Rodriguez have written some of the most engaged stories about homosexuality, repressed sexuality, and the many ways in which gays are oppressed in a patriarchal society. Jun Cruz Reyes, one of the editors of *Ang Aklat Likhaan ng Tula at Maikling Kuwento, 1999*, comments on two of the stories on gays included in the anthology.

"Atseng" by Honorio Bartolome de Dios is not for entertainment. His approach is psychological, almost clinical, not begging for help or understanding. He simply narrates an experience: his initiation to sex when he was a child and its effect on his personhood/character at present. Is there gay angst? This can be found in Rommel Rodriquez' "Bilog ang Tatsulok" (Round is a Triangle), with its philosophical narrative approach. He wants to explain something but it is difficult to understand. Meaning is found only on the fringes. Loneliness knows no gender; everyone is entitled to happiness, whatever it means. (Nadera and Reyes 2002, 41; translation by Rosario Torres-Yu)

Rolando B. Tolentino has been a pioneer in the area of experimental narrative forms and more consistent than others in his goal of reinventing the short story. Exposed to critical studies on literature current in America, where he studied for his doctoral degree, Tolentino, who chairs the young group of fictionists known as KATHA, has written a number of short stories using themes and elements of popular culture. In his story "Palabok" (A Native Dish, 1999), he uses the form of a recipe in a cookbook to narrate a wife's typical experience of her husband. She meticulously prepares her spouse's favorite *merienda* (snack) and is disappointed at the end of the day's work when he hardly appreciates her effort. The story uses this ordinary incident to demonstrate that even the most ordinary experience should be interrogated within the framework of a feminist critique of patriarchy. Tolentino is also a keen observer of the pockets of urban and cosmopolitan culture ironically found in a poor country like the Philippines. His story "Fastfood" (1996) takes up the subject of the proliferation of food chains in Metropolitan Manila and other urban centers. It portrays the day-to-day drama behind the counter and the rhythm and tempo of fast-food production. Its characters are rendered like cogs and screws in a fast-grinding machine.[17]

Revolutionary Movement Stories on the Workers and the Oppressed

If literature is like a *habi,* or woven cloth, the revolutionary movement weaves into this tapestry stories that are dyed red. From the 1970s to the 1990s, writers from the middle class who were sympathetic to the cause of workers and peasants wrote stories about their plight. In subsequent years, the workers and peasants joined these writers. As organic intellectuals trained in the revolutionary movement, they expressed their concrete experiences with greater realism and revolutionary zeal than had their middle-class precursors.

The revolutionary movement and the mass movement on the legal front discovered some of these new writers. The Amado V. Hernandez Resource Center, an NGO, holds literary competitions in poetry and fiction among the workers. It is through these competitions that some writers were discovered such as the couple Cesar and Olivia Cervantes. Olivia Cervantes's "Mga Huling Yugto sa Buhay ng Burges na Manggagawa" (Last Gasps of Breath in the Life of a Bourgeois Worker) depicts the capitalist oppression of workers. Through this story, the readers come to comprehend the insight workers need to strengthen their solidarity in the face of economic oppression. Another writer, Abelardo Cruz, wrote "Ningas ng Apoy" (Light of Fire), which tackles the all too familiar theme of union leaders or sympathizers victimized by capitalist violence. At present, there are a number of middle-class writers whose sympathy continues to be with the workers and peasants.[18]

Conclusion

This discussion has cursively mapped the development of the short story in Filipino and other Philippine languages from its beginnings to the present by foregrounding the important historical, political, and literary conditions that influenced its development. This essay underscores how Filipino writers have tried to master or reinvent the form of the short story in varied political, historical and literary contexts. Their task has been to inscribe the experience of Filipinos and their struggle to define themselves and their future in the short story. This modern literary tradition continues to weave new characters, themes, metaphors, and strategies into the present tapestry of Filipino fiction.

Notes

[1] For an interesting online history of this important magazine see *Pilipino Komiks* (2007). The weekly magazine *Liwayway* (Dawn) published a very popular series of stories by Don Severino Reyes, its cofounder, "Kwento ni Lola Basyang," framed as stories by an old female storyteller. It serialized what would become some of the great Tagalog literary novels and published prose by some of the most talented poets and prose writers at that time, including Lope K. Santos, Iñigo Ed. Regalado, Romualdo Ramos, Francisco Laksamana, Fausto J. Galauran and Pedrito Reyes. [Ed.]

[2] These magazines published works in some of the major Philippine languages such as Tagalog, Cebuano, Iloko, Bikol and Ilonggo. During this time, English was the medium of education and the language of the elite. Editor's note: copies of quite recent versions (2001–02) of four of these magazines (*Liwayway*, *Bannawag*, *Bisaya*, and *Hiligaynon*) can be viewed online at http://home.san.rr.com/bikol/magazines.html.

[3] This provides an interesting parallel to the importance of English as a prestige language among the Peranakan Chinese in Singapore. For further information see Loh and Yamada's essay, Chapter 7 in this collection. However, in the case of the Philippines, the "national" language issue served to complicate political unification; this was not the situation in Singapore.

[4] A *dagli* is similar to a very short or brief narrative without the usual plot structure associated with the short story. It has been typically used to teach a moral lesson. According to Ruth Mabanglo, it came about during the Propaganda period, "developed by writers who cited narratives akin to the parables of Jesus Christ" (e-mail correspondence, 27 August 2008). Guillermo describes it as a "vignette," a type of writing that "has much more success in capturing the essence of a single character or event through telling, concrete details" (1996, 368). [Ed.]

[5] Before its new Tagalog edition late in 1922, *Liwayway* was a multilingual magazine: Spanish, English, and Tagalog. [Ed.]

[6] *Kalendariong Bicol* was originally an almanac, published every January, as early as 1877, in Nueva Caceres. On this history see Jose Perez (2005). [Ed.]

[7] For further information on the nationalist tendencies of Abad, see Jolipa (1996). [Ed.]

[8] Being fined for speaking one's mother tongue and feeling a revulsion against it was also expressed by another established writer, Genoveva Edroza-Matute. For further information see Torres-Yu (1999b).

[9] Some of Calixto's more recognized stories include "Mga Matang Tumtom sa Luha" (Eyes Full of Tears), "Pusong Ilo sa Pagkamoot" (A Heart Orphaned of Love) and "Salawahan" (Jealous).

[10] This story was first published in 1962.

[11] It was named after the Propaganda Movement led by the *ilustrados* against the Spanish colonial regime in the 1800s.

[12] This was an organization of messianic peasants. In 1966, its members, led by Vicente de los Santos and armed only with bolos and *anting-anting* (amulets), marched to Malacanang Palace and were massacred by government troops.

[13] "Utos ng Hari" was also anthologized in Chua, et al (1999, 77, 87). [Ed.]

[14] On this issue, see Kintanar 1992; S. Reyes 1994; and Santiago 1997.

[15] These anthologies are several editions of *Ang Aklat Likhaan ng Tula at Maikling Kuwento*. The 1995 edition by Domingo G. Landicho and Lilia Quindoza Santiago; the 1996 edition was edited by Joi Barrios and Jun Cruz Reyes; the 1997 edition was edited by Virgilio S. Almario and Lilia Quindoza Santiago; the 1998 edition was edited by Aurelio Agcaoili and Jose F. Lacaba; the 1999 edition was edited by Victor Emmanuel Carmelo D. Nadera, Jr., and Jun Cruz Reyes; the 2000 edition was edited by Joi Barrios and Roland Tolentino; and the 2001 edition was edited by Domingo G. Landicho and Lilia Quindoza Santiago. The journal was renamed in 2006–07 *Likhaan Journal of Contemporary Philippine Literature*. Its issue editor was Jose Y. Dalisay, Jr.

[16] Others include Glecy Atienza, Mayette Bayuga, Rolando B. Tolentino, Honorio Bartolome de Dios, Vim Nadera, Jimmuel Naval, Alvin Yapan, Alwin Aguirre, Arlene Bongon-Burgos, Eugene Evasco, Eli Guieb, and Rommel Rodriguez. Many of the works of these authors are published in *Likhaan* and the *KATHA* anthologies. Some are prize-winning works.

[17] Tolentino has published his collection of short stories in Filipino, *Fastfood, Megamall, at iba pang Kwento sa Pagsasara ng Ikalawang Milenyum* (Fastfood, Megamall and other Stories at the Close of the Second Millennium, 1999), *Ali*Bang+Bang at iba pang Kwento* (Ali*Bang+Bang and other Stories, 1994) and three novelettes in *Sapinsaping Pag-ibig at Pagtangis* (Layers of Love and Heartaches, 2000).

[18] These writers are Reynaldo Duque, Ernie Yang, Chit Balmaceda Gutierrez, Tomas Agulto, Cytrus Borja, Reuel Aguila and Jun Cruz Reyes. For further information see E. Ordoñez (1996, 352, 356).

References

Abad, Gémino H., ed. 1998. *The Likhaan Anthology of Philippine Literature in English from 1900 to the Present*. Quezon City: University of the Philippines Press.

Abadilla, Alejandro G., and Clodualdo del Mundo, eds. 1936. *Mga Kuwentong Ginto, 1925–1935* [Golden Stories, 1925–1935]. Manila: A. S. Florentino. Republished in 1972.

Abueg, Efren R. 2000. "Abueg on Abueg." In *In Our Own Words: Filipino Writers in Vernacular Languages*, edited by Isagani R. Cruz, 2–5. Manila: De La Salle University Press.

Abueg, Efren, et al. [1964] 1993. *Mga Agos sa Disyerto* [Streams in the Desert]. Metro Manila: Solar.

Agoncillo, Teodoro A. 1949. *Ang Maikling Kuwentong Tagalog (1886–1948)* [Tagalog Short Story (1886–1948)]. Manila: Inang Wika.

Alburo, Erlinda K., ed. 1998. *Labindalawang Kuwento ni Vicente Sotto* [Twelve Stories of Vicente Sotto]. Translated by Remedios B. Ramos. Lungsod Quezon: Sentro ng Wikang Filipino, Sistemang Unibersidad ng Pilipinas.

Alunan, Merlie M. 2000. "Splitting Tongues: Literary Experience in a Multilingual Culture." Paper read at the conference Philippine Literatures in the New Century, National Seminar for Teachers and Writers, University of the Philippines, 24–26 October.

Alunan, Merlie M., ed. 1998. *Fern Garden: An Anthology of Women Writing in the South*. Manila: National Commission on Culture and the Arts.

Baquiran, Romulo P., Jr., Honorio de Dioes, eds. 1999. *Relasyon: Mga Kuwento ng Paglusong at Pag-ahon*. [Liason: Stories of Initiation and Survival]. Quezon City: Ateneo de Manila University Press.

Barrios, Joi, and Jun Cruz Reyes, eds. 1998. *Ang Aklat Likhaan ng Tula at Maikling Kuwento, 1996* [The Aklat Likhaan of Poetry and Short Stories]. Quezon City: University of the Philippines Creative Writing Center and University of the Philippines Press.

Bayuga, Mayette. 2002. *Virgintarian at iba pang Akda*. [Virgintarian and other Works]. Diliman and Quezon City: University of the Philippines Press.

Beltran, Herminio. 1999. "Ang CCP at ang Pambansang Panitikan" [CCP and the National Literature]. Paper read at the National Conference on National Literature, Rizal Hall, University of the Philippines, 25–26 November.

Chua, Apolonio, Rolando Tolentino, Luna Sicat, Eulalio Guieb III, Rosario Torres-Yu and Delfin Tolentino, eds. 1999. *Linangan* [Cultivation]. Quezon City: Office of the Vice Chancellor for Research and Development, University of the Philippines.

Constantino, Renato and Letizia R. Constantino. 1975. *The Philippines: A Past Revisited*. Quezon City: Tala.

———. 1978. *The Philippines: The Continuing Past*. Quezon City: Foundation for Nationalist Studies.

De Guzman, Mes, and Victor Emmanuel Carmelo D. Nadera, Jr., eds. 1997. *Alagwa* [Falling Kite]. Manila: De La Salle University Press.

De la Rosa, Alvarez and Roland B. Tolentino. 1990. *Engkwentro: Kalipunan ng mga Akda ng Kabataang Manunulat* [Encounter: Anthology of Works by Young Writers]. Manila: Kalikasan Press.

Deriada, Leoncio. 2000. "Notes on the Present Hiligaynon Short Story." Paper read at the conference on Philippine Literatures in the New Century, National Seminar for Teachers and Writers, University of the Philippines, 24–26 October.

Edroza-Matute, Genoveva. 1998a. *Babae at iba pang mga Kuwento* [Women and Other Stories]. Quezon City: New Day.

———. 1998b. *None of the Bitter: The Short Stories and Essays in English*. Manila: University of Santo Tomas Publishing House.

Guillermo, Gelacio. 1996. "The New Mass Art and Literature." In *Nationalist Literature: A Centennial Forum*, edited by Elmer A. Ordonez, 358–78. Quezon City: University of the Philippines Press and Philippine Writers Academy.

Hosillos, Lucila V. 1984. *Originality as Vengeance in Philippine Literature*. Quezon City: New Day.

———. 1992. *Hiligaynon Literature: Texts and Contexts*. Quezon City: Aqua-Land Enterprises.

Jolipa, Nora T. 1996. "Lost Paradise: American Colonialism and the Filipino Writer in Spanish." In *Nationalist Literature: A Centennial Forum*, edited by Elmer A. Ordonez, 24–32. Quezon City: University of the Philippines Press and Philippine Writers Academy.

Kintanar, Thelma, B. ed. 1992. *Women Reading: Feminist Perspectives on Philippine Literary Texts*. Diliman, Quezon City: Center for Women's Studies, University of the Philippines Press.

Lacuesta, Lolita Rodriguez. 2000. "Theme and Technique in the Short Stories of Liwayway A. Arceo from 1941–1950." In *The Likhaan Book of Philippine Criticism (1992–1997)*, edited by J. Neil C. Garcia, 197–215. Quezon City: University of the Philippines Press.

Lumbera, Bienvenido L. 1994. "Ang Panitikan ng Kabataan at ang Pagpapayaman sa Wikang Filipino." [The Literature of the Youth and the Development of Filipino Language]. Interview, Balagtas Day. Commission of Filipino Language, Philippine National University, 5 April.

Lumbera, Bienvenido L., and Cynthia N. Lumbera, eds. 1997. *Philippine Literature: A History and Anthology.* Pasig City: Anvil.

Maceda, Teresita G. 1975. "The Vision of Life in Marcel Navarra's Fiction: A Study of the Cebuano Short Story." MA thesis, Ateneo de Manila University.

———. trans. and ed. 1986. *Marcel M. Navarra: Mga Piling Kuwentong Sebuwano* [Selected Sebuano Stories by Marcel M. Navarra]. Quezon City: University of the Philippines Press.

Melendrez-Cruz, Patricia. 1996. "The Modern Pilipino Short Story (1946–1972): Consciousness and Counter-consciousness." In *Nationalist Literature: A Centennial Forum*, edited by Elmer A. Ordoñez, 148–73. Quezon City: University of the Philippines Press and Philippine Writers Academy.

Nadera, Victor Emmanuel Carmelo D., Jr., and Jun Cruz Reyes, eds. 2002. *Ang Aklat Likhaan ng Tula at Maikling Kuwento*, [*Aklat Likhaan* of Poetry and Short Story]. 1999. Quezon City: University of the Philippines Press.

Ordoñez, Elmer A., ed. 1996. *Nationalist Literature: A Centennial Forum*. Quezon City: University of the Philippines Press and Philippine Writers Academy.

Ordoñez, Rogelio L. 1996. "Literatura ng Uring Anakpawis" [Literature of the Working Class]. In *Nationalist Literature: A Centennial Forum*, edited by Elmer A. Ordoñez, 345–58. Quezon City: University of the Philippines Press and Philippine Writers Academy.

Perez, Jose. 2005. "Naga's Printing Press." www.bicolmarl.com, accessed September 2007.

PilipinoKomiks. 2007. "A History of the Liwayway Magazine." www pilipinokomiks.blogspot.com, accessed 17 September 2007.

Realubit, Maria Lilia F. ca. 2001. *Bikol Literary History*. Naga City: Bikol Heritage Society.

Reyes, Jun Cruz. 1981. *Utos ng Hari at iba pang Kuwento*. [King's Command and Other Stories]. Quezon City: New Day.

———. 1998. "Wika at Kamalayan: Ang Maikling Kuwento sa 1996." [Language and Consciousness: The Short Story in 1996]. In *Ang Aklat Likhaan ng Tula at Maikling Kuwento, 1996* [The Likhaan Book of Poetry and Short Story], edited by Joi Barrios and Jun Cruz Reyes, n.p. Quezon City: University of the Philippines Creative Writing Center and University of the Philippines Press.

Reyes, Pedrito. 1998. *50 Kuwentong Ginto ng 50 Batikang Kuwentista*. [50 Golden Stories of 50 Best Short Story Writers]. Manila: Ateneo de Manila University Press.

Reyes, Soledad. 1991. "Recent Trends in Literary History and the Study of Philippine Literature." In *The Romance Mode in Philippine Popular Literature and Other Essays*, 3–21. Manila: De La Salle University Press.

———. ed. 1994. *Ang Silid na Mahiwaga* [Mysterious Room]. Manila: Anvil.

———. 1997. *Pagbasa ng Panitikan at Kulturang Popular*. [Reading of Literature and Popular Culture.] Manila: Ateneo de Manila University Press.

Rillo, Fidel, Rolando B. Tolentino, and Jim Pascual Agustin, eds. 1999. *Ang Aklat Likhaan ng Tula at Maikling Kuwento, 1997* [The Likhaan Book of Poetry and Short Story, 1997]. Diliman, Quezon City: University of the Philippines Creative Writing Center and University of the Philippines Press.

Salanga, Alfredo Navarro, ed. 1987. *Kamao, mga Kuwento ng Protesta, 1970–1986* [Fist, Stories of Protest, 1970–1986]. Manila: Cultural Center of the Philippines.

Samson, Laura, Ruby Alcantara, Monico Atienza, Nilo Ocampo. eds. 1994. *Patricia Melendez-Cruz: Filipinong Pananaw sa Wika, Panitikan at Lipunan* [Patricia Melendez-Cruz: Filipino Perspective on Language, Literature and Society]. Diliman, Lunsod, Quezon: College of Social Sciences and Philosophy Publications, University of the Philippines Press.

Santiago, Lilia Q. 1997. *Sa Ngalan ng Ina: Sandaang Taon ng Tulang Feminista sa Philipinas, 1889–1989* [In the Name of the Mother: 100 Years of Philippine Feminist Poetry, 1899–1989]. Quezon City: University of the Philippines Press. In English, 2002.

Santos, R. Fulleros and Roland B. Tolentino, eds. 1991. *Habilin: Antolohiya ng KATHA para sa Pambansang Kasarinlan*. [Entrust: Anthology of KATHA for National Sovereignty]. Manila: Kalikasan Press.

Sigwa: Isang Antolohiya ng Maiikling Kuwento [Storm: An Anthology of Short Stories]. 1972. Republished in 1992. Diliman, Quezon City: University of the Philippines Press.

Sugbo, Victor. 2000. "The Waray Writer and His Struggle Against Literary Silencing." Paper read at the conference in Philippine Literatures in the New Century, National Seminar for Teachers and Writers. University of the Philippines, 24–26 October.

Tolentino, Roland B., and Luna Sicat. 1999. *Relasyon: Mga Kuwento ng Paglusong at Pag-ahon* [Liason: Stories of Initiation and Survival]. Quezon City: Ateneo de Manila University Press.

Torres-Yu, Rosario. 1996. "The State of Philippine Literature." In *Nationalist Literature: A Centennial Forum*, edited by Elmer A. Ordoñez, 317–36. Quezon City: University of the Philippines Press and Philippine Writers Academy.

———. 1999a. "Pagpapakilala." In *Relasyon: Mga Kuwento ng Pag-ahon*, [Liason: Stories of Initiation and Survival], edited by Rolando B. Tolentino and Luna Sicat, vii–ix. Quezon City: Ateneo de Manila University Press.

———. 1999b. "Ang Babae sa mga Katha ni Genoveva Edroza-Matute: Pagbasag at Pagbuo ng Bagong Kultura ng Kababaihan" [The Woman in the Stories of Genoveva Edroza-Matute: Destroying and Rebuilding a New Culture of Women]. In *Pagbasag at Pagbuo ng Bagong Kultura ng Kababaihan*, edited by Roland Tolentino, *Lagda* [Signature], No. I (*Journal of the Department of Filipino and Philippine Literature*, University of the Philippines).

———. 2000. *Sarilaysay: Tinig ng 20 Babae sa Sariling Danas Bilang Manunulat* [Sarilaysay: Voices of 20 Women on Writing]. Manila: Anvil.

Literary Authors' Index*

* Please check for both the author's first and last name in alphabetical order in the list (Ed.)

A

Abad, Antonio, 323, 343
Abadilla, Alejandro G., 324–325
Abdul Rahim Kajai, 195
Abueg, Efren, 327, 345
Adibah Amin, 197, 208
Aguila, Cesar Leyco, 309
Aguila, Reuel, 344
Agulto, Tomas, 344
Aguirre, Alwin, 344
Ajidarma, Seno Gumira, 256–257, 263, 265, 267–268
Akatdamkoeng, M.C., Akatsadamkng Raphiphat, 37–38
Alfon, Estrella, 297, 314, 317
Alim, Saadah, 244
Almario, Virgilio S., 344
Amansec, Lilia Pablo, 303
Anchan, 24, 61–64, 66, 74
Anis Sabirin, 197
Anonim, 247, 261, 265
Anthony, Cynthia, 203
Anwar Ridhwan, 198–199, 206, 208
Aquino, César, 303
Arcellana, Francisco, 293, 295, 297, 301, 313–314, 317
Arceo, Liwayway, 324, 327, 334, 347
Arciwals, Juan, 323
Arguilla, Manuel E., 294, 297–298, 317, 324–326
Atienza, Glecy, 340, 344
Aung Thin, 153, 170–171, 175, 178–179, 184, 186
Ayala, José V., 303

B

Bacho, Peter, 309
Bagiuo, Tiburcio, 328
Bao Ninh, 280
Baratham, Gopal, 220, 222, 231, 235–236
Barrios, Joi, 335–336, 339, 341, 344–345, 348
Basilio, Rogelio, 329
Batacan, F. H., 308, 310–311
Batungbakal, Brigido, 326
Bautista, Lualhati, 334–335
Bayuga, Mayette, 334–335, 339–340, 344–345
Benitez, Paz Marquez, 297
Binh Nguyen Loc, 277
Binla Sankalakhiri, 71–72, 74
Bobis, Merlinda, 309
Bongon-Burgos, Arlene, 344
Bounyavong, Outhine ('Uthin Bunnyavong), 84, 90, 106
Brainard, Cecilia Manguerra, 300, 309
Brillantes, Gregorio C., 302, 304, 314–316
Bruine Boonen, 247–248, 265
Bua Kaew Chaleunsi, 85–89, 107
Bulosan, Carlos, 294, 309
Bunao, G. Burce, 303
Bunseun Saengmani, 90, 99–100, 107
Bunthanong Somsaiphon, 90–92, 95–97, 105–108
Busu, Fatima, 199

C

Calixto, Ana T., 324, 344
Carunungan, Celso, 294
Castillo, Erwin, 303, 314
Cervantes, Cesar, 342
Cervantes, Olivia, 342
Chai, Arlene, J., 309
Chambo, Keo, 123, 141
Chamlong Fangcholachit, 28, 48–49, 52, 74–75
Chanthi Deuansavan, 90
Chat (Chart) Kobjitti (Kobchitti), 38, 51–52, 55, 75
Che Husna Azhari, 203
Cheong, Colin, 228, 236, 239
Chiranan Pitpreecha, 24
Chua, Rebecca, 222, 236
Chua, Terence, 227, 236
Chulalongkorn, 20, 36, 38
Cordero-Fernando, Gilda, 300, 302–303, 314
Coscolluela, Elsa Martinez (see Martinez-Coscolluela)
Cruz, Abelardo, 342

D

Dagon Khin Khin Lay, 163,180
Dagon Ta-ya, 160–161, 180–181
Dalisay, Jr., Jose Y., 298, 307, 313, 316, 318, 344
Danarto, 255-256, 263, 266, 269
Dauk Ket (Duangdeuan), 84, 90
Daung Ne Min, 172
Daw Aung San Suu Kyim, 180, 183
Daw Khin Swe U, 184
Dawviang Butnakho (Dao Viang Butnakho), 90, 99, 107
de Dios, Honorio Bartolome, 340–341, 344
de Jesus, Noelle Q. (Noelle Chua), 310
de Perfecto, Nicolasa Ponte, 323

del Mundo, Jr., Clodualdo, 324–325, 345
Deriada, Leoncio, 305, 323, 337–338, 346
Dina Zaman, 203
Dinh, Linh, 282–283, 285–86
Doan Quoc Si, 277
Dok Mai Sot (Dokmai), 21, 36, 38, 48
Duang Champa (Dara), 84, 90, 100–101, 104, 107–108
Duangdeuane (Duangdeuan) Bounyavong, 104, 108
Duangsai Luangphasi, 102–103
Duenwad Pimwana, 61, 64–66, 73, 75
Duong Nghiem Mau, 277
Duong Thi Xuan Qui, 278
Duong Thu Huong, 280–281, 285–286
Duong Ratha, 123
Duque, Reynaldo, 344
Duyen Anh, 277

E

Edroza-Matute, Genoveva, 334, 343, 346, 349
Elangovan, 234
Enriquez, Antonio, 314
Escober, ER, 309
Espina-Moore, Lina, 300
Evasco, Eugene, 340, 344

G

Galang, M. Evelina, 309
Galauran, Fausto J., 343
Gamalinda, Eric, 309
Garcia, Fanny, 329, 335
Gempesaw, Antero, 323
Ghani, Uthuman, 234
Goenawan Mohamad, 253, 266
Goh Sin Tub, 220, 231, 234–236
Gonzales, Alicia Tan, 337–338
Gonzalez, N. V. M., 293-95, 297, 299, 302–304, 318
Gonzalez, Romina 308–309

Gouw Peng Liang, 245
Govindasamy, Naa, 216–217, 234, 239
Groyon, Vicente, 308, 309
Guieb, Eli (Eulalio Guieb III), 336, 344, 346
Gutierrez, Chit Balmaceda, 335, 344

H

Hagedorn, Jessica, 309
Heng Sou Sieu, 139, 287
Hidalgo, Antonio A., 311
Hidalgo, Cristina Pantoja, ix, 305, 315, 318
Ho Anh Thai, 282, 287
Ho Bieu Chanh, 273
Ho Kin San, 221, 236
Ho Mingfong, 236
Hoang Ngoc Phach, 273
Hom Phothaung, 100
Hsin-byu-gyun Aung Thein, 159
Htin Lin, 161–162, 180, 182, 187
Huynh, Jade Ngoc Quang, 285, 287
Huynh Tinh Cua, 273

I

Idrus, 250–252, 261, 267
Ilangkannan, Ma, 234
Ishak Hj. Muhammad, 195–96

J

Javellana, Stevan, 294
Jeyaretnam, Philip, 224–225, 231, 236
Jiraphat Angsumali, 53–55, 75
Joaquin, Nick, 297, 299–301, 304, 313, 318
Jong Chian Li, 200
José, F. Sionil, 301, 303–304, 307, 318–319
Ju, 167, 172–173
Juvenle Kuo, 247

K

K. S. Maniam (see Maniam, K.S.)
Kannabiran, Rama, 217–218, 234
Kanokphong Songsomphan, ix, 31, 37–38, 43, 52–53, 55, 66, 72, 75
Kao Seiha, 130, 136, 146
Karim Raslan, 203–205, 209
Kasim, Muhammad, 244, 260
Kassim Ahmad, 197
Katigbak, Luis, 308–09
Kayam, Umar, 254–255, 262, 267
Keris Mas, 196, 200
Khadtijah Hashim, 199
Khai Hung, 274, 284
Khamliang Phonsena, 90
Khamsing Srinawk, 39
Khin Hnin Yu, 165
Khin Swe U, 165, 180, 184
Khun Srun, 122, 139
Killingley, Siew-Yue, 203
Kim Hak, 115
Kon, S., 222, 224
Kong Bunchoeun (Kong Bun Chhoeun/Chhoeurn), 124, 127
Kwo Lay Yen, 245
Kyeh Ni, 159
Kyi Aye, 160

L

Lacaba Jr., Jose, 304, 344
Lacuesta, Angelo, 308
Laksamana, Francisco, 343
Landicho, Domingo G., 339, 344
Lapcharoensap, Rattawut, 32, 37, 39, 285, 288
Latorena, Paz, 297
Le, Linda, 285–286
Le Luu, 280
Le Minh Khue, 278, 281–282, 285, 287–288
Lee Kok Liang, 200–203, 209

Lee, Ricardo, 329
Lee, Russell, 228, 234, 236–237
Lee Tzu Pheng, 233
Lie Kim Hok, 245, 270
Lim, Catherine, 215, 220–225, 228, 231, 235, 237
Lim, Jaime An, 305
Lim, Shirley Geok-Lin, x, 203, 207, 209, 214–215, 219
Lim, Suchen Christine, 215
Lim Thean Soo, 220, 224, 233, 237
Lim Jr., Paulino, 309
Linh Dinh (see Dinh, Linh)
Linmark, R. Zamora, 309, 311
Loh, Mary (Kwuan), xi, 206, 213, 223, 238
Lopez, Salvador P. 298, 303–304, 313, 315, 319, 326
Lucero, Rosario, 308, 338
Ludu U Hla, 154, 162–163, 178

M

M. Saleh Oemar, 247
Ma Ma Lay, 163–165, 181–182, 187, 189
Ma Sanda, 165–169, 183, 187, 190
Ma Thida (Sangyaung; Le Net), 185, 187
Madrid, Renato, 305
Maha Swe, 156, 165
Maha Sila Viravong, 82, 84, 90, 104, 108
Mai Thao, 277
Madjoindo, A. Dt., 248–249, 268
Man Tin, 158–159, 165, 187
Manat Chanyong, 28
Mandank, Or., 248, 268
Maniam, K.S., 197, 201–203, 207, 209–210
Mao Samnang, 125, 139, 141
Martinez-Coscolluela, Elsa, 305
Maung Htin, 157–159, 187
Maung Lun Kyin, 178
Maung Swan Yi, 182, 184, 187

Maung Tha-ra, 161–162, 166–168, 171, 180, 182–183, 187–188
Maung Thin, 163, 188
Melvin, Reine Arcache, 310
Mey Son Sotheary, 128, 148
Min Shin, 159, 188
Minthuwun, 157–158, 180
Miraflor, Norma, 303, 310
Moey, Nicky, 228, 231, 235, 237
Mongkut, King of Siam, 20, 36, 39
Mo Mo (Inya), 165–166, 170–171, 188
Mo Nyein E, 178
Moles, Lino V., 330
Mona, Matu, 249, 268
Moo, Joash, 229, 237
Mud Sudphathai, 73
Mya Hnaung Nyo, 167
Myint Kyaing (Aung Mo Hsaung) 180, 188
Mya Than Tint, 173–174, 184, 188, 190
Myint Than, 178

N

N. Asia, 249, 268
N. I. Loo, 233
Nadera, Jr., Victor (Vim; V.C.) Emmanuel Carmelo D., 335–336, 341, 344, 346–347
Nam Cao, 274, 288
Naowarat Pongpaiboon, 24
Naval, Jimmuel, 344
Navarra, Marcel M., 325, 347
Ne Win Myint, 174–177, 184, 188, 190
Nery, Peter, 338
Ngo Tat To, 274
Nguyen Ba Hoc, 284
Nguyen Cong Hoan, 274–275, 288
Nguyen Hong, 274
Nguyen Huy Thiep, 279, 280, 282, 285, 288–289, 291
Nguyen Quang Lap, 280

Nguyen Thi Hoang, 278
Nguyen Thi Ngoc Tu, 278
Nguyen Thi Thuy Vu, 278
Nguyen Trong Quan, 273
Nguyen Trong Thuat, 273
Nguyen Tuan, 275, 288
Nguyen Van Vinh, 273
Nguyen Vu, 278
Nguyen Vy, 277
Nha Ca, 278
Nhat Linh, 274–275, 277, 284
Nhem Sopath, 129, 148
Nhok Them, 110, 137, 139
Niti Saiyasaeng, 90
Noi Inthanon, 28
Nolledo, Wilfredo, 304
Nou Hach, 116, 139
Nu Nu Yiy (Inwa), 171–173, 186, 188
Nyi Pu Lay, 178, 188–190

O

Ong, Charlson, 308, 316, 319
Ong Choo Suat, 224
Othman Kelantan, S., 197–199, 210
Op Chaiwasu, 28, 29
Oum Suphany, 124–125
Outhine Bounyavong (see also Bounyavong, Outhine), 84, 90, 108

P

P. Monin, 155–156, 180
Pa Nai (Pakiat), 84
Paiwarin Khao-Ngam, 24
Pal Vannarirak, 124–125, 132, 141
Palanca, Clinton, 308
Pang, Alvin, 231–232
Paritas Hutangkul, 69–71, 75–76
Pe Myint, 178
Pech Sangwawann, 123, 141, 149
Pen Chhornn, 130, 136, 149

Pen-Ek Ratanaruang, 8, 15, 32, 34, 41, 61, 285
Phaitoon Thanya, 44, 46–47, 52, 74, 76, 109
Pham, Andrew X., 285, 289
Pham Duy Ton, 284, 290
Pham Thi Hoai, 281, 285, 289
Phan, Aimee, 285, 289
Phan Nhat Nam, 278
Phan Thi Vang Anh, 281, 285, 289–290
Phanu Traiwet, 73
Phin Santel, 131, 149
Phuangphet Buaphachan, 101–102, 108
Phy Runn, 131, 136, 141, 149
Pian Julamunti, 90
Pin Yathay, 123, 149
Pinyo Srichamlong, 52
Polotan, Kerima (Polotan-Tuvera), 301–302, 304, 314, 319
Pol-Paul Pat, 139, 149
Prabda Yoon (Prapda Yun), 27–32, 34, 37, 39, 56, 58–61, 73, 76
Prachakom Lunachai, 67–69, 76
Pretam Kaur, 203
Puatu, Mar, 309

Q

Que, 247

R

Ramesh, K., 228, 234, 238
Ramos, Romualdo, 343
Ratanachai Manabut, 73
Realuyo, Bino, 309
Regalado, Iñigo Ed., 323, 343
Rendra, 259, 268
Rewat Panpipat, 73
Reyes, Don Severino, 343
Reyes, Jun Cruz, 331–332, 339–340, 344–345, 347–348
Reyes, Pedrito, 324, 343, 348

Riem-Eng (Malai Choopinit), 21
Rim Kin, 115, 137, 139, 148
Rivera-Ford, Aida, 300
Rizal, José, 295–296, 313, 315, 340, 345
Rodriguez, Rommel, 336, 340–341, 344
Roley, Brian Ascalon, 309
Roperos, Godofredo, 328
Rosario, Deogracias, 325
Rosca, Ninotchka, 304, 309
Rotor, Arturo B., 297–298, 319, 324–325
Rusmini, Oka, 257–259, 264, 269

S

S. Othman Kelantan (see Othman, S. Kelantan)
S. P. Somtow (Somtow Sucharitkul), 31–32, 39
Sa O, 184
Saiboo, Makadoom, 216, 234
Saisuvan Phaengphong, 90, 93, 105, 108
Saksiri Meesomsueb, 24, 34
Sam Suphearin, 132
Samarindaan, 247
Samruam Singh, 36, 38
San San Nweh, 180
Sanchez, Wilfredo, 303
Sankar, Uthaya, 200
Santiago, Lilia Quindoza, 335, 339, 344, 348
Santos, Alex C., 338
Santos, Bienvenido, 297–298, 300–301, 304, 309, 319
Santos, Lope K., 343
Sarmiento, Menchu, 308
Sarreal, Nadine, 310
Sathaporn Srisajchang, 52
Seliphap, 90
Seni Sauvapong (Seinee Saowaphong) 37, 39

Sering, Tara FT, 308, 310–311
Shahnon Ahmad, 197–198, 203–204, 206, 208, 210
Shamsuddin Salleh, 195
Shwe U-daung, 155
Siburapha (Kulap Saipradit), 22–23, 37, 39
Sicat-Cleto, Luna (Luna Sicat), 339, 346, 349
Sidaoru'ang, Sridaorueang, Sri Daoruang (Wanna Sawatsri), 24, 26, 36, 38, 39–40, 61–62, 73, 76–77
Sikat (Sicat), Rogelio R., 327, 338
Sila Khomchai, 24, 55–56, 76
Sim, Desmond, 238
Siriworn Kaewkan, ix, 66–67, 76
Sitangsupa, 73
Siti Zainon Ismail, 199, 207, 210
Sitoy, Lakambini, 308, 309
Situmorang, Sitor, 253, 262, 269–270
Siv, Darina, 123, 128, 150
Skinner, Michele, 309
Soeman (Suman) Hs., 244, 260
Soepadmo, R., 245
Somjin Nginn, 81–82
Somsuk Suksavat, 90
Son Nam, 277
Son Ngoc Thanh, 117
Sontani, Utuy Tatang, 253–254, 262, 269–270
Soth Polin, 119–120, 123, 139–140, 147
Sothea, 139
Strom, Dao, 285, 290
Suchart (Suchat) Sawatsri, 26, 36, 43
Sulit, Loreto Paras, 297
Suvanthaun Bupphanuvong, 90
Suwanee Sukhontha (Suwanee Sukhonthieng), 25–26

T

Ta Duy Anh, 280, 285, 288
Tan, Nalla, 225–226, 238, 240
Tanselama, 247
Tay, Simon, 214, 230–231, 238, 240
Ten, Maureen, 203
Teodoro, Luis, 304–305, 320
Thaik Htun Thet, 178
Thaitao Sucharitkul, 32
Tham, Claire, 226–227, 238
Thanh Tam Tuyen, 277
Thao Ken, 82
Thaw-da Swe (Hswei), 160, 189
Theikpan Maung Wa (U Sein Tin), 157–158, 190
Thein Pe Myint, 161, 163, 181–182, 189–190
Thida Bunnak (Thidaa Bunnaak), 38
Thio Tjin Boen, 245
Thitsa Ni, 178
Tiempo, Edilberto, 294, 301
Tiempo, Edith, 300–302, 307, 320
Tiempo-Torrevillas, Rowena, 305, 309
Tin Moe, 180
Tint Teh, 159
To Hoai, 274
Toer, Pramoedya Ananta, 246–247, 251–253, 260–262, 265–268, 270
Tolentino, Rolando B., 335–336, 341, 344, 346, 349
Touchstone, 247
Tran Thi Ngh, 278
Truong, Monique T.D., 282, 285, 290
Trung Duong, 278
Tuvera, Katrina, 308
Tuy Hong, 278
Ty-Casper, Linda, 300, 304, 320

U

U Sam Oeur, 123, 150
Usman Awang, 196, 200
Ussiri Dhammachoti, 24, 44–47
Uthen Promdaeng, 73

V

Vajiravudh, 21
Vandy Kaon (Kaonn), 124–125, 138, 140, 148, 151
Vanich Charoongkij-anant, 24, 49–51, 55, 77
Victorio-Reyes, Ligaya, 297
Vien Linh, 277
Villa, Jose Garcia 294, 297–298, 303, 306, 309, 313, 315, 325
Villanueva, Lydia C., 297
Villanueva, Marianne, 309–310, 316, 320
Viset Savaengseuksa, 90, 94, 101, 105, 108
Vo, Linda, 285, 290
Vo Phien, 277, 291
Vu Bang, 277
Vu Hoang Chuong, 277
Vu Thi Thuong, 278
Vu Trong Phung, 275, 284, 288, 291

W

Wangke, 247
Watchara Sujjasarasin, 73
Win Lyovarin, 27–28, 30–31, 34, 40, 56–58, 61, 66, 73, 77
Win Pe, 158, 174–175, 181, 189
Win Si Thu, 178
Win Win Lat, 168
Wong Meng Voon, 216, 233, 238, 241
Wong Swee Hoon, 220–224, 231, 238
Woo Keng Thye, 224, 238

Y

Y Uyen, 278
Yan Aung (Yan Aung Maung Maung), 156, 182
Yang, Ernie, 344
Yap, Arthur, 219–220, 233–234, 239
Yapan, Alvin, 344
Yeo, Robert, 218, 220, 241
Yin Wyn, 181, 190
Yoeun Saolee, 131, 151
You Bo, 119, 132, 139–140
Yuson, Alfred A., 307, 316, 320

Z

Zaharah Nawawi, 199
Zaleha, 245
Zaw Zaw Aung, 177
Zaw-gyi, 158

GPSR Authorized Representative: Easy Access System Europe, Mustamäe tee
50, 10621 Tallinn, Estonia, gpsr.requests@easproject.com

www.ingramcontent.com/pod-product-compliance
Lightning Source LLC
Chambersburg PA
CBHW030431300426
44112CB00009B/952